T0287645

DISCORDANT NOTES

Discordant Notes

The Voice of Dissent in the Court of Last Resort

Volume 1

Rohinton F. Nariman

PENGUIN
ALLEN
LANE

An imprint of Penguin Random House

ALLEN LANE

USA | Canada | UK | Ireland | Australia
New Zealand | India | South Africa | China

Allen Lane is part of the Penguin Random House group of companies
whose addresses can be found at global.penguinrandomhouse.com

Published by Penguin Random House India Pvt. Ltd
4th Floor, Capital Tower 1, MG Road,
Gurugram 122 002, Haryana, India

Penguin
Random House
India

First published in Allen Lane by Penguin Random House India 2021

ISBN 9780670094394

Typeset in Adobe Garamond Pro by Manipal Technologies Limited, Manipal
Printed at Replika Press Pvt. Ltd, India

www.penguin.co.in

To my two beloved uncles
Adi Nariman and Dr Soli Contractor,
who were my mentors and best friends
as long as they lived

CONTENTS

Preface   ix

The Need for Dissent   1

When the Chips Are Down—the Law in Times of
    War or Emergency   43

The Dissenting Judgment as a Stabilizing
    Force—Don't Unsettle the Law   123

The Dissenting Judgment as an Agent of
    Change—the Appeal to the Brooding Spirit of the Law 229

Great Dissents—the Spirit of the Law Continues to
    Brood, Not Act   315

Index of Cases   417
Index   435

PREFACE

A dissenting judgment, as ordinarily understood, is a judgment or an opinion of a judge, sitting as part of a larger bench, who 'dissents' (i.e. disagrees) with the opinion or judgment of the majority. Dissenting judgments or opinions appear in different ways. A dissent is nonetheless a dissent, despite the fact that it may arrive at the same conclusion as that of the majority, but by an antithetical, or even different, set of reasons. Sometimes, the dissenting judgment may be *total*, in the sense that it distances itself not only from the reasoning of the majority judgment but also from its conclusion. Sometimes, the dissent may be *partial*, in that the dissenting judge agrees with certain points in the majority judgment, but disagrees with some other point or points, and ultimately reaches either the same or a different conclusion. For example, while a majority decision of the Supreme Court of India may call for a high court judgment to be upheld, the dissenting judge may, after dissenting on one or more points, send the matter back to the high court on remand to decide a particular issue/issues afresh. Sometimes, there can even be a wolf hiding in sheep's clothing—a concurring judgment that may be styled as such, but may in fact reach the same conclusion by reasoning which does not square with that of the majority. This book has all the aforesaid examples of judgments which may be categorized as 'dissenting' judgments, in the sense just mentioned.

In this book, I have done a thorough study of all the dissenting judgments of the Supreme Court of India, and have attempted—in my own way—to classify most of them according to their quality, conservatism and, the opposite—foresight.

The impetus for this book has come from two sources. The first is a lecture delivered by me in 2016 at the invitation of Justice Sujata V. Manohar, retired judge of the Supreme Court of India, on the occasion of the Twelfth Memorial Lecture in memory of her father, Justice K.T. Desai. For the purpose of delivering this lecture in Bombay, I had done some basic research into great dissents by great dissenters of the Supreme Court of India—namely, Justices S. Fazl Ali, Vivian Bose, Subba Rao and Chief Justice M. Hidayatullah. The second impetus was on account of the disease that stormed the world in 2020—COVID-19—which has led to people remaining in seclusion. My five-week period of imposed isolation in March 2020 led me to research cases from overseas, as a result of which I have ploughed through a large number of dissenting judgments of the great dissenters of the United States Supreme Court such as Justices Oliver Wendell Holmes and William O. Douglas. Interestingly, among the more recent dissenters is the late Justice Antonin Scalia, whose hysterical style of writing brings out with great clarity why his dissenting opinion is invariably correct, and better still, why the majority opinion is invariably wrong!

Apart from the great dissents of the US Supreme Court, I have also been privileged to study and analyse for this book some of the dissents and dissenters of the English courts, including Lord Shaw, Lord Atkin, Lord Reid, Lord Brown and Lord Denning, amongst others. Another rich haul of dissents has come from Australia, in the judgments of Justices Isaacs, Michael Kirby and Chief Justice Dickson, each of whom has added as much to literature as to the law.

Just like Edward Gibbon, who, after completing his magnum opus, *The History of the Decline and Fall of the Roman Empire*, said that he had lost a companion of twenty years, whose void would never be filled, I feel like I, too, have lost my comrade from those weeks of intense preparation and research putting this book together. I hope the reader enjoys reading this book as much as I did writing it.

Enjoy!

I

THE NEED FOR DISSENT

From time immemorial, different systems of law have thrown up different modalities in seeking to arrive at the elusive goal that has been set up in each of them—the advancement of the cause of justice in accordance with law. In an interesting article, Michael Kirby, retired judge of the Australian High Court, expresses the view that, across the world, civil law systems predominate over the common law tradition.[*]

In several civil law systems in the European continent, the principles of unanimity and certainty—which are bulwarks of public confidence—were considered important enough to trump all other considerations. This may well have been because the European magistrate, unlike the common law magistrate, performs judicial as well as administrative duties, resulting in a blurred distinction between the two.[†] For this reason, even superior courts in these nations deliver one single judgment without naming its author—after all, the judgment is of the 'Court', as a collective body of individuals. It was perceived in some of these nations that unless this were done, the decision would be regarded by the public as being limited and weak.[‡] Remnants of this system are still to be found in as many as seven out of twenty-seven countries of the European Union.[§] As a matter of fact, even today in Germany—apart from the Federal Constitutional Court situated at Karlsruhe—courts do not tolerate any dissenting judgments.[¶]

---

[*] Michael Kirby, 'Judicial Dissent—Common Law and Civil Law Traditions', *Law Quarterly Review*, Vol. 123 (July 2007): p. 379.

[†] Edward Dumbauld, '*Dissenting Opinions in International Adjudication*', *University of Pennsylvania Law Review*, Vol. 90, No. 8 (June 1942): pp. 929 at 932.

[‡] A useful history of the introduction of dissent into the civil-law systems of Europe is given by Edward Dumbauld, '*Dissenting Opinions in International Adjudication*' (supra), pp. 937 and 941.

[§] *Dissenting Opinions in the Supreme Courts of the Member States*, study prepared by the Directorate-General for Internal Policies, European Parliament (2012), 30f at p. 7.

[¶] Edward McGlynn Gaffney Jr, 'The Importance of Dissent and the Imperative of Judicial Civility', *Valparaiso University Law Review*, Vol. 28, No. 2 (1994): pp. 583; 591 (33f).

There is an interesting account of how, pursuant to World War 2, an attempt was made to stifle the delivery of minority opinions in the Tokyo War Crimes Trials which took place from May 1946 to November 1948.* This was done as three of the eleven judges adjudicating the trial had arrived late to the particular meeting in which the other eight judges had agreed that 'there would be no separate or dissenting opinions at the conclusion of the trial'. Justice Radhabinod Pal from India, one of the three judges who had arrived late to the meeting, did not adhere to this agreement, and ended up writing a long dissenting judgment of over 1200 pages.†

In the common law countries, however, English law had one rule for the British Isles and another for its colonies. Insofar as the King's Bench was concerned, judgments were delivered *seriatim*, in order of seniority of all the judges who sat on the bench.‡ It is said that Lord Reid followed this practice in 80 per cent of the appeals he was a part of, and justified it on the ground that judicial prose should not be construed as if it were a statute, and that legal development was best fostered by separate concurring opinions supplementing each other and explaining the principles in such a way so as to leave latitude for further developments in the course of future application of these principles.§ Lord Bingham also favoured this in civil cases, with Justice Frankfurter, of the United States Supreme Court, thinking of this as a 'healthy practice'.¶

---

* J.D. Heydon, 'Threats to Judicial Independence', *Law Quarterly Review*, Vol. 129 (April 2013): pp. 205–22.

† Ibid., pp. 208–09.

‡ William J. Brennan Jr, 'In Defense of Dissents', *Hastings Law Journal*, Vol. 37, No. 3 (1986), p. 432; Ruth Bader Ginsburg, 'The Role of Dissenting Opinions', lecture, Harvard Club of Washington DC, 17 December 2009, p. 2. *Grindley v. Barker* ([1798] 1 Bos and Pul 229 at 238) is an early example in which it was pointed out: 'It is impossible that bodies of men should always be brought to think alike: there is often a degree of coercion and the majority is governed by the minority and vice versa according to the strengths of opinions, tempers, prejudices and even interests.' It was further held that decisions which relate to matters of public concern, as opposed to purely private matters should, in the absence of contrary indication in the context, be decided by majority vote. *See* John Alder, 'Dissents in Courts of Last Resort: Tragic Choices?', *Oxford Journal of Legal Studies*, Vol. 20, No. 2 (2000): pp. 221–46 at 233, 52f.

§ J.D. Heydon, 'Threats to Judicial Independence' (supra), pp. 205, 214.

¶ Ibid., in particular, 41f–44f.

The delivery of numerous judgments *seriatim* can, however, lead to chaotic results. Where a number of concurring judgments of different judges have to be put together in order to determine the correct *ratio* of the decision as a whole, this can be done only with great difficulty, or sometimes, not at all. Two examples of this from the Supreme Court of India will suffice.

Early in the Supreme Court's history, in its judgment in *In re: Delhi Laws Act, 1912* (1951),* seven judges gave seven different verdicts on what amounted to the delegation of an 'essential' legislative function. The difficulty in discovering a *ratio* of this judgment was expressed by a later five-judge bench of the court in *Rajnarain Singh v. Chairman, Patna Administration Committee* (1955).† In *Rajnarain Singh*, after setting out the different opinions in *In re: Delhi Laws*, a *ratio* of the judgment was culled out, stating that two of the seven judges had 'swung the balance', as their opinions embodied the greatest common measure of agreement amongst the seven judges:

> Now what exactly does Section 3(1)(f) authorize? After its amendment it does two things: first, it empowers the delegated authority to pick any section it chooses out of the Bihar and Orissa Municipal Act of 1922 and extend it to 'Patna'; and second, it empowers the Local Government (and later the Governor) to apply it with such 'restrictions and modifications' as it thinks fit.
>
> In the *Delhi Laws Act* case, the following provision was held to be good by a majority of four to three:
>
> 'The Provincial Government may . . . extend with such restrictions and modifications as it thinks fit . . . any enactment which is in force in any part of British India at the date of such notification.'
>
> Mukherjea and Bose, JJ., who swung the balance, held that not only could an entire enactment with modification be extended but also a part of one; and indeed that was the actual decision in *Burah* case on which the majority founded. But Mukherjea and Bose, JJ., both placed a very restricted meaning on the words 'restriction' and 'modification' and, as

---

* (1951) SCR 747.
† (1955) 1 SCR 290.

they swung the balance, their opinions must be accepted as the decision of the Court because their opinions embody the greatest common measure of agreement among the seven Judges.*

Likewise, in *S.R. Bommai v. Union of India* (1994),† a nine-judge bench of the Supreme Court had to decide the judicial reviewability of a Presidential Proclamation under Article 356 of the Constitution, where the President had to be satisfied that the government of a state could not be carried on in accordance with the provisions of the Constitution. Six different judgments were delivered in this case, each of them containing differences as to the judicial reviewability of such a proclamation of emergency. Soli Sorabjee has expressed the difficulty in discovering a *ratio* in this case:‡

> The task of determining the ultimate *ratio* has not been rendered easy because there is no order of the Court signed by all the judges enunciating the conclusions of the Court on the various issues decided by it. The exercise becomes more difficult because of the selective concurrence of Justice Pandian with some of the conclusions reached by Justices Sawant and Kuldip Singh, and his agreement with the reasoning and other conclusions arrived at by Justices Jeevan Reddy and Agrawal.
>
> The legal position is that in ascertaining the law declared by the Supreme Court regard must be had to the judgments of the Judges who are in the majority. Separate concurring judgments form a part of the majority judgment of the Court. In *Guardians of the Poor of the West Derby Union v. Guardians of the Poor of the Atcham Union* it was observed as follows:
>
>> [F]our of the learned Judges in the House of Lords gave judgment. Now we know that each of them considers the matter separately, and they then consider the matter jointly, interchanging their judgments, so that every one of them has seen the judgment of the others. If they mean to differ in

---

* Ibid., at 302 and 303.
† (1994) 3 SCC 1.
‡ Soli Sorabjee, 'Decision of the Supreme Court in *S.R. Bommai v. Union of India*: a Critique', (1994) 3 SCC (Jour) 1.

their view, they say openly when they come to deliver their judgments, and if they do not do this, it must be taken that each of them agrees with the judgment of the others.

In a subsequent decision, *Overseers of Manchester v. Guardians of Ormskirk Union* it was held that 'where in the House of Lords one of the learned Lords gives an elaborate explanation of the meaning of the statute, and some of the learned Lords present concur in the explanation, and none express their dissent from it, it must be taken that all of them agreed in it.'

No doubt, the conclusions arrived at by the judges in the majority have been reached by different processes of reasoning. But they cannot be ignored for that reason because 'one would rather have thought that a conclusion stands more fortified when it can be supported not on one but on several lines of reasoning'.

It is significant that Pandian, J. has not dissented from or disapproved of any of the conclusions reached by Sawant and Kuldip Singh, JJ. Again these conclusions have not been dissented from in the judgment of Jeevan Reddy and Agrawal, JJ. There is a difference in emphasis, but not with the conclusions. Accordingly it is submitted that the judgments of Sawant and Kuldip Singh, JJ. to the extent they are not directly or by necessary implication inconsistent with judgments of Justices Jeevan Reddy and Agrawal, are part of the majority judgment and constitute the law of the land under Article 141 of the Constitution.

There is another difficulty. There are observations in the minority judgments which are not in direct conflict with the reasoning and conclusions reached by the majority. Furthermore the majority judgments have not dissented from nor expressed any reservation about these observations. For example, Justice Ramaswamy in illustrating situations which in his opinion can warrant the inference of breakdown of constitutional machinery has mentioned 'gross mismanagement of affairs by a State Government; corruption or abuse of its power'. Another such situation hinted by the learned Judge is wasteful public expenditure by the Chief Minister of a State whose life-size photo is published in all national and regional dailies everyday at great public expenditure despite sufficient warning by the Centre.

What is the legal effect of these off the cuff observations? Do they constitute the law of the land under Article 141 of the Constitution? How are the High Courts to understand them? Should they be regarded as binding on them? The position is further complicated because the Supreme Court has referred with approval to minority opinion in a judgment because the majority has not expressed any different opinion on the point.

It is respectfully submitted that most of these difficulties would not arise if judges strictly adhered to the wholesome rule evolved by the apex court that in adjudication of constitutional issues it is essential that no opinion should be expressed nor observations made on matters which are not directly in issue. It would also be helpful if judges clearly expressed their disagreement with or reservations about questions on which opinions have been expressed by other members of the bench.

Now to the daunting task: What has the Supreme Court decided in *Bommai*'s case?[*]

The conclusion of the learned author finally is:

The sad part is that at the end of the day it is not possible to deduce with certainty the true *ratio* of the judgment with regard to various other issues on which separate and disparate pronouncements have been made.

An agreed order recording the final conclusions which flow from the majority decision was very necessary. Law, it is rightly said, should be clear and precise. The same wholesome prescription applies to declaration of law by the highest court of the land particularly as we are informed by it that judges are presumed to know the tendency of parties concerned to interpret the language in the judgments differently to suit their purposes and the consequent importance that the words have to be chosen very carefully so as not to give room for controversy.[†]

As opposed to the delivery of judgments by all members of a court, the Judicial Committee of the Privy Council was mandated, by an interdict going back to 1627—the time of Charles I, a Stuart monarch—to only pronounce one judgment without any dissenting opinion.[‡] Viscount

---

[*] Ibid., pp. 9–10.
[†] Id., p. 32.
[‡] R.V.R Heuston, *Lives of the Lord Chancellors 1885–1940* (Oxford: Clarendon Press, 1964), p. 178.

Sankey, Lord Chancellor, in *British Coal Corp. v. The King* (1935),[*] summarized the nature of the appeal to the Privy Council as follows:

> It will be convenient to summarize in the briefest terms the nature of the appeal from Dominion or Colonial Courts to His Majesty in Council. The position of this Board, the Judicial Committee of the Privy Council, in relation to such appeals may first be indicated. The Judicial Committee is a statutory body established in 1833 by an Act of 3 & 4 Will. 4, c. 41, entitled an Act for the better Administration of Justice in His Majesty's Privy Council. It contains (*inter alia*) the following recital: 'And whereas, from the decisions of various courts of judicature in the East Indies, and in the plantations, and colonies and other dominions of His Majesty abroad, an appeal lies to His Majesty in Council.' The Act then provides for the formation of a Committee of His Majesty's Privy Council, to be styled the Judicial Committee of the Privy Council, and enacts that 'all appeals or complaints in the nature of appeals whatever, which either by virtue of this Act or of any law, statute or custom may be brought before His Majesty in Council' from the order of any Court or judge should thereafter be referred by His Majesty to, and heard by, the Judicial Committee, as established by the Act, who should make a report or recommendation to His Majesty in Council for his decision thereon, the nature of such report or recommendation being always stated in open Court. The Act contained a great number of provisions for the conduct of appeals. It is clear that the Committee is regarded in the Act as a judicial body or Court, though all it can do is to report or recommend to His Majesty in Council, by whom alone the Order in Council which is made to give effect to the report of the Committee is made.
>
> But according to constitutional convention it is unknown and unthinkable that His Majesty in Council should not give effect to the report of the Judicial Committee, who are thus in truth an appellate Court of law, to which by the statute of 1833 all appeals within their purview are referred.[†]

---

[*] 1935 A.C. 500.
[†] Ibid., at 510–11.

The difference between Privy Council judgments and those delivered on the European continent was only that the name of the author of the judgment always appeared when a Privy Council judgment was delivered. Originally, the Judicial Committee of the Privy Council was not a 'Court'. This is well brought out by John de Pencier Wright, a former judge of the Superior Court of Ontario, Canada, as follows:

> The Judicial Committee of the Privy Council was (and is) not a court. Proceedings did not go to it as 'appeals' in the formal sense but as petitions for justice 'to the foot of the Throne'. The petitioner asserted that he had gone through the court system and had not received justice. The Monarch appointed 'a Committee of my Privy Councillors' to investigate. The members of the committee did not wear robes. They sat in ordinary suits, although counsel appearing before them appeared in robes and wigs. The members did not sit on a dais. They sat at a table on the same level as counsel. At one time they sat at a long table with an empty chair at the end for the Monarch, who never joined them. Under Lord Haldane, this table was replaced by a semi-circular table, and there is no longer an empty chair. The decisions of the Committee were not 'judgments', they were 'advice' to the Monarch, and were handed down in the form of an Order In Council—tied with a red ribbon and bearing the Great Seal. Historically, only one judge delivered reasons for judgment, and, until 1966, no dissents appeared on the face of the Judicial Committee's record, in accordance with a standing order going back to 1627 prohibiting the disclosure of dissenting opinions. Reform of the judicial functions of the Privy Council was effected by Lord Brougham in 1833. Because the membership of the broad Privy Council was drawn from amongst members of Parliament and others, there was no guarantee that the members would be lawyers. A judicial committee of the Privy Council was deemed advisable, and one was created at that time.*

---

* John de Pencier Wright, 'The Judicial Committee of the Privy Council', 10 *Green Bag* 2D 363, pp. 364–65.

Viscount Haldane, in a speech made in 1921, described the Privy Council with an apocryphal story, which is narrated by Lord Neuberger of Abbotsbury as follows:

> That such disputes came before the JCPC might explain why the institution in the 19th and early 20th centuries had more than a whiff of cultural imperialism about it. In his address, Viscount Haldane described an apocryphal story of the JCPC, said to have been a favourite of 19th and early 20th century after-dinner speakers addressing legal gatherings. It went something like this: 'When crossing India's Rajputana plateau, a nineteenth-century traveller noticed a group of villagers offering sacrifice to a far-off god, who had restored to them certain lands which had been seized by a predatory rajah. Inquiries about the deity they were worshipping drew the response: "We know nothing of him but that he is a good god, and that his name is the Judicial Committee of the Privy Council"'.*

Lord Neuberger also states the role of the sovereign in these proceedings:

> Another aspect of the JCPC concerns the role of the sovereign. In his 1921 address, Viscount Haldane described how at the bench there was 'always a chair left vacant, for a very highly constitutional reason—the Sovereign is supposed to come and sit there, and dispense justice to the whole Empire', although he noted that he could 'not say that [he] ever observed him do so'. Nowadays, you will be unsurprised to hear, there is not merely no monarch present, but no vacant chair.†

It is also perhaps for this reason that only 'advice' was tendered by the Privy Council to the sovereign, such that the sovereign—being unconcerned about dissentient voices in his or her Privy Council—had to act in accordance with the 'advice' given.‡

---

* Lord Neuberger, 'The Judicial Committee of the Privy Council in the 21st Century', *Cambridge Journal of International and Comparative Law*, Vol. 3, Issue 1 (2014): pp. 30–45, 36–37.
† Ibid., p. 39.
‡ In *The Law Lords* (London: Macmillan Press Ltd, 1982), Alan Paterson notes (at pp. 98–99): 'Lord Radcliffe considered it one of the strengths of the Privy Council that,

In Chief Justice P.B. Gajendragadkar's autobiography, *To the Best of My Memory*, an interesting incident is pointed out, involving an Indian Privy Councillor, Justice M.R. Jayakar, as follows:

> As I have observed, the Privy Council wrote only one judgment. M.R. Jayakar, who was a member of the Privy Council, once told me that on a matter of Hindu Law, where he did not agree with the majority, after discussion, the majority view was accepted, and it was Jayakar who was asked to draft the judgment. But then the Privy Council did not pass a decree. It merely rendered advice to the Crown. In the House of Lords, and in the Supreme Court of the United States, separate judgments are common. These courts did not follow the convention that the court should speak through one judgment and only one dissent is expressed separately.*

It can thus be seen that within the common law tradition itself, when matters related to the British Isles, judgments could be delivered *seriatim* by all the judges, but when it came to the colonies, one judgment alone spoke for the highest appellate court.

"The people who were accustomed to being in the Council got rather good at rendering one judgment that reflected the opinion of the others. There was a sort of tradition that you didn't take a strong line unless it was one which could be shared by the others." Other Law Lords were less enthusiastic. Lord Pearce was one of them: "We all know that in the Privy Council it gave quite a bit of weakness over the centuries to a Privy Council judgment that sentences were put in for the man who thought that the appeal was doubtful as to whether it should succeed, and felt that it was more likely it should fail, as against the man who wrote it, who was certain it should succeed, and so he would put in the sentences . . . you are getting a compromise judgment in a sense."' This practice of the Privy Council, of delivering only one judgment, has been criticized by J.D. Heydon, 'Threats to Judicial Independence' (supra), p. 212, as follows: 'Another example of the difficulties that can arise from judgments given in a single composite form is Privy Council advice before 1966. Since neither dissents not separate opinions were permitted, there was no outlet for the expression of internal disagreements—either as to the correctness of the outcome or as to the path to the outcome. This created tensions. These tensions tended to be masked by assertions of an emollient, laconic and conclusory kind unsupported by any, or any detailed, expressed reasoning. This language, perhaps generated by bargaining, did not assist in making the law certain. The same thing can be said of some decisions of the Court of Appeal in criminal cases.'

* P.B. Gajendragadkar, *To the Best of My Memory* (New Delhi: Bharatiya Vidya Bhavan, 2013), pp. 132–33.

In the United States of America, the first Supreme Court—
which opened in New York in 1791—followed the English practice
of judgments being delivered *seriatim* by all the justices of the court.
This practice was ended by Chief Justice John Marshall, who remained
the Chief Justice of the United States for a period of thirty-four years.
The great Chief Justice broke with English tradition and adopted the
practice of announcing the judgments of the court in a single opinion,
almost invariably his own.[*] Interestingly, Justice Ruth Bader Ginsburg,
in her presentation to the Harvard Club of Washington DC,[†] points
out that this was probably because Chief Justice Marshall and the other
associate justices of the early Supreme Court lived and dined together in
the same boarding house/inn when the justices convened in Washington
DC, which was the newly set-up capital to which the court shifted when
Marshall became Chief Justice.[‡] Indeed, Chief Justice Marshall delivered
a number of opinions which were contrary to his own judgments and
vote in conference.[§]

In 1804, President Thomas Jefferson put a major spanner in the works
by appointing Justice William Johnson to the Supreme Court.[¶] The newly
appointed justice issued a concurring opinion in one of the first cases

---

[*] William J. Brennan Jr, 'In Defense of Dissents' (supra), p. 433; Ruth Bader Ginsburg,
'The Role of Dissenting Opinions' (supra), p. 1.

[†] Ruth Bader Ginsburg, 'The Role of Dissenting Opinions' (supra), p. 2.

[‡] Hundreds of years later, Chief Justice Earl Warren achieved the same result in a seminal
decision of the US Supreme Court which ended racial discrimination, namely, *Brown
v. Board of Education* (347 U.S. 483). Four out of nine justices came from the South,
and one Justice Stanley Reed proved particularly intractable in his views. In Bernard
Schwartz's book *A History of the Supreme Court* (Oxford: Oxford University Press, 1993),
the author narrates how dinner diplomacy won Justice Stanley Reed over so that this
seminal decision could be delivered unanimously, *see* p. 295.

[§] David P. Curry, 'The Constitution in the Supreme Court: the Powers of the Federal
Courts, 1801–1835', *University of Chicago Law Review*, Vol. 49, Issue 3 (Summer 1982):
pp. 646 at 648; Donald M. Roper, 'Judicial Unanimity and the Marshall Court: a Road
to Reappraisal', *American Journal of Legal History*, Vol. 9 (April 1965): pp. 118 at 119;
and Karl M. ZoBell, 'Division of Opinion in the Supreme Court: a History of Judicial
Disintegration', *Cornell Law Quarterly*, Vol. 44, Issue 2 (Winter 1959): pp. 186 at 193.

[¶] A whole chapter titled 'William Johnson: Dissenter of the Marshall Court'—being
Chapter 2 in Percival E. Jackson's book *Dissent in the Supreme Court: A Chronology*
(Oklahoma: University of Oklahoma Press, 1969)—has been devoted to this justice, as
being the originator of the dissenting opinion in the Marshall Court.

in which he participated. His colleagues were stunned. Justice Johnson described their reaction in a letter to President Jefferson as follows:

> Some cases soon occurred in which I differed from my brethren, and I felt it a thing of course to deliver my opinion. But during the rest of the Session I heard nothing but lectures on the indecency of judges cutting at each other, and the loss of reputation which the Virginia appellate court had sustained by pursuing such a course.[*]

The short-lived tradition of one unanimous opinion had been broken and, by 1806, Justice Paterson had delivered the first dissenting opinion of the court in *Sims v. Slacum* (1806).[†] After this, dissents were never again a rarity—even Chief Justice Marshall went on to write nine dissents in his thirty-four years as chief justice.[‡]

An early dissenting opinion given by Justice Rush in Pennsylvania illustrates that American judges were aware of the value of dissents, even if dissents occurred infrequently. In *Purviance v. Angus* (1786), the learned justice wrote:

> However disposed to concur with my brethren in this cause, I have not been able to do it. Unanimity in courts of justice, though a very desirable object, ought never to be attained at the expense of sacrificing the judgment.[§]

All this leads us to the fundamental question of whether a dissenting judgment really has some value, or is it a mere exercise in futility, as it cannot be said to have stated the law correctly, and may even be considered irrelevant, as it cannot be cited as precedent. In point of fact, H.L.A. Hart—a distinguished legal philosopher—declared, 'a Supreme Tribunal has the last word in saying what the law is, and when it has said it, the statement that the court was "wrong" has no consequences

---

[*] William J. Brennan Jr, 'In Defense of Dissents' (supra), p. 434.
[†] 7 U.S. 300 (1806).
[‡] William J. Brennan Jr, 'In Defense of Dissents' (supra), p. 434.
[§] 1 Dallas 180 (Pa. Ct. Errors and App. 1786) at 494.

within the system: no one's rights or duties are thereby altered'.* Indeed, judge Learned Hand, another outstanding legal jurist, complained that a dissenting opinion 'cancels the impact of monolithic solidarity on which the authority of a bench of Justice so largely depends'.†

Justice Jackson, also a justice known for his individual views, put it thus:

> The right of dissent is a valuable one. Wisely used on well-chosen occasions, it has been of great service to the profession and to the law. But there is nothing good, for either the Court or the dissenter, in dissenting per se. Each dissenting opinion is a confession of failure to convince the writer's colleagues, and the true test of a judge is his influence in leading, not in opposing, his court.‡

One of the greatest dissenters of all time, Justice Oliver Wendell Holmes, started out cautiously enough, echoing this trend of thought. Thus, in *Northern Securities Company v. The United States* (1903),§ the learned justice's first dissent in the Supreme Court, he stated:

> I am unable to agree with the judgment of the majority of the Court, and although I think it useless and undesirable, as a rule, to express dissent, I feel bound to do so in this case and to give my reasons for it . . . Great cases like hard cases make for bad law. For great cases are called great not by reason of their real importance in shaping the law of the future but because of some accident of immediate overwhelming interest which appeals to the feelings and distorts the judgment. The immediate interests exercise a kind of hydraulic pressure which makes what previously was clear seem doubtful, and before which even well-settled principles of law will bend.¶

---

* H.L.A. Hart, *The Concept of Law* (Oxford: Oxford University Press, 1961), p. 138.
† Learned Hand, *The Bill of Rights* (Cambridge, Massachusetts: Harvard University Press, 1958), p. 72.
‡ R.H. Jackson, *The Supreme Court in the American System of Government* (Cambridge, Massachusetts: Harvard University Press, 1955), p. 18.
§ 193 U.S. 197 (1903).
¶ Alfred Lief, *The Dissenting Opinions of Mr. Justice Holmes* (New York: The Vanguard Press, 1929), p. 164.

However, in perhaps the most important dissent of his life in the following year, disagreeing with the majority judgment in *Lochner v. State of New York* (1905),* the learned justice felt emboldened enough to state:

> I regret sincerely that I am unable to agree with the judgment in this case and that I think it my duty to express dissent.[†]

Also opposed to the view of firing off a dissenting opinion whenever a justice felt the need to, Justice Louis Brandeis in *Di Santo v. Pennsylvania* (1927)[‡] cautioned:

> In most matters it is more important that the applicable rule of law be settled than that it be settled right.[§]

Justice Brandeis's view was felicitously stated by John P. Frank in his book review of Alexander Bickel's *The Unpublished Opinions of Mr Justice Brandeis* (1957) as follows:

> Brandeis was a great institutional man. He realized that . . . random dissents . . . weaken the institutional impact of the Court and handicap it in the doing of its fundamental job. Dissents . . . need to be saved for some major matters if the Court is not to appear indecisive and quarrelsome . . . To have discarded some of [his separate] opinions is a supreme example of [Brandeis's] sacrifice to [the] strength and consistency of the Court. And he ha[d] his reward: his shots were all the harder because he chose his ground.[¶]

Justice Brandeis's view is fleshed out in some detail by Robert Post,** who gives examples of justices who, like Justice Brandeis, had the same

---

198 U.S. 45 (1905).
[†] Alfred Lief, *The Dissenting Opinions of Mr. Justice Holmes* (supra), p. 3.
[‡] 273 U.S. 34 (1927).
[§] Ibid., at 42.
[¶] John P. Frank, 'Book Review', *Journal of Legal Education*, Vol. 10, Issue 3 (1957–58): pp. 401 at 404.
[**] Robert Post, 'The Supreme Court Opinion as Institutional Practice: Dissent, Legal Scholarship, and Decision-making in the Taft Court', *Minnesota Law Review*, Vol. 85,

conservative view towards dissenting judgments.* In fact, Justice Holmes in *Federal Trade Commission v. Beechnut Co.* (1922)[†] deprecated 'persistent expressions of opinions that do not command the agreement of the Court', as reaching the 'obvious limits of propriety'. A *per curiam* opinion in *United States v. Lehigh Valley R.R. Co.* (1920)[‡] also stated:

> The Chief Justice and Mr Justice Holmes . . . if they exercised their independent judgment, would be for affirmance; [they] nevertheless concur in the conclusion now announced by the Court because they consider that they are constrained to it in virtue of the controlling effect of the previous decisions . . . cited in the opinion of the Court.[§]

Blom-Cooper and Drewry[¶] also point out that, very often, a judge of the US Supreme Court or the House of Lords held back from dissenting if he found the matter not important enough, or that a doubt as to the majority view was the highest that the learned judge felt about the case at hand. They put it thus:

> In *Richardson v. Shaw* 209 U.S. 365, 385 (1908) he [Justice Holmes] said: 'A just deference to the views of my brethren prevents my dissenting from the conclusion reached, although I cannot but feel a lingering doubt', and in *Bernheimer v. Conwase* 206 U.S. 516, 535 (1907) he said that 'under the circumstances I shall say no more than that I doubt the result'.
>
> A similar and healthy practice has emerged in the House of Lords in recent years. In *University of Strathclyde v. Carnegie Trustees*, 1968 S.C. (H.L.) 27, 47, Lord Wilberforce said, '. . . as the point is one of construction and as the arguments in favour of the limitation to the four old Universities have been clearly and forcefully put in the unanimous judgments of the First Division, now to be overruled, I see no purpose in diluting them by observations of my own. I must however rank myself

---

No. 5 (May 2001): p. 1267.

* Ibid., at 1340–355.

[†] 257 U.S. 441 (1922) at p. 456.

[‡] 254 U.S. 255 (1920).

[§] Percival E. Jackson, *Dissent in the Supreme Court* (supra), p. 13.

[¶] Louis Blom-Cooper and Gavin Drewry, *Final Appeal: A Study of the House of Lords in its Judicial Capacity* (Oxford: Clarendon Press, 1972).

as dubitans'. In *C.I.R. v. Carron Co.* 1967 S.C. (H.L.) 47, 61, Lord Upjohn said, '. . . as it is a most difficult and border-line case, depending largely on the facts, and in the unanimous opinion of your Lordship, of the judges of the First Division and the Special Commissioners as they may otherwise be described, I shall concur in dismissing the appeal.' In *Pickering v. John Tye & Son Ltd.* (unreported) Lord Donovan said, 'I have had some doubts about this case. But your Lordships, with greater experience of these cases than I possess, have reached the conclusion that these omissions are inadequate grounds upon which to reject the Respondent's argument; and in the circumstances I do not feel so firmly attached to my doubts as to press them to the point of dissent. I must therefore concur in the dismissal of the appeal.'

Lord Reid, in *Vandervell Trustees Ltd. v. White* (1970) 46 T.C. 341 succumbed to a dour Scottish approach when he prefaced his judgment thus: 'I am under the disadvantage that I am not familiar with the practical operation of the English Rules of Court. Treating the matter as an ordinary question of construction, I would have been inclined to agree with the decision of the Court of Appeal. But if your Lordships think otherwise I am not prepared to dissent on the matter.*

On the other hand, Justice Joseph Story, the youngest-ever Supreme Court Justice to have been appointed to the court (at age thirty-two), said in *The Nereide* (1815):†

It is a matter of regret that in this conclusion I have the misfortune to differ from a majority of the court, for whose superior learning and ability I entertain the most entire respect. But I hold it an indispensable duty not to surrender my own judgment, because a great weight of opinion is against me—a weight which no one can feel more sensibly than myself. Had this been an ordinary case I should have contented myself with silence; but believing that no more important or interesting question ever came before a prize tribunal, and that the national rights

---

* Ibid., p. 86, 1f.
† 9 Cranch. 388 at 455 (1815).

suspended on it are of infinite moment to the maritime world, I have thought it not unfit to pronounce my own opinion.

Justice Story also remarked in *Briscoe v. Bank of Kentucky* (1837)[*] that it was his 'duty to give public expression' of his opinions 'when they differed from that of the Court', because 'the public have a right to know the opinion of every judge who dissents from the opinion of the Court and the reasons of his dissent'.[†]

Another great dissenter, Justice William O. Douglas of the US Supreme Court, having written as many as 486 dissenting opinions,[‡] stated:

> The right to dissent is the only thing that makes life tolerable for a Judge of an Appellate court.[§]

Justice Douglas also said:

> It is the right of dissent, not the right or duty to conform, which gives dignity, worth, and individuality to man. As Carl Sandburg recently said, 'There always ought to be beatniks in a culture, hollering about the respectables.'[¶]

Justice Douglas's views on the importance of dissenting opinion are fleshed out in his article 'The Dissent, A Safeguard of Democracy',[**] where he wrote:

---

[*] 11 Pet. 257 (1837) at 329.

[†] Percival E. Jackson (supra), p. 17.

[‡] Bernard Schwartz, *A Book of Legal Lists: The Best and Worst in American Law* (Oxford: Oxford University Press, 1997), p. 283.

[§] William O. Douglas, *America Challenged* (New York: Avon Books, 1960), p. 4. Incidentally, this justice penned the greatest number of opinions as well—1164—in the longest-ever tenure at the US Supreme Court, which lasted over thirty-six years. Over the course of this long stint as a US Supreme Court justice, this gifted individual also wrote over thirty books. The only comparison to this justice in our pantheon of judges is Krishna Iyer, J., who wrote over 400 judgments over the course of his seven-year stint on the Supreme Court, and authored over ninety books.

[¶] J.L. Campbell III, 'The Spirit of Dissent', *Judicature*, Vol. 66 (1983): 305 at 311.

[**] William O. Douglas, 'The Dissent: A Safeguard of Democracy', *Journal of the American Judicature Society*, Vol. 32, Issue 4 (December 1948): p. 104.

[D]issents or concurring opinions may salvage for tomorrow the principle that was sacrificed or forgotten today.*

In this article, Justice Douglas went on to point out:

Certainty and unanimity in the law are possible both under the fascist and communist systems. They are not only possible; they are indispensable; for complete subservience to the political regime is a *sine qua non* to judicial survival under either system. One cannot imagine the courts of Hitler engaged in a public debate over the principles of Der Feuhrer, with a majority of one or four deploring or denouncing the principles themselves. One cannot imagine a judge of a Communist court dissenting against the decrees of the Kremlin. Disagreement among judges is as true to the character of democracy as freedom of speech itself. The dissenting opinion is as genuinely American as Otis' denunciation of the general warrants, as Thomas Paine's, Thomas Jefferson's, or James Madison's briefs for civil liberties.

Democracy, like religion, is full of sects and schisms. Every political campaign demonstrates it. Every session of a legislature proves it. No man or group of men has a monopoly on truth, wisdom or virtue. An idea, once advanced for public acceptance, divides like an amoeba. The ifs and buts and howevers each claim a part; and what was once a whole is soon carved into many separate pieces, some of which are larger than the original itself.†

The justice then observed that in the legislative process, which is one of compromise, the ball eventually lands in the lap of the court, which then has to interpret such legislation. Obviously, therefore, differing points of view would emerge amongst the judges in the court:

And so the bill becomes the law and the law arrives before judges for interpretation. The battle that raged before the legislature is now transferred to the court. The passage of the legislation quieted the conflict

---

* Ibid., pp. 106–07.
† Ibid., p. 105.

only temporarily. It breaks out anew in the process of interpretation in the courts. A storm hits the court room, and the advocates take up the fight where the legislators left off. The same cleavage that appeared in legislative halls now shows up among the judges. Each side has eminent authority for its view since two conflicting ideas found their way into the legislation. It is therefore easy for judge or lawyer or editor to accuse the judge, who takes the opposing view, of usurping the role of the legislature. A more honest, a more objective view would concede that interpretation has legislative as well as judicial characteristics. It cannot be otherwise where the legislature has left the choice of competing theories or ideas to the judges.[*]

Dealing with *stare decisis*, or a body of stable and uniform law built up over the years, in constitutional law, the learned judge stated:

> When we move to constitutional questions, uncertainty necessarily increases. A judge who is asked to construe or interpret the Constitution often rejects the gloss which his predecessors have put on it. For the gloss may, in his view, offend the spirit of the Constitution or do violence to it. That has been the experience of this generation and of all those that have preceded. It will likewise be the experience of those which follow. And so it should be. For it is the Constitution which we have sworn to defend, not some predecessor's interpretation of it. *Stare decisis* has small place in constitutional law. The Constitution was written for all time and all ages. It would lose its great character and become feeble, if it were allowed to become encrusted with narrow, legalistic notions that dominated the thinking of one generation.[†]

All these conflicting views, therefore, lead to a general discussion on the pros and cons of dissenting judgments. Michael Kirby has outlined many reasons as to why the common law tradition favours dissenting judgments.[‡] First and foremost, he argues that the tradition of oral

---

[*] Ibid.
[†] Id., p. 106.
[‡] Michael Kirby, 'Judicial Dissent—Common Law and Civil Law Traditions' (supra), p. 379. Justice Kirby was himself one of the greatest dissenters in the Australian High Court.

argument in the common law—contrasted against written submissions in the civil law systems—would lead to a heightened perception of the pros and cons of each case, and would therefore induce each judge to give his own reasons, albeit orally, according to the seniority of his appointment.

He also points out that the recruitment of judges in the common law system consists mainly of advocates who address the court, as opposed to judges recruited in civil law countries after university, without ever having joined the bar. The common law tradition then results in a judiciary comprising experienced, strong-minded, senior-advocates-turned-judges, accustomed to independent thinking and not considering themselves members of an institutional unit or government service.

Third, notions of the courts' role in adversarial litigation produced strong reasons favouring one side or the other. Also, the difference between what Justice Kirby describes as a 'Kelsenian' approach—as opposed to the American approach to constitutional adjudication, including the doctrine of judicial review—would also lead to judges independently expressing themselves. Notions of governance, including a rule of special restraint in criminal and sentencing appeals, observed in England are not necessarily observed in other common law countries.

Andrew Lynch, in *Great Australian Dissents* (Cambridge: Cambridge University Press, 2016), pp. 8–9, states that Justice Kirby's 'kicks' against the majority judgments were in order that his dissenting view be accepted in the arena of public opinion. Lynch puts it thus: 'Lastly, both took full advantage of the liberty that is afforded the judge writing alone in dissent, free from the deadening effects of compromise and the responsibility to lay down the law with colleagues in the majority, to compose highly memorable opinions replete with "passages of great force, eloquence, and ardor". Justices Kirby and Heydon proved to be highly adept at delivering what, in the former's judgments, were referred to as "kicks" against the position adopted by their colleagues. In Kirby J.'s case, his biographer, Professor A.J. Brown, noted that the kicks became "increasingly poetically drafted, and increasingly noticed", but they were "primarily tactical weapons in his battle for public opinion". In chapter 17, Brown reflects on the different audiences that apparently explain the stark differences between Kirby J.'s dissent and that of Chief Justice Gleeson in the unsuccessful challenge to Australia's immigration detention law in *Al-Kateb v. Godwin*. The appeal to an external audience is a noted feature of some judicial opinions. While that strategy may be particularly understandable in a dissent, Professor Melvin I Urofsky claims that, "unless it can show convincingly how wrong the majority is, it will never—no matter how well it may be written—be more than an angry tirade or enter into the constitutional dialogue". In his contrasting of the opinions in *Al-Kateb v. Godwin*, Brown explores whether the decision to write for the public sacrifices a dissent's appeal to the Court on a later occasion.'

Yet another feature is that the 'Bills of Rights', contained in constitutions like the Indian Constitution, following the US Constitution, leads to the existence of strongly held, and differing, opinions over the broad language in which such laws are cast. The pedagogical function is also referred to, by which a court's judgments can be examined by citizens and non-citizens, by lawyer and by non-lawyer, particularly over the Internet—leading to judges being affected by their individual perceptions of the community's social values at the time. Intellectual integrity is said to be another important rationale for dissent. Another reason for dissenting judgments in common law countries is that they act as an inbuilt safety mechanism for the courts to internalize error prevention, as a dissent may later overrule a majority judgment.

Percival E. Jackson also justifies dissenting opinions as follows:

> However, justification for dissent finds wider ground. The pages of history testify to the need and the value of dissent. 'Dissent is essential to an effective judiciary in a democratic society,' said Justice Frankfurter [*Ferguson v. Moore-McCormack Lines*, 352 U.S. 521, 528 (1957)]. 'It record(s) prophecy and shapes history,' he said elsewhere [Frankfurter, 'Holmes and the Constitution', 41 *Harvard Law Review* 162]. It 'sounds a warning note that legal doctrine must not be pressed too far,' said Chief Justice Stone [Mason, Harlan Fiske Stone, 591]. Justice Cardozo put it thus in his mellifluous Victorian prose, 'The voice of the majority may be that of force triumphant, content with the plaudits of the hour and recking little of the morrow. The dissenter speaks of the future, and his voice is pitched to a key that will carry through the years [Cardozo, 'Law and Literature', 36]. And Chief Justice Hughes remarked, 'A dissent in a court of last resort is an appeal to the brooding spirit of the law, to the intelligence of a future day, when a later decision may possibly correct the error into which the dissenting judge believes the court to have been betrayed [Charles Evans Hughes, *The Supreme Court of the United States* (New York: Columbia University Press, 1928), p. 68].*

In *The Law Lords*, the learned author interviewed various members of the House of Lords and found that they gave the following reasons for dissenting:

---

* Percival E. Jackson (supra).

In an attempt to answer this question I asked the Law Lords what factors lead them to publish dissenting opinions and whether there was any feeling in the Lords that dissents should be discouraged. Commentators have frequently discussed the functions served by publishing dissents. They provide comfort to judges in the lower courts who are being reversed and to losing litigants, they indicate to the layman that unanimity is no easier to obtain in some difficult areas of the law than, for example, in the higher reaches of science or theology, they highlight the areas of law which are developing and uncertain, and they indicate possible limits to the legal doctrines espoused in the majority of opinions. Yet the dissenting judge may, and often will, have intended something quite different in producing the dissent. The issue of timing is important. Circulation of a dissent within the court is not the same as making it public. At the first stage, the dissenter has not given up hope of influencing his colleagues, and his dissent is part of the ongoing interaction between members of the court. For example, Lord Radcliffe told me,

> If I couldn't persuade my colleagues in the course of the hearing
> and the discussion afterwards, I tended to leave it alone and see
> whether, if I really worked hard at my opinion and circulated it
> before the decision was handed down, I might perhaps knock
> somebody off his perch.

Even if the dissenter fails to win more support for his position, his dissent may lead to changes in the majority opinion(s). Thus, John Harlan who dissented in 63 per cent of the votes taken on the Warren Court from 1963 to 1967 was well pleased if his heavily researched dissents were plagiarized in a revised majority opinion since the dialogue had worked to produce a better Court opinion. He was much more frustrated when the majority writer declined to enter into a dialogue since he saw no need to respond to the dissent—this Harlan considered to be bad judicial craftsmanship. Whether successful or not some judges withdraw their dissents at this stage, considering that they serve no further useful purpose.*

---

* Alan Paterson, *The Law Lords* (supra), pp. 100–01.

In contrast, an obvious disadvantage of writing a dissent is the public perception that the law is both stable and secure when delivered in a unanimous judgment. Obvious examples of this are the seminal decisions in *Brown v. Board of Education* (1954)* and *Cooper v. Aaron* (1958),† which ended racial segregation in schools in the US. Any dissenting opinion in either of these judgments would have given greater credibility to, or even led to, mass protests and greater defiance, given the racial discrimination in the United States in the 1950s. Even otherwise, the second judgment, in *Cooper v. Aaron*, became necessary only because of the defiant attitude of the governor of Arkansas, who refused to implement *Brown v. Board of Education* in his state.‡

This fear of dissenting judgments causing instability was echoed by Justice Frankfurter in *United States v. Rabinowitz* (1950),§ where he deprecated the court's 'giving fair ground for the belief that the law is the expression of chance, for instance, of unexpected changes in the Court's composition and the contingencies in the choice of successors'.⁵

In *Smith v. Allright* (1943),** Justice Roberts, in a powerfully worded dissent, bemoaned the fact that the majority judgment of Justice Stanley Reed, speaking for the court, had refused to follow precedent, which resulted in doubt and confusion. He put it thus:

> In *Mahnich v. Southern S.S.* Co. No. 200 of the present term [321 U.S. 96, 105, ante, 561, 64 S Ct 455], I have expressed my views with respect to the present policy of the court freely to disregard and to overrule considered decisions and the rules of law announced in them. This tendency, it seems to me, indicates an intolerance for what those

---

* 347 U.S. 483 (1954).
† 358 U.S. 1 (1958).
‡ Lord Mansfield in *Millar v. Taylor* ([1769] 4 Burrows 2303, 2395) also stressed the importance of unanimity amongst judges, stating that the untarnished unanimity of his court 'gives weight and dispatch to the decisions, certainty to the law and infinite satisfaction to the suitors . . .' However, in this very decision, he went on to acknowledge the division amongst the judges, stating: 'We have all equally tried to convince or be convinced but in vain. We continue to differ. And who ever is right, each is bound to abide by and deliver that opinion which is formed upon the fullest examination.'
§ 339 U.S. 56 at 86 (1950).
⁵ Percival E. Jackson (supra) at p. 8.
** 88 L. ed. 987 (1943).

who have composed this court in the past have conscientiously and deliberately concluded, and involves an assumption that knowledge and wisdom reside in us which was denied to our predecessors. I shall not repeat what I there said for I consider it fully applicable to the instant decisions, which but points to the moral anew.[*]

* * *

The reason for my concern is that the instant decision, overruling that announced about nine years ago, tends to bring adjudications of this tribunal into the same class as a restricted railroad ticket, good for this day and train only. I have no assurance, in view of current decisions, that the opinion announced today may not shortly be repudiated and overruled by justices who deem they have new light on the subject. In the present term the court has overruled three cases.[†]

* * *

It is regrettable that in an era marked by doubt and confusion, an era whose greatest need is steadfastness of thought and purpose, this court, which has been looked to as exhibiting consistency in adjudication, and a steadiness which would hold even in the face of temporary ebbs and flows of opinion, should now itself become the breeder of fresh doubt and confusion in the public mind as to the stability of our institutions.[‡]

The majority judgment of Justice Reed, however, dealt with this criticism as follows:

In reaching this conclusion we are not unmindful of the desirability of continuity of decision in constitutional questions. However, when convinced of former error, this Court has never felt constrained to follow precedent. In constitutional questions, where correction depends

---

[*] Ibid., pp. 998–99.
[†] Id., p. 1000.
[‡] Id., p. 1001.

THE NEED FOR DISSENT 27

on amendment and not upon legislative action this Court throughout its history has freely exercised its power to re-examine the basis of its constitutional decisions. This has long been accepted practice, and this practice has continued to this day. This is particularly true when the decision believed erroneous is the application of a constitutional principle rather than an interpretation of the Constitution to extract the principle itself. Here we are applying, contrary to the recent decision of *Grovey v. Townsend*, the well-established principle of the Fifteenth Amendment, forbidding the abridgment by a state of a citizen's right to vote. *Grovey v. Townsend* is overruled.[*]

Another nail in the coffin of dissenting judgments is the fact that the collegiality of judges—an important value in itself for the smooth functioning of the court—would get disrupted if the feelings of judges were to be wounded. An outstanding example of this is Lord Atkin's dissenting judgment in *Liversidge v. Anderson* (1941),[†] which resulted in a complete breakdown of the relationship between Lord Atkin and his brethren.

Also, *stare decisis* is likely to get disturbed if a dissenting judgment does manage to become the law later, sometimes due to a change in circumstance or changes in the personnel of the court.[‡] Dissent is supposed to sometimes give a judge an opportunity for self-publicity at the public's expense.[§] It has also been argued that a dissent might also muddy the waters by confusing the majority speeches.[¶]

Against these considerations, there are now acknowledged to be a very large number of points in favour of dissenting judgments.

---

[*] Id., p. 998. In 10f (on the same page) of this majority judgment, a large number of judgments involving constitutional interpretation in which earlier judgments were overruled are noted.

[†] (1941) UKHL 1.

[‡] William J. Brennan Jr, 'In Defense of Dissents' (supra), p. 430; Andrew Lynch, 'The Intelligence of a Future Day: The Vindication of Constitutional Dissent in the High Court of Australia, 1981–2003', *Sydney Law Review*, Vol. 29 (2007): p. 206.

[§] John Alder, 'Dissents in Courts of Last Resort: Tragic Choices?' (supra), pp. 221–46 at page 243, paragraph 3, read with 122f.

[¶] Ibid., paragraph 4 read with 125f and 126f.

The importance of dissenting judgments generally is also encapsulated in a brilliant statement made by Chief Justice Charles Evans Hughes— one of the most outstanding chief justices of the US Supreme Court— on the efficacy of such judgments. If ever there was a person who had maximum exposure to the workings of the government as well as the court, it was him. Chief Justice Hughes initially gained prominence as a top practitioner in a New York City law firm in the 1890s. During this time, he also served as a visiting professor at Cornell Law School. In 1906, he successfully ran for, and became, governor of New York, defeating the newspaper magnate William Randolph Hearst, and was re-elected in 1908. In 1910, he was appointed to the US Supreme Court by President Taft; he resigned from the Supreme Court in 1916, having emerged as a leading candidate for the Republican presidential nomination that year, with the backing of former President Theodore Roosevelt.* In 1921, Hughes was appointed the Secretary of State by President Warren Harding; he resigned from the position in 1925 in order to return to private law practice.

It is in this period, in 1928, that Hughes committed to posterity his masterly affirmation of the dissenting opinion as being an important element in the development of the law. In 1930, President Herbert Hoover nominated Hughes to become chief justice of the US Supreme Court, where he served with great distinction, retiring in 1941 at the age of seventy-nine.† Chief Justice Hughes's formulation of the efficacy of dissenting opinions is best put in his own words:

> There are some who think it desirable that dissents should not be disclosed as they detract from the force of the judgment. Undoubtedly, they do. When unanimity can be obtained without sacrifice of conviction, it strongly commends the decision to public confidence. But unanimity which is merely formal, which is recorded at the expense of strong, conflicting views, is not desirable in a court of last resort, whatever may be the effect upon public opinion at the time.

---

* Something similar to this took place in India as well. In 1967, Chief Justice Subba Rao resigned as Chief Justice of India, contested for the role of President of India, and lost.
† Frankfurter, J. compared Hughes leading a conference of the nine justices of the Supreme Court to Toscanini (the greatest conductor of music at the time) leading an orchestra.

This is so because what must ultimately sustain the Court in public confidence is the character and independence of the judges. They are not there simply to decide cases, but to decide them as they think they should be decided, and while it may be regrettable that they cannot always agree, it is better that their independence should be maintained and recognized than that unanimity should be secured through its sacrifice. This does not mean that a judge should be swift to dissent, or that he should dissent for the sake of self-exploitation or because of a lack of that capacity for cooperation which is of the essence of any group action, whether judicial or otherwise. Independence does not mean cantankerousness and a judge may be a strong judge without being an impossible person. Nothing is more distressing on any bench than the exhibition of a captious, impatient, querulous spirit. We are fortunately free from this in our highest courts in Nation and State, much freer than in some of the days gone by. Dissenting opinions enable a judge to express his individuality. He is not under the compulsion of speaking for the court and thus of securing the concurrence of a majority. In dissenting, he is a free lance. A dissent in a court of last resort is an appeal to the brooding spirit of the law, to the intelligence of a future day, when a later decision may possibly correct the error into which the dissenting judge believes the court to have been betrayed.*

Nor is this appeal always in vain. In a number of cases dissenting opinions have in time become the law. In *Rogers v. Burlington* (3 Wallace,

---

* Andrew Lynch in *Great Australian Dissents* (supra), pp. 14–15, however, draws attention to the sobering fact that in most cases, the spirit of the law 'continues to brood rather than act'. The learned author puts it thus: 'However, most of the time, the spirit of the law continues to brood rather than act. Some of the dissents in this book may yet meet with a favourable, albeit delayed, reception. As an examination of a path in the law that was not taken, chapter 16's consideration of Justice Anthony North's dissent in the Federal Court of Australia on native title extinguishment highlights the lost opportunities in this contentious area, so critical to Australia's relationship with its Indigenous peoples and to redressing their dispossession by colonization. The chapter concludes by noting recent signs that the High Court may turn back from the path upon which it set in the case of *Western Australia v. Ward* over a decade ago. Whether the Court will head in the direction that was signalled by North J. or develop some other route remains to be seen. But it is not hard to appreciate that the existence of a clearly stated alternative may enrich the Court's reassessment of the previously dominant approach.'

654), as to validity of municipal bonds, Justices Field, Grier, Miller and Chief Justice Chase dissented and the case was overruled by *Brenham v. German American Bank* (144 U.S. 173). In *Doyle v. Continental Insurance Company* (94 U.S. 535) dealing with the authority of a State to exclude a foreign insurance company from doing business within its borders no matter upon what ground, Justices Bradley, Swayne and Miller dissented. This broad decision was followed in *Security Mutual Life Insurance Company v. Prewitt* (202 U.S. 246) in which Justices Day and Harlan dissented. Both were recently overruled by a unanimous court in *Terral v. Burke Construction Company* (257 U.S. 529); see also, *Hanover Fire Insurance Co. v. Harding* (272 U.S. 494) in which the Court said that the dissenting opinions in the former cases had now become the law of the Court. This was because the Court found it impossible to sustain the proposition that the authority of a State to exclude a foreign corporation could go so far as to compel it to waive a constitutional right, as for example, to resort to a Federal court. The decision in *Henry v. Dick Company* (224 U.S. 1), dealing with restrictions in licenses under patents, a case in which there were three dissents, including that of Chief Justice White, was overruled in the case of *Motion Picture Patents Company v. Universal Film Company* (243 U.S. 502) and Justices who had carried the Court in the first instance found themselves in a minority in the later case. In *Alpha Cement Company v. Massachusetts* (268 U.S. 203) there was definite disapproval of what was said by the Court in *Baltic Mining Company v. Massachusetts* (231 U.S. 68), where Chief Justice White and Justices Van Devanter and Pitney had dissented. These are illustrations of the victory of dissent, to which may be added the legal tender cases to which I have already referred. In other instances, where former decisions have not been overruled, dissenting opinions have had a powerful influence on the development of the law. Dissents in important controversies may be expected because they are cases in which it would be difficult for any body of lawyers freely selected to reach an accord. While the public may not understand division in the Court, because of an illusion as to attainable certitude in opinions as to the law, which is notably absent in other fields, it must be remembered that conviction must have its say and that the conservatism of the Court as a judicial body furnishes all the protection that is needed in the long run against capricious overturning of decisions.[*]

Thus, the first and most important pro, so far as dissenting judgments are concerned, is the statement by Justice Hughes, i.e. that a dissent demonstrates flaws in the majority's legal analysis, and is offered as a corrective in the hope that the court will mend the errors of its ways in a future case. What Oliver Cromwell said to the General Assembly of the Church of Scotland in 1650 comes to mind:

> Brethren by the bowels of Christ I beseech you, bethink you that you may be mistaken.[†]

As proof of the accuracy of Justice Hughes's statement, dissenting judgments of the US Supreme Court (as also of the Supreme Court of India), which have gone on to become the law, are legion. Of the seventy-two dissents of Justice Holmes, a large number have become law in the future, dealing with liberty of contract and economic legislation, free speech, the state's rights vis-à-vis the federal government, usurping power by the state where there is none under the Constitution and taxation, generally.[‡]

In fact, Alan Barth's *Prophets with Honour* (1974)[§]—a must-read for serious practitioners of the law—notes six great dissents that ultimately became the law in diverse fields. John Marshall Harlan's dissent in *Plessy v. Ferguson* (1896),[¶] seeking to end racial discrimination in the

---

[*] C.E. Hughes, *The Supreme Court of the United States: Its Foundation, Methods and Achievements: An Interpretation* (New York: Columbia University Press, 1928), pp. 69–70. This speech is incorrectly attributed to Justice Stone, and not Justice Hughes, in Louis Blom-Cooper and Gavin Drewry, *Final Appeal: A Study of the House of Lords in Its Judicial Capacity* (supra), pp. 88–89.

[†] Laurence Tribe, *God Save This Honourable Court: How the Choice of Supreme Court Justice Shapes Our History* (New York: Random House, 1985), p. 103.

[‡] Like Justice Holmes, Justice Isaac Isaacs delivered a number of dissenting judgments which eventually became law after 1921, while he was still on the bench. *See* Michael Kirby, 'Judicial Dissent', *James Cook University Law Review*, Vol. 12 (2005): p. 2.

[§] Alan Barth, *Prophets with Honour* (Minneapolis, Minnesota: Light and Life Publishers, 1974).

[¶] 163 U.S. 537 (1896).

United States, became the law in *Brown v. Board of Education* (1954).*
Likewise, illegal intrusion into the privacy of a person by wiretapping,
condemned by Louis Brandeis dissenting in *Olmstead v. United States*
(1928),† was corrected, following the dissent, in *Katz v. United States*
(1967).‡ Justice Black's dissent in *Betts v. Brady* (1942),§ dealing
with the Sixth Amendment's assurance of the right to counsel, was
followed in *Gideon v. Wainwright* (1963).⁹ Likewise, Justice Stone's
dissent in *Minersville School District v. Gobitis* (1940),** became the
law in a short period of three years, the majority being reversed by
West Virginia Board of Education v. Barnette (1943),†† by which the
majority judgment upheld a Jehovah's Witness's right not to salute
the US flag—which was mandated by schools in the States—as part
of their religious freedom. Equally, Justice Black's dissent in *Colegrove
v. Green* (1946)‡‡ stated that a question which has a political hue does
not necessarily mean that the Supreme Court must adopt a hands-
off approach. *Baker v. Carr* (1962),§§ one of the most significant and
important decisions of the Warren Court, followed Black's dissent and
discarded the hands-off approach of the majority in *Colgrove* when
it came to political questions. Last, but by no means the least, is the
vision of free speech enunciated by Douglas, J. in minority in *Dennis v.
United States* (1951),⁹⁹ upheld in *Yates v. United States* (1957).*** *Yates*,
while not explicitly overruling *Dennis*, modified it so substantially as to
make it a dead letter when it came to free speech trumping the sedition
sections of the 'Smith' Act.†††

In fact, Justice Kirby goes to the extent of stating:

---

* 347 U.S. 483 (1954).
† 277 U.S. 438 (1928).
‡ 389 U.S. 347 (1967).
§ 316 U.S. 455 (1942).
⁹ 372 U.S. 335 (1963).
** 301 U.S. 586 (1940).
†† 319 U.S. 624 (1943).
‡‡ 328 U.S. 549 (1946).
§§ 369 U.S. 186 (1962).
⁹⁹ 341 U.S. 494 (1951).
*** 354 U.S. 298 (1957).
††† Formally, the 'Alien Registration Act', 54 Stat. 670.

Out of transparent reasons, even disagreement, and not from narrow, formal, syllogistic reasoning or enforced concurrence, wisdom and justice are more likely to emerge.[*]

This vision of dissenting judgments is also brought into sharp focus in Chapter II of this book, which discusses great dissents delivered in times of war and emergency, and which have later gone on to become the law.

Another added advantage of a dissenting judgment is that the vigorous debate that it engenders often improves the majority opinion. In short, it avails of 'the marketplace of ideas', famously adverted to by Justice Holmes in his dissent in *Abrams v. United States* (1919),[†] in which the great justice stated:

Persecution for the expression of opinions seems to me perfectly logical. If you have no doubt of your premises or your power, and want a certain result with all your heart, you naturally express your wishes in law, and sweep away all opposition. To allow opposition by speech seems to indicate that you think the speech impotent, as when a man says that he has squared the circle, or that you do not care wholeheartedly for the result, or that you doubt either your power or your premises. But when men have realized that time has upset many fighting faiths, they may come to believe even more than they believe the very foundations of their own conduct that the ultimate good desired is better reached by free trade in ideas—that the best test of truth is the power of the thought to get itself accepted in the competition of the market, and that truth is the only ground upon which their wishes safely can be carried out. That, at any rate, is the theory of our Constitution. It is an experiment, as all life is an experiment. Every year, if not every day, we have to wager our salvation upon some prophecy based upon imperfect knowledge. While that experiment is part of our system, I think that we should be eternally vigilant against attempts to check the expression of opinions that we loathe and believe to be fraught with death, unless they so imminently

---

[*] Michael Kirby, 'Judicial Dissent—Common Law and Civil Law Traditions' (supra), pp. 379 at 399.
[†] 250 U.S. 616 (1919).

threaten immediate interference with the lawful and pressing purposes of the law that an immediate check is required to save the country.[*]

In fact, Rory K. Little justifies judicial dissents by dividing them into three distinct components, two of which are directly traceable to freedom of speech, as follows:

> Judicial dissent can be broken into three distinct components: expressing disagreement to one's colleagues privately; having one's disagreement with the majority's opinion publicly noted; and issuing a written dissenting opinion in company with the majority's. I wish to consider here a 'complete' judicial right to dissent, one that encompasses all three components: private voting, public non-joinder, and written dissenting opinions. I suggest below that the first two components are supported by the First Amendment. The third component, however—a right to issue dissenting opinions—must be founded on a constitutional conception of Article III 'courts' and 'judges', because the First Amendment likely cannot carry the right that far.[†]

Sometimes, a dissenting judgment brings forth a rejoinder by another learned judge in the same case. Thus, in *Bradley Egg Farm Ltd. v. Clifford and Ors.* (1943),[‡] which was a case relating to vicarious liability on the ground of negligence, L.J. Goddard began his judgment as follows:

> Subject to a short addition drafted by Scott L.J., in which I concur, to explain a little more fully why we differ from Bennett J., this is the judgment of my Lord and myself.[§]

L.J. Scott then delivered a separate concurring judgment, in order to answer the points raised in the dissenting judgment of Bennett, J., as follows:

---

[*] William J. Brennan Jr, 'In Defense of Dissents' (supra), pp. 429–30.
[†] Rory K. Little, 'Reading Justice Brennan: Is There a "Right" to Dissent?', *Hastings Law Journal*, Vol. 50 (1999).
[‡] (1943) 2 All ER 378.
[§] Ibid., p. 379.

Since the joint judgment of Goddard L.J., and myself was written, I have read that of Bennett, J. and given to it the careful consideration it deserves, but find myself unable to agree with his two conclusions. I will try to explain why.*

Likewise, in *Vijay Narain Singh v. State of Bihar* (1984),† a question arose as to whether the petitioner before the court could be called an 'anti-social element', as defined by Section 2(d) of the Bihar Control of Crimes Act, 1981. Stating that the said act is a preventive detention measure and therefore must be construed strictly, the majority judgment of Justice Venkataramiah held that the detenu could not be called an anti-social element on the basis of a single act or omission falling under (i) and (iv) of Section 2(d). Justice A.P. Sen dissented. Justice Chinnappa Reddy then found it necessary to write a separate concurring judgment, stating as to why Justice Sen's dissent could not be said to be the correct view, which is as follows:

> I entirely agree with my brother Venkataramiah, J. both on the question of interpretation of the provisions of the Bihar Control of Crimes Act, 1981 and on the question of the effect of the order of grant of bail in the criminal proceeding arising out of the incident constituting one of the grounds of detention. It is really unnecessary for me to add anything to what has been said by Venkataramiah, J., but my brother Sen, J. has taken a different view and out of respect to him, I propose to add a few lines.‡

Often, a dissenting judgment can be used to emphasize the limit of a majority decision which is otherwise worded broadly.§ Dissenting judgments can also foretell the doom which the majority judgment will

---

* Ibid., p. 386.
† (1984) 3 SCC 14.
‡ Ibid., pp. 18–19.
§ Referred to by William J. Brennan Jr in 'In Defense of Dissents' (supra): William J. Brennan, Jr, 'State Constitutions and the Protection of Individual Rights', *Harvard Law Review*, Vol. 90, No. 3 (1977): p. 489.

have on society generally. Thus, Clarkson, J. in *Oliver v. City of Raleigh* (1937)* stated:

> I know that this, like every other case, will become the parent stock from which a motley progeny will spring. In those after years when this case, elevated to high authority by the cold finality of the printed page, is quoted with the customary, 'It has been said 'perchance another court will say, 'mayhaps the potter's hand trembled at the wheel'. Possibly when that moment comes these words may give the court a chance to say, 'Yea, and a workman standing hard by saw the vase as it cracked'.†

In *Plessy v. Ferguson* (1896),‡ Harlan, J. in his dissent prophesied:

> In my opinion, the judgment this day rendered will, in time, prove to be quite as pernicious as the decision made by this tribunal in the *Dred Scott* Case. It was adjudged in that case that the descendants of Africans who were imported into this country and sold as slaves were not included nor intended to be included under the word 'citizens' in the Constitution, and could not claim any of the rights and privileges which that instrument provided for and secured to citizens of the United States; that, at the time of the adoption of the Constitution, they were considered as a subordinate and inferior class of beings, who had been subjugated by the dominant race, and, whether emancipated or not, yet remained subject to their authority, and had no rights or privileges but such as those who held the power and the government might choose to grant them. The recent amendments of the Constitution, it was supposed, had eradicated these principles from our institutions. But it seems that we have yet, in some of the States, a dominant race—a superior class of citizens, which assumes to regulate the enjoyment of civil rights, common to all citizens, upon the basis of race. The present decision, it may well be apprehended, will not only stimulate aggressions, more or less brutal and irritating, upon the admitted rights of coloured citizens, but will encourage the belief that it is

* 193 S.E. 853 at 857 (1937).
† *See* R.E. Megarry, *A Second Miscellany at Law* (New Delhi: Universal Book Traders, 1996), p. 148.
‡ 163 U.S. 537 (1896).

possible, by means of state enactments, to defeat the beneficent purposes which the people of the United States had in view when they adopted the recent amendments of the Constitution, by one of which the blacks of this country were made citizens of the United States and of the States in which they respectively reside, and whose privileges and immunities, as citizens, the States are forbidden to abridge. Sixty millions of whites are in no danger from the presence here of eight millions of blacks. The destinies of the two races in this country are indissolubly linked together, and the interests of both require that the common government of all shall not permit the seeds of race hate to be planted under the sanction of law. What can more certainly arouse race hate, what more certainly create and perpetuate a feeling of distrust between these races, than state enactments which, in fact, proceed on the ground that coloured citizens are so inferior and degraded that they cannot be allowed to sit in public coaches occupied by white citizens. That, as all will admit, is the real meaning of such legislation as was enacted in Louisiana.[*]

This prophecy came absolutely true when 'blacks' were severely racially discriminated against by the 'Jim Crow' laws enacted by many states in the early 1900s. This state of affairs carried on in the United States until 1954, when the *Plessy v. Ferguson* majority opinion was overruled, leading to the Civil Rights Act of 1964,[†] which finally did away with discrimination based on race.

Sometimes, a dissenting judgment points out that if there is no authority for a certain proposition, it does not mean that the proposition should not be accepted if the justice of the case so required it. Thus, in *Candler v. Crane, Christmas and Co.* (1951),[‡] Denning, L.J. in his dissent, stated:

> Apart from such cases, no action, he said, had ever been allowed for negligent statements, and he urged that this want of authority was a reason against it being allowed now. This argument about the novelty of the action does not appeal to me in the least. It has been put forward in

---

[*] Ibid., pp. 559–60.
[†] 78 Stat. 241.
[‡] (1951) 2 K.B. 164.

all the great cases which have been milestones of progress in our law, and it has always, or nearly always, been rejected. If you read the great cases of *Ashby v. White*, *Pasley v. Freeman* and *Donoghue v. Stevenson* you will find that in each of them the judges were divided in opinion. On the one side there were the timorous souls who were fearful of allowing a new cause of action. On the other side there were the bold spirits who were ready to allow it if justice so required. It was fortunate for the common law that the progressive view prevailed.[*]

Dissenting judgments also often make an important contribution to the integrity of the process of judgment. An impressive dissent can make a judge who has joined the majority change his mind—as an example, in *Bengal Immunity Co. v. State of Bihar* (1955),[†] Justice N.H. Bhagwati recanted changing his view of the law as expressed by him in *State of Bombay v. United Motors* (1953)[‡] in *Bengal Immunity v. State of Bihar*.[§] It has also sometimes happened that before the final judgment is pronounced, a draft dissent was persuasive enough to change the minds of an erstwhile majority, becoming the majority judgment itself.[¶] In *The Law Lords* (1982), the learned author states:

> Sometimes the alternative arena is a law reform body, such as the Law Commission, or even the legislature. Several law lords mentioned the possibility of reform as a reason for publishing a dissent.[**]

---

[*] Ibid., p. 178.

[†] (1955) 2 SCR 603.

[‡] (1953) 4 SCR 1069.

[§] This is a rare occurrence. For example, the majority in *Gobitis* (301 U.S. 586 [1940]) was undone in *West Virginia* (319 U.S. 624 [1943]) within a period of three years, with three justices (joined by two new justices) of the US Supreme Court changing their views in this period. As opposed to this, it can often take twenty years, or sometimes even sixty years, for a dissent to become the law—Holmes J.'s minority view in *Hammer v. Dagenhart* (247 U.S. 251 [1918]) was accepted more than twenty years later in *United States v. Darby Lumber Co.* (312 U.S. 100 [1941]) and Harlan J.'s opinion in *Plessy* (163 U.S. 537 [1896]) only became the law sixty years later in *Brown* (347 U.S. 483 [1954]).

[¶] *See* Ruth Bader Ginsburg, 'The Role of Dissenting Opinions' (supra), p. 4, where she states: 'On occasion—not more than four times per term I would estimate—a dissent will be so persuasive that it attracts the votes necessary to become the opinion of the Court. I had the heady experience of writing a dissent for myself and one other Justice; in time, it became the opinion of the Court from which only three of my colleagues dissented.'

[**] Alan Paterson, *The Law Lords* (supra), p. 101.

He goes on to note:

> For e.g., Lord Hailsham '[when I dissent] I am moved by the necessity
> to express an honest opinion on the case before me and possibly point a
> way for future legislatures in the field of law reform.[*]

The dissenting judgment is then taken up by the legislature, which then legislatively overrules the majority judgment. An example of this is Justice Sikri's dissenting judgment in *Coffee Board, Bangalore v. JCT, Madras* (1969),[†] which became the law by a legislative overruling of the majority judgment when Parliament amended Section 5 of the Central Sales Tax Act in 1975, in line with Justice Sikri's dissenting judgment.

Another great plus-point of a dissenting judgment is that there is no need to accommodate the views of various colleagues. The dissenting judgment, being a personal view, can then be clear, unlike majority judgments, which are often the products of the muddy waters of compromise. Justice Scalia puts it thus:

> To be able to write an opinion solely for oneself, without the need to
> accommodate, to any degree whatsoever, the more-or-less-differing
> views of one's colleagues, to address precisely the points of law that one
> considers important and no others; to express precisely the degree of
> quibble, or foreboding, or disbelief, or indignation that one believes the
> majority's disposition should engender—that is indeed an unparalleled
> pleasure.[‡]

Justice Cardozo, another great judge, observed in this behalf as under:

> Comparatively speaking at least, the dissenter is irresponsible. The
> spokesman of the court is cautious, timid, fearful of the vivid world,
> the heightened phrase. He dreams of an unworthy brood of scions,
> the spawn of careless dicta, disowned by the *ratio decidendi*, to which

---

[*] Ibid., p. 239, 63f.
[†] (1969) 3 SCC 349.
[‡] Antonin Scalia, 'The Dissenting Opinion', *Journal of Supreme Court History*, Vol. 1994, Issue 1 (1994): pp. 33 at 42.

all legitimate offspring must be able to trace their lineage. The result is to cramp and paralyse. One fears to say anything when the peril of misunderstanding puts a warning finger to the lips. Not so, however, the dissenter. He has laid aside the role of the hierophant, which he will be only too glad to resume when the chances of war make him again the spokesman of the majority. For the moment, he is the gladiator making a last stand against the lions. The poor man must be forgiven a freedom of expression, tinged at rare moments with a touch of bitterness, which magnanimity as well as caution would reject for one triumphant.[*]

Another important contribution that a dissenting judgment can make is to an ongoing dialogue between the courts and the legislature. A law can thus be drafted based on aspects taken from both the majority and the minority judgments. This is well brought out in Claire L'Heureux-Dubé's 'The Dissenting Opinion: Voice of the Future?'.[†] Dissenting judgments can also aid in sharpening the wits of a law student. Students taught by the case-law method, as I was in the Campus Law Centre, New Delhi, were given as homework the study of the grey areas of the law, which involved the reading of majority and minority dissenting judgments; this often led to debates in class. Often, if the minority judgment could be supported with independent reasoning by the student, it would trump the majority judgment in the eyes of the professor and the class.

One other interesting aspect of a dissenting judgment is that while it may not appeal to judges in its own jurisdiction, it could, in the future, appeal to judges in other jurisdictions, who are free to choose from either majority or minority judgments overseas on the basis of their reasoning. An interesting example of the borrowing of a minority judgment from overseas to buttress a judgment of the Indian Supreme Court can be seen in *R.D. Shetty v. International Airport Authority of India* (1979),[‡] where Justice Douglas's minority judgment in *Jackson v. Metropolitan Edison Co.* (1974)[§] was preferred to the majority view, holding that the monopolistic

---

[*] Benjamin N. Cardozo, 'Law and Literature', *Yale Review* (1925): pp. 699 at 715.
[†] Clair L'Heureux-Dubé, 'The Dissenting Opinion: Voice of the Future?', *Osgoode Hall Law Journal*, Vol. 38, No. 3 (2000): pp. 496 at 510, 511.
[‡] (1979) 3 SCC 489 at pp. 508–09.
[§] 419 U.S. 345 (1974).

tendency of a non-state actor can make it 'State' within the meaning of Article 12 of the Constitution of India. Another example, this time, of a judiciary overseas choosing an Indian minority judgment over the majority judgment, is of the Federal Court of Malaysia in *Loh Wai Kong v. Malaysia* (1978)* in which Justice Hidayatullah's dissenting view in *Satwant Singh Sawhney v. D. Ramarathnam* (1967)† was preferred over that of the majority and followed.‡

It can thus be seen that the pros of dissenting judgments generally far outweigh the cons. Even unanimity, which is an important con, is often undone by public awareness of the importance of bona fide differing points of view among judges of the highest court.§ Equally, a challenge to collegiality amongst judges, which is also one of the cons of expressing dissenting opinions, has itself an obverse side—collegiality can often be fostered through the 'safety valve' of a dissenting judgment, as the frustration that the potential dissenter feels at not airing his opinion disappears. In fact, such frustration can itself lead to a lack of collegiality.¶

Having examined the dissenting judgment from a philosophical point of view, the stage is now set for an in-depth examination of the great dissents and dissenters of the Supreme Court of India.

---

* Federal Court Civil Appeal No. 87 of 1978 and Originating Motion No. 9 of 1978.

† (1967) 3 SCC 525.

‡ Hidayatullah, J.'s dissenting opinion in *Satwant Singh* ([1967] 3 SCR 525) is discussed in detail in Chapter VI.

§ Justice Kirby in 'Judicial Dissent' (supra) at p. 5 is firmly of the view that: 'There are many in society who hate disagreement, demand unanimity and insist on more consensus, including amongst appellate judges. They speak endlessly of the need for clarity and certainty in the law. Truly, these are goals to be attained if at all possible. But judges must not achieve them at the sacrifice of truth, independence and conscience. There are many failings in the judicial system of Australia for it is a human institution. But amongst its greatest strengths is the role it gives to judges to state their honest opinions. As citizens, we can agree or disagree with those opinions. But we must vigilantly protect, and cherish, these open procedures. And that includes the expression of disagreement, where it exists.'

¶ J.D. Heydon, 'Threats to Judicial Independence' (supra), p. 213, puts it thus: 'It has also been argued that most judges do not like to dissent because it "frays collegiality". It is said that appellate courts need to co-operate and therefore place a premium on co-operative behaviour. It is said collegiate enterprise of appellate judging "does not work well when the judges' relations with one another become tinged with animosity—and that is always a danger because of the way in which the members of the cooperative enterprise are selected". But too high a price can be paid for agreeable personal relationships and internal harmony.'

II

WHEN THE CHIPS ARE
DOWN—THE LAW IN TIMES
OF WAR OR EMERGENCY

A review of the judgments of the highest courts of the land in the UK, USA, Australia and India reveal the truth of Justice Holmes's dissenting opinion in *Northern Securities Company* (1903)[*]—that because of some accident of immediate overwhelming interest, which appeals to the feelings and distorts the judgment, a kind of 'hydraulic pressure' is exercised, which makes what was previously clear seem doubtful, and before which even settled principles of law will bend. This statement of practical expediency is never truer than when the superior courts are faced with the horrors of ongoing war, or internal 'emergency' situations.

World War 1, which broke out in 1914, had as its victims millions of young men each fighting for his own country. In this kind of situation, persons, who, in any sense of the word, 'belonged' to a nation with whom Great Britain was at war, were suspect. One such person was Arthur Zadig, a naturalized British subject of German birth, who was interned by an order made by the Secretary of State under powers given by Regulation 14B, which was made under the Defence of the Realm Consolidation Act, 1914. Having been interned in a jail without trial for a period of eighteen months by the time the judgment of the House of Lords in his case was delivered, Arthur Zadig knocked at the doors of the House of Lords in *Rex v. Halliday* (1917),[†] contending that Regulation 14B was not authorized by the act and was therefore *ultra vires*. Regulation 14B, with which the court was concerned, reads as follows:

> Where on the recommendation of a competent naval or military authority or of one of the advisory committees hereinafter mentioned it appears to the Secretary of State that for securing the public safety or

---

[*] 193 U.S. 197 (1903).
[†] (1917) UKHL 1.

the defence of the realm it is expedient in view of the hostile origin or associations of any person that he shall be subjected to such obligations and restrictions as are hereinafter mentioned, the Secretary of State may by order require that person forthwith, or from time to time, either to remain in, or to proceed to and reside in, such place as may be specified in the order, and to comply with such directions as to reporting to the police, restriction of movement, and otherwise as may be specified in the order, or to be interned in such place as may be specified in the order:

Provided that any such order shall, in the case of any person who is not a subject of a State at war with His Majesty, include express provision for the due consideration by one of such advisory committees of any representations he may make against the order.

If any person in respect of whom any order is made under this regulation fails to comply with any of the provisions of the order he shall be guilty of an offence against these regulations, and any person interned under such order shall be subject to the like restrictions and may be dealt with in like manner as a prisoner of war, except so far as the Secretary of State may relax such restrictions.

The advisory committees for the purposes of this regulation shall be such advisory committees as are appointed for the purpose of advising the Secretary of State with respect to the internment and deportation of aliens, each of such committees being presided over by a person who holds or has held high judicial office.[*]

The order complained of by Mr Zadig was made by the Home Secretary on 15 October 1915 and was as follows:

Whereas, on the recommendation of a competent military authority, appointed under the Defence of the Realm Regulations, it appears to me that, for securing the public safety and the defence of the realm, it is expedient that Arthur Zadig, of 56, Portsdown Road, Maida Vale, W., should, in view of his hostile origin and associations, be subjected to such obligations and restrictions as are hereinafter mentioned.

---

[*] (1917) UKHL 1, pp. 2–3 (page numbers correspond to the online version of the judgment, accessed at https://www.bailii.org/uk/cases/UKHL/1917/1.html).

'I hereby order that the said Arthur Zadig shall be interned in the institution in Cornwallis Road, Islington, which is now used as a place of internment, and shall be subject to all the rules and conditions applicable to aliens there interned.

If within seven days from the date on which this order is served on the said Arthur Zadig he shall submit to me any representations against the provisions of this order, such representations will be referred to the advisory committee appointed for the purpose of advising me with respect to the internment and deportation of aliens and presided over by a judge of the High Court, and will be duly considered by the committee. If I am satisfied by the report of the said committee that this order may be revoked or varied without injury to the public safety or the defence of the realm, I will revoke or vary the order by a further order in writing under my hand. Failing such revocation or variation this order shall remain in force.'

A majority of judges of the House of Lords held that, being a wartime measure, Regulation 14B could not be held to be *ultra vires* and therefore the impugned order made by the Home Secretary was valid. In one of the greatest dissenting judgments of its time, Lord Shaw of Dunfermline began his judgment, stating:

My Lords, I reckon this appeal to be in the first class of importance. My opinion differs from that of your Lordships, and this has led me to consider and reconsider the matter with care. The gravity of the issue, and the respect which I entertain for my noble and learned friends here and for the learned judges of the Courts below, with all of whom I am constrained to differ, these appear to me to demand a statement, fuller than usual, of the grounds of my own position . . . I am clearly the opinion that, although appearing to be a regulation, this is, in truth and essentially, not a regulation at all, and that it was *ultra vires* of His Majesty in Council to issue under the guise of a regulation an authorization for the apprehension, seizure, and internment without trial of any of the lieges. In my view Parliament never sanctioned, either in intention or by

---

* Ibid., pp. 3–4.

reason of the statutory words employed in the Defence of the Realm Acts, such a violent exercise of arbitrary power. It follows that the order or fiat of the Secretary of State which has already been quoted is also *ultra vires*.'

The learned law lord went on to state that an Act of Parliament, even in times of war, could not have intended that despotic power should remain in the hands of the executive:

These are the words: 'His Majesty in Council has power during the continuance of the present war to issue regulations for securing the public safety and the defence of the realm, and as to the powers and duties for that purpose of the Admiralty'. A change has occurred in this consolidation and amendment Act, not in the important words, but in their collocation. The important words referred to are 'for securing the public safety and the defence of the realm'. In the earlier Acts the regulations were to be 'as to the powers and duties of the Admiralty, 'for securing the public safety and the defence of the realm'. Now the regulations issue direct from the King in Council. It is perfectly plain to me how this occurred. The later details of the section show that regulations as to the powers of officers or individuals might cover ground beyond the province of those departments or persons. For example, the Board of Trade, the Post Office, or the Foreign Office might well be concerned in, or in the carrying out of, many of these details. And so the shortest and most comprehensive method was taken, namely, of transferring the general topic dealt with in regulations to the Government of the day—all the rest remaining in substance as before.

It is, in my view, largely owing to this simple change, however, and from the collocation in which the words now stand that the Courts below have come to their conclusion.

From that conclusion positively stupendous results follow. The words, it is said, are perfectly general; the King in Council is vested with powers to judge of what is for the public safety and the defence of the realm, and to act accordingly. All the rest of those statutes as to trial, intimation, notification of rights; every provision for the legal disposal of

---

' Id., p. 9.

the question affecting liberty—all this is on one side, the side of offence against a regulation: on the other side stands this super-eminent power of the Government of the day. In the exercise of that power the plainest teachings of history and dictates of justice demand that, on the one hand, Government power, and, on the other, individual rights—these two— shall face each other as party and party. But it is not so, so it is said; here the Government as a party shall act at its own hand; the subject as a party shall submit and shall not be heard; the Government is at once to be party, judge, and executioner. When—so is the logic of the argument— Parliament took elaborate pains to make a legal course and legal remedy plain to the subject as to all the regulations which were stated in detail, there was one thing which Parliament did not disclose, but left Courts of law to imply—namely, that Parliament, all the time and intentionally, left another deadly weapon in the hands of the Government of the day under which the remainder of those very Acts, not to speak of the entire body of the laws of these islands protective of liberty, would be avoided. As occasion served the Government of the day, despotic force could be wielded, and that whole fabric of protection be gone. My Lords, I do not believe Parliament ever intended anything of the kind. We are not in the region of subtlety or obliquity. Holding the views I do of this parliamentary transaction, and forming these from the language employed, I cannot attribute to the Legislature the intention alleged.

xxx xxx xxx

If once again, and ever so slightly, that prerogative gets into association with executive acts done apart from clear parliamentary authority, it will be an evil day: that way lies revolution. Do not let the thing which has been done—in my opinion a violent thing—be associated for one moment with, or at any point be said to be supported by, Royal prerogative. Its validity depends upon the Act of Parliament alone.

xxx xxx xxx

This reduces to comparative unimportance those apparent safeguards derived not from the Act of Parliament, but inserted into the 'regulations' themselves. The language of the regulation, for instance, 'where it appears to the Secretary of State' and 'on the recommendation of a competent naval or military authority' is simply equivalent to a declaration that the delegate, to judge and issue, is one department of Government, and that that will, of course, act in accord with, and on the recommendation of, those other departments which are presumably versed in the situation. The Government remains master. And a proviso is made for due consideration by an advisory committee of any representations against the order; but it was frankly admitted that the Secretary of State is not bound to comply with the advice received; he may do as he likes: again the Government is master.

As these considerations are resolved the importance of the issue for liberty does not wane. The interpretation put upon this Government power to issue regulations for safety and defence is that of perfect generality. Is this generality limited? it was asked. Yes, replied the Crown; the limitations are two, and two only. In the first place, regulations can only be issued during the war—a limitation in time. In the second place, they can only be issued for the public safety and for the defence of the realm—a limitation of purpose. But who is to judge of that purpose? As to what acts of State are promotive or regardful of that purpose, can a Court of law arrest the hand of a responsible Executive? Extreme cases may be figured in which personal caprice and not public considerations might be imagined, but in everything, from the lighting of a room to the devastation of a province, no Court of law could dare to set up its judgment on the merits of an issue—a public and political issue—of safety or defence. So that this limitation, as a legal limitation, is illusory. The only one that remains is that of time. 'During the war' the Government has been allowed at its own hand to do anything it likes. 'Regulation' covers all: the issue of decrees, arrests, proscription, imprisonment, internment, exile—all are covered comprehensively by the word 'regulations'. Such an issue is made on grounds which are not in the region of law; judges are not fitted to interpose on these: a judgment, nay, possibly even a comment, upon them would besmirch the Bench. That course which alone is safe is, leave the domain of public need or claim or advantage to the undisturbed possession of Parliament and its delegates. I accordingly agree that a plea put forward by a subject against a Government, grounded upon an appeal to Courts of law as to public requirements, would be unavailing in the region of *ultra vires*. Once let the overmastering generality of the principle of regulation be affirmed, as has been done, all is lost; the law itself is overmastered. The only law remaining is that which the Bench must accept from the mouth of the Government: *'Hoc volo, sic jubeo; sit pro ratione voluntas.'*

Lord Shaw then went on to remind the court that a government in the United Kingdom can never, by an Act of Parliament, be authorized to become a 'Committee of Public Safety' (which was known for wielding arbitrary and despotic power during the French Revolution). In ringing words, he also warned the court that it was bringing back the 'Star Chamber', which was a court of politicians enforcing a policy, not a court of judges administering the law, as follows:

But does the principle, or does it not, embrace a power not over liberty alone but also over life? If the public safety and defence warrant the Government under the Act to incarcerate a citizen without trial, do they stop at that, or do they warrant his execution without trial? If there is a power to lock up a person of hostile origin and associations because the Government judges that course to be for public safety and defence, why, on the same principle and in exercise of the same power, may he not be shot out of hand? I put the point to the learned Attorney-General, and obtained from him no further answer than that the graver result seemed to be perfectly logical. I think it is. The cases are by no means hard to figure in which a Government in a time of unrest, and moved by a sense of duty, assisted, it may be, by a gust of popular fury, might issue a regulation applying, as here, to persons of hostile origin or association, saying, 'Let such danger really be ended and done with, let such suspects be shot.' The defence would be, I humbly think, exactly that principle, and no other, on which the judgments of the Courts below are founded—namely, that during the war this power to issue regulations is so vast that it covers all acts which, though they subvert the ordinary fundamental and constitutional rights, are in the

---

* Id., pp. 14–16.

Government's view directed towards the general aim of public safety or defence.

Under this the Government becomes a Committee of Public Safety. But its powers as such are far more arbitrary than those of the most famous Committee of Public Safety known to history. It preserved a form of trial, of evidence, of interrogations. And the very homage which it paid to law discovered the odium of its procedure to the world. But the so-called principle—the principle of prevention, the comprehensive principle—avoids the odium of that brutality of the Terror. The analogy is with a practice, more silent, more sinister—with the *lettres de cachet* of Louis Quatorze. No trial: proscription. The victim may be 'regulated'— not in his course of conduct or of action, not as to what he should do or avoid doing. He may be regulated to prison or the scaffold. Suppose the appellant had been appointed for execution. Public outcry, public passion, public pity—these I can conceive; but I cannot conceive one argument upon the legal construction of this Act of Parliament that would have been different from the one which is now affirmed by Courts of law. It is this last matter with which these are concerned. In my humble opinion the construction is unsound. I think that if Parliament had intended to make this colossal delegation of power it would have done so plainly and courageously and not under cover of words about regulations for safety and defence. The expansions of such language into the inclusion of such a power appear to me to be unwarrantably strained.

The use of the Government itself as a Committee of Public Safety has its conveniences, has its advantages. So had the Star Chamber. 'The Star Chamber,' says Maitland (*Constitutional History of England*, p. 263), 'examining the accused, and making no use of the jury, probably succeeded in punishing many crimes which would otherwise have gone unpunished. But that it was a tyrannical court, that it became more and more tyrannical, and under Charles I was guilty of great infamies, is still more indubitable.' And then occur his memorable words: 'It was a court of politicians enforcing a policy, not a court of judges administering the law.'

There is the basic danger. And may I further emphatically observe that that danger is found in an especial degree whenever the law is not the same for all, but the selection of the victim is left to the plenary discretion whether of a tyrant, a committee, a bureaucracy or any other depositary of despotic power. Whoever administers it, this power of selection of a class, and power of selection within a class is the negation of public safety or defence. It is poison to the Commonwealth.

xxx xxx xxx

And once you have abandoned the line of safety which I have sketched—namely, confining regulations to rules of conduct to be obeyed with safety or punished after trial for the breach—once that is abandoned, how far may you not go? Once a discretion over all things and persons and rights and liberties, so as to secure public safety and defence, what regulations may issue? This one is founded on 'hostile origin or associations.' It enters the sphere of suspicion, founded not on conduct but on presumed opinions, beliefs, motives, or prepossessions arising from the land from which a person sprang. This is dangerous country; it has its dark reminders. It is the proscription, the arrest of suspects, at the will of men in power vested with a plenary discretion. If the power to issue regulations meant thus to warrant a passage from proof to suspicion and from the sphere of action to the sphere of motive or the mind, let us think how much this involves.

No far-fetched illustrations are needed; for, my Lords, there is something which may and does move the actions of men often far more than origin or association, and that is religion. Under its influence men may cherish beliefs which are very disconcerting to the Government of the day, and hold opinions which the Government may consider dangerous to the safety of the realm. And so, if the principle of this construction of the statute be sound, to what a strange pass have we come! A regulation may issue against Roman Catholics—all, or, say, in the South of Ireland, or against Jews—all, or, say in the East of London—they may lose their liberty without a trial. During the war that entire chapter of the removal of Catholic and Jewish disabilities which has made the toleration of Britain famous through the world may be removed—not because her Parliament has expressly said so, but by a stroke of the pen of a Secretary of State.*

---

* Id., pp. 17–19.

Applying principles of interpretation of statutes, which were extant in the law of England at the time, Lord Shaw went on to hold:

> Differing as I unfortunately and respectfully do from your Lordships, it would not be right that I should fail to add that the expanded construction adopted by the Courts below appears to me in every one of these particulars to be inconsistent with those principles of interpretation which have been long recognized. It is, I humbly think, not simple, but strained. It is repugnant to the rest of the Act. It operates repeal of statutes on an important and vast scale. It leads to startling and absurd results and to an upheaval of constitutional right . . . The construction I have ventured to propose appears to me to be not unreasonable, but to square with every familiar and accustomed canon. I think that the judgment of the Courts below is erroneous, and is fraught with grave legal and constitutional danger. In my opinion the appeal should be allowed, the regulation challenged should be declared *ultra vires*, and the appellant should be set at liberty.[*]

Only one law lord forming part of the majority of the bench was stung to the quick by the example given by Lord Shaw, i.e. of a regulation or order issuing against entire communities like the Roman Catholics or the Jews, denying them liberty without a trial. Lord Dunedin endeavoured to deal with these examples as follows:

> It is pointed out that the powers, if interpreted as the unanimous judgment of the Courts below interprets them, are drastic and might be abused. That is true. But the fault, if fault there be, lies in the fact that the British Constitution has entrusted to the two Houses of Parliament, subject to the assent of the King, an absolute power untrammelled by any written instrument obedience to which may be compelled by some judicial body. The danger of abuse is theoretically present; practically, as things exist, it is in my opinion absent.
>
> Were a regulation to be framed, as my noble friend who is to follow me suggests, to intern the Catholics of south Ireland or the Jews of

---

[*] Id., pp. 24 and 26.

London the result would, I think, be the speedy repeal of the Act which authorizes the regulation.

That preventive measures in the shape of internment of persons likely to assist the enemy may be necessary under the circumstances of a war like the present is really an obvious consideration. Parliament has in my judgment, in order to secure this and kindred objects, risked the chance of abuse which will always be theoretically present when absolute powers in general terms are delegated to an executive body; and has thought the restriction of the powers to the period of the duration of the war to be a sufficient safeguard.[*]

It is interesting to note that in dealing with these examples, Lord Dunedin clearly stated that anyone knocking at the doors of the court in times of war would find the door completely closed—the only recourse would be to the 'good sense' of Parliament, which would speedily repeal an act which authorized such a regulation.

However, it is heartening to note that when the war ended, Avory, J. in *Chester v. Bateson* (1920),[†] thought it appropriate, when construing a regulation made under another statute, to rely on the observations of the dissenting judgment of Lord Shaw as follows:

I have based my judgment solely upon the construction of the statute which confers the power to make regulations—'shall not leave to do right' means shall not omit to do right—'notwithstanding that there is a commanding under the great or little seal'. In this connection I think it not inappropriate to quote a passage from the opinion, although it was a dissentient opinion, of Lord Shaw of Dunfermline, in the case of *Rex v. Halliday* where he says: 'Whether the Government has exceeded its statutory mandate is a question of *ultra* or *intra vires* such as that which is now being tried. In so far as the mandate has been exceeded, there lurk the elements of a transition to arbitrary government, and therein of grave constitutional and public danger. The increasing crush of legislative efforts and the convenience to the Executive of a refuge to

---

[*] Id., p. 6.
[†] (1920) 1 K.B. 829.

the device of Orders in Council would increase that danger tenfold were the judiciary to approach any such action of the Government in a spirit of compliance rather than of independent scrutiny.' For these reasons I hold this part of the regulation to be *ultra vires* and invalid; and the appeal therefore should be allowed and the case remitted to the justices to hear and determine.*

Almost a century later, Lord Hope, speaking for the UK Supreme Court in *Her Majesty's Treasury v. Mohommed Jabad Ahmed and Others* (2010)[†] dealt with *R. v. Halliday* by adverting to Lord Shaw's warning against the risk of 'arbitrary government' if the judiciary were to adopt a hands-off approach, as follows:

> It cannot be suggested, in view of the word 'any', that the power is available only for use where the Security Council has called for non-military, diplomatic and economic sanctions to deter aggression between states. But the phrase 'necessary or expedient for enabling those measures to be effectively applied' does require further examination. The closer those measures come to affecting what, in *R v. Secretary of State for the Home Department, Ex p Simms* [2000] 2 AC 115, 131, Lord Hoffmann described as the basic rights of the individual, the more exacting this scrutiny must become. If the rule of law is to mean anything, decisions as to what is necessary or expedient in this context cannot be left to the uncontrolled judgment of the executive. In *Chester v. Bateson*, Avory J. referred to Lord Shaw of Dunfermline's warning in *R v. Halliday* [1917] AC 260, 287 against the risk of arbitrary government if the judiciary were to approach actions of government in excess of its mandate in a spirit of compliance rather than that of independent scrutiny. The undoubted fact that section 1 of the 1946 Act was designed to enable the United Kingdom to fulfil its obligations under the Charter to implement Security Council resolutions does not diminish this essential principle. As Lord Brown says in para 194, the full honouring of these obligations is an imperative. But these resolutions are the product of

---

* Ibid., pp. 836–37.
† (2010) UKSC 2.

a body of which the executive is a member as the United Kingdom's representative. Conferring an unlimited discretion on the executive as to how those resolutions, which it has a hand in making, are to be implemented seems to me to be wholly unacceptable. It conflicts with the basic rules that lie at the heart of our democracy.[*]

It can safely be stated that today, even in times of war, the majority judgment in *R. v. Halliday* will not hold, Lord Shaw's great dissent being the correct view of the law.

The next great dissent in wartime, far better known than Lord Shaw's dissent in *R v. Halliday*, is Lord Atkin's dissent in the celebrated case of *Liversidge v. Anderson* (1942).[†] Lord Atkin's biographer, Geoffrey Lewis, tells us that the judgment was delivered by the House of Lords in late 1941, at a time when the war was going well for Germany and badly for England.[‡] London was being incessantly bombed by the Luftwaffe; the Axis powers had attacked Russia on 22 June 1941; and the United States had yet to enter the war.

In this case, one Mr Jack Perlzweig, who used the alias 'Robert Liversidge', was a British citizen born to Russian parents. He was described as a somewhat shadowy and mysterious figure, who had become a wealthy businessman by the late 1930s. In May 1940, before the battle of Britain, he was serving as a volunteer pilot officer in the Royal Air Force. He challenged his detention in Brixton Prison under Regulation 18B of the Defence (General) Regulations, 1939, which provided that if the Secretary of State made an order in which he recited that he had reasonable cause to believe that a person was of 'hostile association', and that by reason thereof it was necessary that he be detained, the subjective satisfaction of the Secretary of State acting in good faith was sufficient to render such detention as being in accordance with law, and unassailable in courts of law.[§]

---

[*] Ibid at paragraph 45.

[†] 1942 A.C. 206.

[‡] Geoffrey Lewis, *Lord Atkin* (New Delhi: Universal Law Publishing Co. Ltd, 1999), p. 132.

[§] Susan Kiefel, 'Judicial Courage and the Decorum of Dissent', Selden Society Lecture, Supreme Court of Queensland, 28 November 2017, p. 1.

Here, again, only one voice spoke in dissent, namely, the voice of Lord Atkin. Viscount Maugham (the older brother of the novelist William Somerset Maugham) delivered the first of the majority judgments. This was followed by Lord Atkin's dissent, which in turn was followed by the concurring judgments of Lord Macmillan, Lord Wright and Lord Romer. The majority held that the language of the regulation in question made it clear that the entire matter was to be left to the executive discretion of the Secretary of State, with Lord Maugham holding: '[I] cannot myself believe that those responsible for the order in counsel could have contemplated for a moment the possibility of the action of the Secretary of State being subject to the discussion, criticism and control of a judge in a Court of law.'* This view was echoed by the other learned law lords in their majority judgments. Lord Macmillan was quick to point out:

> In the first place, it is important to have in mind that the regulation in question is a war measure. This is not to say that the courts ought to adopt in wartime canons of construction different from those which they follow in peace time. The fact that the nation is at war is no justification for any relaxation of the vigilance of the courts in seeing that the law is duly observed, especially in a matter so fundamental as the liberty of the subject—rather the contrary. But in a time of emergency when the life of the whole nation is at stake it may well be that a regulation for the defence of the realm may quite properly have a meaning which because of its drastic invasion of the liberty of the subject the courts would be slow to attribute to a peace time measure. The purpose of the regulation is to ensure public safety, and it is right so to interpret emergency legislation as to promote rather than to defeat its efficacy for the defence of the realm. That is in accordance with a general rule applicable to the interpretation of all statutes or statutory regulations in peace time as well as in war time.[†]

Lord Atkin's celebrated dissent is wholly unlike the restrained dissent of Lord Shaw of Dunfermline in *R. v. Halliday*. Other learned law lords, both

---

* 1942 A.C. 206, p. 220.
† Ibid., pp. 251–52.

before and after the decision of *Liversidge*, have normally used extremely restrained language in dissent. Before examining Lord Atkin's dissent, a look at three examples of this restraint will suffice.

In *Shaw v. Director of Public Prosecutions* (1962),[*] Lord Reid dissented from the reasoning of the majority on the meaning of the expression 'living on the earnings of prostitution' contrary to Section 30 of the Sexual Offences Act, 1956. The learned law lord referred to the ordinary meaning of these words, and noted the argument against creating new offences. He then held:

> Even if there is still a vestigial power of this kind it ought not, in my view, to be used unless there appears to be general agreement that the offence to which it is applied ought to be criminal if committed by an individual. Notoriously there are wide differences of opinion today as to how far the law ought to punish immoral acts which are not done in the face of the public. Some think that the law already goes too far, some that it does not go far enough. Parliament is the proper place, and I am firmly of opinion the only proper place, to settle that. When there is sufficient support from public opinion, Parliament does not hesitate to intervene. Where Parliament fears to tread it is not for the courts to rush in.[†]

He then adverted to the consequences of holding that a 'general' offence existed from the meaning and application of the words 'deprave' and 'corrupt', and that the meaning of these words must be left to the jury. The learned law lord concluded thus:

> Finally I must advert to the consequences of holding that this very general offence exists. It has always been thought to be of primary importance that our law, and particularly our criminal law, should be certain: that a man should be able to know what conduct is and what is not criminal, particularly when heavy penalties are involved. Some suggestion was made that it does not matter if this offence is very wide:

---

[*] (1962) AC 220.
[†] Ibid., p. 9.

no one would ever prosecute and if they did no jury would ever convict if the breach was venial. Indeed, the suggestion goes even further: that the meaning and application of the words 'deprave' and 'corrupt' (the traditional words in obscene libel now enacted in the 1959 Act) or the words 'debauch' and 'corrupt' in this indictment ought to be entirely for the jury, so that any conduct of this kind is criminal if in the end a jury think it so. In other words, you cannot tell what is criminal except by guessing what view a jury will take, and juries' views may vary and may change with the passing of time. Normally the meaning of words is a question of law for the Court. For example, it is not left to a jury to determine the meaning of negligence: they have to consider on evidence and on their own knowledge a much more specific question—Would a reasonable man have done what this man did? I know that in obscene libel the jury has great latitude, but I think that it is an understatement to say that this has not been found wholly satisfactory. If the trial Judge's charge in the present case was right, if a jury is entitled to water down the strong words 'deprave', 'corrupt' or 'debauch' so as merely to mean lead astray morally, then it seems to me that the Court has transferred to the jury the whole of its functions as censor morum—the law will be whatever any jury may happen to think it ought to be, and this branch of the law will have lost all the certainty which we rightly prize in other branches of our law.*

Equally restrained is a famous judgment of Lord Denning in the celebrated case of *Scruttons Ltd v. Midland Silicones* (1962).† In this case, a majority of the law lords held that when sued for negligence, stevedores were not entitled to the benefit of the provision limiting liability in a contract of carriage, because they were not parties to the contract. Lord Denning dissented. In referring to Lord Justice Scrutton, a judge who had laid down much of the commercial law in England, Lord Denning stated:

My Lords, it is said that, in stating this proposition, for once Homer nodded and that this great master of our commercial law—and the

---

* Id., p. 16.
† 1962 1 All ER 1.

members of this House too—overlooked the 'fundamental principle' that no one who is not a party to a contract can sue or be sued upon it or take advantage of the stipulations or conditions that it contains. I protest they did nothing of the kind. You cannot understand the *Elder Dempster* case without some knowledge of the previous law and I would draw the attention of your Lordships to it.

First of all let me remind your Lordships that this 'fundamental principle' was a discovery of the 19th century. Lord Mansfield and Buller, J. knew nothing of it. But in the 19th century it was carried to the most extravagant lengths. It was held that, where a duty to use reasonable care arose out of a contract, no one could sue or be sued for a breach of that contract except a party to it, see *Winterbottom v. Wright* (1842) 10 M. & W. 109, *Alton v. Midland Rly Co.* (1865) 19 C.B., N.S. 213. In the 19th century if a goods owner had sought to sue stevedores for negligence, as he has in this case, he would have failed utterly. The reason being that the duty of the stevedores to use reasonable care arose out of their contract with the carrier; and no one could sue them for a breach of that duty except the other party to the contract, namely, the carrier. If the goods were damaged, the only remedy of the owner of the goods was against the carrier with whom he contracted, and not against the stevedores with whom he had no contract. If proof were needed that the doctrine was carried so far, it is provided by the many cases in the middle of the nineteenth century where the owner of goods sent them by railway for 'through transit' to a destination on another line. The first carrier carried them safely over his line but they were damaged by the negligence of the second carrier. It was repeatedly held that the goods owner had no remedy against the second carrier: for the simple reason that he had no contract with him.

xxx xxx xxx

What an irony is here! This 'fundamental principle' which was invoked 100 years ago for the purpose of holding that the agents of the carrier were 'not liable at all' is now invoked for the purpose of holding that they are inescapably liable, without the benefit of any of the conditions of carriage. How has this come about? The reason is because in the 19th century negligence was not an independent tort. If you wished to sue a man for negligence, you had to show some special circumstances which put him under a duty of care towards you. You might do it by reason of a contract, by a bailment, by his inviting you on to his premises on business, by his leaving about a thing which was dangerous in itself, and in other ways. But apart from some such special circumstances, there was no general duty to use care.*

In conclusion, dissenting from the view of the majority, Lord Denning held:

My Lords, I have dealt with this case at some length because it is the first case ever recorded in our English books where the owner of goods has sued a stevedore for negligence. If the owner can, by so doing, escape the exceptions in the contract of carriage and the limitations in the Hague Rules, it will expose a serious gap in our commercial law. It has great potentialities too. If you can sue the stevedore for his negligence in unloading, why should you not sue the master and officers of the ship for their negligence in the navigation or management of the ship? No longer need you worry about the limitation to £100 or £200 a package. You can recover the value of the most precious package without disclosing its nature or value beforehand. No longer need you worry about bringing an action within one year. You can bring it within six years. Nor are the potentialities limited to carriage by sea. They can be profitably extended to carriage by air and by road and rail. You have only to sue the servants of the carrier for negligence and you can get round all the exceptions and limitations that have hitherto been devised. No doubt the carrying company will stand behind its servants. It will foot the bill, as any good employer would, for the sake of good relations. But when you find that the carrying company has, in the long run. to pay for the damage, you see at once that you have turned the flank of the Hague Rules (for carriage by sea) and the Warsaw Convention (for carriage by air). The exemptions and limitations which are there so clearly given to the 'carrier' do not avail his servants and agents when they are sued. By suing them, the goods owner will be

---

* Ibid. at pp. 16, 17.

able completely to upset the balance of risks as hitherto covered by insurance. No wonder that Parliament has already found it necessary to step in. It has done so in sections 2 and 3 of the Merchant Shipping (Liabilities of Shipowners and Others) Act, 1958: and sections 1, 5 and 10 and the First Schedule Article 25A of the Carriage by Air Act, 1961, which is not yet in force nor likely to be for some time. But these are only piecemeal efforts of very limited scope. Much more is needed if the law is such as your Lordships today declare it to be. For myself, however, I would not allow this gap to be driven in our commercial law. I would not give the 'fundamental principle' of the 19th century a free rein. It should not have unbridled scope to defeat the intentions of business men. I would stand by the proposition stated by Scrutton, L.J. and affirmed, as I believe, by this House 37 years ago.

I would allow this appeal.[*]

In a recent dissent in *Granatino v. Radmacher* (2010),[†] Baroness Hale, disagreeing with the majority view in a matter in which she felt strongly, put the controversy in the case thus:

The issue in this case is simple: what weight should the court hearing a claim for ancillary relief under the Matrimonial Causes Act 1973 give to an agreement entered into between the parties before they got married which purported to determine the result? I propose to call these 'ante-nuptial agreements' because our legislation already uses the term 'ante-nuptial' to refer to things done before a marriage. I should also point out that, although our judgments talk only of marriage and married couples, our conclusions must also apply to couples who have entered into a civil partnership. The issue may be simple, but underlying it are some profound questions about the nature of marriage in the modern law and the role of the courts in determining it. Marriage is, of course, a contract, in the sense that each party must agree to enter into it and once entered both are bound by its legal consequences. But it is also a status. This means two things. First, the parties are not entirely free to determine

---

[*] Id., p. 22.
[†] (2010) UKSC 42.

all its legal consequences for themselves. They contract into the package which the law of the land lays down. Secondly, their marriage also has legal consequences for other people and for the state. Nowadays there is considerable freedom and flexibility within the marital package but there is an irreducible minimum. This includes a couple's mutual duty to support one another and their children. We have now arrived at a position where the differing roles which either may adopt within the relationship are entitled to equal esteem. The question for us is how far individual couples should be free to re-write that essential feature of the marital relationship as they choose.*

In restrained and dignified language, she pointed out her dissenting view as follows:

It is for that reason that I have chosen to write a separate judgment, for although there is much within the majority judgment with which I agree, there are some points upon which I disagree. Specifically: (1) I disagree with the view, mercifully obiter to the decision in this case, that ante-nuptial agreements are legally enforceable contracts. (2) I disagree with the view, also mercifully obiter to the decision in this case, that it is open to this court to hold that they are. (3) I disagree with the view that, in policy terms, there are no relevant differences between agreements made before and agreements made after a marriage. (4) I disagree with the way in which the majority have formulated the test to be applied by a court hearing an application for financial relief, which I believe to be an impermissible gloss upon the courts' statutory duties. However, I agree that the court must consider the agreement in the light of the circumstances as they now exist and that the way the matter was put by the Privy Council in *MacLeod v. MacLeod* [2008] UKPC 64, [2010] 1 AC 298, was too rigid, and in some cases, too strong; and I broadly agree with the majority upon the relevant considerations which the court should take into account. (5) I disagree with the approach of the Court of Appeal to the actual outcome of this case, which the majority uphold. In my view it is inconsistent with the continued importance

_____

* Ibid., paragraphs 131–32.

attached to the status of marriage in English law. This is independent
of the weight to be attached to the agreement in this case. (6) I consider
that the reform of the law on ante- and post-nuptial agreements should
be considered comprehensively, not limited to agreements catering for
future separation or divorce. I understand that Lord Mance shares my
misgivings on points (1) and (2) above. He also takes the view that the
difference between our formulations of the test, referred to in point (4)
above, is unlikely to be important in practice. As the ultimate question
is what is fair, the starting point is unlikely to matter once all the facts
are before the court. I hope that he is right.*

In marked contrast to Lord Reid, Lord Denning and Baroness Hale, Lord
Atkin's dissent in *Liversidge* is hard-hitting and uses ridicule and satire
throughout. The example given to ram home the point that the plain
words of the regulation cannot be distorted, as was done by the majority
law lords, is as follows:

> It is surely incapable of dispute that the words 'if A has X' constitute a
> condition the essence of which is the existence of X and the having of
> it by A. If it is a condition to a right (including a power) granted to A,
> whenever the right comes into dispute the tribunal whatever it may be
> that is charged with determining the dispute must ascertain whether
> the condition is fulfilled. In some cases the issue is one of fact, in others
> of both fact and law, but in all cases the words indicate an existing
> something the having of which can be ascertained. And the words do
> not mean and cannot mean 'if A thinks that he has'. 'If A has a broken
> ankle' does not mean and cannot mean 'if A thinks that he has a broken
> ankle'. 'If A has a right of way' does not mean and cannot mean 'if A
> thinks that he has a right of way.' 'Reasonable cause' for an action or a
> belief is just as much a positive fact capable of determination by a third
> party as is a broken ankle or a legal right. If its meaning is the subject
> of dispute as to legal rights, then ordinarily the reasonableness of the
> cause, and even the existence of any cause is in our law to be determined
> by the judge and not by the tribunal of fact if the functions deciding

---

* Id., paragraph 138.

law and fact are divided. Thus having established, as I hope, that the plain and natural meaning of the words 'has reasonable cause' imports the existence of a fact or state of facts and not the mere belief by the person challenged that the fact or state of facts existed, I proceed to show that this meaning of the words has been accepted in innumerable legal decisions for many generations, that 'reasonable cause' for a belief when the subject of legal dispute has been always treated as an objective fact to be proved by one or other party and to be determined by the appropriate tribunal. I will go further and show that until June or July of this year in connection with this reg. 18B, there never has been any other construction even submitted to the courts in whatever context the words are found.[*]

Having given this example, Lord Atkin then went on to state:

I have pointed out that the words in question have a plain and natural meaning, that that meaning has been invariably given to them in statements of the common law and in statutes, that there has been one invariable construction of them in the courts, and that the Defence Regulations themselves clearly recognize that meaning, using different words where it is intended that the executive officer should have unqualified discretion.[†]

Then comes the most oft-quoted portion of this celebrated judgment:

I view with apprehension the attitude of judges who on a mere question of construction when face to face with claims involving the liberty of the subject show themselves more executive minded than the executive. Their function is to give words their natural meaning, not, perhaps, in war time leaning towards liberty, but following the dictum of Pollock C.B. in *Bowditch v. Balchin*, cited with approval by my noble and learned friend Lord Wright in *Barnard v. Gorman*: 'In a case in which the liberty of the subject is concerned, we cannot go beyond the natural

---

[*] Id., pp. 227–28.
[†] Id., p. 236.

construction of the statute.' In this country, amid the clash of arms, the laws are not silent. They may be changed, but they speak the same language in war as in peace. It has always been one of the pillars of freedom, one of the principles of liberty for which on recent authority we are now fighting, that the judges are no respecters of persons and stand between the subject and any attempted encroachments on his liberty by the executive, alert to see that any coercive action is justified in law. In this case I have listened to arguments which might have been addressed acceptably to the Court of King's Bench in the time of Charles I.

I protest, even if I do it alone, against a strained construction put on words with the effect of giving an uncontrolled power of imprisonment to the minister. To recapitulate: The words have only one meaning. They are used with that meaning in statements of the common law and in statutes. They have never been used in the sense now imputed to them. They are used in the Defence Regulations in the natural meaning, and, when it is intended to express the meaning now imputed to them, different and apt words are used in the regulations generally and in this regulation in particular. Even if it were relevant, which it is not, there is no absurdity or no such degree of public mischief as would lead to a non-natural construction.

I know of only one authority which might justify the suggested method of construction: 'When I use a word,' Humpty Dumpty said in rather a scornful tone, 'it means just what I choose it to mean, neither more nor less'. 'The question is,' said Alice, 'whether you can make words mean so many different things.' 'The question is,' said Humpty Dumpty, 'which is to be master—that's all.' After all this long discussion the question is whether the words 'If a man has' can mean 'If a man thinks he has'. I am of opinion that they cannot, and that the case should be decided accordingly.*

Lord Atkin then ended his judgment by pouring further ridicule on the theory of 'subjective satisfaction':

Of course, if the subjective theory is right and the Secretary of State has indeed unconditional power of imprisonment, it was enough for

---

* Id., pp. 244–45.

him to say that he exercised the power. But it seemed to be suggested
in argument that, even if the power were conditional, yet it would be
a good return by the Secretary of State to say that he had made the
order in the terms of the regulation. This seems to me, with respect, to
be fantastic. A minister given only a limited authority cannot make for
himself a valid return by merely saying I acted as though I had authority.
His *ipse dixit* avails nothing. A constable would make no valid return by
saying: 'I had reasonable cause for my arrest', or 'I served the criminal
at the time with a written notice that I was arresting him for reasonable
suspicion of felony'. However, on my view of this, the Secretary of State
has made a return sufficient to indicate that the Divisional Court were
right in refusing to order the writ to issue. I think that the appeal in this
case should be dismissed.*

Interestingly, Lord Simon, the Lord Chancellor, did not sit on this
case, but he did his best to dissuade Lord Atkin from using sarcasm and
ridicule as a weapon in his dissenting judgment. What actually happened
is narrated in a speech made by the Hon'ble Susan Kiefel A.C., ex-Chief
Justice of Australia, as follows:

> Lord Simon, the Lord Chancellor, had not sat on the case but came
> to hear about the Humpty Dumpty reference and sought to persuade
> Lord Atkin to 'join the majority or, at least, tone down his dissenting
> opinion'. It might seem strange to some that a judge who disagrees with
> the majority opinion might nevertheless join with them, but it was then
> a well-established tradition that judges refrained from dissenting unless
> a case was of particular importance. Lord Radcliffe said that when he
> joined the House of Lords in 1949 a dissent was 'a serious thing'. The
> justification for the practice appears to have been that the exposure of
> differences of opinion might detract from the authority of the House
> of Lords. Lord Simon was sufficiently concerned about the matter that
> he wrote to Lord Atkin asking him whether he really thought that the
> 'very amusing citation from Lewis Carroll' was necessary. He said 'I
> fear that it may be regarded as wounding to your colleagues who take

---

* Id., p. 247.

the view you satirize, and I feel sure you would not willingly seek to hold them up to ridicule'. Lord Atkin's biographer thought that Lord Simon might be criticized for attempting to edit Atkin's speech. For my part I consider it perfectly proper for a senior judge to seek to persuade another judge to remove references of this kind. Lord Simon himself explained to Lord Atkin that he was principally concerned about the dignity of the court. The likely effect on the feelings of Lord Atkin's colleagues was no doubt another means by which to persuade him. Lord Atkin was not persuaded. In his reply to Lord Simon he said that if he had not had the 'highest esteem' for his colleagues he would have used 'very different language' to what he had used (one can only speculate as to what literary texts might have been employed if he had not regarded his colleagues well). He did not think he was ridiculing them, but rather the method which they had employed in construing the Regulation. He concluded:

'I consider that I have destroyed [the majority view] on every legal ground: and it seems to me fair to conclude with a dose of ridicule.'

He would not alter the opinion. Lord Simon tried once more and pressed Lord Atkin to 'omit the jibe' but it was to no avail. The response of the other members of the House of Lords was to refuse to speak to Lord Atkin or to lunch with him for a considerable time. In English parlance he was 'sent to Coventry'.*

The speeches of all the law lords were read in a temporary chamber on 3 November 1941. The following day, the press gave full coverage to the decision, including Lord Atkin's stinging dissent. Stung to the quick, Lord Maugham, the presiding judge, did something unprecedented—he wrote a letter to *The Times* on 6 November 1941, under the heading 'War and Habeas Corpus'. The letter reads thus:

Sir—Those who took part in the decision of the House of Lords in the case of *Liversidge v. Anderson* could wish for no better statement of the reasons which guided the House, in affirming your leading article of 4 November, but there is one thing which I would like to add.

---

* Susan Kiefel, Judicial Courage and the Decorum of Dissent' (supra), pp. 4–5.

Lord Atkin, in his dissentient speech, stated that he had listened 'to arguments which might have been addressed acceptably to the Court of King's Bench in the time of Charles I'. Counsel, according to the traditions of the Bar, cannot reply even to so grave an animadversion as this. I think it only fair to the Attorney General and Mr Valentine Holmes, who appeared for the Respondents, to say that I presided at the hearing and listened to every word of their arguments, and that I did not hear from them, or anyone else, anything which could justify such a remark.

Yours truly,
Maugham.[*]

Lord Atkin's reaction was in a letter to his daughter, Nancy, in which he wrote:

I suppose you saw Maugham's letter in the Times today. I think he must be suffering from a nervous strain. It is of course quite unprecedented and quite unpardonable for one judge to attack another in the Press, and nothing will induce me to reply.[†]

Feelings were obviously running high. Fortunately, Lord Atkin preserved complete silence, in accordance with the dignity of his high office. Lord Maugham's letter, on the other hand, met with universal disapproval. The *Daily Telegraph*, in a leading article on 7 November 1941, entitled 'A Judge's Lapse', remarked:

The rebuke to Lord Atkin was in fact superfluous; but even if the complaint had been never so well justified that could not have excused the method chosen by Lord Maugham to ventilate it.[‡]

Academic commentators were divided—while Sir William Holdsworth and Professor Goodhart supported the majority judgment, Dr C.K. Allen

---

[*] Geoffrey Lewis, *Lord Atkin* (supra), p. 143.
[†] Ibid., p. 144.
[‡] Id., p. 144.

supported Lord Atkin's view. The immediate aftermath of Lord Atkin's judgment was that Lord Atkin was put by his colleagues into 'Coventry'— from that day on, Lord Atkin had lunch alone. Despite his dissent being generally well accepted at that time, there were comments on the acidity of Lord Atkin's speech. For example, in 'Obiter Dicta', an article written in the *Law Journal* (1941), it was stated:

> It is a pity that Lord Atkin saw fit to add to his forcible judgment . . . matters which were not necessary to his reasoning and, therefore, added nothing to its strength.*

Lord Atkin's final vindication came in 1980, almost forty years after *Liversidge*. The majority judgments in *Liversidge* were expressly overruled, and Lord Atkin's dissent was stated to be a correct view of the law by Lord Diplock in *Inland Revenue Commissioners v. Rossminster Ltd.* (1980)† as follows:

> With the issue of the warrant the functions and responsibilities of the circuit judge come to an end. The power of the officer of the board to seize and remove things that he finds upon the premises which the warrant authorizes him to enter and search, is conferred directly upon him by subsection (3) which limits his powers of seizure and removal to things 'which he has reasonable cause to believe may be required as evidence for the purposes of proceedings' for an offence involving a tax fraud. These words appearing in a statute do not make conclusive the officer's own honest opinion, that he has reasonable cause for the prescribed belief. The grounds on which the officer acted must be sufficient to induce in a reasonable person the required belief before he can validly seize and remove anything under the subsection. This was affirmed in *Nakkuda Ali v. Jayaratne* [1951] A.C. 66, a decision of the Privy Council in which Lord Radcliffe writing for the board expressed the view that the majority speeches in *Liversidge v. Anderson* [1942] A.C. 206, in which a contrary construction had been placed on similar words

---

* 'Obiter Dicta', *Law Journal*, Vol. 91 (1941): pp. 409 at 410.
† (1980) A.C. 952.

in the wartime regulation 18B of the Defence (General) Regulations 1939, should be regarded as an authority for the meaning of that phrase in that particular regulation alone. For my part I think the time has come to acknowledge openly that the majority of this House in *Liversidge v. Anderson* were expediently and, at that time, perhaps, excusably, wrong and the dissenting speech of Lord Atkin was right.[*]

What Lord Atkin did in terms of satire and ridicule way back in 1941, which may have been novel at that time, appears to have lit a flame in other dissenting judges both within and outside the UK. Thus, we find Lord Bridge of Harwich using strong language in his dissent in *Attorney General v. Guardian Papers Ltd.* (1987).[†] This judgment is commonly referred to as the first *Spycatcher* case, in which one W, a former member of the British Security Service, who had access to highly classified and sensitive information, and who proposed to publish his memoirs in Australia, was subjected to government censure—with the British government moving the courts for an injunction against the publication of such a book. This injunction was granted by the majority in *Attorney General*, stating that the right of the public to be protected by the security service in defence of the realm, and the need to prevent the disclosure of information received by W in confidence, prevailed over the right of the public to be fully informed by the press. Lord Bridge's dissent to this proposition was hard-hitting:

> But it is perfectly obvious and elementary that, once information is freely available to the general public, it is nonsensical to talk about preventing its 'disclosure'. Whether the *Spycatcher* allegations are true or false is beside the point. What is to the point is that they are now freely available to the public or, perhaps more accurately, to any member of the public who wants to read them. I deliberately refrain from using expressions such as 'the public domain' which may have technical overtones. The fact is that the intelligence and security services of any country in the

---

[*] Ibid. As a subject of further comment, see Lord Toulson's majority opinion for the UK Supreme Court in *Regina v. Secretary of State for the Home Department* ([2013] 1 W.L.R. 2224 at 2234).

[†] (1987) 3 All ER 316.

world can buy the book *Spycatcher* and read what is in it. The fact is that any citizen of this country can buy the book in America and bring it home with him or order the book from America and receive a copy by post. Some enterprising small traders have apparently found it worth their while to import copies of the book and sell them by the roadside.

xxx xxx xxx

What of the other side of the coin and the encroachment on freedom of speech? Having no written constitution, we have no equivalent in our law to the First Amendment to the Constitution of the United States of America. Some think that puts freedom of speech on too lofty a pedestal. Perhaps they are right. We have not adopted as part of our law the European Convention on Human Rights to which this country is a signatory. Many think that we should. I have hitherto not been of that persuasion, in large part because I have had confidence in the capacity of the common law to safeguard the fundamental freedoms essential to a free society including the right to freedom of speech which is specifically safeguarded by Article 10 of the Convention. My confidence is seriously undermined by your Lordships' decision. All the judges in the courts below in this case have been concerned not to impose any unnecessary fetter on freedom of speech. I suspect that what the Court of Appeal would have liked to achieve, and perhaps set out to achieve by their compromise solution, was to inhibit The Sunday Times from continuing the serialization of *Spycatcher*, but to leave the press at large at liberty to discuss and comment on the *Spycatcher* allegations. If there were a method of achieving these results which could be sustained in law, I can see much to be said for it on the merits. But I can see nothing whatever, either in law or on the merits, to be said for the maintenance of a total ban on discussion in the press of this country on matters of undoubted public interest and concern which the rest of the world now knows all about and can discuss freely. Still less can I approve your Lordships' decision to throw in for good measure a restriction on reporting court proceedings in Australia which the Attorney General had never even asked for. Freedom of speech is always the first casualty under a totalitarian regime. Such a regime cannot afford to allow the free circulation of information and ideas among its citizens. Censorship is the indispensable tool to regulate what the public may and what they may not know. The present attempt to insulate the public in this country from information which is freely available elsewhere is a significant step down that very dangerous road. The maintenance of the ban, as more and more copies of the book *Spycatcher* enter this country and circulate here, will seem more and more ridiculous. If the Government are determined to fight to maintain the ban to the end, they will face inevitable condemnation and humiliation by the European Court of Human Rights in Strasbourg. Long before that they will have been condemned at the bar of public opinion in the free world.

But there is another alternative, The Government will surely want to reappraise the whole *Spycatcher* situation in the light of the views expressed in the courts below and in this House. I dare to hope that they will bring to that reappraisal qualities of vision and of statesmanship sufficient to recognize that their wafer thin victory in this litigation has been gained at a price which no Government committed to upholding the values of a free society can afford to pay.

I add a postscript to record that I have now had the opportunity to read first drafts of the opinions of my noble and learned friends, Lord Templeman and Lord Ackner. I remain in profound disagreement with them.[*]

In the US Supreme Court, Justice Brennan was credited as being one of the most influential justices of his era, indeed, of the twentieth century.[†] He is credited with having written 471 substantive dissenting opinions in his thirty-four terms at the Supreme Court.[‡] When in dissent, as was increasingly the case during the last half of his tenure, he was neither caustic nor trivial.[§] As was noted by his close friend, Abner Mikva, Justice Brennan 'knew how to disagree without being disagreeable'.[¶]

---

[*] Ibid., pp. 345–47.

[†] See Rory K. Little (supra), 11f, p.4.

[‡] Ibid., p. 1.

[§] Id., p. 4.

[¶] Abner J. Mikva, 'Reason, Passion & the Progress of Law: Remaking and Advancing the Constitutional Vision of Justice William J. Brennan', *Harvard Civil Rights—Civil Liberties Law Review*, Vol. 33 (1998): pp. 325, 331.

In contrast, Rehnquist, J. used sarcasm and ridicule in his dissenting judgments to great effect. In *Steelworkers v. Weber* (1979),[*] Justice Rehnquist, joined by Chief Justice Burger, had this to say about the majority judgment:

> Thus, by a *tour de force* reminiscent not of jurists such as Hale, Holmes, and Hughes, but of escape artists such as Houdini, the Court eludes clear statutory language, 'uncontradicted' legislative history, and uniform precedent in concluding that employers are, after all, permitted to consider race in making employment decisions.[†]

Likewise, in *Florida v. Royer* (1983),[‡] Rehnquist, J., with whom Burger C.J. and O'Connor, J. joined, spoke of the majority opinion thus:

> The plurality's meandering opinion contains in it a little something for everyone, and although it affirms the reversal of a judgment of conviction, it can scarcely be said to bespeak a total indifference to the legitimate needs of law enforcement agents seeking to curb trafficking in dangerous drugs. Indeed, in both manner and tone, the opinion brings to mind the old nursery rhyme: 'The King of France/With forty thousand men/Marched up the hill/And then marched back again'.[§]

Following this trend of dissenting judgments using sarcasm and ridicule, one judge of the US Supreme Court—Justice Antonin Scalia—stands out more as an angry young man tilting at the windmills that the majority judgments have set up, than as a sober lifelong justice appointed to the Supreme Court.[¶] Some of his more notable dissenting opinions use

---

[*] 443 U.S. 193 (1979).
[†] Ibid., p. 222.
[‡] 460 U.S. 491 (1983).
[§] Ibid., pp. 519, 520.
[¶] This is in contrast to a famous dissent of yesteryear, namely, the dissent of Justice Curtis in the celebrated judgment of *Dred Scott v. Sandford* (60 U.S. 393 [1857]), where Curtis, J. also used extremely restrained language on an issue which led the United States to civil war. He dissented as follows: 'I dissent, therefore, from that part of the opinion of the majority of the court, in which it is held that a person of African descent cannot be a citizen of the United States; and I regret I must go further, and dissent both from what I

ridicule and satire that can almost be characterized as being hysterical.*

---

deem their assumption of authority to examine the constitutionality of the act of Congress commonly called the Missouri compromise act, and the grounds and conclusions announced in their opinion. Having first decided that they were found to consider the sufficiency of the plea to the jurisdiction of the Circuit Court, and having decided that this plea showed that the Circuit Court had not jurisdiction, and consequently that this is a case to which the judicial power of the United States does not extend, they have gone on to examine the merits of the case as they appeared on the trial before the court and jury, on the issues joined on the pleas in bar, and so have reached the question of the power of Congress to pass the act of 1802. On so grave a subject as this, I feel obliged to say that, in my opinion, such an exertion of judicial power transcends the limits of the authority of the court, as described by its repeated decisions, and, as I understand, acknowledged in this opinion of the majority of the court. I have expressed my opinion and the reasons therefore, at far greater length than I could have wished, upon the different questions on which I have found it necessary to pass, to arrive at a judgment on the case at bar. These questions are numerous, and the grave importance of some of them required me to exhibit fully the grounds of my opinion. I have touched no question which, in the view I have taken, it was not absolutely necessary for me to pass upon, to ascertain whether the judgment of the Circuit Court should stand or be reversed. I have avoided no question on which the validity of that judgment depends. To have done either more or less, would have been inconsistent with my views of my duty.'

* Roscoe Pound, dean emeritus of Harvard Law School, in '*Cacoethes Dissentiendi*: The Heated Judicial Dissent', *American Bar Association Journal*, Vol. 39, No. 9 (September 1953), p. 794, highlighted what he put as the high watermark of 'judicial imitation of forensic advocacy'. Setting out a dissenting judgment of a California Supreme Court justice, Pound observed: 'Perhaps the high-water mark of judicial imitation of forensic advocacy is reached by the same Judge in *Sanguinetti v. Moore Dry Dock* Co. 36 Cal. 2d 812, 823-845 (1951). Here in twenty-two pages of vigorous dissent we are told that the majority "reached a new low in search for a reason to reverse a judgment", that there was "not a scintilla of reason or common sense in such a holding", that it was "so lacking in consideration of the realities of the situation that it may be said to be naïve", that "the reactionary philosophy of the majority opinion is so out of harmony with present day concepts of trial procedure that it resembles some of the skeletons of the dead past" and that "it should be apparent to every unprejudiced mind, as it is to me, that the majority in seizing upon this motion as the sole ground for a reversal of the judgment in this case, is simply creating a mythical error which exists only in hypertechnical illusion."' Finally he sums up: 'In essence what these four judges have done here is to blindly announce a court-made rule which not only finds no support in history, precedent, experience, custom, practice, logic, reason, common sense or natural justice but is in utter defiance of all of these standards'. The doctrines announced by his colleagues are denounced as 'absurd', 'transcending the height of absurdity' and lacking any 'shred of reason, logic or common sense', 'wholly unsound and utterly lacking in either factual or legal foundation'. He tells us that if there is a scintilla or reason or logic behind the doctrine of the majority it is not apparent to him and he doubts whether it would be 'to any unprejudiced mind'. In a similar vein, Justice Scalia used the vehicle of the dissenting judgment far beyond

As an example, in *PGA Tour, Inc. v. Martin* (2001),* which involved a challenge to the Professional Golf Association's rule prohibiting golfers from using motorized carts during tournaments, he wrote:

> I am sure that the Framers of the Constitution, aware of the 1457 edict of King James II of Scotland prohibiting golf because it interfered with the practice of archery, fully expected that sooner or later the paths of golf and government, the law and the links, would once again cross, and that the judges of this august Court would some day have to wrestle with that age-old jurisprudential question, for which their years of study in the law have so well prepared them: Is someone riding around a golf course from shot to shot really a golfer?†

In *Morisson v. Olson* (1988),‡ where the US Supreme Court was seized of the constitutionality of the independent counsel provisions of the Ethics in Government Act, 1978, and a larger question on the separation of powers contemplated in the US Constitution, he wrote in his dissent:

> Frequently an issue of this sort will come before the Court clad, so to speak, in sheep's clothing: the potential of the asserted principle to effect important change in the equilibrium of power is not immediately evident, and must be discerned by a careful and perceptive analysis. But this wolf comes as a wolf.
>
> It is in fact comforting to witness the reality that he who lives by the *ipse dixit* dies by the *ipse dixit*. But one must grieve for the Constitution.§

---

pointing out how the majority justices were incorrect in law. In fact, Andrew Lynch in *Great Australian Dissents* (supra) speaks of Justice Scalia's dissenting opinions in the following terms: 'Scalia has perfected the opinion as attack "ad rhetoric" (Mark Tushnet, *I Dissent—Great Opposing Opinions in Landmark Supreme Court Cases* [Boston: Beacon Press, 2006, p. xxii]). As one commentator remarked on Scalia, J.'s criticisms of the majority reasoning in cases from the court's 2014–15 term: 'Welcome to the era of the judicial dissent as body slam' (Dahlia Lithwick, 'Sunday Book Review: "Dissent and the Supreme Court" by Melvik I Urofksy', *New York Times*, 21 October 2015) (34f, p.9).
* 532 U.S. 661 (2001).
† Ibid. at 700.
‡ 487 U.S. 654 (1988).
§ Ibid. at 699, 726.

Then, in *Atkins v. Virginia* (2002),* where the Supreme Court was tasked with deciding whether the death penalty could be administered upon a convict who was determined to be 'mildly mentally retarded', he wrote:

> Today's decision is the pinnacle of our Eighth Amendment death-is-different jurisprudence. Not only does it, like all of that jurisprudence, find no support in the text or history of the Eighth Amendment; it does not even have support in current social attitudes regarding the conditions that render an otherwise just death penalty inappropriate. Seldom has an opinion of this Court rested so obviously upon nothing but the personal views of its Members.[†]

On a question involving the interpretation of religious freedoms in the United States in *Lee v. Weisman* (1992),[‡] Justice Scalia wrote scathingly, in dissent, of his associate justices thus:

> I find it a sufficient embarrassment that our Establishment Clause jurisprudence regarding holiday displays has come to require scrutiny more commonly associated with interior decorators than with the judiciary. But interior decorating is a rock-hard science compared to psychology practiced by amateurs.[§]

It was in *Lawrence v. Texas* (2003),[⁵] in which the arrest of a male for engaging in consensual homosexual conduct was challenged as being in violation of the 'due process' clause of the Fourteenth Amendment of the US Constitution, where Justice Scalia remarked:

> I do not know what 'acting in private' means; surely consensual sodomy, like heterosexual intercourse, is rarely performed on stage . . . One of the benefits of leaving regulation of this matter to the people rather than to

---

* 536 U.S. 304 (2002).
[†] Ibid. at 338.
[‡] 505 U.S. 577 (1992).
[§] Ibid. at 636.
[⁵] 539 U.S. 558 (2003).

the courts is that the people, unlike judges, need not carry things to their logical conclusion.*

More recently, in *King v. Burwell* (2015),[†] the Patient Protection and Affordable Care Act (commonly known as Obamacare) was the subject matter of discussion. Justice Scalia, with whom Justices Thomas and Alito joined, opens his dissent by stating:

> The Court holds that when the Patient Protection and Affordable Care Act says 'Exchange established by the State' it means 'Exchange established by the State or the Federal Government'. That is of course quite absurd, and the Court's 21 pages of explanation make it no less so.[‡]

He goes on to state:

> Under all the usual rules of interpretation, in short, the Government should lose this case. But normal rules of interpretation seem always to yield to the overriding principle of the present Court: The Affordable Care Act must be saved.
>
> The Court interprets §36B to award tax credits on both federal and state Exchanges. It accepts that the 'most natural sense' of the phrase 'Exchange established by the State' is an Exchange established by a State. (Understatement, thy name is an opinion on the Affordable Care Act!) Yet the opinion continues, with no semblance of shame, that 'it is also possible that the phrase refers to all Exchanges—both State and Federal'. (Impossible possibility, thy name is an opinion on the Affordable Care Act!) The Court claims that 'the context and structure of the Act compel [it] to depart from what would otherwise be the most natural reading of the pertinent statutory phrase . . . Let us not forget, however, why context matters: It is a tool for understanding the terms of the law, not an excuse for rewriting them.'
>
> Ordinary connotation does not always prevail, but the more unnatural the proposed interpretation of a law, the more compelling

---

* Ibid., at 597, 604.
[†] 576 U.S. 988 (2015).
[‡] Ibid., Scalia's dissent, p. 1.

the contextual evidence must be to show that it is correct. Today's interpretation is not merely unnatural; it is unheard of. [*]

xxx xxx xxx

The Court's reading does not merely give 'by the State' a duplicative effect; it causes the phrase to have no effect whatever. [†]

xxx xxx xxx

It is bad enough for a court to cross out 'by the State' once. But seven times?

It is common sense that any speaker who says 'Exchange' some of the time, but 'Exchange established by the State' the rest of the time, probably means something by the contrast. [‡]

xxx xxx xxx

It is presumably in order to avoid these questions that the Court concludes that federal Exchanges count as state Exchanges only 'for purposes of the tax credits' (Contrivance, thy name is an opinion on the Affordable Care Act!). [§]

xxx xxx xxx

The Court's next bit of interpretive jiggery-pokery involves other parts of the Act that purportedly presuppose the availability of tax credits on both federal and state Exchanges. [¶]

xxx xxx xxx

---

[*] Id., pp. 2–3.
[†] Id., p. 5.
[‡] Id., p. 6.
[§] Id., p. 7.
[¶] Id., p. 8.

The Court claims that the Act must equate federal and state establishment of Exchanges when it defines a qualified individual as someone who (among other things) lives in the 'State that established the Exchange,' 42 U.S.C. §18032(f)(1)(A). Otherwise, the Court says, there would be no qualified individuals on federal Exchanges, contradicting (for example) the provision requiring every Exchange to take the "interests of qualified individuals" into account when selecting health plans. Ante, at 11 (quoting §18031(e)(1)(b)). Pure applesauce.[*]

xxx xxx xxx

The Court has not come close to presenting the compelling contextual case necessary to justify departing from the ordinary meaning of the terms of the law. Quite the contrary, context only underscores the outlandishness of the Court's interpretation.

For its next defence of the indefensible, the Court turns to the Affordable Care Act's design and purposes.[†]

xxx xxx xxx

We lack the prerogative to repair laws that do not work out in practice, just as the people lack the ability to throw us out of office if they dislike the solutions we concoct.[‡]

xxx xxx xxx

What a parody today's decision makes of Hamilton's assurances to the people of New York: 'The legislature not only commands the purse but prescribes the rules by which the duties and rights of every citizen are to be regulated. The judiciary, on the contrary, has no influence over . . . the purse; no direction . . . of the wealth of society, and can take no active resolution whatever. It may truly be said to have neither FORCE

---

[*] Id., p. 10.
[†] Id., p. 12.
[‡] Id., p. 18.

nor WILL but merely judgment.' The Federalist No. 78, p. 465 (C. Rossiter ed. 1961).*

xxx xxx xxx

Perhaps the Patient Protection and Affordable Care Act will attain the enduring status of the Social Security Act or the Taft-Hartley Act; perhaps not. But this Court's two decisions on the Act will surely be remembered through the years. The somersaults of statutory interpretation they have performed ('penalty' means tax, 'further [Medicaid] payments to the State' means only incremental Medicaid payments to the State, 'established by the State' means not established by the State) will be cited by litigants endlessly, to the confusion of honest jurisprudence. And the cases will publish forever the discouraging truth that the Supreme Court of the United States favors some laws over others, and is prepared to do whatever it takes to uphold and assist its favorites. I dissent.[†]

Expressions like 'jiggery-pokery', 'pure applesauce' and 'somersaults of statutory interpretation' are expressions which, in my opinion, have no place in a judicial opinion—albeit a dissenting one—of the highest court of the land. Likewise, in *Obergefell v. Hodges* (2015),[‡] which dealt with a state's licensing a marriage between two people of the same sex and of the recognition of such marriage, Justice Scalia, with whom Justice Thomas joined, dissents, saying:

I join The Chief Justice's opinion in full. I write separately to call attention to this Court's threat to American democracy.

The substance of today's decree is not of immense personal importance to me. The law can recognize as marriage whatever sexual attachments and living arrangements it wishes, and can accord them favorable civil consequences, from tax treatment to rights of inheritance. Those civil consequences—and the public approval that conferring the

---

* Id., p. 20.
† Id., p. 21.
‡ 135 S. Ct. 2584 (2015).

name of marriage evidences—can perhaps have adverse social effects, but no more adverse than the effects of many other controversial laws. So it is not of special importance to me what the law says about marriage. It is of overwhelming importance, however, who it is that rules me. Today's decree says that my Ruler, and the Ruler of 320 million Americans coast-to-coast, is a majority of the nine lawyers on the Supreme Court. The opinion in these cases is the furthest extension in fact—and the furthest extension one can even imagine—of the Court's claimed power to create 'liberties' that the Constitution and its Amendments neglect to mention. This practice of constitutional revision by an unelected committee of nine, always accompanied (as it is today) by extravagant praise of liberty, robs the People of the most important liberty they asserted in the Declaration of Independence and won in the Revolution of 1776: the freedom to govern themselves.*

xxx xxx xxx

But the Court ends this debate, in an opinion lacking even a thin veneer of law. Buried beneath the mummeries and straining-to-be-memorable passages of the opinion is a candid and startling assertion: No matter what it was the People ratified, the Fourteenth Amendment protects those rights that the Judiciary, in its 'reasoned judgment', thinks the Fourteenth Amendment ought to protect. That is so because '[t]he generations that wrote and ratified the Bill of Rights and the Fourteenth Amendment did not presume to know the extent of freedom in all of its dimensions . . .' One would think that sentence would continue: '. . . and therefore they provided for a means by which the People could amend the Constitution,' or perhaps '. . . and therefore they left the creation of additional liberties, such as the freedom to marry someone of the same sex, to the People, through the never-ending process of legislation.' But no. What logically follows, in the majority's judge-empowering estimation, is: 'and so they entrusted to future generations a charter protecting the right of all persons to enjoy liberty as we learn its meaning'. The 'we', needless to say, is the nine of us. 'History and

---

* Ibid., Scalia's dissent, pp. 1–2.

tradition guide and discipline [our] inquiry but do not set its outer boundaries.' Thus, rather than focusing on the People's understanding of 'liberty'—at the time of ratification or even today—the majority focuses on four 'principles and traditions' that, in the majority's view, prohibit States from defining marriage as an institution consisting of one man and one woman.

This is a naked judicial claim to legislative—indeed, *super-legislative*—power; a claim fundamentally at odds with our system of government. Except as limited by a constitutional prohibition agreed to by the People, the States are free to adopt whatever laws they like, even those that offend the esteemed Justices' 'reasoned judgment'. A system of government that makes the People subordinate to a committee of nine unelected lawyers does not deserve to be called a democracy.*

xxx xxx xxx

Take, for example, this Court, which consists of only nine men and women, all of them successful lawyers who studied at Harvard or Yale Law School. Four of the nine are natives of New York City. Eight of them grew up in east- and west-coast States. Only one hails from the vast expanse in-between. Not a single Southwesterner or even, to tell the truth, a genuine Westerner (California does not count). Not a single evangelical Christian (a group that comprises about one quarter of Americans), or even a Protestant of any denomination. The strikingly unrepresentative character of the body voting on today's social upheaval would be irrelevant if they were functioning as *judges*, answering the legal question whether the American people had ever ratified a constitutional provision that was understood to proscribe the traditional definition of marriage. But of course the Justices in today's majority are not voting on that basis; *they say they are not*. And to allow the policy question of same-sex marriage to be considered and resolved by a select, patrician, highly unrepresentative panel of nine is to violate a principle even more fundamental than no taxation without representation: no social

---

* Id., pp. 4–5.

transformation without representation . . . But what really astounds is the hubris reflected in today's judicial Putsch.[*]

xxx xxx xxx

They see what lesser legal minds—minds like Thomas Cooley, John Marshall Harlan, Oliver Wendell Holmes, Jr., Learned Hand, Louis Brandeis, William Howard Taft, Benjamin Cardozo, Hugo Black, Felix Frankfurter, Robert Jackson, and Henry Friendly—could not . . . The opinion is couched in a style that is as pretentious as its content is egotistic. It is one thing for separate concurring or dissenting opinions to contain extravagances, even silly extravagances, of thought and expression; it is something else for the official opinion of the Court to do so.[†]

xxx xxx xxx

The world does not expect logic and precision in poetry or inspirational pop-philosophy; it demands them in the law. The stuff contained in today's opinion has to diminish this Court's reputation for clear thinking and sober analysis.

Hubris is sometimes defined as o'erweening pride; and pride, we know, goeth before a fall. The Judiciary is the 'least dangerous' of the federal branches because it has 'neither Force nor Will, but merely judgment; and must ultimately depend upon the aid of the executive arm' and the States, 'even for the efficacy of its judgments'. With each decision of ours that takes from the People a question properly left to them—with each decision that is unabashedly based not on law, but on the 'reasoned judgment' of a bare majority of this Court—we move one step closer to being reminded of our impotence.[‡]

The verbal assault on the judges who wrote the majority opinion could not possibly have been more forthright: great justices of the past were

---

[*] Id., p. 6.
[†] Id., p. 7.
[‡] Id., p. 9.

sarcastically referred to as 'lesser legal minds' than the legal minds of the majority judges; the majority-judgment style of writing was attacked as being 'pretentious' and their contents 'egotistic'. In footnote twenty-two, which is in marked contrast to footnote eleven in *Brown*—being perhaps the most famous footnote in the court's history—the learned justice states that he would hide his head 'in a bag', as the present Supreme Court has descended from the disciplined legal reasoning of John Marshall and Joseph Story to the 'mystical aphorisms of the fortune cookie'. And, as if this were not enough, on the majority judgment's 'showy profundities' on the nature of marriage leading to the realization of other freedoms such as 'expression, intimacy and spirituality', the riposte is to 'ask the nearest hippie' whether marriage curtailed or expanded such freedoms.*

It seems that Lord Atkin's famous dissent has, in using invective and ridicule, opened up a Pandora's box in the English-speaking world, which is now impossible to close.[†]

Continuing with wartime judgments in other jurisdictions, in Australia, an interesting question arose in *Farey v. Burvett* (1916),[‡] with World War 1 in 1916, as to whether, under the legislative powers of the Commonwealth of Australia, the Parliament had been conferred with the

---

* Id., p. 8.

† Sometimes, academic scholars do also criticize a judgment with the use of intemperate language. Professor Glanville Williams, a leading academic authority on criminal law, wrote a scathing attack in his article 'The Lords and Impossible Attempts, or *Quis Custodiet Ipsos Custodes*', *Cambridge Law Journal*, Vol. 45 , Issue 1 (March 1986), p. 33, on the decision of the House of Lords in *Anderton v. Ryan* ([1985] AC 560), which considered the issue of criminal liability for an attempt to commit an impossible crime. The article's criticism is set out in David Pannick's *Judges* (Oxford: Oxford University Press, 1987) at p. 126, as follows: 'The tale I have to tell is unflattering of the higher judiciary. It is an account of how the judges invented a rule based upon a conceptual misunderstanding; of their determination to use the English language so strangely that they spoke what by normal criteria would be termed untruths; of their invincible ignorance of the mess they had made out of the law; and of their immobility on the subject, carried to the extent of subverting an Act of Parliament designed to put them straight.' Pannick then goes on to note: 'In a judgment soon after, abandoning the approach which had been the subject of this rebuke, Lord Bridge grudgingly conceded that he had "had the advantage" of reading the criticism, and that although the language used by Williams was "not conspicuous for its moderation . . . it would be foolish, on that account, not to recognize the force of the criticism and churlish not to acknowledge the assistance I have derived from it."' (*See R v. Shivpuri* [1986] 2 WLR 988, 1002.)

‡ 21 C.L.R 433.

power, during the state of war, to fix within the limits of each locality the highest price which may be charged for bread—food supply being limited, thanks to the war. A majority of judges held that Parliament would have such power. Gavan Duffy and Rich, JJ. dissented, stating:

> In these circumstances what meaning should be attributed to the words 'the naval and military defence of the Commonwealth and of the several States' in sec. 51 (VI.) of the *Constitution?* We venture to think that they extend to the raising, training and equipment of naval and military forces, to the maintenance, control and use of such forces, to the supply of arms, ammunitions and other things necessary for naval and military operations, to all matters strictly ancillary to these purposes, and to nothing more. This, in our opinion, is their natural meaning and to extend it would be to paralyze the States during war time as completely as if there had been no reserve powers, and to subject them at all times to an irritating and embarrassing usurpation of their ordinary functions. The defence of the States would be the defence which King Stork extended to the frogs who invoked his assistance.[*]

xxx xxx xxx

Finally, we were pressed not to withhold from the Commonwealth a power so conducive to the effective conduct of a war in which we are engaged, as we firmly believe, on the side of honour and righteousness. Such an appeal is ill made to Judges who are sworn to administer the law without fear, favour or affection, and whose fundamental duty is to interpret the law as they understand it, not to strain it this way or that at the bidding of expediency. But in our opinion the respondent has wholly failed to show that the power to fix the price of bread in Melbourne and its suburbs at the present time is in any sense conducive to the defence of the Commonwealth, or has any relation whatever to the progress of the War. If we are wrong, and such a power be necessary now, or if it becomes necessary in the future, it can be exercised by the State or delegated by the State to the Commonwealth. It is a gross

---

[*] Ibid. at 465.

and pernicious error to suppose that in the conduct of the present war the interests of the States and the Commonwealth are diverse, they are identical, and the people of Australia will no doubt be as willing to protect and forward those interests through their State Legislatures as through the Commonwealth Parliament.*

This is another dissenting judgment in wartime which strongly rejects the emotive argument, which is the 'hydraulic pressure' spoken of by Justice Holmes, to bend the law in extraordinary times such as war. The Olympian heights have now been reached—judges are reminded of their constitutional oath and their fundamental duty to interpret the law as they understand it, and not to give way to 'hydraulic pressure' by straining it this way or that, at the bidding of expediency.

Our next judgment takes us to the opposite end of the globe, namely, the United States, after it had entered World War 2. The date of the decision in *Korematsu v. United States* (1944)† is 18 December 1944, when the Axis forces had been decisively beaten; so was only a matter of time before World War 2 would end in favour of the Allies. The petitioner, Fred Korematzu, was an American citizen of Japanese descent, and was convicted by a federal district court for remaining in San Leandro, California, in his own house, contrary to Civilian Exclusion Order No. 34 of the Commanding General of the Western Command, US Army, which directed that after 9 May 1942, all persons of Japanese ancestry should be excluded from that area. An interesting aspect was that Fred Korematsu was born in the United States to Japanese parents and was therefore a citizen of the United States by virtue of the Fourteenth Amendment of the US Constitution.

The majority judgment—written by Justice Black, found that under the US Constitution, the Congress has the power to declare war, and hence the executive has the right to exclude those of Japanese ancestry from the war area of the West Coast of the United States at the time they did—was a judgment by the military authorities which cannot be second-guessed by courts of law. The majority judgment was careful. It held that

---

* Id., pp. 467–68.
† 323 U.S. 214 (1944).

the exclusion order is upheld at the time it was made—1942 (at the height of World War 2, and after America had joined the war, and when the petitioner violated this order). Three judges dissented. The first dissent, that of Justice Roberts, found:

> The petitioner, a resident of San Leandro, Alameda County, California, is a native of the United States of Japanese ancestry who, according to the uncontradicted evidence, is a loyal citizen of the nation.
>
> A chronological recitation of events will make it plain that the petitioner's supposed offense did not, in truth, consist in his refusal voluntarily to leave the area which included his home in obedience to the order excluding him therefrom. Critical attention must be given to the dates and sequence of events.[*]

xxx xxx xxx

The Government has argued this case as if the only order outstanding at the time the petitioner was arrested and informed against was Exclusion Order No. 34, ordering him to leave the area in which he resided, which was the basis of the information against him. That argument has evidently been effective. The opinion refers to the *Hirabayashi* case, *supra*, to show that this court has sustained the validity of a curfew order in an emergency. The argument, then, is that exclusion from a given area of danger, while somewhat more sweeping than a curfew regulation, is of the same nature—a temporary expedient made necessary by a sudden emergency. This, I think, is a substitution of an hypothetical case for the case actually before the court. I might agree with the court's disposition of the hypothetical case. The liberty of every American citizen freely to come and to go must frequently, in the face of sudden danger, be temporarily limited or suspended. The civil authorities must often resort to the expedient of excluding citizens temporarily from a locality. The drawing of fire lines in the case of a conflagration, the removal of persons from the area where a pestilence has broken out, are familiar examples.

---

[*] Ibid. at 226.

If the exclusion worked by Exclusion Order No. 34 were of that nature, the *Hirabayashi* case would be authority for sustaining it.

But the facts above recited, and those set forth in *Ex parte Endo, supra*, show that the exclusion was but a part of an over-all plan for forceable detention. This case cannot, therefore, be decided on any such narrow ground as the possible validity of a Temporary Exclusion Order under which the residents of an area are given an opportunity to leave and go elsewhere in their native land outside the boundaries of a military area. To make the case turn on any such assumption is to shut our eyes to reality.[*]

The next dissent came from Justice Murphy, which was much more direct. The dissent states:

This exclusion of 'all persons of Japanese ancestry, both alien and non-alien', from the Pacific Coast area on a plea of military necessity in the absence of martial law ought not to be approved. Such exclusion goes over 'the very brink of constitutional power', and falls into the ugly abyss of racism.[†]

xxx xxx xxx

It must be conceded that the military and naval situation in the spring of 1942 was such as to generate a very real fear of invasion of the Pacific Coast, accompanied by fears of sabotage and espionage in that area. The military command was therefore justified in adopting all reasonable means necessary to combat these dangers. In adjudging the military action taken in light of the then apparent dangers, we must not erect too high or too meticulous standards; it is necessary only that the action have some reasonable relation to the removal of the dangers of invasion, sabotage and espionage. But the exclusion, either temporarily or permanently, of all persons with Japanese blood in their veins has no such reasonable relation. And that relation is lacking because the exclusion order necessarily must rely for its reasonableness upon the

---

[*] Id., pp. 231–32.
[†] Id., p. 233.

assumption that all persons of Japanese ancestry may have a dangerous tendency to commit sabotage and espionage and to aid our Japanese enemy in other ways. It is difficult to believe that reason, logic, or experience could be marshalled in support of such an assumption.[*]

xxx xxx xxx

The main reasons relied upon by those responsible for the forced evacuation, therefore, do not prove a reasonable relation between the group characteristics of Japanese Americans and the dangers of invasion, sabotage and espionage. The reasons appear, instead, to be largely an accumulation of much of the misinformation, half-truths and insinuations that for years have been directed against Japanese Americans by people with racial and economic prejudices—the same people who have been among the foremost advocates of the evacuation.[†]

xxx xxx xxx

No one denies, of course, that there were some disloyal persons of Japanese descent on the Pacific Coast who did all in their power to aid their ancestral land. Similar disloyal activities have been engaged in by many persons of German, Italian and even more pioneer stock in our country. But to infer that examples of individual disloyalty prove group disloyalty and justify discriminatory action against the entire group is to deny that, under our system of law, individual guilt is the sole basis for deprivation of rights. Moreover, this inference, which is at the very heart of the evacuation orders, has been used in support of the abhorrent and despicable treatment of minority groups by the dictatorial tyrannies which this nation is now pledged to destroy. To give constitutional sanction to that inference in this case, however well intentioned may have been the military command on the Pacific Coast, is to adopt one of the cruelest of the rationales used by our enemies to destroy the dignity of the individual and to encourage and open

---

[*] Id., p. 235.
[†] Id., p. 239.

the door to discriminatory actions against other minority groups in the passions of tomorrow.

No adequate reason is given for the failure to treat these Japanese Americans on an individual basis by holding investigations and hearings to separate the loyal from the disloyal, as was done in the case of persons of German and Italian ancestry.*

xxx xxx xxx

I dissent, therefore, from this legalization of racism. Racial discrimination in any form and in any degree has no justifiable part whatever in our democratic way of life. It is unattractive in any setting, but it is utterly revolting among a free people who have embraced the principles set forth in the Constitution of the United States. All residents of this nation are kin in some way by blood or culture to a foreign land. Yet they are primarily and necessarily a part of the new and distinct civilization of the United States. They must, accordingly, be treated at all times as the heirs of the American experiment, and as entitled to all the rights and freedoms guaranteed by the Constitution.†

Justice Jackson's dissent, perhaps the most celebrated of the three dissents, puts it this way:

A citizen's presence in the locality, however, was made a crime only if his parents were of Japanese birth. Had Korematsu been one of four—the others being, say, a German alien enemy, an Italian alien enemy, and a citizen of American-born ancestors, convicted of treason but out on parole—only Korematsu's presence would have violated the order. The difference between their innocence and his crime would result, not from anything he did, said, or thought, different than they, but only in that he was born of different racial stock.

Now, if any fundamental assumption underlies our system, it is that guilt is personal and not inheritable. Even if all of one's antecedents had

---

* Id., pp. 240–41.
† Id., p. 242.

been convicted of treason, the Constitution forbids its penalties to be visited upon him, for it provides that 'no attainder of treason shall work corruption of blood, or forfeiture except during the life of the person attainted'. But here is an attempt to make an otherwise innocent act a crime merely because this prisoner is the son of parents as to whom he had no choice, and belongs to a race from which there is no way to resign. If Congress, in peacetime legislation, should enact such a criminal law, I should suppose this Court would refuse to enforce it.[*]

xxx xxx xxx

A military order, however unconstitutional, is not apt to last longer than the military emergency. Even during that period, a succeeding commander may revoke it all. But once a judicial opinion rationalizes such an order to show that it conforms to the Constitution, or rather rationalizes the Constitution to show that the Constitution sanctions such an order, the Court for all time has validated the principle of racial discrimination in criminal procedure and of transplanting American citizens. The principle then lies about like a loaded weapon, ready for the hand of any authority that can bring forward a plausible claim of an urgent need. Every repetition imbeds that principle more deeply in our law and thinking and expands it to new purposes. All who observe the work of courts are familiar with what Judge Cardozo described as 'the tendency of a principle to expand itself to the limit of its logic.' A military commander may overstep the bounds of constitutionality, and it is an incident. But if we review and approve, that passing incident becomes the doctrine of the Constitution. There it has a generative power of its own, and all that it creates will be in its own image. Nothing better illustrates this danger than does the Court's opinion in this case.[†]

xxx xxx xxx

My duties as a justice, as I see them, do not require me to make a military judgment as to whether General DeWitt's evacuation and detention

---

[*] Id., pp. 243–44.
[†] Id., p. 246.

program was a reasonable military necessity. I do not suggest that the courts should have attempted to interfere with the Army in carrying out its task. But I do not think they may be asked to execute a military expedient that has no place in law under the Constitution. I would reverse the judgment and discharge the prisoner.[*]

This case is perhaps the most shocking example of racial discrimination in wartime, because the persons who were discriminated against included persons born in the United States, most of whom may not even have seen Japan. In the aftermath of the Civil Rights Act being passed in 1964, the Congress also took it upon itself to undo the mischief of the majority decision in *Korematsu* by passing the Civil Liberties Act, 1988, in which reparations for war damage to persons like Fred Korematsu were made. As in some of the other wartime cases, this judgment took a long time— around eighty years—to be finally overruled. In *Trump, President of the United States v. Hawaii* (2018),[†] the majority judgment of Chief Justice Roberts gave the final death-blow to the majority opinions in *Korematsu* as follows:

Finally, the dissent invokes *Korematsu v. United States*, 323 U.S. 214 (1944). Whatever rhetorical advantage the dissent may see in doing so, *Korematsu* has nothing to do with this case. The forcible relocation of U.S. citizens to concentration camps, solely and explicitly on the basis of race, is objectively unlawful and outside the scope of Presidential authority. But it is wholly inapt to liken that morally repugnant order to a facially neutral policy denying certain foreign nationals the privilege of admission. The entry suspension is an act that is well within executive authority and could have been taken by any other President—the only question is evaluating the actions of this particular President in promulgating an otherwise valid Proclamation. The dissent's reference to *Korematsu*, however, affords this Court the opportunity to make express what is already obvious: *Korematsu* was gravely wrong the day it was decided, has been overruled in the

---

[*] Id., p. 248.
[†] 138 S. Ct. 2392.

court of history, and—to be clear—'has no place in law under the Constitution'.*

Even more explicitly, the minority judgment of Sotomayor, J. overruled *Korematsu*, stating:

Today's holding is all the more troubling given the stark parallels between the reasoning of this case and that of *Korematsu v. United States*, 323 U.S. 214 (1944). In *Korematsu*, the Court gave 'a pass [to] an odious, gravely injurious racial classification' authorized by an executive order. As here, the Government invoked an ill-defined national-security threat to justify an exclusionary policy of sweeping proportion. As here, the exclusion order was rooted in dangerous stereotypes about, *inter alia*, a particular group's supposed inability to assimilate and desire to harm the United States. As here, the Government was unwilling to reveal its own intelligence agencies' views of the alleged security concerns to the very citizens it purported to protect. And as here, there was strong evidence that impermissible hostility and animus motivated the Government's policy.

Although a majority of the Court in *Korematsu* was willing to uphold the Government's actions based on a barren invocation of national security, dissenting Justices warned of that decision's harm to our constitutional fabric. Justice Murphy recognized that there is a need for great deference to the Executive Branch in the context of national security, but cautioned that 'it is essential that there be definite limits to [the government's] discretion', as '[i]ndividuals must not be left impoverished of their constitutional rights on a plea of military necessity that has neither substance nor support'. Justice Jackson lamented that the Court's decision upholding the Government's policy would prove to be 'a far more subtle blow to liberty than the promulgation of the order itself', for although the executive order was not likely to be long lasting, the Court's willingness to tolerate it would endure.

In the intervening years since *Korematsu*, our Nation has done much to leave its sordid legacy behind. See, *e.g.*, Civil Liberties Act of 1988, 50

---

* Ibid., Opinion (Roberts), p. 38.

U.S.C. App. §4211 *et seq.* (setting forth remedies to individuals affected by the executive order at issue in *Korematsu*); Non-Detention Act of 1971, 18 U.S.C. §4001(a) (forbidding the imprisonment or detention by the United States of any citizen absent an Act of Congress). Today, the Court takes the important step of finally overruling *Korematsu*, denouncing it as 'gravely wrong the day it was decided' (citing *Korematsu*, 323 U.S., at 248 (Jackson, J., dissenting)). This formal repudiation of a shameful precedent is laudable and long overdue. But it does not make the majority's decision here acceptable or right. By blindly accepting the Government's misguided invitation to sanction a discriminatory policy motivated by animosity toward a disfavored group, all in the name of a superficial claim of national security, the Court redeploys the same dangerous logic underlying *Korematsu* and merely replaces one 'gravely wrong' decision with another.

Our Constitution demands, and our country deserves, a Judiciary willing to hold the coordinate branches to account when they defy our most sacred legal commitments. Because the Court's decision today has failed in that respect, with profound regret, I dissent.[*]

In our country, emergencies declared during times of war or deemed 'internal disturbance' have yielded judgments declaring what the law of the land is in such situations. The most noteworthy of these is the judgment in *Additional District Magistrate, Jabalpur v. Shivakant Shukla* (*ADM Jabalpur*) (1976).[†] In this case, following the declaration of 'Emergency', a Presidential Order issued under Article 359(1) of the Constitution of India made it clear that the fundamental right of 'life and personal liberty' was suspended during the period of the Emergency. A majority of four out of five judges not only upheld the Presidential Order but also closed the doors of all the superior courts, including the Supreme Court, to all detainees, stating that since Article 21—as the sole repository of the right to life and personal liberty—had been suspended, no *habeas corpus* writ could be issued in favour of any detenu under preventive detention law. The majority stated this would apply irrespective of whether the detenu

---

[*] Id., Dissent (Sotomayor), pp. 26–28.
[†] (1976) 2 SCC 521.

could show the court that the detention order did not conform to the statute, and even in cases of mistaken identity, where the person seized was not the person to be detained by the order, as also in cases where such orders could be shown to be *mala fide*.

It is important, at this juncture, to resurrect a judgment of Vivian Bose, J., delivered at the height of World War 2, when he happened to be a judge of the High Court of Nagpur in the Central Provinces and Berar. In *Prabhakar Kesheo Tare v. Emperor* (1943),* Bose, J. quoted from all the judgments in *Liversidge* and arrived at the conclusion that the *habeas corpus* section contained in Section 491 of the Code of Criminal Procedure, 1898, continued to subsist despite the Defence of India Act, 1939, read with the rules thereunder. This judgment is remarkable for its logic and insight, and thwarts the logic of the majority judgments in *ADM Jabalpur*. This judgment is therefore quoted *in extenso*:

> This order will govern Misc. Criminal Cases Nos. 57, 69 and 70 of 1942. We have before us a number of applications under Section 491 of the CrPC, the section popularly known as the *habeas corpus* section, and the first point we have to consider is whether the right to apply subsists. The learned Advocate-General contends that it does not, and though he admits that the section has not been expressly repealed or abrogated he contends that the effect of the Defence of India Act (Act 35 of 1939) read with the rules is to render it nugatory. Now it is beyond dispute that this Court has no power to issue the writ of *habeas corpus*, see, 61 Cal. 197 following 54 Cal. 727, and no one contends that the powers conferred by S. 491 are as wide as those under the Habeas Corpus Act. But one matter is common, namely, the right of any person detained within the limits of this Court's appellate jurisdiction, whether by Government or by any one else, to apply to this Court and demand, either that he be 'dealt with according to law' or that he be 'set at liberty'. Fundamentally, the principles which underlie both provisions are the same. The object of both is to safeguard the liberty of the subject against excesses of the Executive and against an abuse of power. This is the most fundamental right known to the constitution bar only one, namely the right of the

---

* AIR 1943 Nag. 26.

Government of the day to preserve the safety of the realm. The right is prized in India no less highly than in England, or indeed any other part of the Empire, perhaps even more highly here than elsewhere; and it is as jealously guarded by the Courts. In the words of Lord Atkin delivering the judgment of the Privy Council in (1931) A.C. 662 at page 670:

In accordance with British jurisprudence no member of the Executive can interfere with the liberty or property of a British subject except on the condition that he can support the legality of his action before a Court of justice and it is the tradition of British justice that Judges should not shrink from deciding such issues in the face of the Executive.

Now, as I have said, this is one of the most fundamental rights known to the Constitution and the most highly prized, but it does yield place to another matter even more fundamental—the safety of the realm. No one doubts the right of the Legislature, or of such power as takes its place in emergencies, or when it is not functioning, to modify the rights of the subject or even to suspend or take them away altogether, and this in times of peace no less than war; for under the Constitution the Legislature is supreme. But, be it observed, it is the Legislature which is supreme, not the Executive, and so, before the Executive can claim the power to override those rights, it must show that the Legislature has empowered it to do so, and under the constitution the Legislature can only act in particular ways. All empowering must therefore be done properly and formally, deliberately, in the manner laid down by the Constitution. The Executive cannot suddenly step in and claim the right to wield absolute and arbitrary power—not even in war time. For, as Lord Atkin said in his dissenting judgment in (1941) 8 ALL. E.R. 338 (Lords Macmillan and Wright agreeing as to this in principle—there was no difference of opinion on this point):

In this country, amidst the clash of arms, the laws are not silent. They may be changed, but they speak the same language in war as in peace. It has always been one of the pillars of freedom, one of the principles of liberty for which, on recent authority, we are now fighting, that the Judges are no respecters of persons and stand between the subject and any attempted encroachments on his liberty by the Executive; alert to see that any coercive action is justified in law.

I may add that these principles of liberty to which Lord Atkin refers apply as much to India as elsewhere, and it is as relevant for a Judge in India to take judicial notice, in a matter of this kind, of repeated allied pledges that justice will be done after the war and that those of the enemy found guilty of excesses and abuse of power will be brought to book and tried and punished, as it was for the learned law Lords in (1941) 3 ALL. E.R. 333 to take judicial notice of the existence of Quislings and Fifth Columnists, and of Lord Atkin to take notice of the principles of liberty for which on high authority we are now fighting. I gather that the necessities of war will not be a sufficient excuse for excesses or an abuse of power committed by the enemy. I cannot think it is intended that they should be here. Therefore the Courts must enquire into such allegations if they are made. All these considerations weighed heavily with the learned law Lords in (1941) 3 ALL. E.R. 338 when they construed provisions similar in many respects to the one we have here—in fact the learned Advocate-General contended that this is the only case really in point and that it is decisive. In my opinion, such considerations are as relevant and should weigh as heavily with us here. It is my view that the rights conferred by S. 491 subsist and will continue to subsist until either the section is expressly, or by necessary and express implication, abrogated, or the rights are expressly taken away. The learned Advocate-General admitted that the section has not been expressly repealed, but he contended that the effect of the Defence of India Act and the rules made under it was to render it nugatory, and he Contended that in consequence the applicants had no right of audience. I refuse to accept this contention. I refused to accept a similar argument in I.L.R. (1940) Nag. 1 at page 11 when an abuse of power by the then Congress Government of the Province was in question. The Earl of Birkenhead refused to accept something similar in (1923) A.C. 603 at p. 610 and in (1928) A.C. 459 at page 467 Lord Hailsham said that would be a 'startling result'. Such fundamental rights, safeguarded under the constitution with elaborate and anxious care and upheld time and again by the highest tribunals of the realm in language of the utmost vigour, cannot be swept away by implication or removed by some sweeping generality. No one doubts the right and the power of the proper authority to remove, but the removal must be express and unmistakable; and this applies whatever Government be in power, and whether the country is at peace or at war.[*]

xxx xxx xxx

It is relevant to point out here, as Lord Atkin pointed out in (1941) 3 All. E.R. 338, that it is difficult to see how the trial of a *habeas corpus* petition can present greater difficulties than the trial of a spy or of a traitor for treason. Also, it seems anomalous that while spies and traitors can be allowed, and are allowed, all reasonable facilities for placing their cases fully before the Courts, particularly in the shape of interviews with counsel, those against whom no charge is preferred are told on the one hand, as, in my opinion, the law tells them, that their right to apply in *habeas corpus* has not been taken away and still subsists, and on the other that they will nevertheless be refused every facility which tends to make that right a living reality if they try to exercise it. I can see the regrettable necessity for detaining and segregating persons who hamper the war effort or endanger public safety. I can see the desirability of arming the executive with weapons which necessitate the utmost secrecy. I can fully understand, as I believe the decision in (1941) 3 ALL. E.R. 338 to be, that Government is not bound to disclose reasons for an arrest and detention under these special powers. But even when all that is accepted, there is in my opinion still left a residue into which the Courts can and must enquire; and that enquiry cannot be frustrated by executive claims to wield absolute and arbitrary power in this way.[†]

xxx xxx xxx

But to examine this contention more closely. Must the applicants necessarily fail, that is to say, is there nothing left into which the Courts can enquire? The learned Advocate-General, relying on (1941) 3 All. E.R. 338 says no. He says it is enough for the Crown to produce the order of detention. Thereafter, there is nothing left for the Courts to do

---

[*] Id., pp. 27–29.
[†] Id., pp. 30–31.

but to dismiss the petition. Again I do not agree. I hesitate to enter upon this ground in the absence of the other side (in my opinion the other side is not really here), and so I do not intend to give a final opinion. I will only venture upon a tentative one. As I understand (1941) 3 All. E.R. 338 the House of Lords do not hold that the jurisdiction of the Courts is wholly barred and that there is nothing left for them to investigate. It is true they hold that a lot is cut away and that very little is left but I understand them to hold that there is a residue and that residue must be investigated when the issue is raised. All the learned law Lords, except Lord Macmillan, stressed the fact that in the case before them there was no assertion of any want of good faith on the part of the Secretary of State and they implied, as I understand their judgments, that if such an issue had been raised, the Court would have been bound to try it. I need only quote Lords Romer and Wright. Lord Romer said:

For if at the trial the Home Secretary gives rebutting evidence to the effect that in his opinion there were reasonable grounds for his belief his statement being merely a statement as to his opinion must necessarily have to be accepted unless it can be shown that he was not acting in good faith and the onus of showing that would be upon the plaintiff '(that is, upon the person detained).' The materials upon which the Home Secretary founded his opinion would be wholly irrelevant and could not be inquired into by a Court of law.

And Lord Wright said:

The Judge '(of the lower Court)' adds, as is obvious, that the Court might no doubt be called upon to decide questions of bona fides or mistaken identity if they should ever arise.

I have concentrated on (1941) 3 ALL. E.R. 338 because it deals with a war measure, and the learned Advocate-General quite rightly pointed out there is a difference as regards interpretation. But as I see it, that notwithstanding, the residue remains. Allegations of want of good faith must be investigated in spite of the war. Other cases, some of less authority, also reach the same conclusion, though they use different language. Thus, some call it an 'abuse of power', others a 'fraud upon the Act', and so forth. But I think they all come to much the same thing on a final analysis. In 1928 A.C. 459 the Privy Council called it an 'abuse of power' and held that such an allegation, if made, must be investigated, and that was the expression used in (1916) 2 K.B. 742 which incidentally dealt with a war time regulation. The same view has been taken in India. Thus, 60 Cal. 364 at p. 376 holds that the Courts have jurisdiction to see whether there has been a 'fraud upon the Act,' or an 'abuse of the powers granted by the Legislature,' and 61 Cal. 197 follows it. But, the learned Advocate-General argues, none of these cases really apply because there was nothing corresponding to Section 16 of the Defence of India Act, in the measures with which they were dealing. He contended that S. 16 expressly ousts the jurisdiction of the Courts altogether. I do not think so. Section 16 says:

No order made in the exercise of power conferred by or under this Act shall be called in question by any Court.[*]

xxx xxx xxx

If he is not satisfied and yet issues the order, then he cannot be said to be acting upon or under a power conferred by the Act. The point as I see it is exactly the same as in (1941) 3 All. E.R. 338 except that the language used there was if the Secretary of State 'has reasonable cause to believe' in place of 'is satisfied'. In my view, the dissenting opinion of Lord Atkin notwithstanding, there is no substantial difference in meaning between these two phrases. The House of Lords decided that it is enough for the Crown to produce the order of the Secretary of State unless it is alleged that he had not acted in good faith or in abuse of the powers conferred, in which case the Courts would have to investigate the issue. That, in my opinion, is exactly the position here under the Defence of India Act.

It is to be observed that S. 16 requires that the order be passed in the exercise of the power conferred by the Act and not merely in colourable exercise of such power. The difference can be seen at once when one compares the language of S. 99, Penal Code. That section says that there is no right of private defence against any act done, etc., by a public servant acting in good faith 'under colour of his office'. It is not enough therefore that these orders should be passed under colour of the power conferred. They must be done in actual exercise of it and, as

---

[*] Id., p. 32.

I read the law, no power is conferred to make such orders in bad faith, or in abuse of the Act or for the purpose of effecting a fraud on the Act and consequently, these issues must be investigated if they are raised. Now it is plain that the petitions we have before us do not raise such issues, at any rate not with sufficient particularity to enable them to be tried, though the matter was argued. But they do set out that access to legal advice has been cut off, and it may be, if the petitioners are properly advised, they will be able to couch their petitions in language which will properly raise the issues. In any event, the facts placed before us in argument might, if properly placed and substantiated, raise these issues in a proper form. They appear to fall very close to the illustration of bad faith given by Ameer Ali J., in 61 Cal. 197 at p. 215. It may well be in the result that it will be difficult, perhaps almost impossible, to prove bad faith, especially with the limitations which (1941) 3 ALL. E.R. 338 imposes, but if the House of Lords considers that the issue, if raised, must be tried, it is not for Courts in India to shrink from the task however difficult or disagreeable it may be.[*]

xxx xxx xxx

My conclusions are that (1) Section 491 of the CrPC, has not been abrogated in any respect; (2) that any person aggrieved has a right to apply to the High Court and that he has a right to be heard; (3) that though the Provincial Government is entitled to take all proper precautions in the matter of granting interviews, even to legal advisers, it has no power to shut these detained persons off altogether from reasonable and proper legal advice; (4) that the Provincial Government has no power to prevent such issues as I have indicated from being tried in this Court in the ordinary way, if they are raised, subject of course to such reasonable safeguards as the Provincial Government may desire to have observed, that is to say, the trial, despite all safeguards, must be according to what the Privy Council call canons of natural justice, or according 'to the fundamental rules of practice necessary for the due protection of persons and the safe administration of criminal justice', or, I would observe,

---

[*] Id., p. 33.

of any justice; (5) that in so far as these applicants have been refused access to all legal advice there has been an abuse of power; (6) that the jurisdiction of the Courts is not wholly ousted by the Defence of India Act and that there remains a residue of matter into which the Courts can and must enquire; (7) that it is doubtful whether Farquhar had the power to make these orders of detention—that, in my opinion, requires further consideration after the applicants are properly represented before us. The order I would make therefore in this case is that the Provincial Government be directed to afford these detained persons all reasonable facilities for obtaining such legal advice as they desire, subject to such safeguards as may reasonably be necessary; that the applicants should then be permitted to place their grievances before the Court in petitions properly and legally drawn up; and that they should be allowed, subject again to such safeguards as may seem reasonably necessary, to press these petitions in the usual way, if not personally, at least through counsel in whom they have reasonable confidence. I observe that the applicants cannot insist on seeing counsel A, B or C any more than Government can say that only X shall be allowed. There must be reasonableness on both sides.[*]

In one of the most celebrated dissents in the history of the Supreme Court of India, delivered at the height of an emergency which then seemed to be everlasting, Khanna, J. held that Article 21 was not the sole repository of the human right to life and liberty, nor were the courts barred from issuing *habeas corpus* writs under Article 226 of the Constitution of India, particularly in the exceptional cases pointed out hereinabove.

Beginning his dissent by noting the conflict between two principles, namely, the liberty of the individual versus the security of the state, the learned judge went on to review earlier cases which dealt with wartime emergencies. He relied upon observations made in *Makhan Singh v. State of Punjab* (1964)[†] to the effect that if, in challenging the validity of his detention order, the detenu was pleading any right outside the rights

---

[*] Id., p. 34. In *ADM Jabalpur*, Bose, J.'s judgment in *Prabhakar Kesheo Tare* was referred to in passing both by Bhagwati, J. (see paragraph 455) and Khanna, J. (see paragraph 530).
[†] (1964) 4 SCR 797.

specified in the order, his right to move the court was not suspended. Khanna, J. went on to state that where a detenu has been detained in violation of the mandatory provisions of the act, or the detenu has been able to show that his detention order is *mala fide*, it would be open for such detenu to get relief from a superior court. To similar effect are the judgments in *State of Maharashtra v. Prabhakar Pandurang Sangzgiri* (1966)[*] and *Dr Ram Manohar Lohia v. State of Bihar* (1966).[†] While emphasizing the difference in phraseology of the Presidential Orders in the earlier cases and the more widely worded Presidential Order in the present case, the learned judge held:

> 520. The difference in phraseology of the Presidential Order dated June 27, 1975 and that of the earlier Presidential Orders would not, however, justify the conclusion that because of the new Presidential Order dated June 27, 1975 a detention order need not comply with the requirements of the law providing for preventive detention. Such a detention order would still be liable to be challenged in a court on the ground that it does not comply with the requirement of law for preventive detention if ground for such challenge be permissible in spite of and consistently with the new Presidential Order. The effect of the change in phraseology would only be that such observations which were made in the cases mentioned above in the context of the language of the earlier Presidential Orders cannot now be relied upon. Reliance, however, can still be placed upon the observations made in those cases which were not linked with the phraseology of the earlier Presidential Orders.

After tracing the history of Article 21 to the Magna Carta, the statutes of Westminster, the US Constitution and, finally, the more recent Japanese and Irish constitutions, the learned judge went on to hold that even if Article 21 was suspended, the state could not deprive a person of life or liberty without the authority of law, and quoted Lord Mansfield, as follows:

---

[*] (1966) 1 SCR 702.
[†] (1966) 1 SCR 709.

530. Even in the absence of Article 21 in the Constitution, the State has got no power to deprive a person of his life or liberty without the authority of law. This is the essential postulate and basic assumption of the rule of law and not of men in all civilised nations. Without such sanctity of life and liberty, the distinction between a lawless society and one governed by laws would cease to have any meaning. The principle that no one shall be deprived of his life or liberty without the authority of law is rooted in the consideration that life and liberty are priceless possessions which cannot be made the plaything of individual whim and caprice and that any act which has the effect of tampering with life and liberty must receive sustenance from and sanction of the laws of the land. Article 21 incorporates an essential aspect of that principle and makes it part of the fundamental rights guaranteed in Part III of the Constitution. It does not, however, follow from the above that if Article 21 had not been drafted and inserted in Part III, in that event it would have been permissible for the State to deprive a person of his life or liberty without the authority of law. No case has been cited before us to show that before the coming into force of the Constitution or in countries under rule of law where there is no provision corresponding to Article 21, a claim was ever sustained by the courts that the State can deprive a person of his life or liberty without the authority of law. In fact, any suggestion to such a claim was unequivocally repelled. In the case of James Sommersett, Lord Mansfield dealt with a case of a negro named Sommersett, who was being taken in a ship to Jamaica for sale in a slave market. When the ship anchored at the London port, a *habeas corpus* petition was presented by some Englishmen who were moved by the yelling and cries of Sommersett. In opposition to the petition the slave trader took the plea that there was no law which prohibited slavery. Lord Mansfield while repelling this objection made the following observation in respect of slavery which is one of the worst forms of deprivation of personal freedom:

'It is so odious that nothing can be suffered to support it but positive law: whatever inconvenience, therefore, may follow from this decision, I cannot say this case is allowed or approved by the law of England, and therefore the black must be discharged.'

In another case, *Fabrigas v. Mostyn*, Lord Mansfield observed on p. 173:

'To lay down in an English Court of justice that a Governor acting by virtue of Letters Patent, under the great Seal, is accountable only to God and his own conscience; that he is absolutely despotic, and can spoil, plunder, and affect His Majesty's subjects, both in their liberty and property, with impunity, is a doctrine that cannot be maintained.'

In light of the rule of law embodied in Section 491 of the Criminal Procedure Code, 1898, which continued to remain in force by virtue of Article 372 of the Constitution of India, the learned judge found:

535. It has been pointed out above that even before the coming into force of the Constitution, the position under the common law both in England and in India was that the State could not deprive a person of his life and liberty without the authority of law. The same was the position under the penal laws of India. It was an offence under the Penal Code, 1860, as already mentioned, to deprive a person of his life or liberty unless such a course was sanctioned by the laws of the land. An action was also maintainable under the law of torts for wrongful confinement in case any person was deprived of his personal liberty without the authority of law. In addition to that, we had Section 491 of the Code of Criminal Procedure which provided the remedy of *habeas corpus* against detention without the authority of law. Such laws continued to remain in force in view of Article 372 after the coming into force of the Constitution. According to that article, notwithstanding the repeal by this Constitution of the enactments referred to in Article 395 but subject to the other provisions of this Constitution, all the law in force in the territory of India immediately before the commencement of this Constitution shall continue in force therein until altered or repealed or amended by a competent legislature or other competent authority. The law in force, as observed by the majority of the Constitution Bench in the case of *Director of Rationing and Distribution v. Corporation of Calcutta* include not only the statutory law but also custom or usage having the force of law as also the common law of England which was adopted as the law of the country before the coming into force of the Constitution. The position thus seems to be firmly established that at

the time the Constitution came into force, the legal position was that no one could be deprived of his life or liberty without the authority of law.

Next, the learned judge exposed the startling results that would follow on two alternative constructions of the Presidential Order, it being the duty of the court to adopt the construction which obviates such startling results, and which is also in consonance with international law:

538. I agree with the learned Attorney General that if we are to accept his argument about the scope of the Presidential Order of June 27, 1975 in that event we have to accept it in its entirety and go the whole hog; there is no halfway house in between. So let us examine the consequence of the acceptance of the above argument. This would mean that if any official, even a head constable of police, capriciously or maliciously, arrests a person and detains him indefinitely without any authority of law, the aggrieved person would not be able to seek any relief from the courts against such detention during the period of emergency. This would also mean that it would not be necessary to enact any law on the subject and even in the absence of any such law, if any official for reasons which have nothing to do with the security of State or maintenance of public order, but because of personal animosity, arrests and puts behind the bar any person or a whole group or family of persons, the aggrieved person or persons would not be able to seek any redress from a Court of law. The same would be the position in case of threat of deprivation or even actual deprivation of life of a person because Article 21 refers to both deprivation of life as well as personal liberty. Whether such things actually come to pass is not the question before us, it is enough to state that all these are permissible consequences from the acceptance of the contention that Article 21 is the sole repository of the right to life and personal liberty and that consequent upon the issue of the Presidential Order, no one can approach any court and seek relief during the period of emergency against deprivation of life or personal liberty. In other words the position would be that so far as executive officers are concerned, in matters relating to life and personal liberty of citizens, they would not be governed by any law, they would not be answerable to any court and they would be wielding more or less despotic powers.

'542 . . . Articles 8 and 9 of the Universal Declaration of Human Rights in respect of which resolution was passed by the United Nations and was supported by India read as under:

'ARTICLE 8.

Everyone has the right to an effective remedy by the competent national tribunals for acts violating the fundamental rights granted him by the Constitution or by law.

ARTICLE 9.

No one shall be subjected to arbitrary arrest, detention or exile.

543. While dealing with the Presidential Order under Article 359(1), we should adopt such a construction as would, if possible, not bring it in conflict with the above Articles 8 and 9. From what has been discussed elsewhere, it is plain that such a construction is not only possible, it is also pre-eminently reasonable. The Presidential Order, therefore, should be so construed as not to warrant arbitrary arrest or to bar right to an effective remedy by competent national tribunals for acts violating basic right of personal liberty granted by law.

The learned judge then adverted to the fact that Article 226 of the Indian Constitution cannot be suspended, the said article being the foundation for high courts to issue the writ of *habeas corpus*:

566. Our founding fathers made Article 226 which confers power on the High Court to issue *inter alia* writs in the nature of *habeas corpus* an integral part of the Constitution. They were aware that under the U.S. Constitution in accordance with Article 1 Section 9 the privilege of the writ of *habeas corpus* could be suspended when in cases of rebellion or invasion the public safety may require it. Despite that our founding fathers made no provision in our Constitution for suspending the power of the High Courts under Article 226 to issue writs in the nature of *habeas corpus* during the period of emergency. They had perhaps in view the precedent of England where there had been no suspension of writ of *habeas corpus* since 1881 and even during the course of First and Second World Wars. It would, in my opinion, be not permissible to bring about the result of suspension of *habeas corpus* by a strained construction of the Presidential Order under Article 359(1) even

though Article 226 continues to remain in force during the period of emergency.

The judgments in *R v. Halliday* and *Liversidge v. Anderson* were then referred to:

574. No one can deny the power of the State to assume vast powers of detention in the interest of the security of the State. It may indeed be necessary to do so to meet the peril facing the nation. The considerations of security of the State must have a primacy and be kept in the forefront compared to which the interests of the individuals can only take a secondary place. The motto has to be 'Who lives, if the country dies'. Extraordinary powers are always assumed by the Government in all countries in times of emergency because of the extraordinary nature of the emergency. The exercise of the power of detention, it is well-settled, depends upon the subjective satisfaction of the detaining authority and the courts can neither act as courts of appeal over the decisions of the detaining authority nor can they substitute their own opinion for that of the authority regarding the necessity of detention. There is no antithesis between the power of the State to detain a person without trial under a law of preventive detention and the power of the court to examine the legality of such detention. As observed by Lord Atkin in *Rex v. Halliday** while dealing with the argument that the Defence of Realm Consolidation Act of 1914 and the regulation made under it deprived the subject of his right under the several Habeas Corpus Acts, that is an entire misconception. The subject retains every right which those statutes confer upon him to have tested and determined in a Court of law, by means of a writ of *habeas corpus*, addressed to the person in whose custody he may be, the legality of the order or warrant by virtue of which he is given into or kept in that custody. To quote the words of Lord Macmillan in the case of *Liversidge v. Anderson*:

'It is important to have in mind that the regulation in question is a war measure. This is not to say that the courts ought to adopt in wartime

---

* Obviously, what was meant was the dissenting judgment of Lord Shaw in *Rex v. Halliday*, as Lord Atkin had dissented not in *Rex v. Halliday* but in *Liversidge*.

canons of construction different from those they follow in peacetime. The fact that the nation is at war is no justification for any relaxation of the vigilance of the courts in seeing that the law is duly observed, especially in a matter so fundamental as the liberty of the subject. Rather the contrary.

The learned judge then summarized his conclusions and ended the judgment as follows:

593. I may now summarize my conclusions:

'(1) Article 21 cannot be considered to be the sole repository of the right to life and personal liberty.

(2) Even in the absence of Article 21 in the Constitution, the State has got no power to deprive a person of his life or personal liberty without the authority of law. That is the essential postulate and basic assumption of the rule of law in every civilized society.

(3) According to the law in force in India before the coming into force of the Constitution, no one could be deprived of his life or personal liberty without the authority of law. Such a law continued to be in force after the coming into force of the Constitution in view of Article 372 of the Constitution.

(4) Startling consequences would follow from the acceptance of the contention that consequent upon the issue of the Presidential Order in question no one can seek relief from courts during the period of emergency against deprivation of life and personal liberty. If two constructions of the Presidential Order were possible, the court should lean in favour of a view which does not result in such consequences. The construction which does not result in such consequences is not only possible, it is also pre-eminently reasonable.

(5) In a long chain of authorities this Court has laid stress upon the prevalence of the rule of law in the country, according to which the Executive cannot take action prejudicial to the right of an individual without the authority of law. There is no valid reason to depart from the rule laid down in those decisions, some of which were given by Benches larger than the Bench dealing with these appeals.

(6) According to Article 21, no one can be deprived of his life or personal liberty except in accordance with procedure established by law.

Procedure for the exercise of power of depriving a person of his life or personal liberty necessarily postulates the existence of the substantive power. When Article 21 is in force, law relating to deprivation of life and personal liberty must provide both for the substantive power as well as the procedure for the exercise of such power. When right to move any court for enforcement of right guaranteed by Article 21 is suspended, it would have the effect of dispensing with the necessity of prescribing procedure for the exercise of substantive power to deprive a person of his life or personal liberty, it cannot have the effect of permitting an authority to deprive a person of his life or personal liberty without the existence of such substantive power.

(7) A Presidential Order under Article 359(1) can suspend during the period of emergency only the right to move any court for enforcement of the fundamental rights mentioned in the order. Rights created by statutes being not fundamental rights can be enforced during the period of emergency despite the Presidential Order. Obligations and liabilities flowing from statutory provisions likewise remain unaffected by the Presidential Order. Any redress sought from a Court of law on the score of breach of statutory provisions would be outside the purview of Article 359(1) and the Presidential Order made thereunder.

(8) Article 226 under which the High Courts can issue writs of *habeas corpus* is an integral part of the Constitution. No power has been conferred upon any authority in the Constitution for suspending the power of the High Court to issue writs in the nature of *habeas corpus* during the period of emergency. Such a result cannot be brought about by putting some particular construction on the Presidential Order in question.

(9) There is no antithesis between the power of the State to detain a person without trial under a law of preventive detention and the power the court to examine the legality of such detention. In exercising of such power the courts only ensure that the detaining authority acts in accordance with the law providing for preventive detention.

(10) There is no sufficient ground to interfere with the view taken by all the nine High Courts which went into the matter that the Presidential Order dated June 27, 1975 did not affect the maintainability of the *habeas corpus* petitions to question the legality of the detention orders.

(11) The principles which should be followed by the courts in dealing with petitions for writs of *habeas corpus* to challenge the legality of detention are well-established.

(12) The appropriate occasion for this Court to go into the constitutional validity of Section 16-A(9) of MISA and its impact on the power and extent of judicial scrutiny in writs of *habeas corpus* would be when the State or a detenu, whosoever is aggrieved, comes up in appeal against the final judgment in any of the petitions pending in the High Courts. The whole matter would then be at large before this Court and it would not be inhibited by procedural and other constraints. It would not be permissible or proper for this Court to short-circuit the whole thing and decide the matter by bypassing the High Courts who are seized of the matter.

594. Before I part with the case, I may observe that the consciousness that the view expressed by me is at variance with that of the majority of my learned Brothers has not stood in the way of my expressing the same. I am aware of the desirability of unanimity, if possible. Unanimity obtained without sacrifice of conviction commends the decision to public confidence. Unanimity which is merely formal and which is recorded at the expense of strong conflicting views is not desirable in a court of last resort. As observed by Chief Justice Hughes,* Judges are not there simply to decide cases, but to decide them as they think they should be decided, and while it may be regrettable that they cannot always agree, it is better that their independence should be maintained and recognized than that unanimity should be secured through its sacrifice. A dissent in a court of last resort, to use his words, is an appeal to the brooding spirit of the law, to the intelligence of a future day, when a later decision may possibly correct the error into which the dissenting Judge believes the court to have been betrayed.

Of all the dissenting judgments that have been referred to in this chapter, this judgment was perhaps the most courageous. Justice Khanna was in line to become the Chief Justice of India, and would obviously have known that a government headed by Smt. Indira Gandhi, who had, on

---

* Alan Barth, *Prophets with Honour* (supra), pp. 3–6.

an earlier occasion, already superseded three judges who espoused views on the Constitution of India antithetical to her own, would very likely supersede him as well. This turned out to be true, for, before the Janata government came to power, Beg, J. was made chief justice—superseding Justice Khanna—who resigned as a result.* Nani Palkhivala paid tribute to Justice Khanna for this courageous dissent, saying '[T]o the stature of such a man, the Chief Justiceship of India can add nothing'.† Equally, H.M. Seervai, in his *Constitutional Law of India*, had this to say:

> If in this Appendix the dissenting judgment of Khanna, J. has not been considered in detail, it is not for lack of admiration for the judgment, or the courage which he showed in delivering it regardless of the cost and the consequences to himself. It cost him the Chief Justiceship of India, but it gained for him universal esteem not only for his courage but also for his inflexible judicial independence. If his judgment is not considered in detail it is because under the theory of precedents which we have adopted, a dissenting judgment, however valuable, does not lay down the law and the object of a critical examination of the majority judgments in this Appendix was to show that those judgments are untenable in law, productive of grave public mischief and ought to be overruled at the earliest opportunity. The conclusion which Justice Khanna has reached on the effect of the suspension of Article 21 is correct. His reminder that the rule of law did not merely mean giving effect to an enacted law was timely, and was reinforced by his reference to the mass murders of millions of Jews in Nazi concentration camps under an enacted law. However, the legal analysis in this Chapter

---

* Michael Kirby, 'Judicial Dissent—Common Law and Civil Law Traditions' (supra), pp. 379 at 397, pooh-poohed the fear of retaliation by the governments of the day against dissenting opinions. This is one instance of government retaliation only because a dissenting judgment was written, challenging the authority of government to do as it pleases during the period of emergency.

† It may be pointed out that each of the majority judges in *ADM Jabalpur* (supra)—apart from Chief Justice Ray—became chief justices by virtue of the seniority rule followed in this country. A move was made to supersede Y.V. Chandrachud, C.J. from being chief justice during the Janata Party regime, which got scuttled because the seniority rule, which had been breached by Mrs Gandhi, ought not—as a matter of propriety—to be breached in the same fashion by any successor government.

confirms his conclusion though on different grounds from those which he has given.[*]

In his lifetime, Justice Khanna was given the respect accorded to a hero everywhere he went. It is sad that he did not live to see the majority judgment in *ADM Jabalpur* expressly overruled. In *Justice K.S. Puttaswamy (Retd.) v. Union of India* (2017),[†] a nine-judge bench of the Supreme Court expressly overruled the majority judgment in *ADM Jabalpur* and approved of the minority judgment of Justice Khanna. D.Y. Chandrachud, J. did so in the following terms:

> 136. The judgments rendered by all the four Judges constituting the majority in *ADM, Jabalpur* are seriously flawed. Life and personal liberty are inalienable to human existence. These rights are, as recognized in *Kesavananda Bharati*, primordial rights. They constitute rights under Natural law. The human element in the life of the individual is integrally founded on the sanctity of life. Dignity is associated with liberty and freedom. No civilized State can contemplate an encroachment upon life and personal liberty without the authority of law. Neither life nor liberty are bounties conferred by the State nor does the Constitution create these rights. The right to life has existed even before the advent of the Constitution. In recognizing the right, the Constitution does not become the sole repository of the right. It would be preposterous to suggest that a democratic Constitution without a Bill of Rights would leave individuals governed by the State without either the existence of the right to live or the means of enforcement of the right. The right to life being inalienable to each individual, it existed prior to the Constitution and continued in force under Article 372 of the Constitution. Khanna, J. was clearly right in holding that the recognition of the right to life and personal liberty under the Constitution does not denude the existence of that right, apart from it nor can there be a fatuous assumption that in adopting the Constitution the people of India surrendered the most

---

[*] H.M. Seervai, *Constitutional Law of India*, Volume II (New Delhi: Universal Book Traders, 2002), p. 2229.

[†] (2017) 10 SCC 1.

precious aspect of the human persona, namely, life, liberty and freedom to the State on whose mercy these rights would depend. Such a construct is contrary to the basic foundation of the Rule of Law which imposes restraints upon the powers vested in the modern State when it deals with the liberties of the individual. The power of the Court to issue a writ of *habeas corpus* is a precious and undeniable feature of the Rule of Law.

137. A constitutional democracy can survive when citizens have an undiluted assurance that the Rule of Law will protect their rights and liberties against any invasion by the State and that judicial remedies would be available to ask searching questions and expect answers when a citizen has been deprived of these, most precious rights. The view taken by Khanna, J. must be accepted, and accepted in reverence for the strength of its thoughts and the courage of its convictions.

138. When histories of nations are written and critiqued, there are judicial decisions at the forefront of liberty. Yet others have to be consigned to the archives, reflective of what was, but should never have been. The decision of the US Supreme Court in *Buck v. Bell* ranks amongst the latter. It was a decision in which Oliver Wendell Holmes Jr., J. accepted the forcible sterilization by tubular ligation of Carrie Bucks as part of a programme of State sponsored eugenic sterilization. Holmes, J. while upholding the programme opined that: 'three generations of imbeciles is enough'. In the same vein was the decision of the US Supreme Court in *Korematsu v. United* States, upholding the imprisonment of a citizen in a concentration camp solely because of his Japanese ancestry.

139. *ADM, Jabalpur* must be and is accordingly overruled. We also overrule the decision in *Union of India v. Bhanudas Krishna Gawde*, which followed *ADM, Jabalpur*.

Nariman, J., whose reasoning is the most detailed on this score, held as follows:

532. The learned counsel for the petitioners also referred to another important aspect of the right to privacy. According to the learned counsel for the petitioner this right is a natural law right which is inalienable. Indeed, the reference order itself, in para 12, refers to this aspect of the fundamental right contained. It was, therefore, argued before us that

given the international conventions referred to hereinabove and the fact that this right inheres in every individual by virtue of his being a human being, such right is not conferred by the Constitution but is only recognized and given the status of being fundamental. There is no doubt that the petitioners are correct in this submission. However, one important roadblock in the way needs to be got over.

533. In *ADM, Jabalpur* a Constitution Bench of this Court arrived at the conclusion (by majority) that Article 21 is the sole repository of all rights to life and personal liberty, and, when suspended, takes away those rights altogether. A remarkable dissent was that of Khanna, J . . .

534. According to us this is a correct enunciation of the law for the following reasons:

534.1. It is clear that the international covenants and declarations to which India was a party, namely, the 1948 Declaration and the 1966 Covenant both spoke of the right to life and liberty as being 'inalienable'. Given the fact that this has to be read as being part of Article 21 by virtue of the judgments referred to *supra*, it is clear that Article 21 would,.therefore, not be the sole repository of these human rights but only reflect the fact that they were 'inalienable'; that they inhere in every human being by virtue of the person being a human being;

534.2. Secondly, developments after this judgment have also made it clear that the majority judgments are no longer good law and that Khanna, J.'s dissent is the correct version of the law. Section 2(1)(d) of the Protection of Human Rights Act, 1993 recognizes that the right to life, liberty, equality and dignity referable to international covenants and enforceable by courts in India are 'human rights'. And international covenants expressly state that these rights are 'inalienable' as they inhere in persons because they are human beings. In *I.R. Coelho*, this Court noticed in para 29 that:

'76. . . . The decision in *ADM, Jabalpur*, about the restrictive reading of the right to life and liberty stood impliedly overruled by various subsequent decisions.', and expressly held that these rights are natural rights that inhere in human beings thus:

'61. The approach in the interpretation of fundamental rights has been evidenced in a recent case *M. Nagaraj v. Union of India*, in which the Court noted:

'20. This principle of interpretation is particularly apposite to the interpretation of fundamental rights. It is a fallacy to regard fundamental rights as a gift from the State to its citizens. Individuals possess basic human rights independently of any Constitution by reason of the basic fact that they are members of the human race. These fundamental rights are important as they possess intrinsic value. Part III of the Constitution does not confer fundamental rights. It confirms their existence and gives them protection. Its purpose is to withdraw certain subjects from the area of political controversy to place them beyond the reach of majorities and officials and to establish them as legal principles to be applied by the courts. Every right has a content. Every foundational value is put in Part III as a fundamental right as it has intrinsic value. The converse does not apply. A right becomes a fundamental right because it has foundational value. Apart from the principles, one has also to see the structure of the article in which the fundamental value is incorporated. Fundamental right is a limitation on the power of the State. A Constitution, and in particular that of it which protects and which entrenches fundamental rights and freedoms to which all persons in the State are to be entitled is to be given a generous and purposive construction. In *Sakal Papers (P) Ltd. v. Union of India* this Court has held that while considering the nature and content of fundamental rights, the Court must not be too astute to interpret the language in a literal sense so as to whittle them down. The Court must interpret the Constitution in a manner which would enable the citizens to enjoy the rights guaranteed by it in the fullest measure. An instance of literal and narrow interpretation of a vital fundamental right in the Indian Constitution is the early decision of the Supreme Court in *A.K. Gopalan v. State of Madras*. Article 21 of the Constitution provides that no person shall be deprived of his life and personal liberty except according to procedure established by law. The Supreme Court by a majority held that 'procedure established by law' means any procedure established by law made by Parliament or the legislatures of the State. The Supreme Court refused to infuse the procedure with principles of natural justice. It concentrated solely upon the existence of enacted law. After three decades, the Supreme Court overruled its previous decision in *A.K. Gopalan* and held in its landmark judgment in *Maneka Gandhi v. Union of India* that the procedure contemplated by Article 21 must answer the test of reasonableness. The Court further held that the procedure should also be in conformity with the principles of natural justice. This example is given to demonstrate an instance of expansive interpretation of a fundamental right. The expression 'life' in Article 21 does not connote merely physical or animal existence. The right to life includes right to live with human dignity. This Court has in numerous cases deduced fundamental features which are not specifically mentioned in Part III on the principle that certain unarticulated rights are implicit in the enumerated guarantees.'

534.3. Seervai in a trenchant criticism of the majority judgment states as follows:

'30. The result of our discussion so far may be stated thus: Article 21 does not confer a right to life or personal liberty: Article 21 assumes or recognizes the fact that those rights exist and affords protection against the deprivation of those rights to the extent there provided. The expression 'procedure established by law' does not mean merely a procedural law but must also include substantive laws. The word 'law' must mean a valid law, that is, a law within the legislative competence of the legislature enacting it, which law does not violate the limitations imposed on legislative power by fundamental rights. 'Personal liberty' means the liberty of the person from external restraint or coercion. Thus Article 21 protects life and personal liberty by putting restrictions on legislative power, which under Articles 245 and 246 is subject to the provisions of 'this Constitution', and therefore subject to fundamental rights. The precise nature of this protection is difficult to state, first because among other things, such protection is dependent on reading Article 21 along with other Articles conferring fundamental rights, such as Articles 14, 20 and 22(1) and (2); and, secondly, because fundamental rights from their very nature refer to ordinary laws which deal with the subject-matter of those rights.

31. The right to life and personal liberty which inheres in the body of a living person is recognized and protected not merely by Article 21 but by the civil and criminal laws of India, and it is unfortunate that in Habeas Corpus case this aspect of the matter did not receive the attention which it deserved. Neither the Constitution nor any law confers the right to life. That right arises from the existence of a living

human body. The most famous remedy for securing personal liberty, the writ of *habeas corpus*, requires the production before the court of the body of the person alleged to be illegally detained. The Constitution gives protection against the deprivation of life and personal liberty; so do the civil and criminal laws in force in India. . . .'

We are of the view that the aforesaid statement made by the learned author reflects the correct position in constitutional law. We, therefore, expressly overrule the majority judgments in *ADM, Jabalpur*.

535. Before parting with this subject, we may only indicate that the majority opinion was done away with by the Constitution's 44th Amendment two years after the judgment was delivered. By that Amendment, Article 359 was amended to state that where a proclamation of Emergency is in operation, the President may by order declare that the right to move any court for the enforcement of rights conferred by Part III of the Constitution may remain suspended for the period during which such proclamation is in force, excepting Articles 20 and 21. On this score also, it is clear that the right to privacy is an inalienable human right which inheres in every person by virtue of the fact that he or she is a human being.

Kaul, J., agreeing with the opinions of Nariman and Chandrachud, JJ., also overruled the majority in *ADM Jabalpur*, stating:

649. The second aspect is the discussion in respect of the majority judgment in *ADM, Jabalpur v. Shivakant Shukla* in both the opinions. In *I.R. Coelho v. State of T.N.* it was observed that *ADM, Jabalpur* case has been impliedly overruled and that the supervening event was the Forty-fourth Amendment to the Constitution, amending Article 359 of the Constitution. I fully agree with the view expressly overruling *ADM, Jabalpur* case which was an aberration in the constitutional jurisprudence of our country and the desirability of burying the majority opinion ten fathom deep with no chance of resurrection.

Postscript

It is noteworthy that each one of these celebrated dissents has been vindicated, even if such vindication sometimes took over eighty years.

However, the bottom line remains, as was felicitously put by Lord Atkin in his dissent in *Liversidge*:

> Amidst the clash of arms the laws are not silent.

One may add that after hostilities cease, the hydraulic pressure exerted on judges, who are, after all, human beings, also ceases. A vision that is clouded by the dust of war suddenly becomes clear when the dust subsides after the war, or emergency, ends. Hats off to those who can see clearly even when the dust kicked up by war makes opaque what is otherwise clear: that the rule of law under a constitutional democracy can never be sacrificed at the altar of expediency.

III

THE DISSENTING
JUDGMENT AS A
STABILIZING FORCE—
DON'T UNSETTLE THE LAW

One of the major criticisms against a dissenting judgment, as we have seen in Chapter I, is that it acts as a force which destabilizes the law, in that the majority judgment becomes open to doubt, and could potentially be overruled in the future by a mere change of personnel in the concerned court. This chapter presents the other side of the picture. I have chosen eighteen dissenting judgments of the Supreme Court of India, which protest against the majority judgment on the fundamental premise that the law should *not* be destabilized, and that what has been decided earlier ought to continue.

1. *Bengal Immunity Co. Ltd. v. State of Bihar* (1955)

In one of the early judgments of the Supreme Court of India, a seven-judge bench in the celebrated *Bengal Immunity Co. Ltd. v. State of Bihar and Ors.* (1955),* by a majority of 4:3, actually unsettled the law, overruling a Constitution Bench decision rendered by five judges in *State of Bombay v. United Motors* (1953).† The judgments involved an interpretation of Article 286 of the Constitution of India (as it then stood), which reads thus:

> 286. (1) No law of a State shall impose, or authorize the imposition of, a tax on the sale or purchase of goods where such sale or purchase takes place—
> > (a) outside the State; or
> > (b) in the course of the import of the goods into, or export of the goods out of, the territory of India.

---

* (1955) 2 SCR 603.
† (1953) 4 SCR 1069.

Explanation.—For the purposes of sub-clause (a), a sale or purchase shall be deemed to have taken place in the State in which the goods have actually been delivered as a direct result of such sale or purchase for the purpose of consumption in that State, notwithstanding the fact that under the general law relating to sale of goods the property in the goods has by reason of such sale or purchase passed in another State.

(2) Except insofar as Parliament may by law otherwise provide, no law of a State shall impose, or authorize the imposition of, a tax on the sale or purchase of any goods where such sale or purchase takes place in the course of inter-State trade or commerce:

Provided that the President may by order direct that any tax, on the sale or purchase of goods which was being lawfully levied by the Government of any State immediately before the commencement of this Constitution shall, notwithstanding that the imposition of such tax is contrary to the provisions of this clause, continue to be levied until the thirty-first day of March, 1951.

(3) No law made by the legislature of a State imposing, or authorizing the imposition of, a tax on the sale or purchase of any such goods as have been declared by Parliament by law to be essential for the life of the community shall have effect unless it has been reserved for the consideration of the President and has received his assent.

The vexed question before the Constitution Bench in *United Motors* was whether the Explanation to Article 286(1)(a) would allow a state to tax an interstate sale when, under the explanation, a deeming fiction was introduced. This deeming fiction stated that a sale or purchase shall be 'deemed' to have taken place in the state in which the goods have actually been delivered as a direct result of such sale or purchase for the purpose of consumption in that state. Patanjali Sastri, C.J., speaking for three learned judges, held that the Explanation to Article 286(1)(a) would enable the state referred to in the explanation to tax a sale or purchase of goods, notwithstanding the fact that such sale or purchase was interstate. Bhagwati, J., in a separate concurring judgment, arrived at the same conclusion. Vivian Bose, J., however, dissented, as, in his view, the basic idea underlying Article 286 is to prohibit taxation in the case of interstate trade and commerce, until the ban under Article 286(2) is lifted by Parliament. Only when such ban is lifted, can the explanation to Article 286(1)(a) come into play, as it cannot govern Article 286(2), and must be confined to the subject matter of Article 286(1)(a).

In *State of Travancore-Cochin v. Shanmugha Vilas Cashew Nut Factory* (1954),* another appeal was heard by five learned judges—with Patanjali Sastri, C.J. delivering the majority judgment, as he did in *United Motors*. This time, S.R. Das, J., in a separate judgment, agreed with the dissenting view of Bose, J. in *United Motors*, leading to the constitution of a seven-judge bench to reconsider the entire issue.

The majority judgment of S.R. Das, acting C.J., in *Bengal Immunity*, referred to judgments from overseas as to when and in what circumstances a decision of the final appellate court, such as the Supreme Court of India, could be overruled; it then arrived at the conclusion that the majority view in *United Motors* was incorrect and therefore should be set aside. In so holding, the learned acting chief justice bypassed the hurdle of Article 141 of the Constitution of India by stating that it would not apply to the Supreme Court, and then went on to articulate—applying elementary maths to arrive at the conclusion—that if *United Motors* and *State of Travancore-Cochin* were to be put together, coupled with the fact that Bhagwati, J. had changed his view, judicial opinion stood divided 3:3. This would be another reason why it would be open to a bench of seven judges to consider the entire issue afresh. He put it thus:

> Article 141 which lays down that the law declared by this Court shall be binding on all courts within the territory of India quite obviously refers to courts other than this Court. The corresponding provision of the Government of India Act, 1935 also makes it clear that the courts contemplated are the subordinate courts.
>
> There are several circumstances relating to the majority decision of the Court in *State of Bombay v. The United Motors (India) Ltd.* to which reference must be made. That appeal was heard immediately before the hearing of the appeal reported as *State of Travancore-Cochin v. Shanmugha Vilas Cashew Nut Factory* commenced. The two appeals were, as a matter of fact, heard one after the other and judgments were reserved in both of

---

* (1954) SCR 53.

them. The Constitution of the Benches was, however, different. In the first appeal one of the Judges of that Bench expressly differed from the majority decision and another learned Judge did not accept the majority decision on many points. In the second appeal one Judge of the Bench, who was not a party to the first appeal, differed from the majority decision in the first appeal. The result, therefore, was that the majority decision was definitely differed from by two Judges. Bhagwati, J. has now in the judgment he has written in the present appeal which we have had the advantage of reading reconsidered the matter and on further reflection he thinks that the majority decision on the present issue was erroneous and he now agrees substantially with the view of Article 286(1)(a) read with the Explanation and Article 286(2) which was expressed in the two minority judgments referred to above and which is adopted in the judgment now being delivered in the present appeal. If Bhagwati, J. had then expressed the views he is now doing, then the majority in the Bombay appeal would have been 3 to 2 and if we add the opinion of the dissenting Judge in the Travancore-Cochin appeal then judicial opinion would have been divided 3 to 3. In this juxtaposition it is difficult to give the majority decision in the Bombay appeal that amount of sanctity and reverence which is usually attributed to an unretracted majority decision of this Court.[*]

Bhagwati, J. began his separate concurring judgment in *Bengal Immunity* as follows:

> I agree with the reasoning and the conclusions reached in the judgment just delivered by my Brother S.R. Das. Insofar however as I was a party to the judgment in *State of Bombay v. United Motors (India) Ltd.* it is but proper that I should record my reasons for doing so.[†]

The learned judge then went on to discuss, in great detail, the different views taken by different judges in both *United Motors* as well as *Travancore-Cochin* and, ultimately, after discussing the history of Article 286, recanted on his earlier view:

---

[*] (1955) 2 SCR 603 at pp. 628–29.
[†] Ibid., p. 668.

The third restriction was devised to protect inter-State trade or commerce and covered transactions of sale or purchase of any goods where such sale or purchase took place in the course of inter-State trade or commerce except in so far as Parliament might by law otherwise provide. This was still another viewpoint and this restriction was put with a view to safeguard the freedom of trade, commerce and intercourse throughout the territory of India. The imposition of this restriction meant that the States would be deprived of a large part of their income which they used to derive from taxing sales or purchases falling within this category before the commencement of the Constitution. A proviso was therefore enacted that the President may by order direct that any tax on the sale or purchase of goods which was being lawfully levied by the Government of any State immediately before the commencement of the Constitution shall, notwithstanding that the imposition of such tax is contrary to the provisions of Article 286(2), continue to be levied until the thirty-first day of March, 1951. This proviso enabled the State Governments to levy the taxes which they used to levy before the commencement of the Constitution up to the 31st March 1951 within which period they were expected to adjust their economies and replenish their treasuries by having resort to their legitimate powers of taxation. By the 31st March 1951 the States could also make representations to the Centre and induce the Parliament to otherwise provide by appropriate legislation within the meaning of Article 286(2) and authorize them to impose taxes on the sale or purchase of any goods where such sales or purchases took place in the course of inter-State trade or commerce. But until that ban was lifted by appropriate legislation by the Parliament the ban imposed under Article 286(2) was absolute and no transaction of sale or purchase of goods where such sale or purchase took place in the course of inter-State trade or commerce could ever be made the subject-matter of taxation at the instance of a State Legislature, The Explanation to Article 286(1)(a) being expressly for the purpose of sub-clause (a) i.e., for the purpose of determining what transaction of sale or purchase was outside the State or inside the State as above stated could not be read into Article 286(2) nor could it be read as an exception or proviso to Article 286(2). Reading it as such exception or proviso would be contrary to the express terms of the Explanation and would also stultify the purpose of the enactment of Article 286(2) thus taking a large slice out of the transactions falling within that category. The rule as to the exclusion of the general provision by a special provision would also not apply for the simple reason that the object of Article 286(1)(a) and the Explanation thereto is quite distinct from the object of Article 286(2) and the objects being quite different these provisions do not cover the same subject-matter and therefore there would be no occasion for the application of that rule of construction. To this extent the view taken by me in the Bombay sales tax appeal that the Explanation to Article 286(1) (a) was an exception or proviso to Article 286(2) was clearly erroneous.[*]

The learned judge concluded by saying:

> After further and fuller consideration of the matter in the light of the very elaborate arguments which have been addressed before us by the learned Counsel for the appellants and the Respondents and also the Interveners, I feel that the conclusion reached in the Bombay sales tax appeal needs to be revised and I am of the opinion that Article 286(2) puts an absolute restriction on the taxing power of the States where transactions of sale or purchase take place in the course of inter-State trade or commerce unless and until the ban is lifted by Parliament within the terms thereof and until such ban is lifted no delivery State within the meaning of the Explanation to Article 286(1)(a) much less the other States are in a position to impose a tax on transactions of sale or purchase covered by the Explanation.[†]

In accordance with the majority view of the four learned judges, the ultimate order made by the court was as follows:

> BY THE COURT.—The appeal is allowed and an order shall be issued directing that, until Parliament by law provides otherwise, the State of Bihar do forbear and abstain from imposing Sales Tax on out-of-State dealers in respect of sales or purchases that have taken place in the course

---

[*] Id., pp. 714–16.
[†] Id., p. 727.

of inter-State Trade or commerce even though the goods have been delivered as a direct result of such sales or purchases for consumption in Bihar. The State must pay the costs of the appellant in this court and in the court below. The interveners must bear and pay their own costs.

What is interesting to note is that the seven-judge bench consisted of three judges who had already expressed a view on Article 286, with four new entrants. S.R. Das, acting C.J., stuck to the view expressed by him in *Travancore-Cochin*, and Vivian Bose, J. stuck to his dissenting view in *United Motors*. As noted above, Bhagwati, J. switched sides, recanting on his earlier concurring judgment in *United Motors*, and joining the majority judgment in *Bengal Immunity*. Jaffer Imam, J., one of the four new horsemen, joined the majority. Three of the four new horsemen, i.e. Jagannadhadas, Venkatarama Ayyar and B.P. Sinha, JJ., delivered separate dissenting judgments.

The dissenting judgment of Jagannadhadas, J. adverted to the case law on how reconsideration of a recent judgment should only be within very narrow limits—a mere change in the view of the court not being enough. It is only if a decision is manifestly wrong, and its maintenance is productive of 'great public mischief', would a decision on a constitutional point of this importance be overturned.[*] The learned judge then went on to state that the matter had been fully thrashed out in *United Motors*, and after the fullest consideration of all the arguments made both in support and against, only Bose, J. dissented. Further, the decision in *Travancore-Cochin* did not deal with the question that arose directly in *United Motors*. Also, in point of fact, *Himmatlal Harilal Mehta v. State of Madhya Pradesh* (1954),[†] reiterated the law laid down by the majority judgment in *United Motors*, stating that the correctness of this view could no longer be questioned. The learned judge therefore concluded:

> In view of the above facts, it appears to me *prima facie*, that there was no reason for reconsideration except the fact that a different view had been

---

[*] Id., pp. 737–38.
[†] (1954) SCR 1122.

taken by two of the learned Judges of this Court and except the chance
of a differently constituted majority emerging on rehearing.*

The other important point made in this dissenting judgment is that the
prior decision, being only two years old, was sufficient ground for it to not
be reconsidered:

> It has next been said that the impugned decision is a recent one and
> that 'judicial opinion was divided, if not evenly balanced'. It is no doubt
> true that the prior decision is only two years old. But that is not by
> itself a ground for reconsideration. On the other hand, I should have
> thought that the very fact of its being recent should militate against
> reconsideration. The real test to my mind, as indicated by Justice Dixon
> in *Attorney-General for N.S.W. v. Perpetual Trustee Co. Ltd.* is whether it
> was a fully considered judgment and whether any fresh material has been
> brought to the notice of the Court. In considering the question whether
> a decision is open to reconsideration on account of its being recent, it
> is of importance to observe that our decisions become declarations of
> law under Article 141 and must be treated normally as final from the
> very moment they are pronounced. The finality of the decisions of this
> Court, which is the court of last resort, will be greatly weakened and
> much mischief done if we treat our own judgments, even though recent,
> as open to reconsideration.
>
> It has next been suggested that rectification of the error, if any,
> in the view taken by the previous decision, is difficult and that this
> could be brought about only by the amendment of the legislative
> lists necessitating the consent of the requisite number of States. With
> respect, I am unable to appreciate this. The points of difference in
> the two opposing views ultimately boil down to this. (1) Does the
> Explanation to Article 286(1)(a) taken with the relevant legislative
> entry enable the consuming State to tax fictional inside sales? (2) If so,
> does Article 286(2) override this taxing power? If the right construction
> of Article 286(2) is not what has been accepted by the majority in the
> prior decision, what all was required to correct that error would be to

---

* (1955) 2 SCR 603 at p. 740.

amend Article 286(2) so as to make it clear that it overrides Article 286(1)(a) taken with the Explanation by the insertion therein of some appropriate phrase like 'notwithstanding Explanation to Article 286(1) (a)'. The responsibility for any such amendment, if called for, should be left to the Parliament who, as recent experience has shown, is quite capable of bringing about constitutional amendments when it felt the clear necessity for it.*

The second dissenting judgment, that of Venkatarama Ayyar, J., contains a full exposé of the law as to when judgments should be overruled, and then agree with the majority view in *United Motors*. The learned judge begins by setting out the five questions that arose in this case.† The judgment then goes on to state that the object of the explanation to Article 286(1) (a) is that multiple taxation by the states, depending upon situs of sale and territorial nexus, was sought to be avoided.‡ Reference was then made in great detail to the commerce clause of the US Constitution, stating that the framers of the Indian Constitution, in drafting Article 286(1)(a) and subclause (2), were inspired by the American law on the subject.§ The learned judge went on to state:

> The position may thus be summed up: Article 286(2) applies to sales in the course of inter-State trade. The sales which fall within the Explanation are intra-State sales. The grounds covered by the two provisions are distinct and separate. Each has operation within its own sphere, and there is no conflict between them.¶

He states that, even assuming that there is a conflict between the two provisions, Bhagwati, J.'s original view in *United Motors*—i.e. that the explanation deals with a special situation (as against the general situation dealt with by Article 286[2]) and would therefore prevail—would, by

---

* Id., pp. 742–43.
† Id., pp. 763–64.
‡ Id., p. 769.
§ Id., pp. 777–80.
¶ Id., p. 781.

applying the doctrine of harmonious construction, be the correct view.*
Disagreeing with Bose, J.'s dissenting judgment in *United Motors*, he
stated as follows:

> That was the view expressed by Bose, J. in *The State of Bombay v. The
> United Motors (India) Ltd.* and by Das, J. in *State of Travancore-Cochin
> v. Shanmugha Vilas Cashew Nut Factory.* Briefly, according to this view
> Article 286(2) controls the Explanation. Can this be sustained on the
> language of the enactment? The Explanation is not expressed to be subject
> to Article 286(2). Nor does the latter contain the words 'notwithstanding
> anything contained in the Explanation to Article 286(1)(a)'. These are
> simple and familiar expressions used by the legislature when it intends
> that a particular provision in the Statute should be subject to or override
> another. Nor is there anything in the language of the Explanation
> providing that its operation is not to be in praesenti but contingent on
> Parliamentary legislation under Article 286(2). To construe, therefore,
> Article 286(2) as controlling the Explanation, we must import into the
> Statute words which are not there and thereby cut down the operation
> of the Explanation which on its terms is of equal authority and potency
> with Article 286(2).
>
> There being nothing express in the language of the enactment to lead
> to the conclusion that the Explanation is controlled by Article 286(2), it
> has to be seen whether that conclusion can be drawn on a construction
> of the relevant provisions of the Statute. The appellant argues that it
> can be, and relies firstly on the saving clause in Article 286(2), and
> secondly, on the proviso thereto as supporting it. The argument based
> on the saving clause may thus be stated: The contention that Article
> 286(2) controls the Explanation would have resulted in rendering the
> latter wholly nugatory, if the words 'except insofar as Parliament may by
> law otherwise provide' had not been there. But that result is avoided by
> the saving clause under which the Explanation can come into operation
> when there is Parliamentary legislation lifting the ban under Article
> 286(2). This construction, it is argued, gives effect to the plain language
> of the article and also to both the provisions. But when examined, it will

---

* Id., pp. 790–91.

be seen that far from giving effect to both the Explanation and Article 286(2), this construction results in destroying one or the other of them. The harmonious construction which the law favours is one which gives operation to both the provisions at the same time but in their respective spheres. But according to the appellant, if Article 286(2) is in force then the Explanation cannot operate, and if the Explanation is to operate, it can only be if the Parliament puts an end to Article 286(2) by legislation thereunder. This construction, far from reconciling the two provisions and giving operation to both of them, renders them uncompromisingly hostile, and makes their co-existence and cooperation impossible.[*]

Referring to the startling results that would ensue if the majority decision were to be applied, the learned judge held:

Now, let us look at the other side of the picture. Prior to the Constitution, the States had the power to tax even sales in the course of inter-State trade and commerce, and it is stated that a substantial portion of their revenue was derived from this source. The Constitution enacted Article 286(1)(a) with a view to avoid multiple taxation of sales in the course of inter-State trade, and it is the contention of the respondent that the Explanation on its true interpretation provides for a single taxation of those sales, at the stage of consumption. If the contention of the appellant as to the scope of the Explanation and of Article 286(2) is accepted, this tax could not be levied after the 31st March, 1951, and the States would have lost a substantial source of revenue. What is the substitute that the Constitution has provided therefor? None. In the result, there must be, as argued by the respondent, a financial crisis in the affairs of the States. The position, therefore, is that we have to choose between depriving the States of their power to impose a tax on which their very existence depends, and exposing the sellers having business outside their State to the inconvenience of multiple assessment proceedings. In that situation, can there be any doubt as to what our decision should be? Surely, the claim of the State should have precedence over that of individuals.[†]

[*] Id., pp. 792–94.
[†] Id., p. 803.

Adverting then to the law on when judgments can be overruled, the learned judge put it powerfully thus:

> The question then arises as to the principles on which and the limits within which this power should be exercised. It is, of course not possible to enumerate them exhaustively, nor is it even desirable that they should be crystallized into rigid and inflexible rules. But one principle stands out prominently above the rest, and that is, that in general, there should be finality in the decisions of the highest courts in the land, and that is for the benefit and protection of the public. In this connection, it is necessary to bear in mind that next to legislative enactments, it is decisions of courts that form the most important source of law. It is on the faith of decisions that rights are acquired and obligations incurred, and States and subjects alike shape their course of action. It must greatly impair the value of the decisions of this Court, if the notion came to be entertained that there was nothing certain or final about them, which must be the consequence if the points decided therein came to be reconsidered on the merits every time they were raised. It should be noted that though the Privy Council has repeatedly declared that it has the power to reconsider its decisions, in fact, no instance has been quoted in which it did actually reverse its previous decision except in ecclesiastical cases. If that is the correct position, then the power to reconsider is one which should be exercised very sparingly and only in exceptional circumstances, such as when a material provision of law had been overlooked, or where a fundamental assumption on which the decision is based, turns out to be mistaken. In the present case, it is not suggested that in deciding the question of law as they did in *State of Bombay v. United Motors (India) Ltd.* the learned Judges ignored any material provisions of law, or were under any misapprehension as to a matter fundamental to the decision. The arguments for the appellant before us, were in fact, only a repetition of the very contentions which were urged before the learned Judges and negatived by them. The question then resolves itself to this. Can we differ from a previous decision of this Court, because a view contrary to the one taken therein appears to be preferable? I would unhesitatingly answer it in the negative, not because the view previously taken must necessarily be infallible but because it is important in public interest

that the law declared should be certain and final rather than that it should be declared in one sense or the other. That, I conceive, is the reason behind Article 141. There are questions of law on which it is not possible to avoid difference of opinion, and the present case is itself a single example of it. The object of Article 141 is that the decisions of this Court on these questions should settle the controversy, and that they should be followed as law by all the Courts, and if they are allowed to be reopened because a different view appears to be the better one, then the very purpose with which Article 141 has been enacted will be defeated, and the prospect will have been opened of litigants subjecting our decisions to a continuous process of attack before successive Benches in the hope that with changes in the personnel of the Court which time must inevitably bring, a different view might find acceptance. I can imagine nothing more damaging to the prestige of this Court or to the value of its pronouncements. In *James v. Commonwealth* it was observed that a question settled by a previous decision should not be allowed to be reopened 'upon a mere suggestion that some or all of the Members of the later Court might arrive at a different conclusion if the matter was *res integra*. Otherwise, there would be grave danger of want of continuity in the interpretation of the law' (per Griffiths, C.J. at p. 58). It is for this reason that Article 141 invests decisions of this Court with special authority, but the weight of that authority can only be what we ourselves give to it.

It was suggested as a ground for reconsidering the correctness of the decision in *State of Bombay v. United Motors (India) Ltd.* that it had caused great hardship to the business world. I have already held that there is not much of substance in this complaint. On the other hand, acting on the view that the Explanation confers on the delivery States power to tax the sales, several States amended their Sales Tax Acts in 1951 by inserting appropriate provisions and it is represented before us that for some years, taxes have been collected by the States on the basis of these provisions. If we are now to hold that the view taken in *State of Bombay v. United Motors (India) Ltd.* is erroneous, the consequences will be to render the amended provisions inoperative and the collections of taxes made thereunder illegal. The States will then be not merely powerless to tax sales falling within the Explanation in future, but will have actually to refund whatever they might have collected in the past. I can see no end to the chaos, confusion and trouble that must ensue on such a decision—a situation that can be retrieved only by Parliament removing Article 286(2) out of the scene with retrospective operation, and all this, to benefit not the consumers who are the persons really affected but the sellers who are only statutory middlemen for collection, some of whom are stated to have collected sales tax from purchasers outside their States. I consider it wholly inexpedient that our power of reconsideration should be exercised for that end. This, of course, is apart from my conclusion that on a correct interpretation of the Explanation and Article 286(2), the respondents have the power to tax. In the result, this point must be held against the appellant.[*]

The third dissenting judgment, authored by B.P. Sinha, J., agreed with both Jagannadhadas, J. and Venkatarama Ayyar, J., stating that after a full hearing was given to all arguments made in the earlier round of litigation, simply because another view was possible, *United Motors* could not be overruled.[†] Coming to the merits of the case, the learned judge put it thus:

[W]e are all agreed that the Explanation to Article 286(1)(a) of the Constitution has created a legal fiction as a result of which a transaction of sale or a purchase partaking of an inter-state character has been treated as a domestic transaction. The fiction has localized sales or purchases contemplated by the Explanation, by converting such transactions as would otherwise have been inter-State sales or purchases into sales or purchases inside one State in a sense in which it is placed in a class distinct and separate from what is referred to as sales or purchases 'outside the State' in the main body of Article 286(1)(a) which prohibits imposition of tax by any State. There is a general agreement amongst us, I take it, that the main purpose of creating the fiction is to prevent multiple taxation of the same transaction, but, it may be added, not altogether to stop the taxation of such transactions. We are also agreed that full effect must be given to the legal fiction on the supposition that the putative state of affairs is the real one. While thus agreeing on the

---

[*] Id., pp. 809–11.
[†] Id., pp. 837–39.

general principle bearing on the question of the purpose and scope of a legal fiction, we are again divided on the question of how far the legal fiction should be carried in its actual application. For the reasons given by my brother Venkatarama Aiyar, I agree with him that the fiction created by the Explanation brings such a sale within the taxing power of the State within which such a sale is said to have taken place. Such a result is brought about not by holding that the Explanation has conferred positively the power on the relevant State to impose sales tax, but by holding that such an inside sale is beyond the scope of the prohibition contained in the main body of Article 286(1)(a) which interdicts the imposition of a tax on a sale 'outside the State'. The Explanation has got to be read as an integral part of Article 286(1)(a) and thus read, it means negatively that a sale or purchase outside a State cannot be taxed; and by necessary implication, that a sale or purchase inside a State may be taxed by that State as falling outside the mischief of the prohibition directed against the imposition of a tax on a sale or purchase of goods outside a State; in other words, as soon as a sale or purchase of goods is declared to be outside the pale of the prohibition contained in Article 286(1)(a), the State's power of imposing a tax contained in Article 246 read with Item 54 of List II of the 7th Schedule comes into operation. I do not find myself in agreement with the view propounded by my brother S.R. Das chiefly because that view goes beyond the purpose of the creation of the fiction which admittedly was to prevent multiple taxation. The view as propounded by him besides preventing multiple taxation goes to the length of prohibiting any imposition of sales tax by any State. Such, in my opinion, was not the intention of the Constitution. Whereas the imposition of multiple sales tax on transactions of sale or purchase may be an obstacle to the free flow of inland trade and commerce, the imposition of sales tax by a single State in which the sale is deemed to have taken place by virtue of the Explanation cannot be predicated as having such an effect. The view propounded by my learned brother Venkatarama Aiyar is thus not inconsistent with the avowed purpose of the Constitution, as expressed in Article 301, which provides that trade, commerce and intercourse shall be free throughout the territory of India. In my opinion, the view propounded by my learned brother S.R. Das about the actual application of the legal fiction stops short of giving full effect to that fiction. Allied with this question is the controversy as to whether clause (2) of Article 286 is subject to Article 286(1)(a) read with the Explanation or vice versa. In my opinion, for the reasons given by my learned brother Venkatarama Aiyar the better view is that clause (2) of Article 286 of the Constitution is subject to Article 286(1)(a) read with the Explanation. On the whole, therefore, I would agree with the view that the previous decision of this Court in 1953 SCR 1069 should continue to hold good and govern the present controversy also. In that view of the matter, I would dismiss this appeal with costs.[*]

As a result of the majority decision, Parliament had to step in and enact the Central Sales Tax Act, which it did immediately in 1956. Had it not done so, the fears of Venkatarama Ayyar, J., that the states would be substantially deprived of revenue from sales tax—given the majority view—would have come to fruition.

2. *Manohar Lal Chopra v. Rai Bahadur Rao Raja Seth Hiralal* (1962)

In *Manohar Lal Chopra v. Rai Bahadur Rao Raja Seth Hiralal* (1962),[†] an earlier decision in *Padam Sen v. State of Uttar Pradesh* (1961)[‡] fell for consideration before a bench of four learned judges. The majority judgment of Raghubar Dayal, J., who spoke on behalf of three judges, sidestepped *Padam Sen*, holding that the question in *Padam Sen* was whether the inherent power of the court could be used contrary to what was expressly laid down by Section 75 and Order XXVI of the Code of Civil Procedure, 1908. The court held:

> The section itself says that nothing in the Code shall be deemed to limit or otherwise affect the inherent power of the Court to make orders necessary for the ends of justice. In the face of such a clear statement, it is not possible to hold that the provisions of the Code control the inherent

---

[*] Id., pp. 839–41.
[†] (1962) Supp. (1) SCR 450.
[‡] (1961) 1 SCR 884.

power by limiting it or otherwise affecting it. The inherent power has not been conferred upon the Court; it is a power inherent in the Court by virtue of its duty to do justice between the parties before it.

Further, when the Code itself recognizes the existence of the inherent power of the Court, there is no question of implying any powers outside the limits of the Code.[*]

The majority judgment therefore went on to hold that as there was no prohibition in Section 94 against the grant of a temporary injunction in circumstances not covered by Order XXXIX of the Code of Civil Procedure, 1908, the inherent power of the court could be used to grant a temporary injunction in such circumstances.

Shah, J. dissented. In his view:

> Inherent jurisdiction of the court to make orders *ex debito justitiae* is undoubtedly affirmed by Section 151 of the Code, but that jurisdiction cannot be exercised so as to nullify the provisions of the Code. Where the Code deals expressly with a particular matter, the provision should normally be regarded as exhaustive.[†]

The learned judge went on to extract the observations in *Padam Sen*, and, following it, held:

> The Court in that case held that in exercise of the powers under Section 151 of the Code of Civil Procedure, 1908 the Court cannot issue a commission for seizing books of account of the plaintiff—a purpose for which a commission is not authorized to be issued by Section 75.
>
> The principle of the case is destructive of the submission of the appellants. Section 75 empowers the Court to issue a commission for purposes specified therein: even though it is not so expressly stated that there is no power to appoint a commissioner for other purposes, a prohibition to that effect is, in the view of the Court in *Padam Sen's* case, implicit in Section 75. By parity of reasoning, if the power to issue

---

[*] (1962) Supp. (1) SCR 450 at 463.
[†] Ibid., p. 473.

injunctions may be exercised, if it is so prescribed by rules in the orders in Schedule I, it must be deemed to be not exercisable in any other manner or for purposes other than those set out in Order 39 Rules 1 and 2.*

The dissent in this case thus made it clear that the *ratio* of *Padam Sen* could not be sidestepped in the manner done by the majority and instead ought to have been followed. This is because the majority view would now leave it open for a lawyer to argue that in the absence of a prohibition in the Code of Civil Procedure, 1908, the inherent power of the court could be utilized—which is not the *ratio* of *Padam Sen*. The principle in *Taylor v. Taylor* (1875)[†] gets thrown to the winds—i.e. that when a section of the Code of Civil Procedure, 1908, empowers the court to do something for purposes specified therein, then, obviously, no inherent power exists to utilize such power for purposes other than the stated purpose.

3. *Re: Powers, Privileges and Immunities of State Legislatures* (1965)

Another interesting dissenting judgment is that of Sarkar, J. in the celebrated case reported as *Re: Powers, Privileges and Immunities for State Legislatures* (1965),[‡] in which a five-judge bench was faced with the constitutional crisis that arose out of the proceedings in the legislative assembly of the state of Uttar Pradesh; it is summarized as follows:

> The Legislative Assembly of the State of Uttar Pradesh committed one Keshav Singh, who was not one of its members, to prison for its contempt. The warrant of committal did not contain the facts constituting the alleged contempt. While undergoing imprisonment for the committal, Keshav Singh through his Advocate moved a petition under Article 226 of the Constitution and s.491 of the Code of Criminal Procedure, challenging his committal as being in breach of his fundamental rights; he also prayed for interim bail. The High Court (Lucknow Bench) gave

---

* Id., p. 475.
[†] (1875) 1 Ch.D 426.
[‡] (1965) 1 SCR 413.

notice to the Government Counsel who accepted it on behalf of all the respondents including the legislative assembly. At the time fixed for hearing of the bail application the Government Counsel did not appear. Beg and Sahgal JJ. who heard the application ordered that Keshav Singh be released on bail pending the decision of his petition under Art.226. The Legislative Assembly found that Keshav Singh and his Advocate in moving the High Court, and the two Judges of the High Court in entertaining the petition and granting bail had committed contempt of the Assembly, and passed a resolution that all of them be produced before it in custody. The Judges and the Advocate thereupon filed writ petitions before the High Court at Allahabad and a Full Bench of the High Court admitted their petitions and ordered the stay of the execution of the Assembly's resolution against them. The Assembly then passed a clarificatory resolution which modified its earlier stand. Instead of being produced in custody, the Judges and the Advocate were asked to appear before the House and offer their explanation.

At this stage the President of India made a Reference under Art.143(1) of the Constitution in which the whole dispute as to the constitutional relationship between the High Court and the State Legislature including the question whether on the fact of the case Keshav Singh, his Advocate and the two Judges, by their respective acts, were guilty of contempt of the State Legislature, was referred to the Supreme Court for its opinion and Report.[*]

One of the most important points that arose in the case was the interplay of Article 194(3) with Article 19(1)(a) of the Constitution, both of which deal with the freedom of speech—one in the legislative assembly, confined to its members, and one with regard to the citizens of India generally. In order to appreciate the minority view, Articles 194 and 19(1)(a) are set out hereinbelow:

> 194. (1) Subject to the provision of this Constitution and to the rules and standing orders regulating the procedure of the legislature, there shall be freedom of speech in the legislature of every State.

---

[*] Ibid., pp. 413–14.

(2) No member of the legislature of a State shall be liable to any proceedings in any court in respect of anything said or any vote given by him in the legislature or any committee thereof, and no person shall be so liable in respect of the publication by or under the authority of a House of such a legislature of any report, paper, votes, or proceedings.

(3) In other respects, the powers, privileges and immunities of a House of the legislature of a State, and of the members and the committees of a House of such legislature, shall be such as may from time to time be defined by the legislature by law, and, until so defined, shall be those of the House of Commons of the Parliament of the United Kingdom, and of its members and committees, at the commencement of this Constitution.

(4) The provisions of clauses (1), (2) and (3) shall apply in relation to persons who by virtue of this Constitution have the right to speak, in, and otherwise to take part in the proceedings of, a House of the legislature of a State or any committee thereof as they apply in relation to members of that legislature.

19. Protection of certain rights regarding freedom of speech, etc.-

(1) All citizens shall have the right-

(a) To freedom of speech and expression;

* * *

An earlier decision in *Pandit M.S.M. Sharma v. Shri Sri Krishna Sinha and Ors.* (1959),* had held that the privileges of the House of Commons, which were conferred on the Houses of the State Legislature by Article 194(3), take precedence over fundamental rights. In *M.S.M. Sharma*, the Bihar State Legislative Assembly had directed certain parts of its proceedings to be expunged; but, notwithstanding this, the petitioner— the editor of a newspaper called *Searchlight*—published the full account of the proceedings in the House, including what was expunged. A notice was therefore issued to him by the House to show cause as to why steps should not be taken against him for breach of privilege of the House. The petitioner filed a petition under Article 32 of the Constitution of

---

* (1959) Supp. (1) SCR 806.

India, stating that the aforesaid privilege did not control his fundamental right of freedom to speech under Article 19(1)(a) and that therefore the notice ought to be struck down. The majority judgment of four out of five learned judges held that the House possessed this privilege and that it was not subject to the fundamental right of a citizen under Article 19(1)(a).* In dealing with *M.S.M Sharma*, Sarkar, J., in his dissenting judgment in *Re: Powers, Privileges*, held as follows:

> I feel no doubt, however, that the majority judgment in *Sharma* case was perfectly correct when it held that privileges were not subject to fundamental rights. I have earlier set out the first three clauses of Article 194. The first clause was expressly made subject to the provisions of the Constitution—whatever the provisions contemplated were—while the third clause was not made so subject. Both the majority and the minority judgments are agreed that the third clause cannot, therefore, be read as if it had been expressly made subject to the provisions of the Constitution. For myself, I do not think that any other reading is possible. Clause (3) of Article 194 thus not having been expressly made subject to the other provisions of the Constitution, how is a conflict between it and any other provisions of the Constitution which may be found to exist, to be resolved? The majority held that the principle of harmonious construction has to be applied for reconciling the two and Article 194(3) being a special provision must take precedence over the fundamental right mentioned in Article 19(1)(a) which was a general provision. Though Subba Rao, J., said that there was no inherent inconsistency between Article 19(1)(a) and Article 194(3), he nonetheless applied the rule of harmonious construction. He felt that since the legislature had a wide range of powers and privileges and those privileges can be exercised without infringing the fundamental rights, the privilege should yield to the fundamental right. This construction, he thought, gave full effect to both the articles. With great respect to the learned Judge, I find it difficult to follow how this interpretation produced the result of both the articles having effect and thus achieving a harmonious construction.†

---

* Subba Rao, J.'s dissent in *M.S.M Sharma* (supra) is discussed in detail in Chapter VI.
† (1965) 1 SCR 413 at pp. 525–26.

Sarkar, J. differed with the view of the majority, which had distinguished *Sharma* on the footing that it is an authority for the proposition that the privilege of the House, though not subject to the fundamental right under Article 19, would, however, be subject to the fundamental right under Article 21. According to Sarkar, J., this would be in the teeth of the majority decision in *M.S.M. Sharma*, as understood by him. The learned judge therefore concluded:

> In this Court some discussion took place as to the meaning of the words 'subject to the provisions of the Constitution' in clause (1) of Article 194. These words can, in my view, only refer to the provisions of the Constitution laying down the procedure to be observed in the House for otherwise clauses Section (1) and (2) will conflict with each other. I will now make a digression and state that learned advocate for the Assembly pointed out that in Article 194 the Constitution-makers treated the liberty of speech of a member differently by expressly providing for it in clauses Section (1) and (2) and by providing for other privileges, that is, privileges other than that of the freedom of speech in the House, in clause (3). He said that the reason was that if the freedom of speech in the House was conferred by clause (3) it would be controlled by law made by the legislature and then the party in power might conceivably destroy that freedom. The intention was that the freedom of speech in the House should be guaranteed by the Constitution itself so as to be beyond the reach of any impairment by any law made by the legislature. I think that is the only reason why that freedom was treated separately in the Constitution in clauses Section (1) and (2) of Article 194. Therefore those clauses have nothing to do with the case in hand. Nor had they anything to do with the decision in *Sharma*'s case. The result is that in my judgment *Sharma*'s case covers the present case and cannot be distinguished from it.
>
> For the reasons earlier stated I come to the conclusion that when there is a conflict between a privilege conferred on a House by the second part of Article 194(3) and a fundamental right, that conflict has to be resolved by harmonizing the two provisions. It would be wrong to say that the fundamental right must have precedence over the privilege simply because it is a fundamental right or for any other

reason. In the present case the conflict is between the privilege of the House to commit a person for contempt without that committal being liable to be examined by a Court of law and the personal liberty of a citizen guaranteed by Article 21 and the right to move the courts in enforcement of that right under Article 32 or Article 226. If the right to move the courts in enforcement of the fundamental right is given precedence, the privilege which provides that if a House commits a person by a general warrant that committal would not be reviewed by courts of law, will lose all its effect and it would be as if that privilege had not been granted to a House by the second part of Article 194(3). This, in my view, cannot be. That being so, it would follow that when a House commits a person for contempt by a general warrant that person would have no right to approach the courts nor can the courts sit in judgment over such order of committal. It is not my intention to state that there may not be exceptions to the rule but I do not propose to enter into discussion of these exceptions, if any, in the present case. The existence of those exceptions may be supported by the observations of Lord Ellenborough, C.J. in *Burdett v. Abbot. May* at p. 159 puts the matter thus: 'Lord Ellenborough, C.J., left open the possibility that cases might arise in which the courts would have to decide on the validity of a committal for contempt where the facts displayed in the return could by no reasonable interpretation be considered as a contempt'.[*]

4. *Bhagwandas Goverdhandas Kedia v. Girdharilal Pashottamdas and Co.* (1966)

In *Bhagwandas Goverdhandas Kedia v. Girdharilal Pashottamdas and Co.* (1966),[†] an interesting question arose as to which court would have jurisdiction to entertain and decide a suit, depending upon where a contract could be said to be concluded. The contract, in the facts of that case, was concluded by long-distance telephone, the offer being made by the respondent at Ahmedabad, and the acceptance given by the appellant at Khamgaon. The majority judgment of J.C. Shah, J., speaking on behalf

---

[*] Ibid., pp. 533–34.
[†] (1966) 1 SCR 656.

of himself and Wanchoo, J., held that the rule that applies to acceptance by post of a telegram would not apply to contracts made by telephone. The 'acceptance by post' rule, which is contained in Section 4 of the Indian Contract Act, 1872, did not envisage the use of the telephone as a means of conversation between parties and therefore could not have intended to make any rule in that behalf. This being so, the English judgment of *Entores Ltd. v. Miles Far East Corp.* (1955),* was followed. Hidayatullah, J. in a dissenting judgment, which is remarkable both for its learning and its logic, held that since the language of Section 4 of the Indian Contract Act, 1872, would clearly cover even a telephone contract, this section alone can be applied. After setting out the facts, the learned judge stated:

> The rules to apply in our country are statutory but the Contract Act was drafted in England and the English Common law permeates it; however, it is obvious that every new development of the Common law in England may not necessarily fit into the scheme and the words of our statute. If the language of our enactment creates a non-possumus adamant rule, which cannot be made, to yield to any new theories held in foreign courts our clear duty will be to read the statute naturally and to follow it . . . Sir William Anson compared the proposal (offer in English Common law) to a train of gun-powder and the acceptance to a lighted match. This picturesque description shows that acceptance is the critical fact, even if it may not explain the reason underlying it. It is, therefore, necessary to see why the rule about acceptance by post or by telegram was treated as a departure from the general rule of law that acceptance must be communicated.[†]

xxx xxx xxx

The difficulty arises because proposals and acceptances may be in praesentes or inter absentes and it is obvious that the rules must vary. In acceptance by word of mouth, when parties are face to face, the rule gives hardly any trouble. The acceptance may be by speech,

---

* (1955) 2 QBD 327.
† (1966) 1 SCR 656, p. 667.

or sign sufficiently expressive and clear to form a communication of the intention to accept. The acceptance takes effect instantly and the contract is made at the same time and place. In the case of acceptance inter absentes the communication must be obviously by some agency. Where the proposer prescribes a mode of acceptance that mode must be followed. In other cases a usual and reasonable manner must be adopted unless the proposer waives notification. Cases in the last category are offers of reward for some service or fulfilling some condition, such as trying a medicine (*Carlill v. Carbolic Smoke Ball Co.*)]. The offer being to the whole world, the acceptance need not be notified and the contract is made when the condition is fulfilled.[*]

xxx xxx xxx

The principles which underlie the exceptional rule in English Common law are:

'(i) the post office is the agent of the offeror to deliver the offer and also to receive the acceptance;

(ii) no contract by post will be possible, as notification will have to follow notification to make certain that each letter was duly delivered;

(iii) satisfactory evidence of posting the letter is generally available;

(iv) if the offeror denies the receipt of the letter it would be very difficult to disprove his negative; and

(v) the carrier of the letter is a third person over whom the acceptor has no control.[†]

xxx xxx xxx

Professor Winfield (writing in 1939) said that this rule prevailed in Canada, South Africa, New South Wales. Dealing with the European countries he said that three systems are followed: (1) the system of Information under which the offeror must be notified and the contract is formed only when the offeror is so informed. This prevailed in

---

[*] Ibid., p. 669.
[†] Id., p. 671.

Belgium, Italy, Spain, Roumania, Bulgaria and Portugal; (2) the system of declaration, under which the contract is formed from the moment when the recipient of the offer declares his acceptance, even without the knowledge of the offeror.*

xxx xxx xxx

It will be seen from the above discussion that there are four classes of cases which may occur when contracts are made by telephone: (1) where the acceptance is fully heard and understood; (2) where the telephone fails as a machine and the proposer does not hear the acceptor and the acceptor knows that his acceptance has not been transmitted; (3) where owing to some fault at the proposer's end the acceptance is not heard by him and he does not ask the acceptor to repeat his acceptance and the acceptor believes that the acceptance has been communicated; and (4) where the acceptance has not been heard by the proposer and he informs the acceptor about this and asks him to repeat his words. I shall take them one by one.

Where the speech is fully heard and understood there is a binding contract and in such a case the only question is as to the place where the contract can be said to be completed. Ours is that kind of a case. When the communication fails and the acceptance is not heard, and the acceptor knows about it, there is no contract between the parties at all because communication means an effective communication or a communication reasonable in the circumstances. Parties are not ad idem at all. If a man shouts his acceptance from such a long distance that it cannot possibly be heard by the proposer he cannot claim that he accepted the offer and communicated it to the proposer as required by Section 3 of our Contract Act. In the third case, the acceptor transmits his acceptance but the same does not reach the proposer and the proposer does not ask the acceptor to repeat his message. According to Lord Denning the proposer is bound because of his default. As there is no reception at the proposer's end, logically the contract must be held to be complete at the proposer's end. Bringing in considerations of estoppel do not

---

* Id., p. 672.

solve the problem for us. Under the terms of Section 3 of our Act such communication is good because the acceptor intends to communicate his acceptance and follows a usual and reasonable manner and puts his acceptance in the course of transmission to the proposer. He does not know that it has not reached. The contract then results in much the same way as in the case of acceptance by letter when the letter is lost and in the place where the acceptance was put in course of transmission. In the fourth case if the acceptor is told by the offeror that his speech cannot be heard there will be no contract because communication must be effective communication and the act of acceptor has not the effect of communicating it and he cannot claim that he acted reasonably.[*]

xxx xxx xxx

It is plain that the law was framed at a time when telephones, wireless, Telstar and Early Bird were not contemplated. If time has marched and inventions have made it easy to communicate instantaneously over long distance and the language of our law does not fit the new conditions it can be modified to reject the old principles. But we cannot go against the language by accepting an interpretation given without considering the language of our Act.[†]

xxx xxx xxx

Regard being had to the words of our statute I am compelled to hold that the contract was complete at Khamgaon. It may be pointed out that the same result obtains in the conflict of laws as understood in America and quite a number of other countries such as Canada, France, etc. also apply the rule which I have enunciated above even though there is no compulsion of any statute. I have, therefore, less hesitation in propounding the view which I have attempted to set down here.[‡]

---

[*] Id., pp. 678–79.
[†] Id., p. 681.
[‡] Id., p. 682.

Despite the powerful dissent, Parliament has not thought it fit to amend the Indian Contract Act, 1872. The majority judgment therefore continues to be the law of the land.

5. *Superintendent & Legal Remembrancer, State of West Bengal v. Corporation of Calcutta* (1967)

Superintendent & Legal Remembrancer, State of West Bengal v. Corporation of Calcutta (1967)[*] is one of the few nine-judge-bench judgments of the Supreme Court of India. Nine judges were constituted in order to determine whether the Constitution Bench judgment in *Director of Rationing v. Corporation of Calcutta* (1961),[†] should be overruled. In that case, the Constitution Bench had held that the English rule of the Crown not being bound by statute—save by express words or by necessary implication—would be followed in India; this resulted in the position that the central and state governments would not be bound by statutes like the ordinary citizen, unless it is expressly so stated or can be culled out by necessary implication. The majority view of eight learned judges held that the common law rule of construction that the Crown is not, unless expressly named or clearly intended, bound by statute, was not accepted as a rule of construction throughout India, and was not statutorily recognized in India. In any case, the majority declared that an archaic rule based on the prerogative of the Crown had no relevance to a democratic republic; it is inconsistent with the rule of law based on the doctrine of equality. Therefore, the normal construction—that an enactment applies to citizens as well as the state, unless such an enactment expressly or by necessary implication exempts the states from its operation—would be the correct position in law. This being so, the majority judgment overruled *Director of Rationing*.

Shah, J. was the sole dissenter in this case. According to him:

The rule of interpretation was, as already stated, a settled rule and was law in force in the territory of India within the meaning of Article 372

---

[*] (1967) 2 SCR 170.
[†] (1961) 1 SCR 158.

of the Constitution. I am unable to agree with the contention that a rule of interpretation is not 'law in force' within the meaning of Article 372.*

xxx xxx xxx

I do not think that the guarantee of the equal protection clause of the Constitution extends to any differential treatment which may result in the application of a special rule of interpretation between the State and the citizens. Nor can it be said that under our Constitution equality in matters of interpretation between the State and the citizens is predicated in all respects. It must be remembered that our Constitutional set-up is built up not anew, but on the foundations of our old institutions. The political set-up is indisputably changed, but can it be said that our concept of a State is so fundamentally altered that the traditional view about State privileges, immunities and rights must be abandoned because they had a foreign origin, on the supposed theory of equality between the State and the citizens—a theory which seeks to equate common good of the people represented by the State with the rights and obligations of the individual—the court should decline to give effect to the State privileges and immunities? If it be granted that the State in making laws is entitled to select itself for special treatment different from the treatment accorded to the citizen—and it is not denied that in order to achieve public good it can do so even if there is a differential treatment between the State and the citizen—is there any reason to suppose that a statute which evidently was framed on the basis of the well-settled rule of the pre-Constitution days which accorded to the State a special treatment in the matter of interpretation of statutes must be deemed to have a different meaning on the supposition that the Constitution has sought to impose equality between the State and the citizen? The fact that in our federal set-up sovereignty is divided between the Union and the States, and in the application of the rule that the State is not bound by a statute, unless expressly named or clearly implied, conflicts between the State enacting a law and the Union, or another State may arise does not give rise to any insuperable difficulty which renders the

---

* (1967) 2 SCR 170, p. 198.

rule in applicable to the changed circumstances, for it is the State which enacts a legislation in terms general which alone may claim benefit of the rule of interpretation, and not any other State.[*]

xxx xxx xxx

Under the provisions of the Calcutta Municipal Act the owner or occupier of a market is required to take out a license. But there is no express reference to the State: nor is there anything peculiar in the nature, purpose and object or in the language used in the enactment relating to the issue of licenses which may suggest that the State must by necessary implication be bound by its provisions. I am, therefore, of the view that the High Court was in error in holding that the State of West Bengal was bound by the provisions relating to the issue of licenses for occupation or conduct of a market.[†]

The protest of Shah, J. in the minority view, however, has no real legs to stand on. Even in the Magna Carta, way back in 1215, King John had accepted the fact that even though he may make the law, he had to obey it as well. This is what led Bracton to state *'quod Rex non debet esse sub-homine sed sub Deo et lege'*, meaning 'because the king ought not to be subservient to man, but under God and the law'. This statement of Bracton, made shortly after the Magna Carta was declared, was pressed into service by Sir Edward Coke, the then Chief Justice of the Common Pleas, with his sovereign, King James I of England and Scotland, thus:

The question between them was whether the King, in his own person might take what causes he pleased from the determination of the Judges and determine them himself. This is what Coke says happened: 'Then the King said that he thought the law was founded upon reason and that he and others had reason as well as the Judges; to which it was answered by me, that true it was that God had endowed His Majesty with excellent science and great endowments of nature, but His Majesty

---

[*] Ibid., p. 199.
[†] Id., p. 200.

was not learned in the laws of his realm of England, and causes which concern the life, or inheritance, or goods, or fortunes of his subjects, are not to be decided by natural reason but by the artificial reason and judgment of law, which law is an act which requires long study and experience before that a man can attain to the cognizance of it; and that the law was the golden metwand and measure to try the causes of the subjects; and which protected His Majesty in safety and peace: with which the King was greatly offended, and said, that then he should be under the law, which was treason to affirm, as he said: to which I said that Bracton saith, *quod Rex non debet esse sub-hominesed sub Deo et lege.*' It would be hard to find a single paragraph in which more of the essence of English constitutional law and history could be found. The King ought not to be under a man, *non debet esse sub-homine,* but under God and the law, *sed sub Deo et lege.*`

6. *Gandhi Faiz-E-Am College v. University of Agra and Anr.* (1975)

In *Gandhi Faiz-E-Am College v. University of Agra and Anr.* (1975),[†] Statute 14A of the Agra University came up for consideration, which required each non-government college already affiliated, or when affiliated to the University of Agra, to constitute a governing body of the college on which the staff of the college would be represented by the principal and at least one teacher who would hold office for one academic year. The appellant was a Muslim-minority educational institution which challenged the constitutional validity of Statute 14A, stating that it violated its right to administer, i.e. manage, a minority institution of its choice under Article 30(1) of the Constitution of India, as held in the nine-judge bench in *Ahmedabad St. Xavier College Society v. State of Gujarat* (1974).[‡] The majority judgment sidestepped the finding in the *Ahmedabad St. Xavier College*, holding that Statute 14A is a regulatory clause aimed at improving the administration of the college, and not to inhibit its autonomy. Mathew,

---

[*] Quoted by Mathew, J. in *Indira Gandhi v. Raj Narain* ([1976] 2 SCR 347 at 520 [1f]).
[†] (1975) 2 SCC 283.
[‡] (1974) 1 SCC 717.

J., one of the members of the nine-judge bench in *Ahmedabad St. Xavier College*, dissented, stating:

35. I should have thought that the matter was concluded by the decision of this Court in *Ahmedabad St. Xavier's College Society v. State of Gujarat*. Section 33-A(1)(a) of the Gujarat University Act, 1949, which fell for consideration in that case, among other matters, read:

'33-A.(1) Every college (other than a Government college or a college maintained by the Government) affiliated before the commencement of the Gujarat University (Amendment) Act, 1972 (hereinafter in this section referred to as 'such commencement')—

(a) shall be under the management of a governing body which shall include amongst its members the Principal of the college, a representative of the University nominated by the Vice-Chancellor, and three representatives of the teachers of the college and at least one representative each of the members of the non-teaching staff and the students of the college, to be elected respectively from amongst such teachers, members of the non-teaching staff and students.'

This provision was challenged in that case as violating the fundamental right under Article 30(1) of the minority community in question there. This Court held by a majority that the provision was bad as it offended the fundamental right of the religious minority under Article 30(1) to administer its educational institution. The reason was that the provision required the inclusion, in the governing body of the college, of persons whom the religious minority did not want to include. When Article 30(1) speaks that a religious or linguistic minority has the right to administer educational institutions of its choice, it means that the right to carry on the administration of the institution must be left to the managing body consisting of persons in whom the religious or linguistic minority has faith and confidence.

36. The learned Chief Justice, speaking for himself and Palekar, J., after referring to the provisions of Section 33-A(1)(a) said in that case that the right to administer is the right to conduct and manage the affairs of the institution and that this right is exercised 'through a body of persons in whom the founders of the institution have faith and confidence and who have full autonomy in that sphere'. He further

said that the right to administer is subject to permissible regulatory measures and that permissible regulatory measures are those which do not restrict the right of administration but facilitate it and ensure better and more effective exercise of the right for the benefit of the institution and through the instrumentality of the management of the institution and without displacing the management. He was of the view that if the administration has to be improved, it should be done through the agency or the instrumentality of the existing management and not by displacing it. The learned Chief Justice further observed that autonomy in administration means right to administer effectively and to manage and conduct the affairs of the institutions, that the right of administration means day to day administration and that the choice in the personnel of management is a part of the administration. He concluded by saying:

'The provisions contained in Section 33-A(1)(a) of the Act have the effect of displacing the management and entrusting it to a different agency. The autonomy in administration is lost. New elements in the shape of representatives of different types are brought in. The calm waters of an institution will not only be disturbed but also mixed. These provisions in Section 33-A(1)(a) cannot therefore apply to minority institutions.'

37. Jaganmohan Reddy, J. speaking for himself and Alagiriswami, J. agreed with the view expressed by the learned Chief Justice on the question of the validity of Section 33-A(1)(a) in its application to the minority.

38. Khanna, J. in his concurring judgment said that the argument that a law or regulation could not be deemed unreasonable unless it was totally destructive of the right of the minority to administer educational institutions was fallacious and was negatived by this Court by its previous decisions and that a law which interferes with the minorities choice of a governing body or management council would be violative of the right guaranteed by Article 30(1). This view has been consistently taken by this Court in the cases of *Rt. Rev. S.K. Patro, Mother Provincial and D.A.V. College (affiliated to the Guru Nanak University) (supra)*.

Section 33-A which provides for a new governing body for the management of the college and also for selection committees as well as the constitution thereof would consequently have to be quashed so far as the minority educational institutions are concerned because of the contravention of Article 30(1).

39. On behalf of Chandrachud, J. and myself, I said:

The requirement that the college should have a governing body which shall include persons other than those who are members of the governing body of the Society of Jesus would take away the management of the college from the governing body constituted by the Society of Jesus and vest it in a different body. The right to administer the educational institution established by a religious minority is vested in it. It is in the governing body of the society of Jesus that the religious minority which established the college has vested the right to administer the institution and that body alone has the right to administer the same. The requirement that the college should have a governing body including persons other than those who constitute the governing body of the Society of Jesus has the effect of divesting that body of its exclusive right to manage the educational institution. That it is desirable in the opinion of the Legislature to associate the Principal of the college or the other persons referred to in Section 33-A(1)(a) in the management of the college is not a relevant consideration. The question is whether the provision has the effect of divesting the governing body as constituted by the religious minority of its exclusive right to administer the institution. Under the guise of preventing maladministration, the right of the governing body of the college constituted by the religious minority to administer the institution cannot be taken away.'

xxx xxx xxx

'42. The provisions of Statute 14A are in pari materia with those of Section 33-A(1)(a) of the Act which fell for consideration in *Ahmedabad St. Xavier's College* case *(supra)* except that only the principal and the seniormost member of the staff alone are required to be included in the managing committee of the college in question here. But, in principle, that makes no difference. The principle, as I said, is that the minority community has the exclusive right to vest the administration of the college in a body of its own choice, and any compulsion from an outside authority to include any other person in that body is an abridgment of its fundamental right to administer the educational institution.

43. It is, no doubt, true that it is upon the principal and the teachers that the whole temper and the tone of a college depend. But that does not mean that the principal and the teachers should be members of the governing council of a college. It was only in the context of the right of the religious or linguistic minority to appoint the principal and teachers of the college established by it that we said in *Ahmedabad St. Xavier's College* case *(supra)*:

'It is upon the principal and teachers of a college that the tone and temper of an educational institution depend. On them would depend its reputation, the maintenance of discipline and its efficiency in teaching. The right to choose the principal and to have the teaching conducted by teachers appointed by the management after an overall assessment of their outlook and philosophy is perhaps the most important facet of the right to administer an educational institution. We can perceive no reason why a representative of the University nominated by the Vice-Chancellor should be on the Selection Committee for recruiting the Principal or for the insistence of head of the department besides the representative of the University being on the Selection Committee for recruiting the members of the teaching staff. So long as the persons chosen have the qualifications prescribed by the University, the choice must be left to the management. That is part of the fundamental right of the minorities to administer the educational institution established by them.'

44. While affirming the correctness of the observation in the context in which it was made, I think it necessary to repudiate its relevance and application here.

45. I would, therefore, allow the appeal without any order as to costs.

It must never be forgotten that a fundamental right is to be given the widest reach so as to fulfil its potential—particularly an absolute right such as the right contained in Article 30(1) of the Constitution, which is not subject to reasonable restrictions made by the state; it is only subject to reasonable regulations made, not in the public interest, but in the interest of the minority institution itself. Sidestepping a binding nine-judge-bench judgment by using some observations in support of whittling down the fundamental right, without referring to the other observations which deal with the picture of the fundamental right as a whole, was rightly exposed by Mathew, J. in his dissent, stating that a *pari materia* provision in the state of Gujarat had been held inapplicable to minority institutions.

7. *State of Kerala v. N.M. Thomas* (1976)

State of Kerala v. N.M. Thomas (1976)[*] is one of those seminal decisions in which the law relating to reservation in favour of Scheduled Castes, Scheduled Tribes and Other Backward Communities was completely revamped by a seven-judge bench of the Supreme Court of India. The earlier view—that reservation of posts in the government under Article 16 of the Constitution is an exception to the general rule of equality stated in that article—was done away with by the majority judgments. It was stated that Article 16(1) is only part of a comprehensive scheme to ensure equality in all spheres and is an instance of the larger concept of equality of law. Thus, Article 16(4) cannot be viewed as an exception to Article 16(1), but only as something which logically emanates from Article 16(1). The corollary of this of course is that reservation is not the only means of reaching the goal of equality by affirmative action in favour of those who are downtrodden. In fact, on the facts of this case, Rule 13AA of the Kerala State and Subordinate Services Rules, which empowered the state government to further exempt, for a specified period, members of Scheduled Castes and Scheduled Tribes already in service from passing certain departmental tests, in order that they may be promoted without passing those tests, was held to be constitutionally valid. Khanna, J. and Gupta, J., however, dissented. In Khanna, J.'s view, a constitution is to be construed as a vehicle for the life of a nation and deals with the practical problems of the government. He put it thus:

> 213. In construing the provisions of the Constitution we should avoid a doctrinaire approach. A Constitution is the vehicle of the life of a

---

[*] (1976) 2 SCC 310.

nation and deals with practical problems of the Government. It is, therefore, imperative that the approach to be adopted by the courts while construing the provisions of the Constitution should be pragmatic and not one as a result of which the court is likely to get lost in a maze of abstract theories. Indeed, so far as theories are concerned, human thinking in its full efflorescence, free from constraints and inhibitions, can take such diverse forms that views and reasons apparently logical and plausible can be found both in favour of and against a particular theory. If one eminent thinker supports one view, support for the opposite view can be found in the writings of another equally eminent thinker. Whatever indeed may be the conclusion, arguments not lacking in logic can be found in support of such conclusion. The important task of construing the articles of a Constitution is not an exercise in mere syllogism. It necessitates an effort to find the true purpose and object which underlies that article. The historical background, the felt necessities of the time, the balancing of the conflicting interests must all enter into the crucible when the court is engaged in the delicate task of construing the provisions of a Constitution. The words of Holmes that life of law is not logic but experience have a direct relevance in the above context.

214. Another thing which must be kept in view while construing the provisions of the Constitution is to foresee as to what would be the impact of that construction not merely on the case in hand but also on the future cases which may arise under those provisions. Out of our concern for the facts of one individual case, we must not adopt a construction the effect of which might be to open the door for making all kinds of inroads into a great ideal and desideratum like that of equality of opportunity. Likewise, we should avoid, in the absence of compelling reason, a course that has the effect of unsettling a constitutional position, which has been settled over a long term of years by a series of decisions.

215. The liberal approach that may sometimes have been adopted in upholding classification under Article 14 would in the very nature of things be not apt in the context of Article 16 when we keep in view the object underlying Article 16. Article 14 covers a very wide and general field of equality before the law and the equal protection of the laws. It is, therefore, permissible to cover within its ambit manifold classifications

as long as they are reasonable and have a rational connection with the object thereof. As against that Article 16 operates in the limited area of equality of opportunity for all citizens in matters relating to employment or appointment to an office under the State. Carving out classes of citizens for favoured treatment in matters of public employment, except in cases for which there is an express provision contained in clause (4) of Article 16, would as already pointed out above in the very nature of things run counter to the concept underlying clause (1) of Article 16.

216. The matter can also be looked at from another angle. If it was permissible to accord favoured treatment to members of backward classes under clause (1) of Article 16, there would have been no necessity of inserting clause (4) in Article 16. Clause (4) in Article 16 in such an event would have to be treated as wholly superfluous and redundant. The normal rule of interpretation is that no provision of the Constitution is to be treated as redundant and superfluous. The Court would, therefore, be reluctant to accept a view which would have the effect of rendering clause (4) of Article 16 redundant and superfluous.

xxx xxx xxx

220. The matter can also be looked at from another angle. Departmental tests are prescribed to ensure standards of efficiency for the employees. To promote 34 out of 51 persons although they have not passed the departmental tests and at the same time not to promote those who have passed the departmental tests can hardly be conducive to efficiency. There does not, therefore, appear to be any infirmity in the finding of the High Court that the impugned promotions are also violative of Article 335 of the Constitution.

221. It may state that there is no dispute so far as the question is concerned about the need to make every effort to ameliorate the lot of backward classes, including the members of the scheduled castes and the scheduled tribes. We are all agreed on that. The backwardness of those sections of population is a stigma on our social set-up and has got to be erased as visualized in Article 46 of the Constitution. It may also call for concrete acts to atone for the past neglect and exploitation of those classes with a view to bring them on a footing of equality,

real and effective, with the advanced sections of the population. The question with which we are concerned, however, is whether the method which has been adopted by the appellants is constitutionally permissible under clause (1) of Article 16. The answer to the above question, in my opinion, has to be in the negative. Apart from the fact that the acceptance of the appellants' contention would result in undermining the principle of equality of opportunity enshrined in clause (1) of Article 16, it would also in effect entail overruling of the view which has so far been held by this Court in the cases of *Champakam, Rangachari* and *Devadasan*. I find no sufficient ground to warrant such a course. The State, in my opinion has ample power to make provision for safeguarding the interest of backward classes under clause (4) of Article 16 which deals with reservation of appointments or posts for backward classes not adequately represented in the services under the State. Inaction on the part of the State under clause (4) of Article 16 cannot, in my opinion, justify strained construction of clause (1) of Article 16. We have also to guard against allowing our supposed zeal to safeguard the interests of members of scheduled castes and scheduled tribes to so sway our mind and warp our judgment that we drain off the substance of the contents of clause (1) of Article 16 and whittle down the principle of equality of opportunity in the matter of public employment enshrined in that clause in such a way as to make it a mere pious wish and teasing illusion. The ideals of supremacy of merit, the efficiency of services and the absence of discrimination in sphere of public employment would be the obvious casualties if we once countenance inroads to be made into that valued principle beyond those warranted by clause (4) of Article 16.

Gupta, J. also dissented, agreeing with the view of Khanna, J. The learned judge invoked the principle of harmonious construction of various provisions of the Constitution of India, thus:

224. The lower division clerks working in the Registration Department of the State of Kerala have to pass within a fixed time certain departmental tests to be eligible for promotion as upper division clerks. For some of these lower division clerks who happen to belong to scheduled castes

or scheduled tribes, the time for passing the tests has been extended by successive orders made by the Government in exercise of the power conferred by Rule 13-AA of the Kerala State and Subordinate Services Rules 1958. The High Court of Kerala held that Rule 13-AA was violative of Article 16(1) and (2) of the Constitution and set aside the orders made under that rule. On behalf of the appellant, State of Kerala, and some of the respondents and interveners, validity of Rule 13-AA is sought to be justified on a construction of Article 16(1) which, it is claimed, is based on the provisions of Articles 46 and 335 of the Constitution. It is contended that Article 16(1) should be read in the light of the other two articles. I am not clear as to what exactly that means; neither Article 46 and Article 335 mention Article 16(1), nor Article 16(1) refers to either of them. All the three articles coexist in the Constitution which we, the People of India, have given to ourselves, and if it is correct to say that one of them should be read in the light of the other two, it is equally right to suggest that the two of them should be read in the light of other. This means that the various parts of an organic instrument like the Constitution ought to be harmoniously construed, but that is not the same thing as suggesting that even where the scope and ambit of one part is clear, it should be abridged, extended or amended to prove its affinity with another part. Each limb of the body has its own function, and to try to make one of them do the work of another is both unnecessary and unwise; this might throw the entire system out of gear.

xxx xxx xxx

231. All I have said above relates to the scope of Article 16(1) only, because Counsel for the appellant has built his case on this provision alone. Clause (4) of Article 16 permits reservation of appointments on posts in favour of backward classes of citizens notwithstanding Article 16(1); I agree with the views expressed by Khanna, J., on Article 16(4) which comes in for consideration incidentally in this case. The appalling poverty and backwardness of large sections of the people must move the State machinery to do everything in its power to better their condition but doling out unequal favours to members of the clerical staff does not

seem to be a step in that direction: tilting at the windmill taking it to be a monster serves no useful purpose.

232. It may be pertinent in this connection to refer to the observations of Gajendragadkar, J. (as he then was) in *M.R. Balaji v. State of Mysore* which, though made in the context of Article 15(4), has relevance for this case also:

'When Article 15(4) refers to the special provision for the advancement of certain classes or scheduled castes or scheduled tribes, it must not be ignored that the provision which is authorized to be made is a special provision; it is not a provision which is exclusive in character, so that in looking after the advancement of those classes, the State would be justified in ignoring altogether the advancement of the rest of the society. It is because the interests of the society at large would be served by promoting the advancement of the weaker elements in the society that Article 15(4) authorizes special provision to be made. But if a provision which is in the nature of an exception completely excludes the rest of the society, that clearly is outside the scope of Article 15(4). It would be extremely unreasonable to assume that in enacting Article 15(4) the Parliament intended to provide that where the advancement of the backward classes or the scheduled castes and tribes was concerned, the fundamental rights of the citizens constituting the rest of the society were to be completely and absolutely ignored.'

More recently, in *State of J&K v. T.N. Khosa* this Court has sounded a note of caution:

'. . . let us not evolve, through imperceptible extensions, a theory of classification which may subvert, perhaps submerge, the precious guarantee of equality. The eminent spirit of an ideal society is equality and so we must not be left to ask in wonderment: what after all is the operational residue of equality and equal opportunity?'

I believe these words are not just so much rhetoric, but meant to be taken seriously.

233. I concur with the order proposed by Khanna, J.

The courts have had a difficult time balancing the rights of the Scheduled Castes, Scheduled Tribes and Other Backward Classes with the demand for efficiency in administration and excellence in spheres of activity as higher posts are reached. Despite a Herculean effort to cut the Gordian knot by a majority of nine judges in *Indra Sawhney v. Union of India* (1992),* restricting reservations generally to 50 per cent and cutting out reservation in promotion, the Constitution has been amended to entrench reservation in promotion by introducing Articles 16(4-A) and 16(4-B), which have in turn been upheld as not having damaged or destroyed the basic structure of the Constitution.†

8. *Bangalore Water Supply & Sewerage Board, etc. v. R. Rajappa* (1978)

Bangalore Water Supply & Sewerage Board, etc. v. R. Rajappa & Others (1978),‡ is an attempt by a seven-judge bench of the Supreme Court of India to expand the definition of the term 'industry' in Section 2(j) of the Industrial Disputes Act so as to give it its maximum reach. In so doing, the majority judgment overruled a number of earlier Constitution Bench decisions of the Supreme Court. Y.V. Chandrachud, C.J., Jaswant Singh and Tulzapurkar, JJ. dissented. Y.V. Chandrachud, C.J. held that *State of Bombay v. Hospital Mazdoor Sabha* (1960)§—one of the judgments overruled by the majority—was correctly decided:

> 177. These exceptions which the Court engrafted upon the definition of 'industry' in Section 2(j) in order to give to the definition the merit of reasonableness, became in course of time as many categories of activities exempted from the operation of the definition clause. To an extent, it seems to me clear that though the decision in *Hospital Mazdoor Sabha* that a Government-run hospital was an industry proceeded upon the rejection of the test of '*noscitur a sociis*', it is this very principle which constitutes the rationale of the exceptions carved out by the Court. It was said that the principle of '*noscitur a sociis*' is applicable in cases of doubt and since the language of the definition admitted of no doubt, the

---

* (1992) Supp. (3) SCC 217.
† *M. Nagaraj and Ors. v. Union of India and Ors.* ([2006] 8 SCC 212).
‡ (1978) 2 SCC 213.
§ AIR 1960 SC 610.

principle had no application. But if the language was clear, the definition had to be given the meaning which the words convey and there can be no scope for seeking exceptions. The contradiction, with great respect, is that the Court rejected the test of 'association of words' while deciding whether the Government-run hospital is an industry but accepted that very test while indicating which categories of activities would fall outside the definition. The question then is: If there is no doubt either as to the meaning of the words used by the legislature in Section 2(j) or on the question that these are words of amplitude, what justification can one seek for diluting the concept of industry as envisaged by the legislature?

178. On a careful consideration of the question I am of the opinion that *Hospital Mazdoor Sabha* was correctly decided insofar as it held that the J.J. group of hospitals was an industry but, respectfully, the same cannot be said in regard to the view of the Court that certain activities ought to be treated as falling outside the definition clause.

179. One of the exceptions carved out by the Court is in favour of activities undertaken by the Government in the exercise of its inalienable functions under the Constitution, call it regal, sovereign or by any other name. I see no justification for excepting these categories of public utility activities from the definition of 'industry'. If it be true that one must have regard to the nature of the activity and not to who engages in it, it seems to me beside the point to enquire whether the activity is undertaken by the State, and further, if so, whether it is undertaken in fulfilment of the State's constitutional obligations or in discharge of its constitutional functions. In fact, to concede the benefit of an exception to the State's activities which are in the nature of sovereign functions is really to have regard not so much to the nature of the activity as to the consideration who engages in that activity; for, sovereign functions can only be discharged by the State and not by a private person. If the State's inalienable functions are excepted from the sweep of the definition contained in Section 2(j), one shall have unwittingly rejected the fundamental test that it is the nature of the activity which ought to determine whether the activity is an industry. Indeed, in this respect, it should make no difference whether, on the one hand, an activity is undertaken by a corporate body in the discharge of its statutory functions or, on the other, by the State itself in the exercise of its inalienable

functions. If the water supply and sewerage schemes or firefighting establishments run by a Municipality can be industries, so ought to be the manufacture of coins and currency, arms and ammunition and the winning of oil and uranium. The fact that these latter kinds of activities are, or can only be, undertaken by the State does not furnish any answer to the question whether these activities are industries. When undertaken by a private individual they are industries. Therefore, when undertaken by the State, they are industries. The nature of the activity is the determining factor and that does not change according to who undertakes it. Items 8, 11, 12, 17 and 18 of the First Schedule read with Section 2(n)(vi) of the Industrial Disputes Act render support to this view. These provisions which were described in *Hospital Mazdoor Sabha* as 'very significant' at least show that, conceivably, a defence establishment, a mint or a security press can be an industry even though these activities are, ought to be and can only be undertaken by the State in the discharge of its constitutional obligations or functions. The State does not trade when it prints a currency note or strikes a coin. And yet, considering the nature of the activity, it is engaged in an industry when it does so.

Equally, *National Union of Commercial Employees v. M.R. Meher* (1962),[*] was held to be correctly decided, stating that it is not possible to accept the broad formulation that a solicitor's establishment is an 'industry'. Clubs were also stated to be outside 'industry'.[†] Likewise, Jaswant Singh, J., speaking for himself and Tulzapurkar, J., also held:

185. The definition of the term 'industry' as contained in Section 2(j) of the Industrial Disputes Act which is in two parts being vague and too wide as pointed out by Beg, C.J. and Krishna Iyer, J., we have struggled to find out its true scope and ambit in the light of plethora of decisions of this Court which have been laying down fresh tests from time to time making our task an uphill one. However, bearing in mind the collocation of the terms in which the definition is couched and applying the doctrine of *noscitur a sociis which, as pointed out by this Court in*

---

[*] AIR 1962 SC 1080.
[†] (1978) 2 SCC 213, paragraphs 181–82.

State of *Bombay v. Hospital Mazdoor Sabha*, means that, when two or more words which are susceptible of analogous meaning are coupled together they are understood to be used in their cognate sense. They take as it were their colour from each other, that is, the more general is restricted to a sense analogous to a less general. Expressed differently, it means that the meaning of a doubtful word may be ascertained by reference to the meaning of words associated with it, we are of the view that despite the width of the definition it could not be the intention of the legislature that Categories 2 and 3 of the charities alluded to by our learned Brother Krishna Iyer in his judgment, hospitals run on charitable basis or as a part of the functions of the Government or local bodies like municipalities and educational and research institutions whether run by private entities or by Government and liberal and learned professions like that of doctors, lawyers and teachers, the pursuit of which is dependent upon an individual's own education, intellectual attainments and special expertise should fall within the pale of the definition. We are inclined to think that the definition is limited to those activities systematically or habitually undertaken on commercial lines by private entrepreneurs with the co-operation of employees for the production or distribution of goods or for the rendering of material services to the community at large or a part of such community. It is needless to emphasize that in the case of liberal professions, the contribution of the usual type of employees employed by the professionals to the value of the end product (viz. advice and services rendered to the client) is so marginal that the end product cannot be regarded as the fruit of the co-operation between the professional and his employees.

186. It may be pertinent to mention in this connection that the need for excluding some callings, services and undertakings from the purview of the aforesaid definition has been felt and recognized by this Court from time to time while explaining the scope of the definition of 'industry'. This is evident from the observations made by this Court in *State of Bombay v. Hospital Mazdoor Sabha; Secretary, Madras Gymkhana Club Employees Union v. Management of the Gymkhana Club and Management of Safdarjung Hospital, New Delhi v. Kuldip Singh Sethi.* Speaking for the Bench in *State of Bombay v. Hospital Mazdoor Sabha*, Gajendragadkar, J. (as he then was) observed in this connection thus:

'It is clear, however, that though Section 2(j) uses words of very wide denotation, a line would have to be drawn in a fair and just manner so as to exclude some callings, services or undertakings. If all the words used are given their widest meaning, all services and all callings would come within the purview of the definition; even service rendered by a servant purely in a personal or domestic matter or even in a casual way would fall within the definition. It is not and cannot be suggested that in its wide sweep the word "service" is intended to include service howsoever rendered in whatsoever capacity and for whatsoever reason. We must, therefore, consider where the line should be drawn and what limitations can and should be reasonably implied in interpreting the wide words used in Section 2(j), and that no doubt is a somewhat difficult problem to decide.'

187. In view of the difficulty experienced by all of us in defining the true denotation of the term 'industry' and divergence of opinion in regard thereto—as has been the case with this Bench also—we think, it is high time that the legislature steps in with a comprehensive bill to clear up the fog and remove the doubts and set at rest once for all the controversy which crops up from time to time in relation to the meaning of the aforesaid term rendering it necessary for larger Benches of this Court to be constituted which are driven to the necessity of evolving a working formula to cover particular cases.

In 1982, Parliament did step in and redefine 'industry', following the minority judgment in *Bangalore Water Supply*, as follows:[*]

(j) 'industry' means any systematic activity carried on by co-operation between an employer and his workmen (whether such workmen are employed by such employer directly or by or through any agency, including a contractor) for the production, supply or distribution of goods or services with a view to satisfy human wants or wishes (not being wants or wishes which are merely spiritual or religious in nature), whether or not,—

---

[*] Section 2(c), Act 46 of 1982.

(i) any capital has been invested for the purpose of carrying on such activity; or

(ii) such activity is carried on with a motive to make any gain or profit,

and includes—

(a) any activity of the Dock Labour Board established under section 5A of the Dock Workers (Regulation of Employment) Act, 1948;

(b) any activity relating to the promotion of sales business or both carried on by an establishment,

but does not include—

(1) any agricultural operation except where such agricultural operation its carried on in an integrated manner with any other activity (being any such activity as is referred to in the foregoing provisions of this 0.ause) and such other activity is the predominant one.

Explanation,—For the purposes of this sub-clause, 'agricultural operation' does not include any activity carried on in a plantation as defined in clause (f) of section 2 of the Plantations Labour Act, 1951; or

(2) hospitals or dispensaries; or

(3) educational, scientific, research or training institutions; or

(4) institutions owned or managed by organizations wholly or substantially engaged in any charitable, social or philanthropic service; or

(5) khadi or village industries; or

(6) any activity of the Government relatable to the sovereign functions of the Government including all the activities carried on by the departments of the Central Government dealing with defence research, atomic energy and space; or

(7) any domestic service; or

(8) any activity, being a profession practised by an individual or body of individuals, if the number of persons employed by the individual or body of individuals in relation to such profession is less than ten; or

(9) any activity, being an activity carried on by a cooperative society or a club or any other like body of individuals, if the number of persons employed by the co-operative society, club or other like body of individuals in relation to such activity is less than ten;

However, over two decades later, the law remains in limbo for two reasons—this amended definition has not yet been brought into force, and the majority judgment in *Bangalore Water Supply* has been referred to a bench of nine judges for reconsideration.*

9. *Supreme Court Advocates-on-Record Association v. Union of India* (1993)

The judgment of a nine-judge bench in *Supreme Court Advocates-on-Record Association and another v. Union of India* (1993),[†] popularly referred to as the 'Second Judges' case, is of seminal importance in the constitutional scheme of the appointment of judges to the higher judiciary in this country. Nine learned judges of the Supreme Court overturned the settled position on the appointment of judges, which had stood from 1950 till 1993, taking the view that the majority decision in the 'First Judges' case—*S.P. Gupta and Ors. v. Union of India and Ors.* (1981)[‡]—was incorrect and therefore overruling it. The focal point of *Supreme Court Advocates-on-Record Association* hinged upon whether the expression 'consultation' in Article 124(2) of the Constitution would mean 'concurrence', which would imply that the ultimate decision to appoint a member of the superior judiciary vests with the Chief Justice of India. A majority of seven out of the nine learned judges took this view. Justices Ahmadi and Punchhi dissented. In a tour de force, Ahmadi, J. candidly admitted that the Constitution is what the judges say it is.[§] This being so, it is all the more important that complete objectivity be maintained while interpreting constitutional provisions which relate to the power of the judiciary. The learned judge put it felicitously thus:

> 271. A word of caution before we proceed further. The Constitution is what the Judges say it is. That is because the power to interpret the Constitution vests in the Judges. A heavy responsibility lies on the

---

* *Bangalore Water Supply* (supra) was referred to a nine-judge bench in *State of Uttar Pradesh v. Jai Bir Singh* ([2017] 3 SCC 311).
[†] (1993) 4 SCC 441.
[‡] (1981) Supp. SCC 87.
[§] (1993) 4 SCC 441, paragraph 271.

Judges when they are called upon to interpret the Constitution, the responsibility is all the more heavier when the provisions to be construed relate to the powers of the judiciary. It is essential that complete objectivity is maintained while interpreting the constitutional provisions relating to the power of the judiciary vis-à-vis the executive in the matter of appointments to the superior judiciary to avoid any feeling amongst the other constitutional functionaries that there has been usurpation of power through the process of interpretation. This is not to say that the judiciary should be unduly concerned about such criticism but merely to emphasize that the responsibility is greater in such cases. To put it differently where the language of the Constitution is plain and the words used are not ambiguous, care should be taken to avoid giving an impression that fancied ambiguities have been conjured with a view to making it possible to place a convenient construction on the provisions. If the words are plain and unambiguous, effect must be given to them, for that is the constituent body's intent, whether you like it or not, and any seeming attempt to depart therefrom under the guise of interpretation of imaginary ambiguities would cast a serious doubt on the credibility and impartiality of the judiciary. It would seem as if judges have departed from their sworn duty; any such feeling would rudely shock peoples' confidence and shake the very foundation on which the judicial edifice stands. The concern of the judiciary must be to faithfully interpret the constitutional provisions according to its true scope and intent because that alone can enhance public confidence in the judicial system.

After dealing with the English and American systems of appointment of judges, the learned judge stated that our founding fathers adopted a middle course—by conferring power on the executive to appoint judges, but only after consultation with the Chief Justice of India. The learned judge was at pains to point out that it is the executive who appoints the higher judiciary in these nations, as well as in Australia, Canada and New Zealand.*

The learned judge went on to state that as a matter of pure language, the word 'consultation' had been very carefully selected, as it was used in Articles 217 and 222 as well, whereas the expression 'consent' was used by

---

* Ibid., paragraphs 277–79.

way of contrast in Article 224-A.* Going then to the articles which deal with the lower judiciary, Ahmadi, J. noted that the high court is given a pivotal role in their appointment. However, in this case, the appointment of a high court judge must be preceded by consultation with three constitutional functionaries—the Chief Justice of India, the chief justice of the state high court and the Governor of the state. The proposal to appoint, as a matter of constitutional convention, comes from the chief justice of the high court, who knows about the professional competence of the person. The executive's role is to find out how such person is otherwise, namely, the antecedents of the individual, his political affiliations, his associations, his other interests in life, and so on. The learned judge put it thus:

> 290. Insofar as appointment to the High Court is concerned, the same is governed by Article 217(1). We have reproduced the text of this article earlier. The appointment has to be made by the President by warrant under his hand and seal. But it must be preceded by 'consultation' with the Chief Justice of India, the Chief Justice of the State and the Governor of the State. Consultation with these three functionaries is a condition precedent and a *sine qua non* to appointment. It is common knowledge that the proposal ordinarily emanates from the Chief Justice of the High Court who forwards it to the Chief Minister. The Chief Minister scrutinizes the proposal and if he needs any clarification he must interact with the Chief Justice. If he or the Governor has any suggestion to make or names to propose they may do so and forward the same to the Chief Justice who may examine the suggestions and send his response. The Chief Minister must then forward the proposal, with the comments of the Chief Justice, if any, in consultation with the Governor to the Minister of Law and Justice in the Central Government. The Minister of Law and Justice would then consult the Chief Justice of India and the Prime Minister and then forward the papers with the advice to the President who will thereupon issue the warrant of appointment. On a plain reading of Article 217(1) it becomes clear that the President is empowered to make the appointment 'after' consultation with the three constitutional functionaries. The article does not give any

---

* Id., paragraph 284.

indication of any hierarchy among the three consultees. These three functionaries are those who are consulted, they have a consultative role to play in the appointment of a High Court Judge but the ultimate power of appointment rests in the President who must act in accordance with Article 74(1) of the Constitution. The power conferred on the President is not an absolute or arbitrary power but the same is checked, circumscribed and conditioned by the requirement of prior consultation with the three constitutional functionaries. The consultation must be complete, purposive and meaningful and cannot be treated as a mere idle formality. If the consultation is found to be a mere empty formality without effective exchange of views, the appointment would be vitiated and the whole exercise may ultimately turn out to be love's labour lost. Each of the three constitutional functionaries holds a high constitutional position and it is difficult to see how, in the absence of express words, it can be said that there is a hierarchy envisaged by the said provision. It must be remembered that the Chief Justice of the High Court must be attributed intimate knowledge regarding the quality of legal acumen of the members of the Bar chosen by him for appointment. Since he has the opportunity to watch the performance of the members of the Bar at close quarters, he is best suited to assess the worth of the candidate relating to his legal knowledge, acumen and similar other qualities, including his willingness to work hard and his temperament to discharge judicial functions. From that point of view great weight must be attached to the opinion of the Chief Justice of the High Court. On other matters, such as, the antecedents of the individual, his political affiliations, if any, his other interests in life, his associations etc. the executive alone may provide the information. Similarly, the executive would be able to collect information regarding the honesty and integrity of the individual and certain other related matters which may have a bearing on his appointment. Thus the opinion of the executive in this area would be equally important. From both these opinions would emerge the personality of the candidate proposed for appointment. The Chief Justice of India being 'paterfamilias' of the judiciary in India would have the advantage of the views of both these consultees and, where necessary, he may also be able to interact with the Chief Justice of the High Court as well as colleagues on the Supreme Court Bench from that Court, if any, before formulating his view finally in the matter. His view, thus formulated would certainly be entitled to greater weight since he had the benefit of filtering the views of the other two consultees on the question of suitability of the proposed candidate, but can it mean that his view will totally eclipse the view of the others forbidding the executive to evaluate it before formulating its advice to be tendered to the President? We will leave this as a poser for the present and proceed to consider the process of appointment under Article 124(2) of the Constitution.

Stressing the language used in Article 124(2), and comparing it with the language used in various other articles, the learned judge put it thus:

> 293. From the relevant provisions of the Constitution concerning the judiciary which we have referred to and reproduced hereinbefore, it is evident that the Constitution has used different expressions to meet with different situations. The word 'consultation' is used in Articles 124(2), 217(1) and (3) and 233(1), the expression 'previous consent' is used in Articles 127, 128 and 224-A, the word 'recommended' is used in Article 233(2), and the word 'approval' is used in Article 145 and proviso to Article 229(2) of the Constitution. Reference to these provisions is illustrative and not exhaustive.

After going into the legislative history of Article 124 and the *Constituent Assembly Debates*—in particular the amendment proposed by Mr B. Pocker Sahib, that the expression 'concurrence' be used in the place of 'consultation', which was rejected by the Constituent Assembly—the learned judge came to the conclusion:

> 303. . . . There being no hierarchy contemplated by Article 217(1) each consultee has a definite contribution to make which need not be ignored. The opinions of the consultees both under Article 124(2) and 217(1) are intended to act as checks on the exercise of discretion by the executive which will be accountable to the people. It would be in exceptional cases that the executive would depart from the collective uniform advice of all the consultees. Take even a case where the Chief Justice of India expresses an opinion after consulting two of his colleagues. What if the opinion of his colleagues differs? Still his opinion will prevail! Then the President consults a few Judges of the Supreme Court and the High Courts and

their uniform opinion conflicts with that of the Chief Justice of India. It would be unfair if the opinion of the other consultees is rendered redundant because it does not concur with the opinion of the Chief Justice of India. It is one thing to say that great weight should be attached to the opinion of the Chief Justice of India and another thing to say that amongst the consultees his word will be final. We, therefore, find it difficult to hold that the opinion of the entire judiciary is symbolized in the view of the Chief Justice of India and the President is bound to act in accordance therewith under Article 74(1) of the Constitution. Such a view may tend to make the Chief Justice of India insensitive to the views of the other consultees and may embroil him in avoidable litigation. If the President has to act on the aid and advice of the Council of Ministers it is difficult to hold that he is bound by the opinion of the Chief Justice of India unless we hold that the Council of Ministers including the Prime Minister would be bound by the opinion of the Chief Justice of India, a construction which to our mind is too artificial and strained to commend acceptance. We think, such an interpretation of the constitutional provisions would tantamount to rewriting the Constitution under the guise of interpretation which would distort the judicature fabric found woven into the Constitution. Therefore, however convincing it may sound to the ideal of judicial independence that the views of the Chief Justice of India must have primacy as his views expressed after consulting his two senior most colleagues would be symbolic of the views of the entire judiciary, the submission cannot be accepted unless the Constitution is amended. As the constitutional provisions presently stand, the submission based on this line of reasoning is unacceptable. For the foregoing reasons, but subject to the qualifications in the concluding paragraph, we do not think the majority view in *S.P. Gupta* case articulated in the judgments of Bhagwati, Fazal Ali, Desai and Venkataramiah, JJ. requires reconsideration on this aspect of the matter.

Ahmadi, J.'s final conclusion was stated thus:

313. We conclude:

i.   The concept of judicial independence is deeply ingrained in our constitutional scheme and Article 50 illuminates it. The degree of independence is near total after a person is appointed and inducted in the judicial family.

ii.   The method of selecting a judge for the Supreme Court and the High Court is outlined in Articles 124(2) and 217(1) of the Constitution. While in the United States, the United Kingdom, Australis and Canada appointments to the superior judiciary are exclusively by the executive, our Constitution has charted a middle course by providing for 'prior consultation' with the judiciary before the President, i.e. the executive, makes the appointment to the Supreme Court or the High Courts. Therefore, however convincing it may sound to the ideal of judicial independence that the views of the Chief Justice of India must have primacy as his views expressed after consulting his two senior most colleagues would he symbolic of the views of the entire judiciary, the submission cannot be accepted unless the Constitution is amended. As the constitutional provisions presently stand, the submission based on this line of reasoning is unacceptable.

iii. Under our constitutional scheme prior consultation with the Chief Justice of India is a must under Articles 124(2), 217(1), 217(3) and 222(1) but the weight to be attached to the views of the Chief Justice of India would depend on whether it is at the pre-appointment stage or the post-appointment stage and whether he is one of the consultees or the sole consultee.

iv.   The concept of primacy to be accorded to the views of the Chief Justice of India has three elements, namely, (a) primacy as 'pater familias' of Indian Judiciary, (b) primacy to be accorded to his views amongst the consultees mentioned in Articles 124(2), 217(1) and (c) primacy in the sense that the opinion of the Chief Justice of India would be binding on the President, i.e., the executive.

The position of the Chief Justice of India under the Constitution is unique, in that, on the judicial side he is primus inter pares, i.e. first among equals, while on the administrative side he enjoys limited primacy in regard to managing of the court business. As regards primacy to be accorded to his views vis-à-vis the President, i.e. the executive, although his views may be entitled to great weight he does not enjoy a right of veto, in the sense that the President is not bound to act according to his views. However, his views would be of higher value vis-à-vis the views of his colleagues, more so if he has expressed them after assessing the views of his colleagues but his view will not eclipse the views of his colleagues forbidding the President, i.e. the executive, from relying of them. The weight to be attached to his views would be much greater as compared to the weight to be accorded to the views of the other consultees under Article 217(1) since he has had the advantage of filtering their views and ordinarily his views should prevail except for strong and cogent reasons to the contrary but that does not mean that the views of the other consultees would be rendered irrelevant or non-est forbidding the President, i.e. executive, from noticing or relying on them. The views of the Chief Justice of India would be entitled to even greater weight when he is the sole consultee under the constitution, e.g. Article 222(1), more so when it concerns a member of the judicial family and ordinarily his view should be accepted and acted upon by the President, i.e. the executive, unless there are compelling reasons to act otherwise to be recorded in writing so that the apprehension of the executive having acted in a manner tantamounting to interference with judicial independence is dispelled. Thus graded weight has to be attached to the views of the Chief Justice of India as indicated hereinabove.

v.   There is nothing in the language of Article 222(1) to rule out a second transfer of a once transferred judge without his consent but ordinarily the same must be avoided unless there exist pressing circumstances making it unavoidable. Ordinarily a transfer effected in public interest may not be punitive but all the same the Chief Justice of India must take great care to ensure that in the guise of public interest the judge is not being penalized.

vi.   The question of fixation of judge-strength under Article 216 is justiciable, in that, a limited *mandamus* can issue to the executive to perform its constitutional duty within a reasonable time in the manner and to the extent indicated in the direction given by Venkataramiah, J. *S.P. Gupta*'s case. But this would be in the rarest of rare cases where there exist glaring and compelling circumstance which would force the hands of the Court.

vii. We respectfully do not agree with the observations made in the judgment of Brother Verma, J. in regard to the application of the principle of seniority and legitimate expectation, etc. for reasons stated hereinbefore.

Punchhi, J. agreed with Ahmadi, J., and set forth his disagreement with the majority judgment as follows:

> 510. I am in disagreement, though regretfully but respectfully, with the views of the majority in virtually rewriting the Constitution to assign a role to the Chief Justice of India, in the whole conspectus of the Constitution, as symbolic in character and to his being a mere spokesman representing the supposed views of entire judiciary. I also disagree, likewise, in the creation of and vesting of powers assumed, in the hands of the oligarchy representing the judiciary as a whole created by adding words to the Constitution by interpretative exercise so as to silence the singular voice of the Chief Justice of India for ever. I also disagree to the denial of judicial review on the subject on the supposition that it would be the judiciary's act, as that is against the basic structure of the Constitution. Subject to the views afore-expressed, I am, by and large, in respectful agreement with the opinion of my learned brother Ahmadi, J. Necessarily and sequelly, save to the views afore-expressed by me, I am in respectful disagreement with the views of my learned Brethren Pandian and Kuldip Singh, JJ. since they are supportive of the majority view, save and except where their views accord with mine and that of brother Ahmadi, J.

As is well known, the aftermath of this judgment was the enactment of the Constitution (Ninety-Ninth Amendment) Act, 2014, the establishment of a 'National Judicial Appointments Commission', which would consist of the Chief Justice of India, the two senior-most judges, the law minister and two eminent persons who were to be selected by the mandated procedure. This constitutional amendment in turn became the subject matter of challenge and was struck down as unconstitutional by a five-judge bench in *Supreme Court Advocates on Record Association v. Union of India* (2016)[*] by a majority of four judges, with Chelameswar, J. dissenting.[†]

The constitutional position since 1993 has therefore continued. India is perhaps the only nation where a collegium of judges, headed by the Chief Justice of India, has the final say in judicial appointments to the higher judiciary. How well this system has worked has been the subject matter of intense debate. However, many legal experts regard the present system as being the lesser of two evils.[‡]

10. *Mafatlal Industries v. Union of India* (1997)

In *Mafatlal Industries v. Union of India* (1997),[§] a nine-judge bench of the Supreme Court overruled a Constitution Bench decision in *Sales Tax Officer, Benaras & Ors. v. Kanhaiya Lal Mukundlal Saraf* (1959),[⁷] in which it was held that Section 72 of the Indian Contract Act, 1872, could be invoked so that the refund of an illegal tax may be granted to an assessee as a matter of law, without taking into consideration whether such assessee would be unjustly enriched thereby. The majority judgment of B.P. Jeevan Reddy, J., on behalf of himself and four other learned judges, overruled *Kanhaiya Lal*, holding that the doctrine of unjust enrichment is a just and salutary doctrine in which no person can seek to collect duty

---

[*] (2016) 5 SCC 1.

[†] Chelameswar, J.'s dissent in *Supreme Court Advocates on Record Association* (supra) is discussed in detail in Chapter VII.

[‡] Justice Kirby strongly believes that politicians alone should appoint judges; in 'Appellate Courts and Dissent', New South Wales Judicial Officers' Bulletin (2004), p. 5, he says: 'Contrary to received wisdom, the capacity of politicians, elected by the people, to influence over time the composition of important courts in Australia, is not a weakness of our constitutional and judicial system. It is a strength. It is precisely how the Constitution is expected to work. I do not agree with the idea of judicial appointment commissions made up mainly of judges, lawyers and other worthies from the elite. Such bodies, almost certainly would, clone-like, reproduce judges just like themselves. We do not need this. I witnessed the strength of diversity in the judiciary in the Court of Appeal of New South Wales. I discovered, truly, that diversity of judicial outlook was a most precious intellectual commodity. The conception of invariable certainty about the law, or incontestable judicial outcomes, is an infantile belief. Contemporary judges owe it to the people whom they serve to explain why this is so.'

[§] (1997) 5 SCC 536.

[⁷] (1959) SCR 1350.

from his purchaser at one end, and also claim refund of the same duty from the state on the ground that it has been levied and collected contrary to law. It was further held that Section 72 of the Indian Contract Act, which incorporates a rule of equity must therefore take into account other equitable considerations as well. S.C. Sen, J. differed from this viewpoint. According to him, there was no need to revisit *Kanhaiya Lal*:

> 209. To sum up, under the Central Excises and Salt Act, 1944, there is only one duty and that has been imposed on manufacture. This duty has to be paid before clearance. This duty has to be paid in the manner and mode laid down by the Act. The Act does not impose any other duty. The Act is not concerned with what happens after the goods have been cleared. If the duty has been erroneously imposed, the refund of the duty must be made to the person on whom it is imposed. Refund of tax must not be confused with restitution or compensation. In my judgment, there is only one taxpayer and it is the person who pays the tax at the time of clearance of goods. There is no other tax imposed by the Central Excise Act. How the burden of tax is borne or its economic impact on the manufacturer are not matters within the purview of the Central Excise Act. No notice of these considerations can be taken in deciding the application for refund by the Excise Officer. Article 265 of the Constitution enjoins that no duty shall be levied and collected except in accordance with law. If it is found that a manufacturer has been asked to pay more than what he is liable to pay under the Central Excise Act, he is immediately entitled to get the refund of the wrongfully collected duty. This constitutional guarantee cannot be sidetracked in any manner.

Dealing with the argument based on unjust enrichment, the learned judge held:

> 248. In my view, the entire argument based on 'unjust enrichment' is founded on a false premise. It will be wrong to assume that the duty element can be included in the price and that no prejudice will be caused to the manufacturer by the levy or enhancement of the duty. To take this position is to ignore the economic realities.

249. There may also be a situation when a manufacturer will not be able to certify that he has not passed on the duty even though he has borne it. Supposing a manufacturer is charging Rs 100 per unit of goods. The price of Rs 100 is calculated on the basis of Rs 80 as costs, Rs 10 as profits and Rs 10 as excise duty. The excise duty element is enhanced unlawfully by Rs 5. In such a case, the manufacturer may either raise the price of the goods by Rs 5 or he may decide to reduce his profit to Rs 5 and sell the goods at the same price. In the second case when the manufacturer reduces the profit element to Rs 5 and sells the goods at Rs 100, can it be said that he has passed on the burden of excise duty to his customers. The price is inclusive of the duty element. In a sense, the burden of duty borne by the manufacturer has been passed on. But then again, the manufacturer has suffered diminution of profit. Can it be said in such a case that if the manufacturer manages to get an order of refund of duty, it will be unethical for him to get the amount because this will be 'unlawful enrichment'? The manufacturer in a case like this will not be in a position to certify that the burden of duty has not been included in the price of the goods but the fact remains that in order to maintain the price of goods at the optimum level the manufacturer had to suffer loss of profit. The Central Government has been empowered to exempt, generally or absolutely by notification, excisable goods from the whole or any part of the duty imposed thereon. Judicial notice must be taken that in very many cases, having regard to the hardship suffered by the industry and representations made by the industry, duties have been reduced or exempted by issuing appropriate notifications or even by legislation.

Dealing with Section 64-A of the Sale of Goods Act, 1930, the learned judge then held:

268. The position gets curiouser after the deposit. After adjustment of the tax against the deposit, the surplus amount is not returned to the manufacturer. It has to be credited to the Fund or paid to the person who has borne the incidence of tax, i.e., the ultimate consumer. In other words, the manufacturer will be robbed of a portion of his sale price for no rhyme or reason. This may also have the effect of nullifying the sale contract entered into by the manufacturer with the buyer. The buyer had agreed to pay an agreed price which may include the duty element.

The seller agreed to sell the goods to the buyer at that price. Section 64-A of the Sale of Goods Act protects the interests of both. How can a portion of that price be taken away and credited to a Fund or paid to the ultimate consumer? What will happen to the contract? The only effect of Section 11-D is to rob the manufacturer of a portion of his legitimate dues. These provisions are not in aid of the charge on manufacture levied by the Central Excise Act, but are in excess of the charge and are confiscatory in nature and have to be struck down.

In this view of the matter, it was therefore concluded:

278. In conclusion, I hold that the Government is permitted to levy and retain only that much of excise duty which can be lawfully levied and collected under the Central Excise Act read with the Central Excise Tariff Act, 1985 and the Central Excise Rules and various notifications issued from time to time. Anything collected beyond this is unlawful and cannot be retained by the Government under any pretext. The illegal levy and collection of duty violates not only the Central Excise Act and the Rules but also offends Article 265 of the Constitution of India.

279. I am of the view that the provision of Section 11-B is a device for denying the claim for refund of duty to a taxpayer and must be struck down as violative of Article 265 of the Constitution. It in effect tries to perpetuate an illegal levy without altering the basis of the law under which the levy was made in any way. It is also a colourable piece of legislation and must be struck down.

280. Section 11-D imposes unreasonable restriction on the right to carry trade and violates Article 19(1)(g). Excise authority cannot deny the manufacturer the freedom to commerce and trade and take away a portion of the contract price even without raising any demand or giving any hearing. The Excise Officer cannot under any circumstance give the balance to the ultimate consumer or credit the amount to the Fund. Section 11-D is arbitrary and is a colourable piece of legislation and is hereby struck down.

281. Sections 12-C and 12-D are parts of a device to withhold refunds of unlawfully gathered tax. These provisions are also violative of Article 265 of the Constitution.

11. *ITC. Ltd. v. Agricultural Produce Market Committee & Ors.* (2002)

In *ITC Limited v. Agricultural Produce Market Committee & Ors.* (2002),[*] the question that arose was whether the Tobacco Board Act, 1975, was constitutionally valid; and consequently, whether the Agricultural Produce Markets Acts of certain states (to the extent these state legislations deal with the sale of tobacco in market areas) were constitutionally valid.

In an earlier round of litigation, in *ITC Ltd. v. State of Karnataka* (1985),[†] a three-judge bench decided—by a majority of 2:1—that Agricultural Produce Markets Acts made under Entry 28 of List II of the Seventh Schedule to the Constitution of India were *ultra vires*, to the extent that they dealt with the sale of tobacco in market areas—the said field being an 'abstracted' field of legislation under the Tobacco Board Act, 1975, read with the declaration made under Section 2 thereof.

By a majority of 3:2, the judgment in *ITC v. Agricultural Produce Market Committee* overruled the majority opinion in the earlier *ITC* case. It did so by referring to a Constitution Bench decision in *Tika Ramji v. State of U.P.* (1956),[‡] stating that the expression 'industry' in Entry 52 of List I of the Seventh Schedule has a restricted meaning—it includes the process of manufacture or production, but does not include processes antecedent or subsequent thereto, such as the acquisition of raw material and the disposal of the finished products of that industry. G.B. Patnaik, J., joined by Bharucha, C.J., differed with the majority judgment. The three questions that arose for determination were set out thus:

> 182. Though several counsel have raised contentions in different forms as indicated earlier, but essentially the following questions arise for our determination:
>
> 1. Whether the Tobacco Board Act enacted by Parliament under Entry 52 of List I can be held to be constitutionally valid and within the legislative competence of Parliament, so far as the provisions

---

[*] (2002) 9 SCC 232.
[†] (1985) Supp. SCC 476.
[‡] (1956) SCR 393.

contained in the same in relation to the growing of tobacco and sale of raw materials are concerned, and this in turn would depend upon the question whether the word 'industry' used in Entry 52 of List I should be given a restricted meaning;

2. Even if the Tobacco Board Act is held to be constitutionally valid and the Agricultural Produce Markets Act is also held to be constitutionally valid and within the powers of the State Legislature, so far as the purchase and sale of tobacco within the market area is concerned, whether both the Acts can be allowed to operate, as was held by the minority judgment in *ITC* case;

3. If there is repugnancy between the two then whether the Central Act would prevail, as was held by the majority judgment in *ITC* case.

The relevant Entries in the Seventh Schedule of the Constitution were then set out as follows:

List I
7. Industries declared by Parliament by law to be necessary for the purpose of defence or for the prosecution of war.

* * *

52. Industries, the control of which by the Union is declared by Parliament by law to be expedient in the public interest.
List II
24. Industries subject to the provisions of Entries 7 and 52 of List I.

* * *

27. Production, supply and distribution of goods subject to the provisions of Entry 33 of List III.
28. Markets and fairs.

The minority judgment then went on to deal with the sheet anchor of the majority view—the reliance upon *Tika Ramji*, which constricted the scope of the word 'industry' occurring in Entry 52 of List I, as stated hereinabove. The minority judgment made it clear that *Tika Ramji* and its progeny would not apply to Entry 52 of List I, as that case dealt with different legislation, made under a different Entry:

189. . . It would, therefore, be necessary to examine what really this Court in Tika Ramji has held. At the outset, it may be noticed that in none of these cases, relied upon by Mr Dwivedi, namely, *Tika Ramji, Calcutta Gas, Kannan Devan*, and *Ganga Sugar* the competence of Parliament to make any law referable to Entry 52 of List I had not been questioned. In Tika Ramji the question for consideration was whether the Act passed by the State Legislature and notification issued thereunder are repugnant to the Parliament Act and notification issued thereunder. On examining the provisions of the State Act, namely, the Sugarcane Act, the Court held that the said law concerns solely with the regulation of supply and purchase of sugarcane and in no way trenched upon the jurisdiction of the Centre with regard to sugar and on scrutiny of Section 18-G of the Industries (Development and Regulation) Act, the Court held that the Act, more specifically Section 18-G did not cover sugarcane nor even Parliament's intention to cover the entire field could be inferred. The Court was required to find out the meaning of the expression 'any article or class of articles relatable to any scheduled industry' used in Section 18-G and it held that it did not refer to the raw materials but only to the finished products. The Court went into the object of the Central Act which was equitable distribution and availability of manufactured articles at fair prices. The argument that had been advanced in that case was that the Sugarcane Act enacted by the State Legislature though appears to be a legislation in regard to sugarcane required for use in the sugar factory but in pith and substance its true nature is a legislation in regard to sugar industry which had been declared under the Industries (Development and Regulation) Act and control of the industry has been taken over by the Union. Negativing that contention and on examining the contents of Entry 24 of List II and Entry 27 of the said List II, the Court observed that the controlled industries were relegated to Entry 52 of List I which was the exclusive province of Parliament leaving the other industries within Entry 24 of List II. In that case, the Court was not required to examine the content and scope of the expression 'industry'

in Entry 52 of List I and in fact the Court observed that it was concerned with as to whether the raw materials of an industry which form an integral part of the process are within the topic of 'industry' which form the subject-matter of Item 52 of List I. The Central legislation which was under consideration in that case as well as the notifications issued by the Central Government were held to have been enacted by Parliament in exercise of the legislative power conferred upon it by Entry 33 of List III and was an exercise of concurrent jurisdiction and once the law is made by Parliament in exercise of its concurrent jurisdiction, then it would not deprive the Provincial Legislatures of similar powers which they had under the Provincial Legislative List. It is important to notice the findings of the Court in that case:

'It also follows as a necessary corollary that, even though sugar industry was a controlled industry, none of these Acts enacted by the Centre was in exercise of its jurisdiction under Entry 52 of List I.'

Whatever observations the Court made on which Mr Dwivedi placed strong reliance, therefore, cannot be made use of indicating the ambit and contents of the expression 'industry' under Entry 52 of List I. When the Court observed that the term 'industry' which would be capable of comprising three different aspects: (i) raw materials which are an integral part of the industrial process, (ii) the process of manufacture or production, and (iii) the distribution of the products of the industry, and held that raw materials should be goods which would be comprised of Entry 27 of List II and the process of manufacture or production would be comprised in Entry 24 of List II, except where the industry was a controlled industry when it would fall under Entry 52 of List I, the Court was obviously not examining the contents of the expression 'industry' under Entry 52 of List I and that is why the Court observed that the legislation which was enacted by the Centre in regard to sugar and sugarcane could fall within Entry 52 of List I. When the legislation in question that was under consideration was held not to be legislation under Entry 52 of List I, the question of applying the *ratio* in the case of *Tika Ramji* in the context of Parliament's power to make a law under Entry 52 of List I and the content and scope of such law or the scope and content of the expression 'industry' under Entry 52 of List I cannot have any application and consequently, on the basis of the judgment of this Court in Tika Ramji it cannot be contended that the expression 'industry' in Entry 52 of List I must have a restricted meaning. It is further apparent from the conclusion of the Court in that case when it refused to import the pith-and-substance argument, holding that the same cannot be imported for the simple reason that both the Centre as well as the State Legislatures were operating in the concurrent field and, therefore there was no question of any trespass upon the exclusive jurisdiction vested in the Centre under Entry 52 of List I. In other words in Tika Ramji neither this Court was called upon to examine the content of the expression 'industry' under Entry 52 of List I nor had the relevant Central law which was under consideration been enacted with reference to power under Entry 52 of List I. This being the position, we do not find much force in the submission of Mr Dwivedi that the conclusion recorded by the majority view in *ITC* case is vitiated, as it had not noticed observations of the Constitution Bench decision in Tika Ramji. In our opinion, it would be wholly inappropriate for this Court to apply the observations made in *Tika Ramji* case with regard to raw materials of 'industry'. The Court in *Tika Ramji* case having not been called upon to determine the question whether the expression 'industry' in Entry 52 of List I should be given a restricted meaning at all as contended by Mr Dwivedi, it would be wholly inappropriate to import the observations in Tika Ramji for construing the ambit and content of the subject head of legislation 'industry' under Entry 52 of List I. Since the Court was examining the provisions of the Industries (Development and Regulation) Act, which regulated the manufacturing process until Section 18-G was brought in amendment in the year 1953 and the Industries (Development and Regulation) Act did not purport to regulate the trade and commerce in the raw materials, namely, sugarcane and the Court in fact was scrutinizing whether the State Act enacted by the State Legislature could be held to be repugnant to the Central legislation, it found that there exists no repugnancy and the two Acts cover two different fields and would coexist. In this view of the matter any observations or conclusion of the Court in Tika Ramji will be of no assistance to us for arriving at a decision as to whether the term 'industry' in Entry 52 of List I would have a restricted meaning or would have a wide meaning, which is the normal interpretation of every entry in the respective lists. In *Calcutta Gas* case no doubt Tika Ramji had been followed and the Court was examining the two competing entries in List II itself of the Seventh Schedule of the Constitution, namely, Entries 24 and 25. While Entry 24 of List II is 'industry', Entry 25 is 'gas and gasworks' and the question, therefore was whether law made by the State Legislature on the subject head 'gas and gasworks' would prevail over a law made by the State Legislature over the subject 'industry' and the Court held that 'gas and gasworks' being a special subject head, law made thereunder would prevail over any law made under the general head 'industries'. It may be observed that in *Calcutta Gas* case, it has been held:

'It is not necessary in this case to attempt to define the expression "industry" precisely or to state exhaustively all its ingredients.'

In view of the aforesaid observations, we fail to understand how this decision can be pressed into service for ascertaining the true import and content of the expression 'industry' which is the subject head under consideration in the case in hand.

With *Tika Ramji* and its progeny out of the way, the minority judgment then went on to refer to earlier decisions of the Supreme Court, stating that the Entries in the Lists contained in the Seventh Schedule of the Constitution of India should be given a liberal and generous construction:

192. In the aforesaid premises, we are of the considered opinion that the Tobacco Board Act enacted by Parliament under Entry 52 of List I is constitutionally valid and all the provisions therein, including the provisions relating to growing of tobacco and sale and purchase of tobacco are within the legislative competence of Parliament. We are further of the opinion that the word 'industry' in Entry 52 of List I cannot be given a restricted meaning, particularly when a conspectus of all the decisions interpreting entry in any of the lists of the Constitution including the minority view of Mukharji, J. in *ITC* case is to the effect that the entries in the list should be given liberal and generous construction and it is a well-accepted cardinal rule of interpretation that the words in a constitutional document, conferring legislative powers should be construed most liberally and in their widest amplitude.

The dissenting judges then found that the provisions of Sections 3,8 and 32 of the Tobacco Board Act, 1975, and Sections 4(2) and 15 of the Agricultural Produce Markets Act came into direct collision with each other, resulting in the Tobacco Board Act prevailing over the Agricultural Produce Markets Act, insofar as it related to a levy of fee for sale and purchase of tobacco within the market area.[*]

Here, again, the minority judgment was conscious of the fact that the majority judgment in the earlier *ITC* case had been relied upon, and followed; persons having settled their affairs on the basis that fees would be levied and collected under the central enactment, and not under the state enactments. The upsetting of this view of the law, even if incorrect—that too by a majority of 3:2, brings back echoes of *Bengal Immunity*. What is also noteworthy is the resultant confusion caused by the unsettling of settled law owing to a different bench hearing and deciding the very issue that was decided earlier by a bench whose members happened to be different.

12. *Pradeep Kumar Biswas v. Indian Institute of Chemical Biology* (2002)

The question which arose before a seven-judge bench in *Pradeep Kumar Biswas v. Indian Institute of Chemical Biology & Ors.* (2002),[†] was whether the Council of Scientific and Industrial Research was correctly held to be 'State' within the meaning of Article 12 of the Constitution of India, as declared by a bench of five judges in *Sabhajit Tewary v. Union of India* (1975).[‡] In *Pradeep Kumar Biswas*, a majority of five of the seven learned judges held that *Sabhajit Tewary* was wrongly decided, and overruled it.[§] Two learned judges, namely, Justices Lahoti and Raju, differed. In order to appreciate the controversy raised in this case, it is necessary to first set out Article 12 of the Constitution of India. Article 12 reads thus:

---

[*] (2002) 9 SCC 232 at paragraph 193.
[†] (2002) 5 SCC 111.
[‡] (1975) 1 SCC 485.
[§] (2002) 5 SCC 111 at paragraph 66.

In this part, unless the context otherwise requires, 'the State' includes the Government and Parliament of India and the Government and the Legislatures of each of the States and all local or other authorities within the territory of India or under the control of the Government of India.

After an exhaustive review of all the relevant decisions on which 'agency' or 'instrumentality' could be said to be 'State' within the meaning of Article 12, the dissenting judgment strongly disapproved of the judgment in *Ajay Hasia v. Khalid Mujib Sehravardi & Ors.* (1981)* as follows:

87. Here itself we have a few comments to offer. Firstly, the distinction between 'instrumentality and agency' on the one hand, and 'authority (for the purpose of 'other authorities')' on the other, was totally obliterated. In our opinion, it is one thing to say that if an entity veiled or disguised as a corporation or a society or in any other form is found to be an instrumentality or agency of the State then in that case it will be the State itself in a narrower sense acting through its instrumentality or agency and therefore, included in 'the State' in the wider sense for the purpose of Article 12. Having found an entity whether juristic or natural to be an instrumentality or agency of the State, it is not necessary to call it an 'authority'. It would make a substantial difference to find whether an entity is an instrumentality or agency or an authority. Secondly, *Ajay Hasia* was the case of a registered society; it was not an appropriate occasion for dealing with corporations or entities other than society. On the inferences drawn by reading of the memorandum of association of the Society and rules framed thereunder, and subjecting such inferences to the tests laid down in the decision itself, it was found that the Society was an instrumentality or agency of the State and on tearing the veil of the Society what was to be seen was the State itself though in disguise. It was not thereafter necessary to hold the Society an 'authority' and proceed to record 'that the Society is an instrumentality or the agency of the State and the Central Governments and it is an 'authority' within the meaning of Article 12' (SCC p. 740, para 15), entirely obliterating, the dividing line between 'instrumentality or agency of the State' and 'other authorities'. This has been a source of

* (1981) 1 SCC 722.

confusion and misdirection in thought process as we propose to explain a little later. Thirdly, though six tests are laid down but there is no clear indication in the judgment whether in order to hold a legal entity the State, all the tests must be answered positively and it is the cumulative effect of such positive answers which will solve the riddle or positive answer to one or two or more tests would be enough to find out a solution. It appears what the Court wished was reaching a final decision on an overall view of the result of the tests. Compare this with what was said by Bhagwati, J. in *Ramana*'s case. We have already noticed that in *Ajay Hasia*, Bhagwati, J. has in his own words summarized the test laid down by him in *Ramana*'s case. In *Ramana*'s case he had said that the question whether a corporation is a governmental instrumentality or agency would depend on a variety of factors which defy exhaustive enumeration and moreover even amongst these factors described in *Ramana*'s case 'Court will have to consider the cumulative effect of these various factors and arrive at its decision'.

The dissenting judges then went on to hold:

96. The terms instrumentality or agency of the State are not to be found mentioned in Article 12 of the Constitution. Nevertheless they fall within the ken of Article 12 of the Constitution for the simple reason that if the State chooses to set up an instrumentality or agency and entrusts it with the same power, function or action which would otherwise have been exercised or undertaken by itself, there is no reason why such instrumentality or agency should not be subject to the same constitutional and public law limitations as the State would have been. In different judicial pronouncements, some of which we have reviewed, any company, corporation, society or any other entity having a juridical existence if it has been held to be an instrumentality or agency of the State, it has been so held only on having been found to be an alter ego, a double or a proxy or a limb or an offspring or a mini-incarnation or a vicarious creature or a surrogate and so on—by whatever name called— of the State. In short, the material available must justify holding of the entity wearing a mask or a veil worn only legally and outwardly which on piercing fails to obliterate the true character of the State in disguise. Then it is an instrumentality or agency of the State.

97. It is this basic and essential distinction between an 'instrumentality or agency' of the State and 'other authorities' which has to be borne in mind. An authority must be an authority *sui juris* to fall within the meaning of the expression 'other authorities' under Article 12. A juridical entity, though an authority, may also satisfy the test of being an instrumentality or agency of the State in which event such authority may be held to be an instrumentality or agency of the State but not vice versa.

98. We sum up our conclusions as under:

(1) Simply by holding a legal entity to be an instrumentality or agency of the State it does not necessarily become an authority within the meaning of 'other authorities' in Article 12. To be an authority, the entity should have been created by a statute or under a statute and functioning with liability and obligations to the public. Further, the statute creating the entity should have vested that entity with power to make law or issue binding directions amounting to law within the meaning of Article 13(2) governing its relationship with other people or the affairs of other people—their rights, duties, liabilities or other legal relations. If created under a statute, then there must exist some other statute conferring on the entity such powers. In either case, it should have been entrusted with such functions as are governmental or closely associated therewith by being of public importance or being fundamental to the life of the people and hence governmental. Such authority would be the State, for, one who enjoys the powers or privileges of the State must also be subjected to limitations and obligations of the State. It is this strong statutory flavour and clear indicia of power—constitutional or statutory, and its potential or capability to act to the detriment of fundamental rights of the people, which makes it an authority; though in a given case, depending on the facts and circumstances, an authority may also be found to be an instrumentality or agency of the State and to that extent they may overlap. Tests 1, 2 and 4 in *Ajay Hasia* enable determination of governmental ownership or control. Tests 3, 5 and 6 are 'functional' tests. The propounder of the tests himself has used the words suggesting relevancy of those tests for finding out if an entity was instrumentality or agency of the State. Unfortunately thereafter the tests were considered relevant for testing if an authority is the State and this fallacy has occurred because of difference between 'instrumentality

and agency' of the State and an 'authority' having been lost sight of *sub silentio*, unconsciously and undeliberated. In our opinion, and keeping in view the meaning which 'authority' carries, the question whether an entity is an 'authority' cannot be answered by applying *Ajay Hasia* tests.

(2) The tests laid down in *Ajay Hasia* case are relevant for the purpose of determining whether an entity is an instrumentality or agency of the State. Neither all the tests are required to be answered in the positive nor a positive answer to one or two tests would suffice. It will depend upon a combination of one or more of the relevant factors depending upon the essentiality and overwhelming nature of such factors in identifying the real source of governing power, if need be by removing the mask or piercing the veil disguising the entity concerned. When an entity has an independent legal existence, before it is held to be the State, the person alleging it to be so must satisfy the court of brooding presence of the Government or deep and pervasive control of the Government so as to hold it to be an instrumentality or agency of the State.

As a result of this conclusion, the minority judgment found that *Sabhajit Tewary* was rightly decided, and ought not to be overruled.[*]

The trend of subsequent decisions has been in accordance with the majority judgment. However, a discordant note was struck in *Zee Telefilms Ltd. & Anr. v. Union of India* (2005),[†] which held that despite the fact that the Board of Control for Cricket in India had a monopoly status and complete control over the sport of cricket, it would not be 'State' within the meaning of Article 12.[‡] *Zee Telefilms* was also a judgment delivered by a majority of 3:2.[§] Even prior to *Pradeep Kumar Biswas*, the question of expanding the scope of Article 12 so as to include within its scope private parties was expressly left open by the judgment in *M.C. Mehta v. Union of India* (1987),[¶] with Bhagwati, J. observing:

---

[*] (2002) 5 SCC 111 at paragraph 104.
[†] (2005) 4 SCC 649.
[‡] Ibid., at paragraph 36.
[§] The dissenting judgments of S.B. Sinha and S.N. Variava, JJ. in *Zee Telefilms* (supra) are discussed in detail in Chapter VII.
[¶] (1987) 1 SCC 395.

29. We were, during the course of arguments, addressed at great length by counsel on both sides on the American doctrine of State action. The learned counsel elaborately traced the evolution of this doctrine in its parent country. We are aware that in America since the Fourteenth Amendment is available only against the State, the courts in order to thwart racial discrimination by private parties, devised the theory of State action under which it was held that wherever private activity was aided, facilitated or supported by the State in a significant measure, such activity took the colour of State action and was subject to the constitutional limitations of the Fourteenth Amendment. This historical context in which the doctrine of State action evolved in the United States is irrelevant for our purpose especially since we have Article 15(2) in our Constitution. But it is the principle behind the doctrine of State aid, control and regulation so impregnating a private activity as to give it the colour of State action that is of interest to us and that also to the limited extent to which it can be Indianized and harmoniously blended with our constitutional jurisprudence . . .'

30. Before we part with this topic, we may point out that this Court has throughout the last few years expanded the horizon of Article 12 primarily to inject respect for human rights and social conscience in our corporate structure. The purpose of expansion has not been to destroy the raison d'etre of creating corporations but to advance the human rights jurisprudence. *Prima facie* we are not inclined to accept the apprehensions of learned counsel for Shriram as well founded when he says that our including within the ambit of Article 12 and thus subjecting to the discipline of Article 21, those private corporations whose activities have the potential of affecting the life and health of the people, would deal a death blow to the policy of encouraging and permitting private entrepreneurial activity. Whenever a new advance is made in the field of human rights, apprehension is always expressed by the status quo-ists that it will create enormous difficulties in the way of smooth functioning of the system and affect its stability. Similar apprehension was voiced when this Court in *R.D. Shetty* case brought public sector corporations within the scope and ambit of Article 12 and subjected them to the discipline of fundamental rights. Such apprehension expressed by those who may be affected by any new and innovative expansion of human

rights need not deter the court from widening the scope of human rights and expanding their reach and ambit, if otherwise it is possible to do so without doing violence to the language of the constitutional provision. It is through creative interpretation and bold innovation that the human rights jurisprudence has been developed in our country to a remarkable extent and this forward march of the human rights movement cannot be allowed to be halted by unfounded apprehensions expressed by status quoists. But we do not propose to decide finally at the present stage whether a private corporation like Shriram would fall within the scope and ambit of Article 12, because we have not had sufficient time to consider and reflect on this question in depth. The hearing of this case before us concluded only on December 15, 1986 and we are called upon to deliver our judgment within a period of four days, on December 19, 1986. We are therefore, of the view that this is not a question on which we must make any definite pronouncement at this stage. But we would leave it for a proper and detailed consideration at a later stage if it becomes necessary to do so.'

All of this keeps the pot of litigation boiling. However, it is most unlikely that any future Constitution Bench would harken back to the minority view taken in *Pradeep Kumar Biswas*. Thus, in the ultimate analysis, *Sabhajit Tewary* is unlikely to raise its head again.

13. *State of Punjab v. Devans Modern Breweries Ltd.* (2004)

The question in *State of Punjab v. Devans Modern Breweries Ltd.* (2004)* arose because of a reference made to five judges questioning the correctness of a Constitution Bench decision in *Kalyani Stores v. State of Orissa and Ors.* (1966).† In *Kalyani Stores*, it was held that Article 301 of the Constitution of India would apply in relation to trade in potable liquor. The reference order found that *Kalyani Stores* would, *prima facie*, clash with at least four other judgments of the court, which had consistently taken the view that trade in potable liquor, being *res extra commercium*

---

* (2004) 11 SCC 26.
† (1966) 1 SCR 865.

(literally, 'a thing outside commerce'), could not be said to be 'trade, commerce or intercourse', which fell within the protection of Article 19(1) (g) of the Constitution and, consequently, would be outside the scope of the expression 'trade' in Article 301.

By a razor-thin majority of 3:2, the majority judgment in *Devans Modern Breweries* sidestepped *Kalyani Stores*, stating that it would not apply to the facts of the case—*Kalyani Stores* having dealt with the Punjab Excise Act, 1914, which was an existing law enacted prior to the Constitution of India, and which was expressly saved by Articles 305 and 372, rendering it immune from attack under Article 301.

B.N. Agrawal and S.B. Sinha, JJ. wrote separate dissenting judgments. Agrawal, J. held, relying primarily upon *K.K. Narula v. State of Jammu and Kashmir & Ors.* (1967),* that a discordant note had been struck by the previous decisions of the Supreme Court on whether trade in potable liquor would receive the protection of Article 19(1)(g) of the Constitution. The learned judge then concluded:

51. From the analysis of decisions rendered by this Court in *Cooverjee B. Bharucha, R.M.D. Chamarbaugwala, Har Shankar* or *Khoday Distilleries* it will appear that a person cannot claim any right to deal in any obnoxious substance on the ground of public morality. The State, therefore, is entitled to completely prohibit any trade or commerce in potable liquor. Such prohibition, however, has not been imposed. Once a licence is granted to carry on any trade or business, can it be said that a person is committing a crime in carrying on business in liquor although he strictly complies with the terms and conditions of licence and the provisions of the statute operating in the field? If the answer to the said question is to be rendered in the affirmative it will create havoc and lead to anarchy and judicial vagaries. When it is not a crime to carry on such business having regard to the fact that a person has been permitted to do so by the State in compliance with the provisions of the existing laws, indisputably he acquires a right to carry on business. Even in respect to trade in food articles or other essential commodities either complete prohibition or restrictions are imposed in the matter of

* (1967) 3 SCR 50.

carrying on any trade or business, except in terms of a licence granted in that behalf by the authorities specified in that behalf. The distinction between a trade or business being carried out legally or illegally having regard to the restrictions imposed by a statute would have, therefore, to be judged by the fact as to whether such business is being carried out in compliance with the provisions of the statute(s) operating in the field or not. In other words, so long it is not made impermissible to carry on such business by reason of a statute, no crime can be said to have been committed in relation thereto. The doctrine of *res extra commercium*, thus, would not be attracted, whence a person carries on business under a licence granted in terms of the provisions of the regulatory statutes.

xxx xxx xxx

55. Once the regulations restricting the right to carry on business in potable liquor are attributed to the reasonable restrictions and public interest clause contained in clause (6) of Article 19 of the Constitution, the fundamental right to carry on trade under Article 19 is conceded. Once such a right is conceded, it cannot be said that although a person has a fundamental right to carry on trade or business for the purpose of Article 19(1)(g), subject to imposition of reasonable restrictions by a law made in terms of clause (6) of Article 19, he does not have such a right in terms of Article 301 of the Constitution or for that matter Article 14 thereof. Articles 303 and 304 of the Constitution also provide for imposition of restrictions and thus even a freedom guaranteed to a person under Article 301 is not an absolute one, but subject to the constitutional limitations provided therefor. Article 301 confers freedom but not a licence. The protection from discrimination as envisaged in *Khoday Distilleries* would not only operate against the State which is the licensor but having regard to the constitutional goals to be achieved by the commerce clause contained in Article 301, must be extended to another State which seeks to impose restrictions on import.

Dealing with *Kalyani Stores*, the learned judge then held:

93. Once it is held that the principle of *res extra commercium* is not applicable, the decisions in *Kalyani Stores, H. Anraj* and *Bhailal Bhai* having been rendered by a Constitution Bench would constitute binding precedents. Once it is held that the legislature has no power to levy any excise duty on imported liquor in excess of the countervailing duty within the State, having regard to the constitutional limitation imposed in terms of Entry 51 List II of the Seventh Schedule to the Constitution, such discriminatory levy must be held to be violative of Articles 303(1) and 304(a) of the Constitution. As import fee is an impost, thus, levy thereof in addition to countervailing duty would clearly attract the wrath of Article 304(a) of the Constitution. It has not been and could not have been contended that the tax is compensatory in nature as was the case in *Automobile*. I am, therefore, of the opinion that the impugned impost cannot be upheld.

Sinha, J., in a separate dissent, reviewed the case law on *res extra commercium*, and agreed with Agrawal, J. that the said expression cannot possibly apply once the liquor trade is licensed by the state and not prohibited.* The learned judge then referred to *Kalyani Stores* and found that it would apply on all fours to these cases as well:

338. *Kalyani Stores* is a Constitution Bench judgment. A Constitution Bench has unequivocally held that Article 301 of the Constitution shall apply to trade of liquor. Once this Court comes to the conclusion that the doctrine of *res extra commercium* was not applicable, *Kalyani Stores* must be applied on all fours. In any event, the decision of a Constitution Bench cannot be brushed aside as having been passed *'sub silentio'* or on the basis of the doctrine of *'per incuriam'*.

339. Judicial discipline envisages that a coordinate Bench follow the decision of an earlier coordinate Bench. If a coordinate Bench does not agree with the principles of law enunciated by another Bench, the matter may be referred only to a larger Bench. But no decision can be arrived at contrary to or inconsistent with the law laid down by the coordinate Bench. *Kalyani Stores* and *K.K. Narula* both have been rendered by the

* (2004) 11 SCC 26 at paragraph 217.

Constitution Benches. The said decisions, therefore, cannot be thrown out for any purpose whatsoever; more so when both of them if applied collectively lead to a contrary decision proposed by the majority.

340. In *Halsbury's Laws of England* (4th Edn.), Vol. 26 at pp. 297–98, para 578, it is stated:

'A decision is given *per incuriam* when the court has acted in ignorance of a previous decision of its own or of a court of coordinate jurisdiction which covered the case before it, in which case it must decide which case to follow (*Young v. Bristol Aeroplane Co. Ltd.*) In *Huddersfield Police Authority v. Watson Lord Goddard*, C.J. said that a decision was given *per incuriam* when a case or statute had not been brought to the court's attention and the court gave the decision in ignorance or forgetfulness of the existence of the case or statute); or when it has acted in ignorance of a House of Lords decision, in which case it must follow that decision; or when the decision is given in ignorance of the terms of a statute or rule having statutory force (*Young v. Bristol Aeroplane Co. Ltd., KB* at p.729, See also *Lancaster Motor Co. (London) Ltd. v. Bremith Ltd.* For a Divisional Court decision disregarded by that court as being *per incuriam*, see *Nicholas v. Penny*). A decision should not be treated as given *per incuriam*, however, simply because of a deficiency of parties (*Morelle Ltd. v. Wakeling*), or because the court had not the benefit of the best argument (*Bryers v. Canadian Pacific Steamships Ltd.*, per Singleton, L.J.; affd. sub nom. *Canadian Pacific Steamships Ltd. v. Bryers*), and, as a general rule, the only cases in which decisions should be held to be given *per incuriam* are those given in ignorance of some inconsistent statute or binding authority (*A. and J. Mucklow Ltd. v. IRC*; *Morelle Ltd. v. Wakeling*). See also *Bonsor v. Musicians' Union* where the *per incuriam* contention was rejected and, on appeal to the House of Lords, although the House overruled the case which bound the Court of Appeal, the House agreed that that court had been bound by it. Even if a decision of the Court of Appeal has misinterpreted a previous decision of the House of Lords, the Court of Appeal must follow its previous decision and leave the House of Lords to rectify the mistake (*Williams v. Glasbrook Bros. Ltd.*).'

341. In *Vijay Laxmi Sadho (Dr.) v. Jagdish* it has been observed as follows:

'33. As the learned Single Judge was not in agreement with the view expressed in *Devilal's* case it would have been proper, to maintain judicial discipline, to refer the matter to a larger Bench rather than to take a different view. We note it with regret and distress that the said course was not followed. It is well settled that if a Bench of coordinate jurisdiction disagrees with another Bench of coordinate jurisdiction whether, on the basis of 'different arguments' or otherwise, on a question of law, it is appropriate that the matter be referred to a larger Bench for resolution of the issue rather than to leave two conflicting judgments to operate, creating confusion. It is not proper to sacrifice certainty of law. Judicial decorum, no less than legal propriety forms the basis of judicial procedure and it must be respected at all costs.'

342. In *State of Bihar v. Kalika Kuer* a Bench of this Court upon taking a large number of decisions into consideration observed:

'10. Looking at the matter, in view of what has been held to mean by *per incuriam,* we find that such element of rendering a decision in ignorance of any provision of the statute or the judicial authority of binding nature, is not the reason indicated by the Full Bench in the impugned judgment, while saying that the decision in the case of *Ramkrit Singh* was rendered *per incuriam.*'

It was further opined:

'The earlier judgment may seem to be not correct yet it will have the binding effect on the later Bench of coordinate jurisdiction. Easy course of saying that earlier decision was rendered *per incuriam* is not permissible and the matter will have to be resolved only in two days—either to follow the earlier decision or refer the matter to a larger Bench to examine the issue, in case it is felt that earlier decision is not correct on merits.'

343. It is also trite that the binding precedents which are authoritative in nature and are meant to be applied should not be ignored on application of the doctrine of *sub silentio* or *per incuriam* without assigning specific reasons therefor. I, for one, do not see as to how *Kalyani Stores* and *K.K. Narula* read together can be said to have been passed *sub silentio* or rendered *per incuriam.*'

The effect of the majority judgment in this case is that *Kalyani Stores*, though not expressly overruled, has been rendered toothless. The prevailing view—that trade in liquor is *res extra commercium*, is obviously incorrect. The proceeds from a licensed trade can never be equated with the proceeds from crime. In point of fact, the Constitution of India, in providing in a Directive Principle of State Policy that it is open to the state to enforce prohibition of potable liquor,[*] also gives the states the power, under Entry 51 of List II of the Seventh Schedule of the Constitution, to impose excise duty on intoxicating liquor. What is therefore envisaged by the Constitution itself, is that where a state does not prohibit, in its entirety, the manufacture or sale of liquor, but instead licenses it, the state can levy and collect excise duty/sales tax on potable liquor. In the latter situation, it is obvious that with respect to legitimate trade being carried on, once licensed, the state cannot behave unreasonably or arbitrarily, therefore bringing in the fundamental rights under Articles 14 and 19(1) (g) as well as the constitutional right under Article 301.

14. *State of West Bengal v. Kesoram Industries Ltd.* (2004)

In *State of West Bengal v. Kesoram Industries Ltd. & Ors* (2004)[†]—the primary issue raised before a bench of five judges about the binding nature of an earlier seven-judge-bench decision of the court in *India Cement Ltd. v. State of Tamil Nadu* (1990).[‡] In effect, the seven-judge-bench judgment in *India Cement* was sidestepped by the majority judgment of R.C. Lahoti, J. in *Kesoram Industries*—speaking on behalf of a majority of four judges—by arriving at a conclusion opposite to that which was arrived at in *India Cement*. The question which arose for consideration was whether the levy of cess by states on coal-bearing land and other mineral-bearing lands would be *ultra vires*, in that, the legislative field relating to coal and other minerals would stand abstracted from the state's legislative competence, owing to Entry 54 of List I of the Seventh Schedule of the Constitution, and the declaration made in Section 2 of the Mines and Minerals Act, 1957.

S.B. Sinha, J., in a lengthy sole dissent, arrived at the conclusion that the cess that was imposed under three acts pertaining to the state of West

---

[*] Article 47, Constitution of India.
[†] (2004) 10 SCC 201.
[‡] (1990) 1 SCC 12.

Bengal were *ultra vires* and unconstitutional, inasmuch as the judgment in *India Cement* covered these cases. In arriving at this conclusion, the learned judge first held that the Constitution of India has laid down that India would be quasi-federal or a hybrid-federal state.[*] The learned judge then went on to consider *India Cement* and its progeny, and concluded:

> '352. The principles of reading a judgment is well known. What is binding in terms of Article 141 of the Constitution of India is the *ratio* of the judgment. The *ratio decidendi* of a judgment is the reason assigned in support of the conclusion. If the reasons contained in a judgment do not appeal to a subsequent Bench, the matter may be referred to a larger Bench but so long the same is not done, the *ratio* can neither be watered down nor brushed aside. *India Cement, Orissa Cement* and other judgments of Coordinate Benches are binding on us. Correctness or otherwise of the said judgments has not been questioned. It would, therefore, not be proper for this Court to read something in the judgment which does not appear therefrom or to exclude from our consideration reasoning on the basis whereof, the conclusions of the judgment had been reached.'

Entry 49 of List II of the Seventh Schedule, which was strongly relied upon, was put out of harm's way by stating that what could be taxed under the said Entry by the states is only the surface area, and not the minerals underneath.[†] In any event, Sinha, J. held that Entry 49 of List II could not trench upon the legislative field carved out from the states by the Parliament under Entries 52 and 54 of List I.[‡] The cesses in question were held to be not imposts on land directly as a unit, as held by previous judgments of the Supreme Court, but were, in substance, taxes on minerals produced.[§] Entry 50 of List II, also relied upon, was put out of harm's way by reliance upon Wanchoo, J.'s dissenting judgment in *Hingir Rampur Coal Co. Ltd. v. State of Orissa* (1961)[¶] as follows:

---

[*] (2004) 10 SCC 201 at paragraph 215.
[†] Ibid., at paragraph 380.
[‡] Id., at paragraph 362.
[§] Id., at paragraphs 371–74.
[¶] (1961) 2 SCR 537.

Wanchoo, J. in *Hingir Rampur Coal Co. Ltd. v. State of Orissa* observed:

'Thus tax on mineral rights would be confined, for example, to taxes on leases of mineral rights and on premium or royalty for that. Taxes on such premium and royalty would be taxes on mineral rights while taxes on the minerals actually extracted would be duties of excise.'

The learned Judge further observed:

'There would be no difficulty where an owner himself works the mine to value the mineral rights on the same principles on which leases of mineral rights are made and then to tax the royalty which, for example, the owner might have got if instead of working the mine himself he had leased it out to somebody else. There can be no doubt therefore that taxes on mineral rights are taxes of this nature and not taxes on minerals actually produced.'

Finally, *Ajoy Kumar Mukerjee v. Local Board of Barpetta* (1965),* a decision strongly relied upon by the majority judgment in order to undermine the *ratio* of *India Cement*, was distinguished by Sinha, J. as follows:

564. Furthermore, it is one thing to say that a land is being used as a *haat* as was in the case of *Ajoy Mukherjee* or forest as was in the case of *Moopil Nair* but it is another thing to say that a tax is imposed on activities of land confined to extraction of mineral, which is clearly beyond the power of the State Legislature. On the same analogy levy of house tax is permissible having regard to the nature and object thereof wherefor there can be a valid classification. The annual valuation of the house on the basis of income must be considered for the purpose of quantifying the tax. But the said principle would not apply in the case of tax on production of minerals.

565. We, having regard to the decisions of this Court in *Buxa Dooars* and *India Cement* which are directly on the point, do not think that the approach to the questions involved in the instant case should be different. In imposing tax, having regard to political or economical considerations, it may be permissible to allow some concession to the small owners or income arising from the land may be taken into

---

* (1965) 3 SCR 47.

consideration but as would be noticed from the decisions, the validity of such taxes has been upheld in relation to the land or the structures standing thereupon or a tax on circumstances and properties.'

Finally, a summary of the learned judge's findings was set out as follows:

593. This Court while interpreting binding judgments cannot in effect and substance overrule the same or read down the principles of law enunciated therein.

Summary of our findings

(i) Federalism under the Indian context points out to the supremacy of Parliament and the legislative entries contained in different lists of the Seventh Schedule must be construed accordingly.

(ii) The interpretation of legislation will depend upon the legislative entries to which it relates and intent and purport of the makers of the Constitution and no principle of interpretation can be introduced to the effect that the Court should lean towards a State.

(iii) Tea and coal being subjects of great importance, Parliament has taken over the complete control of the entire field in respect thereof and other minerals in terms of the Tea Act, 1953 and the Mines and Minerals (Regulation and Development) Act, 1957 respectively.

(iv) Having regard to the purport and object of the said parliamentary Acts and the declarations contained in Section 2 of the 1957 Act and the 1953 Act, the State must be held to be denuded of its power to levy any tax on coal or tea, particularly having regard to the provisions of Sections 9, 9-A, 13, 18 and 25 of the 1957 Act and Sections 10, 13, 15, 25 and 30 of the Tea Act. Field of taxation on minerals is also covered by Section 25 of the 1957 Act. The field of taxation under the Tea Act is specifically covered by Section 25 thereof.

(v) The State being owner of the minerals and grant of mineral rights being controlled by the parliamentary statute, the State is denuded of its power to impose any tax on mineral rights in terms of Entry 50 of List II of the Seventh Schedule of the Constitution.

(vi) Having regard to the underlying object of the 1953 Act and the 1957 Act, even if the doctrine of pith and substance is applied, it may not be possible to hold that the State Legislature has only incidentally encroached upon the legislative field occupied by Parliament.

(vii) Levy of tax on coal-bearing lands and mineral-bearing lands where mining operations are being carried out through the process of incline or digging pits is illegal, inasmuch as the underground mining right would be larger in area than the surface right and, thus, it is not possible to uphold the validity of such statute with reference to the extent of the surface right as mineral is being extracted from a larger underground area. Different rights may belong to different persons over the same surface land and similarly different rights may belong to different persons in respect of or over underground rights and the impugned statutes having not made any provision of different methods of levy, the impugned statutes are *ultra vires*.

The impugned provisions do not specify who would be liable to pay in relation to different rights and who would be considered to be the owner of the land and to what extent. If the extent of surface land is treated to be the unit, the same having regard to different mining rights granted to different persons over different minerals, would all be liable to pay cess although they may not have any right over the surface at all or exercise such right thereover only over a part thereof.

As mineral-bearing lands cannot be treated as an independent unit in respect of which tax can be invoked, the impugned Acts must be held to be unconstitutional.

(viii) Tax on lands and buildings in terms of Entry 49 of List II of the Seventh Schedule of the Constitution of India can be levied on land as a unit and not otherwise.

(ix) As green tea leaves are marketable, the decision in Goodricke Group having mainly been rendered on the premise that green tea leaves are not marketable must be held to have passed *sub silentio* and, thus, does not lay down correct legal position.

(x) In view of the definitions of 'land' and 'immovable property' contained in the Bengal Cess Act, 1880, as no road cess or public works cess can be imposed on standing crops or any kind of structures, houses, shops or other buildings which would include factories and workshops for processing tea, no levy by way of cess can be imposed by reason of the impugned Acts either on the mining leasehold or the tea estate containing standing crops as also houses and buildings.

(xi) Measure of a tax although may not be determinative of the nature thereof, the same will play an important role in determining the character thereof particularly keeping in view the purpose and object the parliamentary Acts seek to achieve. In determining the legislative competence the taxing event also plays an important role.

(xii) The Tea Act having been enacted in terms of Entries 10 and 14 of List I as also Article 253 of the Constitution, the State is completely denuded of its legislative power in relation thereto. The expression 'tea' should be given a broad meaning and Entry 52 of List I of the Seventh Schedule of the Constitution should be interpreted in relation to tea having regard to the purport and object it seeks to achieve.'

The correctness of the majority judgment in *Kesoram Industries* is itself the subject matter of a reference order to a bench of nine learned judges.[*] Here, again, the law on a very important point relating to the taxation power of the states is in limbo, and is yet to be settled by an authoritative and conclusive decision of the Supreme Court.

15. *State of Gujarat v. Mirzapur Moti Kureshi Kassab* (2005)

The question which arose before a seven-judge bench in *State of Gujarat v. Mirzapur Moti Kureshi Kassab* (2005)[†] related to the constitutional validity of Section 2 of the Bombay Animal Preservation (Gujarat Amendment) Act, 1994, which introduced certain amendments in Section 5 of the Bombay Animal Preservation Act, 1954. The Statement of Objects and Reasons for the said amendment was set out in the majority judgment as follows:

The existing provisions of the Bombay Animal Preservation Act, 1954 provides for prohibition against the slaughter of cow, calf of a cow, and

---

[*] *Mineral Area Development Authority v. Steel Authority of India and Ors.* ([2011] 4 SCC 450).

[†] (2005) 8 SCC 534.

the bulls and bullocks below the age of sixteen years. It is an established fact that the cow and her progeny sustain the health of the nation by giving them the life-giving milk which is so essential an item in a scientifically balanced diet.

The economy of the State of Gujarat is still predominantly agricultural. In the agricultural sector, use of animals for milch, draught, breeding or agricultural purposes has great importance. It has, therefore, become necessary to emphasize preservation and protection of agricultural animals like bulls and bullocks. With the growing adoption of non-conventional energy sources like biogas plants, even waste material has come to assume considerable value. After the cattle cease to breed or are too old to do work, they still continue to give dung for fuel, manure and biogas, and therefore, they cannot be said to be useless. It is well established that the backbone of Indian agriculture is, in a manner of speaking, the cow and her progeny and have on their back, the whole structure of the Indian agriculture and its economic system.

In order to give effect to the policy of the State towards securing the principles laid down in Articles 47, 48 and clauses (b) and (c) of Article 39 of the Constitution, it was considered necessary also to impose total prohibition against slaughter of progeny of cow.

As the Gujarat Legislative Assembly was not in session the Bombay Animal Preservation (Gujarat Amendment) Ordinance, 1993 to amend the said Act was promulgated to achieve the aforesaid object in the interest of the general public. This Bill seeks to replace the said Ordinance by an Act of the State Legislature.

At the time, *Mohd. Hanif Quareshi v. State of Bihar* (1959)[*] was the leading judgment in this field. The effect of *Quareshi* was summed up by the majority judgment as follows:

26. Their Lordships referred to other documents as well. The findings of fact arrived at, based on such evidence may briefly be summed up. In the opinion of Their Lordships, cow progeny ceased to be useful as a draught cattle after a certain age and they, although useful otherwise,

---

[*] (1959) SCR 629.

became a burden on the limited fodder available which, but for the so-called useless animals, would be available for consumption by milch and draught animals. The response of the States in setting up gosadans (protection homes for cows and cow progeny) was very poor. It was on appreciation of the documentary evidence and the deduction drawn therefrom which led Their Lordships to conclude that in spite of there being a presumption in favour of the validity of the legislation and respect for the opinion of the legislatures as expressed by the three impugned enactments, they were inclined to hold that a total ban of the nature imposed could not be supported as reasonable in the interests of the general public.

This necessitated the constitution of the seven-judge bench in order to ascertain whether *Quareshi* needed to be revisited, and if so, whether the Gujarat Amendment made to the Bombay Act would be valid as a result. The majority judgment of six learned judges, Lahoti, C.J., speaking for the majority, overruled *Quareshi*, and consequently upheld the Gujarat Amendment in its entirety.* One judge alone dissented—Justice A.K. Mathur. The learned judge stated that the question posed before the court

---

* Interestingly, the six majority judges in *Mirzapur Moti* (supra) were vegetarians. There is no doubt that if a chief justice, as master of the roster, wishes to ensure a certain result, he can so constitute a bench which may overrule an earlier judgment, based on personal preference and predilection, rather than constitutional law. By way of contrast, the composition of the bench in *Shayara Bano v. Union of India* ([2017] 9 SCC 1) would show that the bench was carefully selected by the then chief justice so that when dealing with the constitutional validity of the practice of 'Triple Talaq', the bench consisted of one Hindu, one Sikh, one Christian, one Muslim and one Parsi. The composition of the bench therefore yielded three judgments. The dissenting judgment of Khehar, C.J., accepted by Nazeer, J., did not strike down Triple Talaq as being unconstitutional, observing that the said practice was part of the personal law of Sunni Muslims and could not therefore violate fundamental rights, not being 'law' under Article 13 of the Constitution of India. However, Khehar, C.J. would have injuncted the practice of Triple Talaq until appropriate legislation was passed by Parliament to regulate it. Nariman, J., joined by Lalit, J., was of the view that Section 2 of the Muslim Personal Law (Shariat) Application Act, 1937—which recognized and enforced the practice of Triple Talaq—was manifestly arbitrary and therefore violative of Article 14. Joseph, J. concurred with Nariman, J. in the end result, declaring Triple Talaq unconstitutional, by observing that it was against the tenets of the Quran, properly read. He also concurred with Nariman, J. that legislation which is manifestly arbitrary can be struck down under Article 14, but agreed with Khehar, C.J. that the 1937 act had no application to the practice of Triple Talaq.

was no longer *res integra*, having been authoritatively decided in at least
five judgments of the Supreme Court.* The conclusion in *Quareshi* was
thereafter set out as follows:

> 152. His Lordship has discussed the question of reasonable restriction
> under Article 19(6) and after considering all material placed before the
> Court, and adverting to social, religious, utility point of view in most
> exhaustive manner finally concluded thus:
>
> 'After giving our most careful and anxious consideration to the pros
> and cons of the problem as indicated and discussed above and keeping
> in view the presumption in favour of the validity of the legislation
> and without the least disrespect to the opinions of the legislatures
> concerned we feel that in discharging the ultimate responsibility cast on
> us by the Constitution we must approach and analyse the problem in
> an objective and realistic manner and then make our pronouncement
> on the reasonableness of the restrictions imposed by the impugned
> enactments. So approaching and analysing the problem, we have
> reached the conclusion (i) that a total ban on the slaughter of cows of
> all ages and calves of cows and calves of she-buffaloes, male and female,
> is quite reasonable and valid and is in consonance with the directive
> principles laid down in Article 48; (ii) that a total ban on the slaughter
> of she-buffaloes or breeding bulls or working bullocks (cattle as well as
> buffaloes) as long as they are as milch or draught cattle is also reasonable
> and valid, and (iii) that total ban on the slaughter of she-buffaloes, bulls
> and bullocks (cattle or buffalo) after they cease to be capable of yielding
> milk or of breeding or working as draught animals cannot be supported
> as reasonable in the interest of the general public.

Quareshi's progeny was thereafter referred to, and the doctrine of *stare
decisis* invoked, stating that it would not be proper to reverse a view which
has held good for a long spell of time—from 1958 to 1996—there being
no material change in any ground reality warranting a reversal of these
decisions.† Articles 48A and 51, which were not there at the time *Quareshi*

---

* (2005) 8 SCC 534 at paragraph 150.
† Ibid at paragraph 168.

was decided, spoke, respectively about the protection and improvement of the environment, and the safeguarding of the wildlife of the country, and the fundamental duty, in particular, under Article 51A(g), to have compassion for living creatures. Though these two articles came later, the minority judgment held that copious extracts were made from various scriptures in *Quareshi* to show that a proper consideration of our cattle wealth was present at the forefront even in that case.* *Stare decisis* was then invoked by the minority judgment, stating:

> 174. Therefore the hallmarks of the law are certainty, predictability and stability unless the ground reality has completely changed. In the present case, as discussed above, in my opinion the ground reality has not changed and the law laid down by this Court holds good and is relevant. Some advancement in technology and more and more use of cow dung and urine is not such a substantial factor to change the ground realities so as to totally do away with the slaughtering of the aged bulls and bullocks. It is true my Lord the Chief Justice has rightly observed that the principle of *stare decisis* is not a dogmatic rule allergic to logic and reason; it is a flexible principle of law operating in the province of precedents providing room to collaborate with the demands of changing times dictated by social needs, State policy and judicial conscience. There is no quarrel with this proposition, but the only question is whether the earlier decisions are not logical or they have become unreasonable with the passage of time. In my humble opinion, those decisions still hold good in the present context also. Therefore, I do not think that there are compelling reasons for reversal of the earlier decisions either on the basis of advancement of technology or reason, or logic, or economic consideration. Therefore, in my humble opinion, there is no need to reverse the earlier decisions.

The aftermath of this decision has been that bovine cattle, other than the cow, who are no longer useful as draught or milk cattle, cannot now be slaughtered for food. We must not forget that India is a diverse country, with various differences in the cultures of its people, including with regard to different dietary habits. Unfortunately, Article 29(1), which deals with

---

* Id at paragraphs 169–70.

the preservation of culture in a diverse country such as ours, was also completely missed by the majority in *Mirzapur Moti*. Article 29(1) states:

> Any section of the citizens residing in the territory of India or any part thereof having a distinct language, script or culture of its own shall have the right to conserve the same.

That 'culture' is a compendious expression, which includes the food habits of people, was not argued before the court. In the North-East of India as well as in the south, non-draught and non-milk-giving cattle comprise the staple diet of a large number of persons. The wisdom of the majority decision ought to be revisited, not only on the ground that *stare decisis* has been unsettled, but that great public mischief would also ensue if millions of useless cattle are turned out by their owners on to the streets and are free to ravage the countryside for food, roaming freely all over India, causing road accidents and other major problems.

16. *Standard Chartered Bank v. Directorate of Enforcement* (2005)

In *Standard Chartered Bank v. Directorate of Enforcement* (2005),* the subject matter for discussion before a Constitution Bench of five learned judges of the Supreme Court was corporate criminal liability under Section 56(1)(i) of the Foreign Exchange Regulation Act, 1973. The section reads:

> 56. Offences and prosecutions.—(1) Without prejudice to any award of penalty by the adjudicating officer under this Act, if any person contravenes any of the provisions of this Act other than Section 13, clause (a) of sub-section (1) of Section 18, Section 18-A, clause (a) of sub-section (1) of Section 19, sub-section (2) of Section 44 and Sections 57 and 58, or of any rule, direction or order made thereunder, he shall, upon conviction by a court, be punishable,—
>
> (i) in the case of an offence the amount or value involved in which exceeds one lakh of rupees, with imprisonment for a term which shall

---

* (2005) 4 SCC 530.

not be less than six months, but which may extend to seven years and
with fine:

> Provided that the court may, for any adequate and special reasons
> to be mentioned in the judgment, impose a sentence of imprisonment
> for a term of less than six months.

The question that arose before the court was whether a 'company', as a
separate legal entity, can be said to violate this provision. By a thin majority
of 3:2, the majority judgment held in favour of prosecution of a corporate
person as follows:

> 31. As the company cannot be sentenced to imprisonment, the court
> cannot impose that punishment, but when imprisonment and fine is
> the prescribed punishment the court can impose the punishment of fine
> which could be enforced against the company. Such a discretion is to be
> read into the section so far as the juristic person is concerned. Of course,
> the court cannot exercise the same discretion as regards a natural person.
> Then the court would not be passing the sentence in accordance with
> law. As regards company, the court can always impose a sentence of fine
> and the sentence of imprisonment can be ignored as it is impossible to
> be carried out in respect of a company. This appears to be the intention
> of the legislature and we find no difficulty in construing the statute
> in such a way. We do not think that there is a blanket immunity for
> any company from any prosecution for serious offences merely because
> the prosecution would ultimately entail a sentence of mandatory
> imprisonment. The corporate bodies, such as a firm or company
> undertake a series of activities that affect the life, liberty and property
> of the citizens. Large-scale financial irregularities are done by various
> corporations. The corporate vehicle now occupies such a large portion
> of the industrial, commercial and sociological sectors that amenability of
> the corporation to a criminal law is essential to have a peaceful society
> with stable economy.
>
> 32. We hold that there is no immunity to the companies from
> prosecution merely because the prosecution is in respect of offences
> for which the punishment prescribed is mandatory imprisonment (sic
> and fine). We overrule the views expressed by the majority in *Velliappa*

Textiles on this point and answer the reference accordingly. Various other contentions have been urged in all appeals, including this appeal, they be posted for hearing before an appropriate Bench.

The dissenting judgment of B.N. Srikrishna, J., on behalf of himself and N. Santosh Hegde, J., found that the majority judgment in *Assistant Commissioner, Assessment (ii), Bangalore & Ors. v. M/s. Velliappa Textiles Ltd. & Anr.* (2003)* did not need to be upset, as it was a well-considered judgment which considered two reports of the Law Commission of India, of 1941 and 1947, and which also referred to the same problem in various foreign jurisdictions, including Australia, France, Canada, the Netherlands and Belgium. Reference was also made in *Velliappa* to the fact that Parliament had proposed an IPC (Amendment) Bill, 1972, clause 72(a) of which was specifically intended to take care of a situation where the offender was a company, and the offence was mandatorily punishable with imprisonment, in which case the option was given to the court to sentence such a corporate offender to a fine only.[†] The minority judgment then went on to state that it is the function of the court to *interpret*, and not *make*, law,[‡] and that the majority was guilty of carrying out a legislative exercise thinly disguised as a judicial act.[§] The argument of consequence was rejected emphatically by the minority stating:

> 73. A final argument, more in terrorem than based on reason, put forward was that, if the majority view in *Velliappa* is upheld, it would be impossible to prosecute a number of offenders in several statutes where strict liability has been imposed by the statute. If that be so, so be it. As already pointed out, the judicial function is limited to finding solutions within specified parameters. Anything more than that would be 'judicial heroics' and 'naked usurpation of legislative function'.

---

* (2003) 11 SCC 405.
† (2005) 8 SCC 534 at paragraph 56.
‡ Ibid., at paragraphs 61, 62.
§ Id., at paragraph 68.

The minority then expressly supported the majority view in *Velliappa* as follows:

> 75. Para 57 of the judgment in *Velliappa* specifically notices that corporate criminal liability cannot be imposed without making corresponding legislative changes such as the imposition of fine in lieu of imprisonment. That such requisite legislative changes were introduced in Australia, France (Penal Code of 1992), the Netherlands (the Economic Offences Act, 1950 and Article 51 of the Criminal Code) and Belgium (in 1934 Cour de Cassation) is already referred to in *Velliappa*.
>
> 76. We see nothing special in the Indian context which requires us to take a different view. In all these jurisdictions, the view that prevailed was that, where a statute imposes mandatory imprisonment plus fine, such a provision would not enable the punishment of a corporate offender. If the legislatures of these countries stepped in to resolve the problem by appropriate legislative enactments giving option to the courts to impose fine in lieu of imprisonment in the case of a corporate offender, we see nothing special in the Indian context as to why such a course cannot be adopted. Merely because the situation confronts the courts in a number of statutes, the court need not feel deterred in construing the statute in accordance with reason.
>
> xxx xxx xxx
>
> 79. For all these reasons, we are of the opinion that the majority view of this Court in *Velliappa* is correct and does not require any reconsideration by this Bench. All the matters comprised in this group be placed before appropriate Benches for disposal in accordance with law.

The minority judgment in this case is a textbook example of a dissenting judgment acting as a stabilizing force, stating that an earlier binding view of the Supreme Court ought not to be unsettled, particularly in view of the fact that Parliament was cognizant of the problem posed in the case and, despite one abortive attempt made way back in 1972 to rectify the situation, has not yet rectified the same.

17. *SBP & Co. v. Patel Engineering Ltd.* (2005)

A seven-judge bench in *SBP & Co. v. Patel Engineering Ltd.* (2005)[*] was concerned with the correctness of a five-judge-bench decision in *Konkan Railway Corporation Ltd. & Anr. v. Rani Construction Pvt. Ltd.* (2002),[†] which had held that the power exercised by the chief justice of the high court or the Chief Justice of India under Section 11(6) of the Arbitration and Conciliation Act, 1996 (i.e. to appoint an arbitrator) is an 'administrative' and not a 'judicial' power. The majority judgment of P.K. Balasubramanian, J. in *SBP*, speaking on behalf of himself and five other learned judges, summarized the majority decision as follows:

47. We, therefore, sum up our conclusions as follows:

(i)   The power exercised by the Chief Justice of the High Court or the Chief Justice of India under Section 11(6) of the Act is not an administrative power. It is a judicial power.

(ii) The power under Section 11(6) of the Act, in its entirety, could be delegated, by the Chief Justice of the High Court only to another Judge of that Court and by the Chief Justice of India to another Judge of the Supreme Court.

(iii) In case of designation of a Judge of the High Court or of the Supreme Court, the power that is exercised by the designated Judge would be that of the Chief Justice as conferred by the statute.

(iv) The Chief Justice or the designated Judge will have the right to decide the preliminary aspects as indicated in the earlier part of this judgment. These will be his own jurisdiction to entertain the request, the existence of a valid arbitration agreement, the existence or otherwise of a live claim, the existence of the condition for the exercise of his power and on the qualifications of the arbitrator or arbitrators. The Chief Justice or the designated Judge would be entitled to seek the opinion of an institution in the matter of nominating an arbitrator qualified in terms of Section 11(8) of the Act if the need arises but the order appointing the arbitrator could only be that of the Chief Justice or the designated Judge.

---

[*] (2005) 8 SCC 618.
[†] (2002) 2 SCC 388.

(v)   Designation of a District Judge as the authority under Section 11(6) of the Act by the Chief Justice of the High Court is not warranted on the scheme of the Act.

(vi) Once the matter reaches the Arbitral Tribunal or the sole arbitrator, the High Court would not interfere with the orders passed by the arbitrator or the Arbitral Tribunal during the course of the arbitration proceedings and the parties could approach the Court only in terms of Section 37 of the Act or in terms of Section 34 of the Act.

(vii) Since an order passed by the Chief Justice of the High Court or by the designated Judge of that Court is a judicial order, an appeal will lie against that order only under Article 136 of the Constitution to the Supreme Court.

(viii)There can be no appeal against an order of the Chief Justice of India or a Judge of the Supreme Court designated by him while entertaining an application under Section 11(6) of the Act.

(ix) In a case where an Arbitral Tribunal has been constituted by the parties without having recourse to Section 11(6) of the Act, the Arbitral Tribunal will have the jurisdiction to decide all matters as contemplated by Section 16 of the Act.

(x)   Since all were guided by the decision of this Court in *Konkan Rly. Corpn. Ltd. v. Rani Construction (P) Ltd.* and orders under Section 11(6) of the Act have been made based on the position adopted in that decision, we clarify that appointments of arbitrators or Arbitral Tribunals thus far made, are to be treated as valid, all objections being left to be decided under Section 16 of the Act. As and from this date, the position as adopted in this judgment will govern even pending applications under Section 11(6) of the Act.

(xi) Where District Judges had been designated by the Chief Justice of the High Court under Section 11(6) of the Act, the appointment orders thus far made by them will be treated as valid; but applications if any pending before them as on this date will stand transferred, to be dealt with by the Chief Justice of the High Court concerned or a Judge of that Court designated by the Chief Justice.

(xii) The decision in *Konkan Rly. Corpn. Ltd. v. Rani Construction (P) Ltd.* is overruled.

C.K. Thakker, J. was the sole dissenting judge. The learned judge referred to the history of the litigation in the Supreme Court under Section 11 of the Indian Arbitration Act—the earlier view of the court was that the chief justice, or his designate, acts under Section 11(6) in a purely administrative capacity, and hence his decision, not being a judicial decision, would not be appealable under Article 136 of the Constitution of India. This view was doubted, as a result of which, after a series of judgments, a five-judge bench was constituted in order to test whether the decision of the three learned judges in *Konkan Railway Corpn. Ltd. & Ors v. M/s. Mehul Construction Co.* (2000)* was correct. Five learned judges in the second *Konkan Railway* case in 2002 then held that the earlier *Konkan Railway* decision was correct, and that the function performed by the chief justice or his designate was administrative, and did not contain any adjudicatory process. Thus, the order passed by the chief justice, or his designate, under Section 11(6) could not be challenged before the Supreme Court under Article 136 of the Constitution. One would have thought that this being an authoritative pronouncement of five learned judges, the law was now settled once and for all. However, within three years of this decision, the matter was placed before a seven-judge bench in order to consider whether the five-judge bench, which was set up specifically to settle the law and pronounce authoritatively, was itself correct.

Justice Thakker in his dissent relied strongly upon the fact that the chief justice need not himself appoint an arbitrator, but that any person or institution designated by him may do so. This, according to the learned judge, would conclusively show that the said function is administrative and not judicial, and that therefore the decision of the earlier five-judge bench should not be disturbed. Thakker, J. put it thus:

> 94. But there is another important reason why the function of the Chief Justice under Section 11 should be considered administrative. All the three sub-sections (4), (5) and (6) of the said section empower the Chief Justice or 'any person or institution designated by him' to exercise the power of the Chief Justice. No provision similar to the one in hand was present in the 1940 Act. Parliament, therefore, has consciously and

---

* (2000) 7 SCC 201.

intentionally made the present arrangement for the first time allowing exercise of the power by the Chief Justice himself or through 'any person or institution designated by him', since the function is administrative in character and is required to be performed on *prima facie* satisfaction under sub-section (6) of Section 11 of the Act.

The learned judge then went on to discuss Section 16(1) of the Arbitration Act, which enables the arbitrator to decide his own jurisdiction, subject of course to ultimate court control. This was determined to be another strong indicator that the function performed by the learned chief justice under Section 11(6) of the Arbitration Act is administrative, as follows:

> 114. Though the submission weighed with the majority, I express my inability to agree with it for several reasons. Firstly, as earlier noted, it proceeds on the basis that the function of the Chief Justice is judicial or quasi-judicial, which is not correct. In my view, it is administrative which is apparent from the language of Section 11 and strengthened by Section 16 which enables the Arbitral Tribunal to rule on its own jurisdiction. Secondly, a court of law must give credit to Parliament that it is aware of settled legal position that judicial or quasi-judicial function cannot be delegated and if the function performed by the Chief Justice is judicial or quasi-judicial in nature, keeping in view legal position, it would not have allowed delegation of such function to 'any person or authority'. Thirdly, the majority held, and I am in respectful agreement with it, that the conferment of power on the Chief Justice is not as *'persona designata'*. Hence, the power can be delegated. Finally, if the legislative intent is the exercise of power by the Chief Justice alone, one fails to understand as to how it can be exercised by a 'colleague' of the Chief Justice as well.
>
> 115. In my opinion, acceptance of the submission of Mr Nariman would result in rewriting of a statute. The scheme of the legislation does not warrant such construction. No court much less the highest court of the country would interpret one provision (Section 11) of an Act of Parliament which would make another provision (Section 16) totally redundant, otiose and nugatory. The legislature has conferred power on the Chief Justice to appoint an arbitrator in certain contingencies.

By the same pen and ink, it allowed the Chief Justice to get that power exercised through 'any person or institution'. It is not open to a court to ignore the legislative mandate by making artificial distinction between the power to be exercised by the Chief Justice or by his 'colleague' and the power to be exercised by other organs though legislature was quite clear on the exercise of power by the persons and authorities specified therein. I accordingly reject the argument.

As a result thereof, the learned judge found that there was no need to revisit the judgment in the second *Konkan Railway* case. The aftermath of the majority judgment in this case led to several complications, including the vexed question as to what would be the width of the jurisdiction of the chief justice in deciding the preliminary questions at the stage of referral of the case to arbitration. The Law Commission of India, headed by Justice Ajit Prakash Shah, looked into the matter and recommended as follows:

28. The Act recognizes situations where the intervention of the Court is envisaged at the pre-arbitral stage i.e. prior to the constitution of the Arbitral Tribunal, which includes Sections 8, 9, 11 in the case of Part I arbitrations and Section 45 in the case of Part II arbitrations. Sections 8, 45 and also Section 11 relating to 'reference to arbitration' and 'appointment of the tribunal', directly affect the constitution of the Tribunal and functioning of the arbitral proceedings. Therefore, their operation has a direct and significant impact on the 'conduct' of arbitrations. Section 9, being solely for the purpose of securing interim relief, although having the potential to affect the rights of parties, does not affect the 'conduct' of the arbitration in the same way as these other provisions. It is in this context the Commission has examined and deliberated the working of these provisions and proposed certain amendments.

29. The Supreme Court has had occasion to deliberate upon the scope and nature of permissible pre-arbitral judicial intervention, especially in the context of Section 11 of the Act. Unfortunately, however, the question before the Supreme Court was framed in terms of whether such a power is a 'judicial' or an 'administrative' power—which

obfuscates the real issue underlying such nomenclature/description as to—

—the scope of such powers—i.e. the scope of arguments which a court (Chief Justice) will consider while deciding whether to appoint an arbitrator or not—i.e. whether the arbitration agreement exists, whether it is null and void, whether it is voidable, etc.; and which of these it should leave for decision of the Arbitral Tribunal.

—the nature of such intervention—i.e. would the court (Chief Justice) consider the issues upon a detailed trial and whether the same would be decided finally or be left for determination of the Arbitral Tribunal.

30. After a series of cases culminating in the decision in *SBP & Co. v. Patel Engg. Ltd.*, the Supreme Court held that the power to appoint an arbitrator under Section 11 is a 'judicial' power. The underlying issues in this judgment, relating to the scope of intervention, were subsequently clarified by Raveendran, J. in *National Insurance Co. Ltd. v. Boghara Polyfab (P) Ltd.*, where the Supreme Court laid down as follows:

'22.1. The issues (first category) which Chief Justice/his designate will have to decide are:

(a) Whether the party making the application has approached the appropriate High Court?

(b) Whether there is an arbitration agreement and whether the party who has applied under Section 11 of the Act, is a party to such an agreement?

22.2. The issues (second category) which the Chief Justice/his designate may choose to decide are:

(a) Whether the claim is a dead (long barred) claim or a live claim?

(b) Whether the parties have concluded the contract/transaction by recording satisfaction of their mutual rights and obligation or by receiving the final payment without objection?

22.3. The issues (third category) which the Chief Justice/his designate should leave exclusively to the Arbitral Tribunal are:

(a) Whether a claim made falls within the arbitration clause (as for example, a matter which is reserved for final decision of a departmental authority and excepted or excluded from arbitration)?

(b) Merits of any claim involved in the arbitration.'

31. The Commission is of the view that, in this context, the same test regarding scope and nature of judicial intervention, as applicable in the context of Section 11, should also apply to Sections 8 and 45 of the Act—since the scope and nature of judicial intervention should not change upon whether a party (intending to defeat the arbitration agreement) refuses to appoint an arbitrator in terms of the arbitration agreement, or moves a proceeding before a judicial authority in the face of such an arbitration agreement.

32. In relation to the nature of intervention, the exposition of the law is to be found in the decision of the Supreme Court in *Shin-Etsu Chemical Co. Ltd. v. Aksh Optifibre Ltd.* (in the context of Section 45 of the Act), where the Supreme Court has ruled in favour of looking at the issues/controversy only *prima facie*.

33. It is in this context, the Commission has recommended amendments to Sections 8 and 11 of the Arbitration and Conciliation Act, 1996. The scope of the judicial intervention is only restricted to situations where the court/judicial authority finds that the arbitration agreement does not exist or is null and void. Insofar as the nature of intervention is concerned, it is recommended that in the event the court/judicial authority is *prima facie* satisfied against the argument challenging the arbitration agreement, it shall appoint the arbitrator and/or refer the parties to arbitration, as the case may be. The amendment envisages that the judicial authority shall not refer the parties to arbitration only if it finds that there does not exist an arbitration agreement or that it is null and void. If the judicial authority is of the opinion that *prima facie* the arbitration agreement exists, then it shall refer the dispute to arbitration, and leave the existence of the arbitration agreement to be finally determined by the Arbitral Tribunal. However, if the judicial authority concludes that the agreement does not exist, then the conclusion will be final and not *prima facie*. The amendment also envisages that there shall be a conclusive determination as to whether the arbitration agreement is null and void. In the event that the judicial authority refers the dispute to arbitration and/or appoints an arbitrator, under Sections 8 and 11 respectively, such a decision will be final and non-appealable. An appeal can be maintained under Section 37 only in

the event of refusal to refer parties to arbitration, or refusal to appoint an arbitrator.[*]

Legislative correction, therefore, took place in 2015 in the shape of Section 11(6-A), which gives credence to the wisdom of the minority view as follows:

11. Appointment of arbitrators.—

xxx xxx xxx

(6-A) The Supreme Court or, as the case may be, the High Court, while considering any application under sub-section (4) or sub-section (5) or sub-section (6), shall, notwithstanding any judgment, decree or order of any court, confine to the examination of the existence of an arbitration agreement.

This statutory provision makes it clear that Thakker, J.'s minority view on leaving preliminary matters to the arbitrator under Section 16(1) of the Arbitration Act was probably correct. However, by a recent amendment in 2019, the arbitration-appointment procedure has now moved on to institutional appointments of arbitrators.[†] In this view of the matter, Section 11(6-A) itself has been deleted.[‡] However, this provision, at the time of writing this book, is yet to be notified.

18. *Mohd. Arif v. The Registrar, Supreme Court of India & Ors.* (2014)

A Constitution Bench of five judges in *Mohd. Arif v. The Registrar, Supreme Court of India & Ors.* (2014)[§] was tasked with determining the contours of the hearing of review petitions in death-sentence cases, which hitherto were being disposed of by circulation in judges' chambers without any oral

---

[*] Report No. 246 (August 2014).
[†] Section 3(i), Arbitration and Conciliation (Amendment) Act, 2019.
[‡] Section 3(iv), Arbitration and Conciliation (Amendment) Act, 2019.
[§] (2014) 9 SCC 737.

argument in court. The question which was raised before the court was whether *P.N. Eswara Iyer v. The Registrar, Supreme Court of India* (1980),* a decision of a bench of five learned judges, would stand in the way of granting an oral hearing in review petitions filed in death-sentence cases. The other subsidiary question before the court was whether petitions in which the death sentence had been awarded should be heard by a bench of at least three learned judges, having regard to the fact that once a death sentence is carried out, no corrective measure could bring the dead body back to life.

The majority judgment delivered by Nariman, J., on behalf of himself and three other learned judges, found no difficulty in dealing with the judgment in *P.N. Eswara Iyer* as follows:

> 33. The validity of no oral hearing rule in review petitions, generally, has been upheld in *P.N. Eswara Iyer* which is a binding precedent. Review petitions arising out of death sentence cases is carved out as a separate category as oral hearing in such review petitions is found to be mandated by Article 21. We are of the opinion that the importance of oral hearing which is recognized by the Constitution Bench in *P.N. Eswara Iyer* itself, would apply in such cases. We are conscious of the fact that while awarding a death sentence, in most of the cases, this Court would generally be affirming the decision on this aspect already arrived at by two Courts below namely the trial court as well as the High Court. After such an affirmation, the scope of review of such a judgment may be very narrow. At the same time, when it is a question of life and death of a person, even a remote chance of deviating from such a decision while exercising the review jurisdiction, would justify oral hearing in a review petition. To borrow the words of Justice Krishna Iyer, J. in *P.N. Eswara Iyer*:
>
> '23. The magic of the spoken word, the power of the Socratic process and the instant clarity of the bar-Bench dialogue are too precious to be parted with . . .'
>
> 34. We feel that this oral hearing, in death sentence cases, becomes too precious to be parted with. We also quote the following observations from that judgment:

---

* (1980) 4 SCC 680.

'29-A. The possible impression that we are debunking the value of oral advocacy in open court must be erased. Experience has shown that, at all levels, the bar, through the spoken word and the written brief, has aided the process of judicial justice. Justicing is an art even as advocacy is an art. Happy interaction between the two makes for the functional fulfilment of the court system. No judicial "emergency" can jettison the vital breath of spoken advocacy in an open forum. Indeed, there is no judicial cry for extinguishment of oral argument altogether.'

35. No doubt, the Court thereafter reminded us that the time has come for proper evaluation of oral argument at the review stage. However, when it comes to death penalty cases, we feel that the power of the spoken word has to be given yet another opportunity even if the ultimate success rate is minimal.

36. If a pyramidical structure is to be imagined, with life on top, personal liberty (and all the rights it encompasses under the new doctrine) immediately below it and other fundamental rights below personal liberty it is obvious that this judgment will apply only to death sentence cases. In most other cases, the factors mentioned by Krishna Iyer, J. in particular the Supreme Court's overcrowded docket, and the fact that a full oral hearing has preceded judgment of a criminal appeal on merits, may tilt the balance the other way.

37. It is also important to advert to Shri Luthra, learned Amicus Curiae's submission. Review Petitions are inartistically drafted. And oral submissions by a skilled advocate can bring home a point which may otherwise not be succinctly stated, given the enlarged scope of review in criminal matters, as stated in *P.N. Eswara Iyer* case. The fact that the courts overcrowded docket would be able to manage such limited oral hearings in death sentence cases only, being roughly 60 per annum, is not a factor to which great weight need be accorded as the fundamental right to life is the only paramount factor in these cases.

It was further held that at least three judicially trained minds needed to apply their minds at the final stage of the journey of a convict on death row. The review petitions that would be set down for oral hearing before three learned judges were, however—given the crowded docket of the court—restricted to a maximum of thirty minutes for oral arguments.* Chelameswar, J. was the sole dissenter. The learned judge found it impossible to get out of *P.N. Eswara Iyer*, which he stated would apply to all review petitions and which would therefore be binding. The learned judge observed:

> 71. As observed by this Court in *Eswara Iyer* case, it has never been held, either in this country or elsewhere, that the rule of *audi alteram partem* takes within its sweep the right to make oral submissions in every case. It all depends upon the demands of justice in a given case. *Eswara Iyer* case clearly held that review applications in this Court form a class where an oral hearing could be eliminated without violating any constitutional provision. Therefore, I regret my inability to agree with the conclusion recorded by my learned Brother Nariman, J. that the need for an oral hearing flows from the mandate of Article 21.
>
> 72. In my opinion, in the absence of any obligation flowing from Article 21 to grant an oral hearing, there is no need to grant an oral hearing on any one of the grounds recorded by my learned Brother for the following reasons:
>
> 72.1. That review petitions are normally heard by the same Bench which heard the appeal. Therefore, the possibility of different judicial minds reaching different conclusions on the same set of facts does not arise.
>
> 72.2 The possibility of the 'remote chance of deviation' from the conclusion already reached in my view is—though emotionally very appealing in the context of the extinguishment of life—equally applicable to all cases of review.

xxx xxx xxx

> 74. I do not see any reason to take a different view—whether the 'developments' subsequent to *Eswara Iyer* case, either in law or practice

---

* (2005) 8 SCC 618 at paragraph 43.

of this Court, demand a reconsideration of the rule, in my opinion, should be left to the Court's jurisdiction under Article 145.'

The aftermath of this case has, however, shown that as a matter of fact, pursuant to oral hearings in review petitions in death-penalty cases, the death penalty at this final judicial stage has sometimes been commuted to life imprisonment.*

---

* See, for example, *X v. State of Maharashtra* ([2019] 7 SCC 1); *Jagdish v. State of Madhya Pradesh* ([2019] SCC OnLine 250); and *Md. Mannan v. State of Bihar* ([2019] SCC OnLine 737).

IV

THE DISSENTING JUDGMENT AS AN AGENT OF CHANGE—THE APPEAL TO THE BROODING SPIRIT OF THE LAW

1. *A.K. Gopalan v. The State* (1950); *Romesh Thappar v. State of Madras* (1950); and *Brij Bhushan v. State of Delhi* (1950)

Three remarkable judgments of the Supreme Court of India, in its opening phase, all delivered by Fazl Ali, J., demonstrate the importance of the dissenting judgment as an agent of change. This far-sighted judge, whose stint in the court was only a little over two years, still managed to be a prophet or a seer, looking deep into the future and laying down law which would ultimately be adopted in preference to the law declared by the majority judgment.[*]

In *A.K. Gopalan v. the State* (1950),[†] the Preventive Detention Act, 1950, was challenged, *inter alia*, on the ground that it violated the fundamental rights contained in Articles 19(1)(d), 21 and 22. The majority judgments upheld the act, holding that the fundamental right under Articles 19 and 21 were in mutually exclusive compartments, and that Article 21 dealt only with the fact that there should be a 'law' in order that the fundamental right to life or personal liberty be validly interfered with. Fazl Ali, J. differed on both counts. The learned judge began by asking two questions, both relating to the fundamental right under Article 19(1)(d):

> It is also argued that since preventive detention amounts to a total deprivation of freedom of movement, it is not a violation of the right granted under Article 19(1)(d) in regard to which the word 'restriction' and not 'deprivation' has been used in clause (5). This argument also does not appeal to me. There are really two questions which fall to be

---

[*] The remaining dissents authored by Fazl Ali, J. are discussed in detail in Chapter VI.
[†] (1950) SCR 88.

decided in this case viz. (a) Does preventive detention take away the right guaranteed by Article 19(1)(d)?; and (b) if so, what are the consequences, if any? It seems obvious to me that preventive detention amounts to a complete deprivation of the right guaranteed by article (19)(d).*

The learned judge then went on to state that fundamental rights cannot be abridged because of 'vague and unfounded fears', as follows:

[A]part from this aspect of the matter, I agree with one of the learned Judges of the Calcutta High Court in his remark that 'no calamitous or untoward result will follow even if the provisions of the Penal Code become justiciable'. I am certain that no Court would interfere with a code which has been the law of the land for nearly a century and the provisions of which are not in conflict with the basic principles of any system of law. It seems to me that this Court should not be deterred from giving effect to a fundamental right granted under the Constitution, merely because of a vague and unfounded fear that something catastrophic may happen.†

Then comes the important passage as to how the fundamental rights granted in various articles are not independent of each other, and must be read together. This most significant passage is as follows:

58. To my mind, the scheme of the Chapter dealing with the fundamental rights does not contemplate what is attributed to it, namely, that each article is a code by itself and is independent of the others. In my opinion, it cannot be said that Articles 19, 20, 21 and 22 do not to some extent overlap each other. The case of a person who is convicted of an offence will come under Articles 20 and 21 and also under Article 22 so far as his arrest and detention in custody before trial are concerned. Preventive detention, which is dealt with in Article 22, also amounts to deprivation of personal liberty which is referred to in Article 21, and is a violation of the right of freedom of movement dealt

---

* Ibid., at p. 143.
† Ibid., at p. 145.

with in Article 19(1)(d). That there are other instances of overlapping of articles in the Constitution may be illustrated by reference to Article 19(1)(f) and Article 31 both of which deal with the right to property and to some extent overlap each other. It appears that some learned High Court Judges, who had to deal with the very question before us, were greatly impressed by the statement in the report of the Drafting Committee of the Constituent Assembly on Article 15 (corresponding to the present Article 21), that the word 'liberty' should be qualified by the insertion of the word 'personal' before it for otherwise it may be construed very widely so as to include the freedoms dealt with in Article 13 (corresponding to the present Article 19). I am not however prepared to hold that this statement is decisive on the question of the construction of the words used in Article 19(1)(d) which are quite plain and can be construed without any extraneous help. Whether the report of the Drafting Committee and the debates on the floor of the House should be used at all in construing the words of a statute, which are words of ordinary and common use and are not used in any technical or peculiar sense, is a debatable question; and whether they can be used in aid of a construction which is a strain upon the language used in the clause to be interpreted is a still more doubtful matter. But, apart from these legal considerations, it is, I think, open to us to analyse the statement and see whether it goes beyond adding a somewhat plausible reason—a superficially plausible reason—for a slight verbal change in Article 21. It seems clear that the addition of the word 'personal' before 'liberty' in Article 21 cannot change the meaning of the words used in Article 19, nor can it put a matter which is inseparably bound up with personal liberty beyond its place. Personal liberty and personal freedom, in spite of the use of the word 'personal', are, as we find in several books, sometimes used in a wide sense and embrace freedom of speech, freedom of association etc. These rights are some of the most valuable phases or elements of liberty and they do not cease to be so by the addition of the word 'personal'. A general statement by the Drafting Committee referring to freedom in plural cannot take the place of an authoritative exposition of the meaning of the words used in Article 19(1)(d), which has not been specifically referred to and cannot be such an overriding consideration as to compel us to put a meaning opposed to reason and authority. The words used in Article 19(1)(d) must be construed as they stand, and we have to decide upon the words themselves whether in the case of preventive detention the right under Article 19(1)(d) is or is not infringed. But, as I shall point out later, however literally we may construe the words used in Article 19(1)(d) and however restricted may be the meaning we may attribute to those words, there can be no escape from the conclusion that preventive detention is a direct infringement of the right guaranteed in Article 19(1)(d).*

Equally important is the following passage, in which the learned judge found that the freedom or right of movement overlaps with the juristic concept of 'personal liberty'. This was felicitously stated as follows:

Having dealt with the principal objections, I wish to revert once again to the main topic. The expressions 'personal liberty' and 'personal freedom' have, as we find in several books, a wider meaning and also a narrower meaning. In the wider sense, they include not only immunity from arrest and detention but also freedom of speech, freedom of association etc. In the narrower sense, they mean immunity from arrest and detention. I have shown that the juristic conception of 'personal liberty', when these words are used in the sense of immunity from arrest, is that it consists in freedom of movement and locomotion. I have also pointed out that this conception is at the root of the criminal law of England and of this country, so far as the offences of false imprisonment and wrongful confinement are concerned. The gravamen of these offences is restraint on freedom of movement. With these facts in view, I have tried to find out whether there is any freedom of movement known in England apart from personal liberty used in the sense of immunity from arrest and detention, but I find no trace of any such freedom. In *Halsbury's Laws of England* (2nd Edn., Vol. 6, p. 391), the freedoms mentioned are the right to personal freedom (or immunity from detention or confinement), the right to property, the right to freedom of speech, the right of public meeting, the right of association etc. Similar classifications will be found in Dicey's *Introduction to the Study of the Law of the Constitution* and

---

* Ibid., at p. 148.

Keith's *Constitutional Law* and other books on constitutional subjects, but there is no reference anywhere to any freedom or right of movement in the sense in which we are asked to construe the words used in Article 19(1)(d). In the Constitutions of America, Ireland and many other countries where freedom is prized, there is no reference to freedom or right of movement as something distinct from personal liberty used in the sense of immunity from arrest and confinement. The obvious explanation is that in legal conception no freedom or right of movement exists apart from what personal liberty connotes and therefore a separate treatment of this freedom was not necessary. It is only in the Constitution of the Free City of Danzig, which covers an area of 791 square miles, that we find these words in Article 75: 'All nationals shall enjoy freedom of movement within the City'. There is however no authoritative opinion available to support the view that this freedom is anything different from what is otherwise called personal liberty. The problem of construction in regard to this particular right in the Constitution of Danzig is the same as in our Constitution. Such being the general position, I am confirmed in my view that the juristic conception that personal liberty and freedom of movement connote the same thing is the correct and true conception, and the words used in Article 19(1)(d) must be construed according to this universally accepted legal conception.[*]

Explaining why the expression 'due process' was not borrowed from the American Constitution, the learned judge found:

In the course of the arguments, the learned Attorney-General referred us to the proceedings in the Constituent Assembly for the purpose of showing that the article as originally drafted contained the words 'without due process of law' but these words were subsequently replaced by the words 'except according to procedure established by law'. In my opinion, though the proceedings or discussions in the Assembly are not relevant for the purpose of construing the meaning of the expressions used in Article 21, especially when they are plain and unambiguous, they are relevant to show that the Assembly intended to avoid the use of the

[*] Ibid., at pp. 150–51.

expression 'without due process of law'. That expression had its roots in the expression *per legem terrae* (law of the land) used in Magna Carta in 1215. In the reign of Edward III, however, the words 'due process of law' were used in a statute guaranteeing that no person will be deprived of his property or imprisoned or indicted or put to death without being brought in to answer by due process of law (28, Edward III, Chapter III). The expression was afterwards adopted in the American Constitution and also in the Constitutions of some of the constituent States, though some of the States preferred to use the words 'in due course of law' or 'according to the law of the land'.

xxx xxx xxx

It seems plain that the Constituent Assembly did not adopt this expression on account of the very elastic meaning given to it, but preferred to use the words 'according to procedure established by law' which occur in the Japanese Constitution framed in 1946.*

After setting out propositions emanating from a few US Supreme Court judgments, the learned judge found:

Thus, in America, the word 'law' does not mean merely State-made law or law enacted by the State and does not exclude certain fundamental principles of justice which inhere in every civilized system of law and which are at the root of it. The result of the numerous decisions in America has been summed up by Professor Willis in his book on *Constitutional Law* at p. 662, in the statement that the essentials of due process are: (1) notice, (2) opportunity to be heard, (3) an impartial tribunal, and (4) orderly course of procedure. It is pointed out by the learned author that these essentials may assume different forms in different circumstances, and so long as they are conceded in principle, the requirement of law will be fulfilled. For example, a person cannot require any particular form or method of hearing, but all that he can require is a reasonable opportunity to be heard. Similarly, an impartial tribunal does not necessarily mean

---

* Ibid., at pp. 158–59.

a judicial tribunal in every case. So far as orderly course of procedure is concerned, he explains that it does not require a court to strictly weigh the evidence but it does require it to examine the entire record to ascertain the issues, to discover whether there are facts not reported and to see whether or not the law has been correctly applied to facts. The view expressed by other writers is practically the same as that expressed by Professor Willis, though some of them do not expressly refer to the fourth element viz. orderly course of procedure. The real point however is that these four elements are really different aspects of the same right viz. the right to be heard before one is condemned.[*]

The learned judge then went on to state:

[T]he question envisages something which is not likely to happen, but it does raise a legal problem which can perhaps be met only in this way that if the expression 'procedure established by law' simply means any procedure established or enacted by statute it will be difficult to give a negative answer to the question, but if the word 'law' includes what I have endeavoured to show it does, such an answer may be justified. It seems to me that there is nothing revolutionary in the doctrine that the words 'procedure established by law' must include the four principles set out in Professor Willis' book, which, as I have already stated, are different aspects of the same principle and which have no vagueness or uncertainty about them. These principles, as the learned author points out and as the authorities show, are not absolutely rigid principles but are adaptable to the circumstances of each case within certain limits. I have only to add that it has not been seriously controverted that 'law' in this article means valid law and 'procedure' means certain definite rules of proceeding and not something which is a mere pretence for procedure.[†]

In dealing with the interplay between Articles 19 and 22, the learned judge held:

---

[*] Ibid., at pp. 162–63.
[†] Ibid., at p. 169.

It was argued that Article 22 is a code by itself and the whole law of preventive detention is to be found within its four corners. I cannot however easily subscribe to this sweeping statement. The article does provide for some matters of procedure, but it does not exhaustively provide for them. It is said that it provides for notice, an opportunity to the detenu to represent his case, an Advisory Board which may deal with his case, and for the maximum period beyond which a person cannot be detained. These points have undoubtedly been touched, but it cannot be said that they have been exhaustively treated. The right to represent is given, but it is left to the legislature to provide the machinery for dealing with the representation. The Advisory Board has been mentioned, but it is only to safeguard detention for a period longer than three months. There is ample latitude still left to Parliament, and if Parliament makes use of that latitude unreasonably, Article 19(5) may enable the court to see whether it has transgressed the limits of reasonableness.[*]

The judgments in *R v. Halliday* and *Liversidge v. Anderson* were then discussed:

I have only to add a few concluding remarks to my judgment. In studying the provisions of the impugned Act, I could not help instituting a comparison in my own mind between it and similar legislation in England during the last two world wars. I could not also help noticing that the impugned Act purports to be a peacetime Act, whereas the legislation to which I have referred was enacted during the war. During the first war as well as the second, a number of persons were detained and a number of cases were brought to Court in connection with their detention, but the two leading cases which will be quoted again and again are *Rex v. Halliday* and *Liversidge v. Sir John Anderson*. We are aware that in America certain standards which do not conform to ordinary and normal law have been applied by the Judges during the period of the war and sometimes they are compendiously referred to as being included in 'war power'. The two English cases to which I have referred also illustrate the same principle, as will appear from

---

[*] Ibid. at pp. 183–84.

two short extracts which I wish to reproduce. In *Rex v. Halliday* Lord Atkinson observed as follows: 'However precious the personal liberty of the subject may be, there is something for which it may well be, to some extent, sacrificed by legal enactment, namely, national success in the war, or escape from national plunder or enslavement.

In *Liversidge v. Sir John Anderson* Lord Macmillan struck the same note in these words:

'The liberty which we so justly extol is itself the gift of the law and as Magna Carta recognizes may by the law be forfeited or abridged. At a time when it is the undoubted law of the land that a citizen may by conscription or requisition be compelled to give up his life and all that he possesses for his country's cause it may well be no matter for surprise that there should be confided to the Secretary of State a discretionary power of enforcing the relatively mild precaution of detention.'

These passages represent the majority view in the two cases, but the very elaborate judgments of Lord Shaw in *Rex v. Halliday* and that of Lord Atkin in *Liversidge v. Sir John Anderson* show that there was room for difference of opinion as well as for a more dispassionate treatment of the case and the points involved in it. It is difficult to say that there is not a good substratum of sound law in the celebrated dictum of Lord Atkin that even amidst the clash of arms the laws are not silent and that they speak the same language in war as in peace. However that may be, what I find is that in the regulations made in England during the first war as well as the second war there was an elaborate provision for an Advisory Board in all cases without any exception, which provided a wartime safeguard for persons deprived of their liberty. There was also a provision in the Act of 1939 that the Secretary of State should report at least once in every month as to the action taken under the regulation including the number of persons detained under orders made thereunder. I find that these reports were printed and made available to the public. I also find that the Secretary of State stated in the House of Commons on 28 January, 1943, that the general order would be to allow British subjects detained under the Regulation to have consultations with their legal advisers out of the hearing of an officer. This order applied to consultations with barristers and solicitors but not to cases where solicitors sent to interview a detained person a clerk who was not an officer of the High Court. The impugned Act suffers in comparison, on account of want of such provisions, though, so far as I can see, no great harm was likely to have been caused by setting up a machinery composed of either administrative or Judicial Authorities for examining the cases of detained persons so as to satisfy the essentials of fairness and justice. The Act also suffers in comparison with some of the later Provincial Acts in which the safeguard of an Advisory Board is, expressly provided for. I find that there is a provision in Section 12(2) of the Act for the review of the cases of detenus after six months, but this is quite different from examining the merits of the case. The object of such a review is obviously to find out whether by reason of any change in the circumstances, a review of the original order is required.

I hope that in pointing out the shortcomings of the Act I will not be misunderstood. I am aware that both in England and in America and also in many other countries, there has been a reorientation of the old notions of individual freedom which is gradually yielding to social control in many matters. I also realize that those who run the State have very onerous responsibilities, and it is not correct to say that emergent conditions have altogether disappeared from this country. Granting then that private rights must often be subordinated to the public good, is it not essential in a free community to strike a just balance in the matter? That a person should be deprived of his personal liberty without a trial is a serious matter, but the needs of society may demand it and the individual may often have to yield to those needs. Still the balance between the maintenance of individual rights and public good can be struck only if the person who is deprived of his liberty is allowed a fair chance to establish his innocence, and I do not see how the establishment of an appropriate machinery giving him such a chance can be an impediment to good and just Government.[*]

The effects of this judgment were only felt after it lay dormant for a period of twenty years. The learned judge did not live to see that his view of the law was expressly accepted by an eleven-judge bench in *R.C. Cooper*

---

[*] Ibid. at pp. 186–88.

v. Union of India (1970),[*] in which the majority view in *Gopalan* was overruled.[†]

Two cases came before the first Supreme Court in which the fundamental right to the freedom of speech and of the press was invoked under Article 19(1)(a) of the Constitution—*Romesh Thappar v. State of Madras* (1950)[‡] and *Brij Bhushan v. State of Delhi* (1950).[§] In *Romesh Thappar*, the validity of the Madras Maintenance of Public Order Act, 1949, in particular, Section 9(1-A), came before the court for consideration. Likewise, in *Brij Bhushan*, the validity of Section 7(1)(c) of the East Punjab Public Safety Act, 1949, was at stake. The majority judgments in both cases held both provisions unconstitutional, inasmuch as Article 19(2)—at the time of the framing of the Constitution—did not contain the expression 'public order'. As originally enacted, Article 19(2) read:

> Nothing in sub clause (a) of Clause (1) shall affect the operation of any existing law in so far as it relates to, or prevents the State from making any law relating to libel, slander, defamation, contempt of court or any matter which offends against decency or morality or which undermines the security of, or tends to overthrow the state.

Fazl Ali dissented in both cases, which—in the words of the learned judge—involved practically the same question.[¶] Therefore, in *Romesh Thappar*, Fazl Ali, J. adopted his reasoning in *Brij Bhushan*, where he held that 'public order' came within the scope of the expression 'undermines the security of . . . the State', stating that the narrower concept of 'sedition' was not to be found in Article 19(2), as it stood at that time, reasoning:

> The framers of the Constitution must have therefore found themselves face to face with the dilemma as to whether the word 'sedition' should

---

[*] (1970) 3 SCR 530.

[†] Ibid. at pp. 573, 577 and 578. *See* also the views of Bhagwati and Krishna Iyer, JJ. in *Maneka Gandhi v. Union of India* ([1978] 2 SCR 621), pp. 669–74, 722–25.

[‡] (1950) SCR 594.

[§] (1950) SCR 605.

[¶] (1950) SCR 594, pp. 603–04.

be used in Article 19(2) and if it was to be used in what sense it was to be used. On the one hand, they must have had before their mind the very widely accepted view supported by numerous authorities that sedition was essentially an offence against public tranquillity and was connected in some way or other with public disorder; and, on the other hand, there was the pronouncement of the Judicial Committee that sedition as defined in the Indian Penal Code did not necessarily imply any intention or tendency to incite disorder. In these circumstances, it is not surprising that they decided not to use the word 'sedition' in clause (2) but used the more general words which cover sedition and everything else which makes sedition such a serious offence. That sedition does undermine the security of the State is a matter which cannot admit of much doubt. That it undermines the security of the State usually through the medium of public disorder is also a matter on which eminent Judges and jurists are agreed. Therefore it is difficult to hold that public disorder or disturbance of public tranquillity are not matters which undermine the security of the State.

xxx xxx xxx

It must be recognized that freedom of speech and expression is one of the most valuable rights guaranteed to a citizen by the Constitution and should be jealously guarded by the Courts. It must also be recognized that free political discussion is essential for the proper functioning of a democratic Government, and the tendency of modern jurists is to deprecate censorship though they all agree that 'liberty of the press' is not to be confused with its 'licentiousness'. But the Constitution itself has prescribed certain limits for the exercise of the freedom of speech and expression and this Court is only called upon to see whether a particular case comes within those limits. In my opinion, the law which is impugned is fully saved by Article 19(2) and if it cannot be successfully assailed it is not possible to grant the remedy which the petitioners are seeking here.*

---

* Ibid., pp. 616, 619.

Shortly after these two judgments, the first amendment to the Constitution*
was passed in 1951, in which Article 19(2) was replaced as follows:

> (2) Nothing in sub-clause (a) of clause (1) shall affect the operation of
> any existing law, or prevent the State from making any law, in so far
> as such law imposes reasonable restrictions on the exercise of the right
> conferred by the said sub-clause in the interests of the security of the
> State, friendly relations with foreign States, public order, decency or
> morality, or in relation to contempt of court, defamation or incitement
> to an offence.

What is interesting to note is that the very Constituent Assembly
which framed Article 19(2) passed the first amendment as a provisional
Parliament until national elections were held in 1952 to elect the first
elected Parliament of the country. The Constituent Assembly, acting as
a provisional Parliament, was of the opinion that Fazl Ali, J. correctly
understood what was sought to be portrayed by the words used in Article
19(2) as originally drafted, and made the necessary amendment to reflect
their original intent, which Fazl Ali, J. alone was clearly able to see.

2. *State of Bombay v. The United Motors (India) Ltd* (1953)

State of Bombay v. The United Motors (India) Ltd (1953)† has been dealt
with in great detail in Chapter III earlier. Bose, J.'s dissenting judgment in
this case was adopted as the correct view of the law by a majority of 4:3 in
Bengal Immunity Co. Ltd. v. State of Bihar and Ors. (1955),‡ also discussed
extensively earlier.

The explanation to Article 286(1)(a) of the Constitution of India
was held by Bose, J. as governing only Article 286(1), and not Article
286(2), as a result of which, if a sale falls within the explanation, then,
notwithstanding that it may be an interstate sale, the legal fiction enacted
in the explanation must be given full effect, and the aforesaid sale must be

---

* The Constitution (First Amendment) Act, 1951.
† (1953) 4 SCR 1069.
‡ (1955) 2 SCR 603.

treated as an intra-state sale which the state may tax under Article 286(1)
(a). This was so held by the learned judge as follows:

> Coming back to the Explanation, its object is, I think, to resolve
> the difficulty regarding the situs of a sale. The Constitution having
> decided that the only State which can tax a sale or a purchase is the
> State in which the transaction takes place, and having before it the
> conflict of views regarding nexus and situs, resolved the problem by
> introducing the fiction embodied in the Explanation. The purpose of
> the Explanation is, in my view, to explain what is not outside the
> State and therefore what is inside. With respect I cannot agree that the
> Explanation is really an exception, and I do not think the *non obstante*
> clause means that under the general law the place where the property
> passes was regarded as the place where the sale takes place, for that
> in itself would be a fiction. There is no such law. In my opinion, all
> it means is that there was a school of thought which regarded that as
> the crucial element on the nexus view and that the Constitution has
> negatived that idea.
>
> I am also unable to agree that the Explanation governs clause (2)
> of Article 286, for it limits itself in express terms to sub-clause (a) of
> clause (1). It says that is an Explanation 'for the purposes of sub-clause
> (a)'. In view of that I do not feel justified in carrying it over to clause
> (2) and holding that it governs there as well. In my judgment, the only
> purpose of the Explanation is to explain where the situs of a sale is.
> Clause (2) has a different object. Its purpose is to prohibit taxation on
> sales and purchases which take place in the course of inter-State trade
> or commerce.
>
> If the Explanation is carried over to clause (2) it must, in my
> judgment, be equally applicable to sub-clause (b) of clause (1). As I
> understand the argument, the reasoning is this. The Explanation turns
> an inter-State sale into an intra-State sale by means of a fiction.[*]

On this view of the law, the Bombay Sales Tax Act, 1952, was held to be
ultra vires the Constitution of India.

---

[*] (1953) 4 SCR 1069, pp. 1103–104.

3. *Director of Rationing and Distribution v. The Corporation of Calcutta* (1961)

In *Director of Rationing and Distribution v. The Corporation of Calcutta* (1961),* the respondent-corporation filed a complaint against the appellant under Section 386(1)(a) of the Calcutta Municipal Act, 1923. The magistrate acquitted the appellant, holding that this provision did not bind the government, whom the appellant represented. The high court, however, reversed this decision. In the majority judgment of Sinha, C.J., speaking on behalf of himself and two other learned judges, joined by a separate concurring judgment of Sarkar, J., the Supreme Court held that the rule of interpretation of statutes, i.e. that the state is not bound by a statute unless provided expressly or by necessary implication, continues to be good law even after the Constitution of India has come into force. This being so, the high court's judgment was set aside and that of the learned magistrate restored. Wanchoo, J. dissented. He held:

> In our country the Rule of Law prevails and our Constitution has guaranteed it by the provisions contained in Part III thereof as well as by other provisions in other Parts: (see *Virendra Singh v. State of Uttar Pradesh*). It is to my mind inherent in the conception of the Rule of Law that the State, no less than its citizens and others, is bound by the laws of the land. When the King as the embodiment of all power— executive, legislative and judicial has disappeared and in our republican Constitution, sovereign power has been distributed among various organs created thereby, it seems to me that there is neither justification nor necessity for continuing the rule of construction; based on the royal prerogative. It is said that though the King has gone, sovereignty still exists and therefore what was the prerogative of the King has become the prerogative of the sovereign. There is to my mind a misconception here. It is true that sovereignty must exist under our Constitution; but there is no sovereign as such now. In England, however, the King is synonymous with the sovereign and so arose the royal prerogative. But in our country it would be impossible now to point to one person or institution and

---

* (1961) 1 SCR 158.

to say that he or it is the sovereign under the Constitution. A further question may arise, if one is in search of a sovereign now, whether the State Government with which one is concerned here is sovereign in the same sense as the English King (though it may have plenary powers under the limits set under our Constitution). This to my mind is another reason why there being no King or sovereign as such now in our country, the rule of construction based on the royal prerogative can no longer be invoked.*

xxx xxx xxx

Further it appears to me that the royal prerogative where it deals with substantive rights of the Crown as against its subjects, as, for example, the priority of Crown debts over debts of the same nature owing to the subject, stands on a different footing from the royal prerogative put forward in the present case, which is really no more than a rule of construction of statutes passed by Parliament. Where, for example, a royal prerogative dealing with a substantive right has been accepted by the courts in India as applicable here also, it becomes a law in force which will continue in force under Article 372(1) of the Constitution. But where the royal prerogative is merely a rule of construction of statutes based on the existence of the Crown in England and for historical reasons, I fail to see why in a democratic republic, the courts should not follow the ordinary principle of construction that no one is exempt from the operation of a statute unless the statute expressly grants the exemption or the exemption arises by necessary implication. On the whole therefore I am of opinion that the proper rule of construction which should now be applied, at any rate after January 26, 1950, is that the State in India whether in the Centre or in the States is bound by the law unless there is an express exemption in favour of the State or an exemption can be inferred by necessary implication. The view taken by the Calcutta High Court in this connection should be accepted and the view expressed by the Privy Council in *Province of Bombay v. Municipal Corporation of the City of*

---

* Ibid., pp. 185–86.

Bombay should no longer be accepted as the rule for construction of statutes passed by Indian legislatures.[*]

As noted in Chapter III above, in the Supreme Court in *Superintendent & Legal Remembrancer, State of West Bengal v. Corporation of Calcutta* (1967),[†] a nine-judge bench was constituted in order to decide whether *Director of Rationing and Distribution* was correct. Subba Rao, J.'s judgment on behalf of himself and six other learned judges held that the dissenting view taken by Wanchoo, J. in *Director of Rationing and Distribution* was the correct view of the law and therefore proceeded to overrule the majority judgments as follows:

> While Sinha, C.J., took the view that the common law of England, including the rule of construction, was accepted as the law of this country and was, therefore, the law in force within the meaning of the said Article, Wanchoo, J., took the view that whatever might be said of the substantive laws, a rule of construction adopted by the common law of England and accepted by the Privy Council at a time when the Crown was functioning in India, was not the law in force within the meaning of the said Article.[‡]

xxx xxx xxx

> To sum up: some of the doctrines of common law of England were administered as the law in the Presidency towns of Calcutta, Bombay and Madras. The Common Law of England was not adopted in the rest of India. Doubtless some of its principles were embodied in the statute law of our country. That apart, in the mofussil, some principles of Common Law were invoked by courts on the ground of justice, equity and good conscience. It is, therefore, a question of fact in each case whether any particular branch of the Common Law became a part of the law of India or in any particular part thereof. The aforesaid rule of construction is

---

[*] Id., pp. 188–89.
[†] (1967) 2 SCR 170.
[‡] Ibid., p. 178.

only a canon of interpretation, it is not a rule of substantive law. Though it was noticed in some of the judgments of the Bombay High Court, the decisions therein mainly turned upon the relevant statutory provisions. One decision even questioned its correctness. There is nothing to show that it was applied in other parts of the country on the ground of justice, good conscience and equity. In Madras, it was not considered to be a binding rule of law, but only as a simple canon of construction. In Calcutta there was a conflict: one Bench accepted the construction and the other rejected it. The Privy Council gave its approval to the rule mainly on the concession of advocates and that decision related to Bombay City. It is, therefore, clear that the said rule of construction was not accepted as a rule of construction throughout India and even in the Presidency towns it was not regarded as inflexible rule of construction. In short it has not become a law of the land.

Let us now proceed on the assumption that it has been accepted as a rule of construction throughout India. This leads us to the question whether the said rule of construction is the law of the land after the Constitution came into force. Under Article 372, all the laws in force in the territory of India immediately before the commencement of this Constitution shall continue in force therein until altered or repealed or amended by a competent legislature or other competent authority. Can it be said that the said canon of construction was a 'law in force' which can only be amended by a legislature? Under Explanation (1) to the said Article, the expression 'law in force' shall include a law passed or, made by a legislature or other competent authority in the territory of India before the commencement of the Constitution. It has been held by this Court that the said expression includes not only enactments of the Indian Legislatures but also the Common Law of the land which was being administered by the courts in India. (See *Director of Rationing and Distribution v. Corporation of Calcutta* and *V.S. Rice and Oil Mills v. State of Andhra Pradesh*). But it is not possible to hold that a mere rule of construction adopted by English courts, and also by some of the Indian courts to ascertain the intention of the legislature was a law in force within the meaning of this term. There is an essential distinction between a law and a canon of construction. This distinction between law and the canon of construction has been noticed by us earlier and we have held that a canon of construction is not a rule of law. We are not concerned here with the statutory rules of interpretation. We are, therefore, of the opinion that a rule of construction is not a 'law in force' within the meaning of Article 372.[*]

Shah, J. wrote a separate dissenting judgment. This dissent in *Superintendent & Legal Remembrancer*, is discussed in detail in Chapter III.

4. *Atiabari Tea Co. Ltd. v. State of Assam and Ors.* (1961)

The dissent of B.P. Sinha, C.J. in *Atiabari Tea Co. Ltd. v. State of Assam and Ors.* (1961)[†] was only one of three views expressed by the court on whether taxes that were levied by Parliament or the state legislatures could be said to impede the movement of goods and persons, so as to infract Article 301 of the Constitution of India. Article 301 states:

Subject to the other provisions of this Part, trade, commerce and intercourse throughout the territory of India shall be free.

The majority judgment of Gajendragadkar, J., speaking for himself and two other learned judges, held that when a tax directly and immediately affects the free flow of trade, such tax must be held to impinge upon the freedom granted under Article 301, and unless saved by any other provision in Chapter XIII of the Constitution, must be held to be invalidly imposed. Two other views were forthcoming. Sinha, C.J. held that taxation, per se, was outside the clutches of Article 301 and could not infract the said article, except if such taxation erected trade barriers, tariff walls and imposts which had a deleterious effect on the free flow of trade, commerce and intercourse. Justice Shah was of the exactly opposite view, stating that the freedom mentioned in Article 301 includes not only freedom from discriminatory tariffs and trade barriers, but from all taxation on trade and commerce.

Sinha, C.J.'s view began with the following statement of the law:

---

[*] Id., pp. 186–87.
[†] (1961) 1 SCR 809.

In short, Part XII is a self-contained series of provisions relating to the finances of the Union and of the States and their inter-relation and adjustments (ignoring the provisions in Chapter 2 of that Part relating to borrowing and Chapter 3 relating to property contracts etc.). Like Part XIII, Part XII also is not expressed to be subject to the other provisions of the Constitution. Hence, both Parts XII and XIII are meant to be self-contained in their respective fields. It cannot, therefore, be said that the one is subject to the other.[*]

The learned judge therefore found:

Viewed in this all comprehensive sense taxation on trade, commerce and intercourse would have many ramifications and would cover almost the entire field of public taxation, both in the Union and in the State Lists. It is almost impossible to think that the makers of the Constitution intended to make trade, commerce and intercourse free from taxation in that comprehensive sense. If that were so, all laws of taxation relating to sale and purchase of goods on carriage of goods and commodities, men and animals, from one place to another, both inter-State and intra-State, would come within the purview of Article 301 and the proviso to Article 304 (b) would make it necessary that all Bills or Amendments of pre-existing laws shall have to go through the gamut prescribed by that proviso. That will be putting too great an impediment to the power of taxation vested in the States and reduce the States' limited sovereignty under the Constitution to a mere fiction. That extreme position has, therefore, to be rejected as unsound.

In this connection, it is also pertinent to bear in mind that all taxation is not necessarily an impediment or a restraint in the matter of trade, commerce and intercourse. Instead of being such impediments or restraints, they may, on the other hand, provide the wherewithals to improve different kinds of means of transport, for example, in cane growing areas, unless there are good roads, facility for transport of sugarcane from sugarcane fields to sugar mills may be wholly lacking or insufficient. In order to make new roads as also to improve old ones,

---

[*] Ibid., p. 824.

cess on the grower of cane or others interested in the transport of this commodity has to be imposed, and has been known in some parts of India to have been imposed at a certain rate per maund or ton of sugarcane transported to sugar factories. Such an imposition is a tax on transport of sugarcane from one place to another, either intra-State or inter-State. It is the tax thus realized that makes it feasible for opening new means of communication or for improving old ones. It cannot, therefore, be said that taxation in every case must mean an impediment or restraint against free flow of trade and commerce. Similarly, for the facility of passengers and goods by motor transport or by railway, a surcharge on usual fares or freights is levied, or may be levied in future. But for such a surcharge, improvement in the means of communication may not be available at all. Hence, in my opinion, it is not correct to characterize a tax on movement of goods or passengers as necessarily connoting an impediment, or a restraint, in the matter of trade and commerce. That is another good reason in support of the conclusion that taxation is not ordinarily included within the terms of Article 301 of the Constitution.

In my opinion, another very cogent reason for holding that taxation *simpliciter* is not within the terms of Article 301 of the Constitution is that the very connotation of taxation is the power of the State to raise money for public purposes by compelling the payment by persons, both natural and juristic, of monies earned or possessed by them, by virtue of the facilities and protection afforded by the State. Such burdens or imposts, either direct or indirect, are in the ultimate analysis meant as a contribution by the citizens or persons residing in the State or dealing with the citizens of the State, for the support of the Government, with particular reference to their respective abilities to make such contributions. Thus public purpose is implicit in every taxation, as such. Therefore, when Part XIII of the Constitution speaks of imposition of reasonable restrictions in public interest, it could not have intended to include taxation within the generic term 'reasonable restrictions'.*

The learned judge then stated his view on Part XIII as follows:

---

* Id., pp. 827–28.

Thus, on a fair construction of the provisions of Part XIII, the following propositions emerge: (1) trade, commerce, and intercourse throughout the territory of India are not absolutely free, but are subject to certain powers of legislation by Parliament or the Legislature of a State; (2) the freedom declared by Article 301 does not mean freedom from taxation *simpliciter*, but does mean freedom from taxation which has the effect of directly impeding the free flow of trade, commerce and intercourse; (3) the freedom envisaged in Article 301 is subject to non-discriminatory restrictions imposed by Parliament in public interest (Article 302); (4) even discriminatory or preferential legislation may be made by Parliament for the purpose of dealing with an emergency like a scarcity of goods in any part of India [Article 303(2)]; (5) reasonable restrictions may be imposed by the Legislature of a State in the public interest [Article 304(b)]; (6) non-discriminatory taxes may be imposed by the Legislature of a State on goods imported from another State or other States, if similar taxes are imposed on goods produced or manufactured in that State [Article 304(a)]; and lastly (7) restrictions imposed by existing laws have been continued, except insofar as the President may by order otherwise direct (Article 305).[*]

In this view of the matter, Sinha, C.J. upheld the statute in question in the following manner:

It will be seen from the bare summary of the relevant provisions of the statute that it is a taxing statute *simpliciter* without the least suggestion even of any attempt at discrimination against dealers and producers outside the State of Assam or of preference in favour of those inside the State. On the face of it, therefore, the Act does not suffer from any of the vices against which Part XIII of the Constitution was intended. It has not been suggested that the Act imposes a heavy burden on the dealer or the producer as the case may be. On the terms of the Statute, it cannot be said that it is intended to put obstacles or impediments in the way of free flow of traffic in respect of jute and tea. On the face of it, it would not be in the interest of the State of Assam to put any such impediments,

---

[*] Id., pp. 831–32.

because Assam is a large producer of those commodities and the market for those commodities is mainly in Calcutta. In those circumstances, it is difficult, if not impossible, to come to the conclusion that the Act comes within the purview of Article 301 of the Constitution. If that is so, no further consideration arising out of the other provisions of Part XIII of the Constitution calls for any decision. It will be seen from the bare summary of the relevant provisions of the statute that it is a taxing statute *simpliciter* without the least suggestion even of any attempt at discrimination against dealers and producers outside the State of Assam or of preference in favour of those inside the State. On the face of it, therefore, the Act does not suffer from any of the vices against which Part XIII of the Constitution was intended. It has not been suggested that the Act imposes a heavy burden on the dealer or the producer as the case may be. On the terms of the Statute, it cannot be said that it is intended to put obstacles or impediments in the way of free flow of traffic in respect of jute and tea. On the face of it, it would not be in the interest of the State of Assam to put any such impediments, because Assam is a large producer of those commodities and the market for those commodities is mainly in Calcutta. In those circumstances, it is difficult, if not impossible, to come to the conclusion that the Act comes within the purview of Article 301 of the Constitution. If that is so, no further consideration arising out of the other provisions of Part XIII of the Constitution calls for any decision.[*]

At the time B.P. Sinha, C.J. espoused this view, it was considered to be as extreme a view as Justice Shah's, who had arrived at the opposite conclusion. It is no wonder that when a seven-judge bench was convened to have a relook into these very provisions in *Automobile Transport (Rajasthan) Ltd. v. The State of Rajasthan and Others* (1963),[†] the majority judgment of S.K. Das, J. accepted the majority view of Gajendragadkar, J. in *Atiabari*, with the rider that 'compensatory' or 'regulatory' taxes would not be violative of Article 301.[‡]

---

[*] Id., pp. 833–34.

[†] (1963) 1 SCR 491.

[‡] Hidayatullah J.'s dissenting opinion in *Automobile Transport* is discussed in detail in Chapter VI.

However, what seemed to have been settled by the seven-judge bench in *Automobile Transport* was revisited by a nine-judge bench in *Jindal Stainless Steel v. State of Haryana* (2017).[*] The majority of the nine-judge bench, in overruling both *Atiabari* and *Automobile Transport*, expressly approved the view of Sinha, C.J. in *Atiabari*, stating that taxation per se is outside the ken of Article 301. Chief Justice Thakur, speaking for the majority, referred to Sinha C.J.'s judgment in paragraph 41, and then held:

> 59. While J.C. Shah, J. in *Atiabari* took the view that all taxes regardless of whether they are discriminatory or otherwise would constitute an impediment on free trade and commerce guaranteed under Article 301 of the Constitution of India, Sinha, C.J., held that taxes per se were totally outside the purview of Article 301 and could never constitute a restriction except where the same operated as a fiscal barrier that prevented free trade, commerce and intercourse. The view taken by Shah, J. was not supported by any one of the counsel appearing for the parties for it was candidly accepted that the same was an extreme view that was legally unsupportable.

In paragraph 116 Sinha, C.J.'s judgment was upheld, with the caveat that insofar as it speaks of taxes which create high tariff walls and which would therefore be within the ken of Article 301, the judgment does not elaborate as to what this high tariff wall would be. Paragraph 116 is set out hereinbelow:

> 116. Reliance by the counsel for the dealers upon the judgment of Sinha, C.J. is also, in our opinion, of no avail to them. After holding taxes to be outside the purview of Part XIII of the Constitution, his Lordship made the following observations:
>
> > '16. . . . If a law is passed by the legislature imposing a tax which in its true nature and effect is meant to impose an impediment to the free flow of trade, commerce and intercourse, for example, by imposing a high tariff wall, or by preventing imports into or exports out of a State, such a law is outside the significance of taxation, as such, but

---

[*] (2017) 12 SCC 1.

assumes the character of a trade barrier which it was the intention of the Constitution-makers to abolish by Part XIII.'

A careful reading of the above would show that Sinha, C.J. had two situations in mind. One, where the State prevents imports into and exports out of the State and the other where the State imposes the high tariff wall with a view to imposing an impediment to the free flow of trade, commerce and intercourse. Insofar as the first category viz. laws that forbid imports into and exports out of a State are concerned, the same would work as a restriction in terms of restrictions within the contemplation of Part XIII and may be permissible in the manner and to the extent the said Part permits to do so, but, in the second case viz. legislature imposing a high tariff wall so as to operate as an impediment to free flow of trade, commerce and intercourse, there are considerable difficulties. That is so because the judgment does not elaborate as to what would constitute a high tariff wall for the tax to operate as a restriction/impediment.

The conclusion reached by the learned chief justice was stated as follows:

> 127. In the light of what we have said above, we answer Question (i) in the negative and declare that a non-discriminatory tax does not per se constitute a restriction on the right to free trade, commerce and intercourse guaranteed under Article 301. Decisions taking a contrary view in *Atiabari* case followed by a series of later decisions shall, therefore, stand overruled including the decision in *Automobile* Transport declaring that taxes generally are restrictions on the freedom of trade, commerce and intercourse but such of them as are compensatory in nature do not offend Article 301.

In a separate concurring judgment by S.K. Singh, J. (Chief Justice B.P. Sinha's grandson), the learned judge adopted Sinha C.J.'s view in *Atiabari*:

> 163. The entire discussion in my view leads to a fair conclusion that the views summarized by Sinha, C.J. in para 18 of his judgment in *Atiabari* case depict the law emanating from Part XIII of the Constitution in the correct perspective. However same cannot be said of the observations in para 16 where his Lordship used the expression:

'16. . . . If a law is passed by the legislature . . . imposing a high tariff wall . . . assumes the character of a trade barrier which it was the intention of the Constitution-makers to abolish by Part XIII.'

These observations do create practical difficulties of insurmountable proportions. Hence these deserve to be treated as obiter or interpreted in the light of the entire passage, to mean such taxes which impose an impediment to the free flow of trade, commerce and intercourse by creating discriminatory tariff wall/trade barrier (emphasis supplied). For Part XIII there can be no real impediment through tax unless the so-called wall or barrier is one of hostile discrimination between local goods and outside goods.

Ramana, J., in a separate concurring judgment, also adopted the reasoning of Sinha, C.J. in *Atiabari* in paragraphs 228 and 229, and concluded:

236. In *Atiabari*, the majority held that the legislative competence of the legislature will have to be judged in the light of relevant Articles of Part XIII and that what entries will attract Article 301 will depend on the content of freedom guaranteed. In Jaiprakash, this Court ruled that concept of compensatory tax evolved in *Automobile* does not apply to general notion of entry tax. As pointed out earlier *Atiabari* is a case dealing with tax under Entry 56, whereas *Automobile* is a case under Entry 57. In view of this it would not be safe to apply the majority opinion in *Atiabari* and *Automobile* while dealing with entry tax. I am therefore compelled to hold that tax law *simpliciter* is not contemplated in Article 301 of the Constitution.'

Banumati, J., in a separate judgment concurring with the chief justice on this point, referred to Sinha C.J.'s dissenting judgment in *Atiabari* in paragraph 340, and adopted his view as follows:

348. In *Atiabari*, Sinha, C.J. took a different view of Article 301 than the one taken by the majority and concluded as under:

'18. . . . (2) the freedom declared by Article 301 does not mean freedom from taxation *simpliciter*, but does mean freedom from taxation which has the effect of directly impeding the free flow of trade, commerce and intercourse;'

'16. In my opinion, another very cogent reason for holding that taxation *simpliciter* is not within the terms of Article 301 of the Constitution is that the very connotation of taxation is the power of the State to raise money for public purposes by compelling the payment by persons, both natural and juristic, of monies earned or possessed by them, by virtue of the facilities and protection afforded by the State. Such burdens or imposts, either direct or indirect, are in the ultimate analysis meant as a contribution by the citizens or persons residing in the State or dealing with the citizens of the State, for the support of the Government, with particular reference to their respective abilities to make such contributions. Thus public purpose is implicit in every taxation, as such. Therefore, when Part XIII of the Constitution speaks of imposition of reasonable restrictions in public interest, it could not have intended to include taxation within the generic term 'reasonable restrictions'.'

According to Sinha, C.J., every tax including a tax on 'movement of goods or passengers' was not necessarily an impediment or restraint in the matter of trade, commerce and intercourse. As per Sinha, C.J. taxation by its very nature could not be included within the term 'reasonable restriction' used in Part XIII. The view of Sinha, C.J. is a correct view and is in consonance with the consistent view taken by this Court that taxing statutes are not per se a 'restriction'.

Finally, the order of the court reflects the fact that Chief Justice Sinha's minority view is now the law, with the caveat aforementioned, as follows:

Order of the Court

1159. By majority the Court answers the reference in the following terms:

1159.1. Taxes *simpliciter* are not within the contemplation of Part XIII of the Constitution of India. The word 'free' used in Article 301 does not mean 'free from taxation'.

1159.2. Only such taxes as are discriminatory in nature are prohibited by Article 304(a). It follows that levy of a non-discriminatory tax would not constitute an infraction of Article 301.

1159.3. Clauses (a) and (b) of Article 304 have to be read disjunctively.

1159.4. A levy that violates Article 304(a) cannot be saved even if the procedure under Article 304(b) or the proviso thereunder is satisfied.

1159.5. The Compensatory Tax Theory evolved in *Automobile Transport* case and subsequently modified in *Jindal* case has no juristic basis and is therefore rejected.

1159.6. The decisions of this Court in *Atiabari, Automobile Transport and Jindal* cases and all other judgments that follow these pronouncements are to the extent of such reliance overruled.

5. New India Sugar Mills Ltd. v. Commissioner of Sales Tax, Bihar (1963)

In *M/s New India Sugar Mills Ltd. v. Commissioner of Sales Tax, Bihar,*[*] sales tax was levied under the Bihar Sales Tax Act, 1947, on sugar that was sold pursuant to the directions of the controller under the Sugar Products Control Order, 1946. A majority of two learned judges of the court held that compulsory sales made pursuant to orders or directions of the controller would not amount to a sale of goods within the meaning of Entry 48 of List II, Seventh Schedule of the Government of India Act, 1935. This was done following *State of Madras v. Gannon Dunkerley & Company (Madras) Ltd.* (1959).[†] Hidayatullah, J. dissented. After setting out in detail all the statutory provisions and the case law of the Federal Court, the English courts and the Supreme Court, Hidayatullah, J. described the origin of sales tax as follows:

> Before considering the facts of this case in the light of the Sugar and Sugar Products Order 1946, I shall summarize what I have said so far. Sales tax is a tax which may be laid on goods or services. It assumes numerous shapes and forms. It is a modern tax being the product of the First World War. The concept of 'sale' is of course much older and even the English Sale of Goods Act, 1893 on which our own statute is based, was prior to the first imposition of tax in modern times. In India, the tax was first levied in 1937 under laws made under Entry 48 which

---

[*] (1963) Supp. (2) SCR 459.
[†] (1959) SCR 379.

read—'Taxes on the sale of goods'. It was introduced as the main source of revenue to the Provinces under a scheme of Provincial Autonomy. Being a commodity tax it came into competition with other commodity taxes like excise but it was held that the entry comprised, wholesale, retail and turnover taxes from the stage of manufacture or production to consumption. Later textual interpretation based on statutes relating to sale of goods and books on the subject of sale, pointed out intrinsic limitations. One such limitation was that the term 'sale' was used in the limited sense it bears in that part of the law of contract which is now incorporated in the Sale of Goods Act. As a result of this fundamental consideration 'forward contracts' were held to be outside the scope of the Entry. The sale, it was held, had to be a completed sale with passing of property before the tax could became payable. A further limitation was pointed out in certain cases relating to building contracts in which it was held that though property in materials passed, it did so without an agreement, express or implied, in that behalf, and only when the materials ceased to be goods and became immovable property. It was held that the supremacy of the Provincial Legislatures did not extend to levying a tax on sales in these circumstances by modifying the definition of sale. It was however held that if the parties agreed to divide a works contract into labour plus materials, the tax might be leviable. It was also held that a tax on building materials was leviable by the legislature having power to levy a tax not expressly mentioned. It was, however, held that if the taxing Province had the goods at the time of the contract or there was other substantial connection with the contract by reason of some element having taken place there, the Legislature could validly make a law which treated the whole transaction as having taken place in the Province.[*]

Pointing out that this very controversy featured many centuries ago even in Roman Law, the learned judge pointed out how a compulsory sale would be a sale nonetheless, as follows:

I shall now analyse the whole transaction and see how the element of compulsion and control affect the existence of a sale. First there is the

---

[*] (1963) Supp. (2) SCR 459, pp. 509–10.

fixation of price by the Controller. Can it be said that there is no sale because the price is fixed by a third person and not by the buyer and seller. This is the old controversy between Labeo and Proculus that if price is fixed by a third person a contract of sale results or not. Labeo with whom Cassius agreed, held that there was not, while Proculus was of the contrary opinion:

'Pretium autem certum esse debet. Nam alioquin si ita inter nos conve-nerit ut guanti Titius rem aestemauerit, tanti sit empta, Labeo negavit ullam uim hoc negotium habere, cuius optnionem Cassius probat. Ofilius et eam emptionem et uenditionem; cuius opinionem Proculus secultus est,' (Gaius 111,140).

This was solved by Justinian holding that there was:

'Sed nostra decisio ita hoc constituti.' (Inst. 111,23,1).

I do not think the modern law is any different. So long as the parties trade under controls at fixed price and accept these as any other law of the realm because they must, the contract is at the fixed price both sides having or deemed to have agreed to such a price. Consent under the law of contract need not be express, it can be implied. There are cases in which a sale takes place by the operation of law rather than by mutual agreement express or implied.[*]

Finally, the learned judge concluded:

But sales often take place without volition of a party. A sick man is given medicines under the orders of his doctor and pays for them to the chemist with tax on the price. He does not even know the names of the medicines. Did he make an offer to the chemist from his sick bed? The affairs of the world are very complicated and sales are not always in their elementary forms. Due to short supply or maldistribution of goods, controls have to be imposed. There are permits, price controls, rationing and shops which are licensed. Can it be said that there is no sale because mutuality is lost on one account or another? It was not said in the *Tata Iron and Steel* case which was a case of control, that there was no sale. The entry should be interpreted in a liberal spirit and not cut down by narrow technical considerations. The entry in other words should not

---

[*] Ibid., pp. 511–12.

be shorn of all its content to leave a mere husk of legislative power. For the purposes of legislation such as on sales tax it is only necessary to see whether there is a sale express or implied. Such a sale was not found in 'forward' contracts and in respect of materials used in building contracts. But the same cannot be said of all situations. I for one would not curtail the entry any further. The entry has its meaning and within its meaning there is a plenary power. If a sale express or implied is found to exist then the tax must follow. I am of the opinion that in these transactions there was a sale of sugar for a price and the tax was payable. I would, therefore, dismiss these appeals with costs.[*]

Justice Hidayatullah's view was eventually approved. In *Vishnu Agencies (Pvt.) Ltd. Etc. v. Commercial Tax Officer & Ors.* (1978),[†] a seven-judge bench of the Supreme Court authoritatively held that Hidayatullah J.'s view in *New India Sugar Mills* was the correct view:

We are of the opinion that the true position in law is as is set out in the dissenting judgment of Hidayatullah, J. and that, the view expressed by Kapur and Shah, JJ. in the majority judgment, with deference, cannot be considered as good law. Bachawat, J. in Andhra Sugars was, with respect, right in cautioning that the majority judgment of Kapur and Shah, JJ. in *New India Sugar Mills* 'should not be treated as an authority for the proposition that there can be no contract of sale under compulsion of a statute' (pp. 715–16). Rather than saying what, in view of the glowing uncertainty of the true legal position on the question, we are constrained to say, namely, that the majority judgment in *New India Sugar Mills* is not good law, Bachawat, J. preferred to adopt the not unfamiliar manner of confining the majority decision to 'the special facts of that case'.

xxx xxx xxx

It all began with the reliance in *Gannon Dunkerley* (pp. 396–98) on the statement in the 8th Edn. (1950) of *Benjamin on Sale* that to constitute

---

[*] Id., pp. 513–14.
[†] (1978) 1 SCC 520.

a valid sale there must be a concurrence of four elements, one of which is 'mutual assent'. That statement is a reproduction of what the celebrated author had said in the second and last edition prepared by himself in 1873. The majority judgment in *New India Sugar Mills* (p. 467) also derives sustenance from the same passage in Benjamin's eighth edition. But as observed by Hidayatullah, J. in his dissenting judgment in that case, consent may be express or implied and offer and acceptance need not be in an elementary form (p. 510). It is interesting that the General Editor of the 1974 edition of *Benjamin's Sale of Goods* says in the preface that the editors decided to produce an entirely new work partly because commercial institutions, modes of transport and of payment, forms of contract, types of goods, market areas and marketing methods, and the extent of legislative and governmental regulation and intervention, had changed considerably since 1868, when the first edition of the book was published. The formulations in Benjamin's second edition relating to the conditions of a valid 'sale' of goods, which are reproduced in the eighth edition, evidently require modification in the light of regulatory measures of social control. Hidayatullah, J., in his minority judgment referred to above struck the new path; and Bachawat, J. who spoke for the Court in Andhra Sugars went a step ahead by declaring that 'the contract is a contract of sale and purchase of cane, though the buyer is obliged to give his assent under compulsion of a statute' (p. 716)."

Beg, C.J., wrote a separate concurring judgment which, instead of overruling the majority opinion in *New India Sugar Mills*, distinguished the same.[†]

6. *Kharak Singh v. State of U.P. & Ors.* (1964)

Yet another instance of a dissenting judgment later becoming the law is to be found in *Kharak Singh v. State of U.P. & Ors.* (1964).[‡] In this case, Regulation 236 of the U.P. Police Regulations was challenged, contending

---

[*] Ibid., pp. 454, 464.
[†] Id., p. 440.
[‡] (1964) 1 SCR 332.

that it violated the right guaranteed to citizens by Articles 19(1)(d) and 21 of the Constitution of India. The regulation reads as follows:

> Without prejudice to the right of Superintendents of Police to put into practice any legal measures, such as shadowing in cities, by which they find they can keep in touch with suspects in particular localities or special circumstances, surveillance may for most practical purposes be defined as consisting of one or more of the following measures:
>
> (a) Secret picketing of the house or approaches to the houses of suspects;
> (b) domiciliary visits at night;
> (c) through periodical inquiries by officers not below the rank of sub-inspector into repute, habits, associations, income, expenses and occupation;
> (d) the reporting by constables and chaukidars of movements and absences from home;
> (e) the verification of movements and absences by means of inquiry slips;
> (f) the collection and record on a history-sheet of all information bearing on conduct.

The majority judgment of Rajagopala Ayyangar, J., along with two other learned judges, struck down only Regulation 236(b), and that too only on the ground that, being an executive regulation and not 'law', the said regulation violated Article 21 of the Constitution of India. Subba Rao, J., along with J.C. Shah, J., held that the entire regulation was unconstitutional on the ground that it infringed both Articles 19(1)(d) and 21 of the Constitution of India. Harkening back to Fazl Ali's view in *Gopalan*, the dissenting judgment spoke of how fundamental rights are not independent of each other, but must be read together:

> At this stage it will be convenient to ascertain the scope of the said two provisions and their relation inter se in the context of the question raised. Both of them are distinct fundamental rights. No doubt the expression 'personal liberty' is a comprehensive one and the right to move freely

is an attribute of personal liberty. It is said that the freedom to move freely is carved out of personal liberty and, therefore, the expression 'personal liberty' in Article 21 excludes that attribute. In our view, this is not a correct approach. Both are independent fundamental rights, though there is overlapping. There is no question of one being carved out of another. The fundamental right of life and personal liberty have many attributes and some of them are found in Article 19. If a person's fundamental right under Article 21 is infringed, the State can rely upon a law to sustain the action; but that cannot be a complete answer unless the said law satisfies the test laid down in Article 19(2) so far as the attributes covered by Article 19(1) are concerned. In other words, the State must satisfy that both the fundamental rights are not infringed by showing that there is a law and that it does amount to a reasonable restriction within the meaning of Article 19(2) of the Constitution. But in this case no such defence is available, as admittedly there is no such law. So the petitioner can legitimately plead that his fundamental rights both under Article 19(1)(d) and Article 21 are infringed by the State.[*]

The impugned regulation was then struck down under Article 21 as follows:

Further, the right to personal liberty takes in not only a right to be free from restrictions placed on his movements, but also free from encroachments on his private life. It is true our Constitution does not expressly declare a right to privacy as a fundamental right, but the said right is an essential ingredient of personal liberty. Every democratic country sanctifies domestic life; it is expected to give him rest, physical happiness, peace of mind and security. In the last resort, a person's house, where he lives with his family, is his 'castle'; it is his rampart against encroachment on his personal liberty. The pregnant words of that famous Judge, Frankfurter J., in *Wolf v. Colorado* pointing out the importance of the security of one's privacy against arbitrary intrusion by the police, could have no less application to an Indian home as to an American one. If physical restraints on a person's movements affect his personal liberty, physical encroachments on his

---

[*] Ibid., pp. 356–57.

private life would affect it in a larger degree. Indeed, nothing is more deleterious to a man's physical happiness and health than a calculated interference with his privacy. We would, therefore, define the right of personal liberty in Article 21 as a right of an individual to be free from restrictions or encroachments on his person, whether those restrictions or encroachments are directly imposed or indirectly brought about by calculated measures. It so understood, all the acts of surveillance under Regulation 236 infringe the fundamental right of the petitioner under Article 21 of the Constitution.[*]

Speaking of Article 19(1)(d), the learned judge stated:

This leads us to the second question, namely, whether the petitioner's fundamental right under Article 19(1)(d) is also infringed. What is the content of the said fundamental right? It is argued for the State that it means only that a person can move physically from one point to another without any restraint. This argument ignores the adverb 'freely' in clause (d). If that adverb is not in the clause, there may be some justification for this contention; but the adverb 'freely' gives a larger content to the freedom. Mere movement unobstructed by physical restrictions cannot in itself be the object of a person's travel. A person travels ordinarily in quest of some objective. He goes to a place to enjoy, to do business, to meet friends, to have secret and intimate consultations with others and to do many other such things. If a man is shadowed, his movements are obviously constricted. He can move physically, but it can only be a movement of an automaton. How could a movement under the scrutinizing gaze of the policemen be described as a free movement? The whole country is his jail. The freedom of movement in clause (d) therefore must be a movement in a free country i.e. in a country where he can do whatever he likes, speak to whomsoever he wants, meet people of his own choice without any apprehension, subject of course to the law of social control. The petitioner under the shadow of surveillance is certainly deprived of this freedom. He can move physically, but he cannot do so freely, for all his activities are watched and noted. The

---

[*] Id., p. 359.

shroud of surveillance cast upon him perforce engender inhibitions in him and he cannot act freely as he would like to do. We would, therefore, hold that the entire Regulation 236 offends also Article 19(1)(d) of the Constitution.

Assuming that Article 19(1)(d) of the Constitution must be confined only to physical movements, its combination with the freedom of speech and expression leads to the conclusion we have arrived at. The act of surveillance is certainly a restriction on the said freedom. It cannot be suggested that the said freedom is also bereft of its subjective or psychological content, but will sustain only the mechanics of speech and expression. An illustration will make our point clear. A visitor, whether a wife, son or friend, is allowed to be received by a prisoner in the presence of a guard. The prisoner can speak with the visitor; but, can it be suggested that he is fully enjoying the said freedom? It is impossible for him to express his real and intimate thoughts to the visitor as fully as he would like. But the restrictions on the said freedom are supported by valid law. To extend the analogy to the present case is to treat the man under surveillance as a prisoner within the confines of our country and the authorities enforcing surveillance as guards, without any law of reasonable restrictions sustaining or protecting their action. So understood, it must be held that the petitioner's freedom under Article 19(1)(a) of the Constitution is also infringed.[*]

Subba Rao, J.'s vision of the law in this dissenting judgment was expressly vindicated fourteen years later in *Maneka Gandhi v. Union of India* (1978)[†] as follows:

> It was in *Kharak Singh v. State of U.P.* that the question as to the proper scope and meaning of the expression 'personal liberty' came up pointedly for consideration for the first time before this Court. The majority of the Judges took the view 'that 'personal liberty' is used in the article as a compendious term to include within itself all the varieties of rights which go to make up the 'personal liberties' of man other than those dealt with

---

[*] Id., pp. 360–61.
[†] (1978) 2 SCR 621 at 669.

in the several clauses of Article 19(1). In other words, while Article 19(1) deals with particular species or attributes of that freedom, 'personal liberty' in Article 21 takes in and comprises the residue. The minority Judges, however, disagreed with this view taken by the majority and explained their position in the following words: 'No doubt the expression 'personal liberty' is a comprehensive one and the right to move freely is an attribute of personal liberty. It is said that the freedom to move freely is carved out of personal liberty and, therefore, the expression 'personal liberty' in Article 21 excludes that attribute. In our view, this is not a correct approach. Both are independent fundamental rights, though there is overlapping. There is no question of one being carved out of another. The fundamental right of life and personal liberty has many attributes and some of them are found in Article 19. If a person's fundamental right under Article 21 is infringed, the State can rely upon a law to sustain the action, but that cannot be a complete answer unless the said law satisfies the test laid down in Article 19(2) so far as the attributes covered by Article 19(1) are concerned.' There can be no doubt that in view of the decision of this Court in *R.C. Cooper v. Union of India* the minority view must be regarded as correct and the majority view must be held to have been overruled.

7. *T. Devadasan v. The Union of India* (1964)

T. Devadasan v. The Union of India (1964)[*] contains one of the most celebrated dissents in the history of the Supreme Court, in that Subba Rao J.'s vision of affirmative action qua Scheduled Castes and Scheduled Tribes ultimately became the law. A 'carry-forward' rule, by which unfilled vacancies to posts reserved for the Scheduled Castes and Scheduled Tribes were to be carried forward to subsequent years was challenged as being violative of Article 16 read with Article 335 of the Constitution of India.

The majority judgment of Mudholkar, J., speaking for himself and three other learned judges, held that since the working of the carry-forward rule, in that case, resulted in the Scheduled Castes and Scheduled Tribes getting more than 50 per cent of the vacancies in a particular year, it was unconstitutional, as it was against the balance struck by Article 16(4).

---

[*] (1964) 4 SCR 680.

Subba Rao, J., after setting out Articles 16(1) and 16(4), 46 and 335, held that Article 335 would have no bearing on the correct interpretation of Article 16(4).* In a celebrated passage, the learned judge laid down his vision of the equality provisions of the Constitution thus:

Article 14 lays down the general rule of equality. Article 16 is an instance of the application of the general rule with special reference to opportunity of appointments under the State. It says that there shall be equality of opportunity for all citizens in matters relating to employment or appointment to any office under the State. If it stood alone, all the backward communities would go to the wall in a society of uneven basic social structure; the said rule of equality would remain only an utopian conception unless a practical content was given to it. Its strict enforcement brings about the very situation it seeks to avoid. To make my point clear, take the illustration of a horse race. Two horses are set down to run a race—one is a first class race horse and the other an ordinary one. Both are made to run from the same starting point. Though theoretically they are given equal opportunity to run the race, in practice the ordinary horse is not given an equal opportunity to compete with the race horse. Indeed, that is denied to it. So a handicap may be given either in the nature of extra weight or a start from a longer distance. By doing so, what would otherwise have been a farce of a competition would be made a real one. The same difficulty had confronted the makers of the Constitution at the time it was made. Centuries of calculated oppression and habitual submission reduced a considerable section of our community to a life of serfdom. It would be well nigh impossible to raise their standards if the doctrine of equal opportunity was strictly enforced in their case. They would not have any chance if they were made to enter the open field of competition without adventitious aids till such time when they could stand on their own legs. That is why the makers of the Constitution introduced clause (4) in Article 16. The expression 'nothing in this article' is a legislative device to express its intention in a most emphatic way that the power conferred thereunder is not limited in any way by the main provision but falls

---

* Ibid., pp. 699–700.

outside it. It has not really carved out an exception, but has preserved a power untrammelled by the other provisions of the article.[*]

He then concluded:

> In the instant case, the State made a provision; adopting the principle of 'carry forward'. Instead of fixing a higher percentage in the second and third selections based upon the earlier results, it directed that the vacancies reserved in one selection for the said Castes and Tribes but not filled up by them but filled up by other candidates, should be added to the quota fixed for the said Castes and Tribes in the next selection and likewise in the succeeding selection. As the posts reserved in the first year for the said Castes and Tribes were filled up by non-Scheduled Caste and non-Scheduled Tribe applicants, the result was that in the next selection the posts available to the latter was proportionately reduced. This provision certainly caused hardship to the individuals who applied for the second or the third selection, as the case may be, though the non-Scheduled Castes and non-Scheduled Tribes, taken as one unit, were benefited in the earlier selection or selections. This injustice to individuals, which is inherent in any scheme of reservation cannot, in my view, make the provision for reservation anytheless a provision for reservation.[†]

This celebrated dissent was commented upon favourably by the majority judgments in *State of Kerala v. N.M. Thomas* (1976),[‡] and ultimately became the law in *Indra Sawhney v. Union of India* (1992),[§] with Jeevan Reddy, J. speaking for the majority expressly overruling the majority judgment in *Devadasan*, preferring the dissenting judgment of Subba Rao, J.[¶]

---

[*] Id., p. 700.

[†] Id., p. 705.

[‡] (1976) 2 SCC 310; and *see* the judgment of Krishna Iyer, J., paragraph 136, and Fazal Ali, J., paragraph 187.

[§] (1992) Supp. 3 SCC 217.

[¶] Ibid., paragraph 817.

8. *Sajjan Singh v. State of Rajasthan* (1965)

Sometimes, doubts cast by judges can have the salutary effect of the constitution of a larger Bench to have a relook at the law. This is what happened in *Sajjan Singh v. State of Rajasthan* (1965).* In this judgment, the Constitution (Seventeenth Amendment) Act, 1964, was upheld by the court. The judgment was delivered by P.B. Gajendragadkar, C.J., joined by two other learned judges. M. Hidayatullah, J., concurred with the judgment of the court, but nevertheless raised the following doubts on the existing state of the law:

> I would require stronger reasons than those given in *Shankari Prasad* case to make me accept the view that fundamental rights were not really fundamental but were intended to be within the powers of amendment in common with the other parts of the Constitution and without the concurrence of the States. No doubt Article 19 by clauses numbered 2 to 6 allows a curtailment of rights in the public interest. This shows that Part III is not static. It visualizes change and progress but at the same time it preserves the individual rights. There is hardly any measure of reform which cannot be introduced reasonably, the guarantee of individual liberty notwithstanding. Even the agrarian reforms could have been partly carried out without Articles 31-A and 31-B but they would have cost more to the public exchequer. The rights of society are made paramount and they are placed above those of the individual. This is as it should be. But restricting the fundamental rights by resort to clauses 2 to 6 of Article 19 is one thing and removing the rights from the Constitution or debilitating them by an amendment is quite another. This is the implication of *Shankari Prasad* case. It is true that such things would never be, but one is concerned to know if such a doing would be possible.
>
> It may be said that the words of Article 368 are quite explicit. Article 368 does not give power to amend 'any provision' of the Constitution. At least the article does not say so. Analysed by the accepted canons of interpretation it is found to lay down the manner of the amendment

---

* (1965) 1 SCR 933.

of 'this Constitution' but by 'this Constitution' it does not mean each individual article wherever found and whatever its language and spirit. The Constitution itself indicates in some places a contrary intention expressly (See Articles 4, 169 and the former Article 240) and in some others by implication (See Article 11). What Article 368 does is to lay down the manner of amendment and the necessary conditions for the effectiveness of the amendment. The contrast between the opening part and the proviso does not show, that what is outside the proviso is necessarily within the powers of amendment. The proviso merely puts outside the exclusive power of Parliament to amend those provisions on which our federal structure rests. It makes it incumbent that a majority of the States should also agree. The proviso also preserves the structure of the higher judiciary so vital to a written Constitution and to a Democracy such as ours. But the article nowhere says that the preamble and every single article of the Constitution can be amended by two-thirds majority despite any permanency in the language and despite any historical fact or sentiment.

The Constitution gives so many assurances in Part III that it would be difficult to think that they were the play things of a special majority. To hold this would mean *prima facie* that the most solemn parts of our Constitution stand on the same footing as any other provision and even on a less firm ground than that on which the articles mentioned in the proviso stand. The anomaly that Article 226 should be somewhat protected but not Article 32 must give us pause. Article 32 does not erect a shield against private conduct but against state conduct including the legislatures (See Article 12). Can the legislature take away this shield? Perhaps by adopting a literal construction of Article 368 one can say that. But I am not inclined to play a grammarian's role. As at present advised I can only say that the power to make amendments ought not ordinarily to be a means of escape from absolute constitutional restrictions.[*]

In a separate concurring judgment, Mudholkar, J. also concurred with the ultimate judgment of the court, but stated:

---

[*] Ibid., pp. 961–63.

We may also have to bear in mind the fact that ours is a written Constitution. The Constituent Assembly which was the repository of sovereignty could well have created a sovereign Parliament on the British model. But instead it enacted a written Constitution, created three organs of State, made the union executive responsible to Parliament and the State executives to the State Legislatures; erected a federal structure and distributed legislative power between Parliament and the State Legislatures, recognized certain rights as fundamental and provided for their enforcement; prescribed forms of oaths of office or affirmations which require those who subscribe to them to owe true allegiance to the Constitution and further require the members of the Union Judiciary and of the higher judiciary in the States, to uphold the Constitution. Above all, it formulated a solemn and dignified preamble which appears to be an epitome of the basic features of the Constitution. Can it not be said that these are indicia of the intention of the Constituent Assembly to give a permanency to the basic features of the Constitution?

It is also a matter for consideration whether making a change in a basic feature of the Constitution can be regarded merely as an amendment or would it be, in effect, rewriting a part of the Constitution; and if the latter, would it be within the purview of Article 368?

The Constitution has enjoined on every member of Parliament before entering upon his office to take an oath or make an affirmation to the effect that he will bear true faith and allegiance to the Constitution. On the other hand under Article 368 a procedure is prescribed for amending the Constitution. If upon a literal interpretation of this provision an amendment even of the basic features of the Constitution would be possible it will be a question for consideration as to how to harmonize the duty of allegiance to the Constitution with the power to make an amendment to it. Could the two be harmonized by excluding from the procedure for amendment, alteration of a basic feature of the Constitution? It would be of interest to mention that the Supreme Court of Pakistan has in *Mr Fazlul Quader Chowdhry v. Mr Mohd. Abdul Haque* held that franchise and form of Government are fundamental features of a Constitution and the power conferred upon the President by the Constitution of Pakistan to remove difficulties does not extend to making an alteration in a fundamental feature of the Constitution.

For striking down the action of the President under, what he calls 'sub-constitutional power' Cornelius, C.J., relied on the Judges' oath of office. After quoting the following passage from Cooley's *Constitutional Limitations*:

'For the constitution of the State is higher in authority than any law, direction, or order made by anybody or any officer assuming to act under it, since such body or officer must exercise a delegated authority, and one that must necessarily be subservient to the instrument by which the delegation is made. In any case of conflict the fundamental law must govern, and the act in conflict with it must be treated as of no legal validity.'

The learned Chief Justice observed:

'To decide upon the question of constitutional validity in relation to an act of a statutory authority, how-high-so-ever, is a duty devolving ordinarily upon the superior courts by virtue of their office, and in the absence of any bar either express or implied which stands in the way of that duty being performed in respect of the Order here in question it is a responsibility which cannot be avoided' (p. 506).

The observations and the passage from Cooley, quoted here for convenience support what I have said earlier regarding the power of the Courts to pronounce upon the validity of amendments to the Constitution.

xxx xxx xxx

Before I part with this case I wish to make it clear that what I have said in this judgment is not an expression of my final opinion but only an expression of certain doubts which have assailed me regarding a question of paramount importance to the citizens of our country: to know whether the basic features of the Constitution under which we live and to which we owe allegiance are to endure for all time—or at least for the foreseeable future—or whether they are no more enduring than the implemental and subordinate provisions of the Constitution.*

---

* Id., pp. 966–69.

The divergent opinions in these judgments led to a relook at the law—with Subba Rao, C.J. constituting a eleven-judge bench for this purpose. In *I.C. Golaknath & Ors. v. State of Punjab & Anr.* (1967),[*] a majority of six learned judges held that Parliament has no power—while amending the Constitution—to amend the fundamental rights chapter so as to abridge or curtail any of those rights. This was laid down expressing the opinion that Article 13(2) of the Constitution would interdict not only statutory law but also amendments made to the Constitution—the power of amendment not being found in Article 368, which deals only with the procedure to amend the Constitution.

The majority judgments in *Golaknath* were in turn overruled in *Kesavananda Bharati Sripadagalvaru & Ors. v. State of Kerala & Anr.* (1973).[†] By a razor-thin majority of 7:6, the majority judgments in *Kesavananda Bharati* held that though the power to amend the Constitution resides in Article 368, and that 'law' in Article 13 refers only to statutory and not constitutional law, Parliament still cannot amend the Constitution so as to damage or destroy its 'basic structure'.

In the long run, it is Mudholkar, J. who turned out to be the prophet, for it is his doubt that was cast in *Sajjan Singh* that ultimately became the law, and continues to be the law, in this country.

9. *Madhya Pradesh Industries Ltd. v. Union of India* (1966)

The question which arose in *Madhya Pradesh Industries Ltd. v. Union of India* (1966)[‡] was whether Rule 55 of the Mineral Concession Rules, which spoke of the revisional jurisdiction of the Central government, was a rule which required the Central government to act in a quasi-judicial capacity, which imposed a duty upon it to give a personal hearing and give reasons for its orders. The majority judgment delivered by Bachawat, J., on behalf of himself and Mudholkar, J., held that since the order of the government of Bombay was only a recommendation to the Central government to grant a mining lease to the appellant, no personal hearing was owed to the

---

[*] (1967) 2 SCR 762.
[†] (1973) 4 SCC 225.
[‡] (1966) 1 SCR 466.

appellant before the Central government heard, and rejected, the revision application. Further, it was not incumbent on the Central government, having agreed with the reasons given by the government of Maharashtra, to give full reasons in its order for rejecting the application. Subba Rao, J. dissented. He referred first to Rule 55, which reads as follows:

> Where a petition for revision is made to the Central Government under Rule 54, it may call for the record of the case from the State Government, and after considering any comments made on the petition by the State Government or other authority, as the case may be, may confirm, modify or set aside the order or pass such other order in relation thereto as the Central Government may deem just and proper:
>
> Provided that no order shall be passed against an applicant unless he has been given an opportunity to make his representations against the comments, if any, received from the State Government or other authority.

The learned judge then went on to hold that the entire scheme of the rules posits a judicial procedure, and that the Central government is constituted as a tribunal to dispose of a revision under Rule 55.[*] Having so held, Subba Rao, J. went on to find:

> The question cannot be disposed of on purely technical considerations. Our Constitution posits a welfare State; it is not defined, but its incidents are found in Chapters III and IV thereof i.e. the Parts embodying fundamental rights and directive principles of State Policy respectively. 'Welfare State' as conceived by our Constitution is a State where there is prosperity, equality, freedom and social justice. In the context of a welfare State, Administrative Tribunals have come to stay. Indeed, they are the necessary concomitants of a welfare State. But arbitrariness in their functioning destroys the concept of a welfare State itself. Self-discipline and supervision exclude or at any rate minimize arbitrariness. The least a tribunal can do is to disclose its mind. The compulsion of disclosure guarantees consideration. The condition to

---

[*] Ibid., p. 471.

give reasons introduces clarity and excludes or at any rate minimizes arbitrariness; it gives satisfaction to the party against whom the order is made; and it also enables an appellate or supervisory court to keep the tribunals within bounds. A reasoned order is a desirable condition of judicial disposal.*

xxx xxx xxx

It is said that this principle is not uniformly followed by appellate courts, for appeals and revisions are dismissed by appellate and revisional courts in limine without giving any reasons. There is an essential distinction between a court and an Administrative Tribunal. A Judge is trained to look at things objectively, uninfluenced by considerations of policy or expediency; but, an executive officer generally looks at things from the standpoint of policy and expediency. The habit of mind of an executive officer so formed cannot be expected to change from function to function or from act to act. So it is essential that some restrictions shall be imposed on tribunals in the matter of passing orders affecting the rights of parties; and the least they should do is to give reasons for their orders. Even in the case of appellate courts invariably reasons are given, except when they dismiss an appeal or revision in limine and that is because the appellate or revisional court agrees with the reasoned judgment of the subordinate court or there are no legally permissible grounds to interfere with it. But the same reasoning cannot apply to an Appellate Tribunal, for as often as not the order of the first tribunal is laconic and does not give any reasons. That apart, when we insist upon reasons, we do not prescribe any particular form or scale of the reasons. The extent and the nature of the reasons depend upon each case. Ordinarily, the Appellate or Revisional Tribunal shall give its own reasons succinctly; but in a case of affirmance where the original tribunal gives adequate reasons, the Appellate Tribunal may dismiss the appeal or the revision, as the case may be, agreeing with those reasons. What is essential is that reasons shall be given by an appellate or revisional tribunal expressly

---

* Id., p. 472.

or by reference to those given by the original tribunal. The nature and the elaboration of the reasons necessarily depend upon the facts of each case. In the present case, neither the State Government's nor the Central Government's order discloses the reasons for rejecting the application of the appellant. In the circumstances the Central Government's order is vitiated, as it does not disclose any reasons for rejecting the revision application of the appellant.*

As a result thereof, Subba Rao, J. would have set aside the Central government order. However, the Supreme Court in *Travancore Rayon Ltd. v. Union of India* (1970),[†] while considering the revisional jurisdiction of the Central government, this time under Section 36 of the Central Excise and Salt Act, 1944, held that Subba Rao, J.'s view in *Madhya Pradesh Industries*, on the necessity for reasons being given, is the correct view of the law, as a subsequent decision in *Bhagat Raja v. The Union of India & Ors.* (1967)[‡] had 'in effect' overruled the judgment of the majority in *Madhya Pradesh Industries*:

> In a later judgment *Bhagat Raja v. Union of India* the Constitution Bench of this Court in effect overruled the judgment of the majority in *Madhya Pradesh Industries Ltd.* case. The Court held that the decisions of tribunals in India are subject to the supervisory powers of the High Court under Article 227 of the Constitution and of appellate powers of this Court under Article 136. The High Court and this Court would be placed under a great disadvantage if no reasons are given and the revision is dismissed by the use of the single word 'rejected' or 'dismissed'. The Court in that case held that the order of the Central Government in appeal did not set out any reasons of its own and on that account set aside that order. In our view, the majority judgment of this Court in *Madhya Pradesh Industries Ltd.* case has been overruled by this Court in *Bhagat Raja* case.[§]

---

* Id., pp. 472–73.
† (1970) 3 SCR 40.
‡ (1967) 3 SCR 302.
§ (1970) 3 SCR 40, p. 45.

10. *Northern India Caterers Private Ltd., & Anr. v. State of Punjab* (1967)

In *Northern India Caterers Private Ltd., & Anr. v. State of Punjab* (1967),* Section 5 of the Punjab Public Premises and Land (Eviction and Recovery) Act of 1955 came up for consideration before the court. Section 5 of the said act provided a summary procedure by which a person who is found on 'public premises', as defined under the act, could be evicted after issue of a show-cause notice to him. The appellant argued that the occupants of public premises could be arbitrarily proceeded against, either by way of a summary procedure provided by the said act, or by way of a suit, as a result of which the said section would violate Article 14 of the Constitution of India. Agreeing with this contention, the majority judgment of Shelat, J., speaking on behalf of himself and two other learned judges, struck down the aforesaid provision. Bachawat, J. differed, stating:

> The constitutional guarantee of Article 14 requires that there shall be no unjust discrimination and all persons shall be treated alike under like circumstances and conditions. The article sustains a rich diversity of laws and permits reasonable classification and differential treatment based on substantial differences having reasonable relation to the object of the legislation. The protection of Article 14 extends to procedural laws, but the legislature may adopt one or more types of procedure for one class of litigation and a different type for another so long as the classification satisfies the test of reasonableness. Thus without violating Article 14, the law may prohibit cross examination of witnesses in proceedings for externment of undesirable persons, see *Gurbachan Singh v. State of Bombay.*
>
> Article 14 permits differential treatment of the government in matters of both substantive law and procedure. The legislature may reasonably provide a longer period of limitation for suits by the government, see *Nav Rattanmal v. State of Rajasthan* give the government the right of priority in payment of its claims, see *Builders Supply Corporation v. Union of India* and deny the protection of the Rent Act to tenants of

---

* (1967) 3 SCR 399.

premises belonging to the government while extending its protection to the government, see *Baburao Shantaram More v. Bombay Housing Board.*

It is settled by our previous decisions that the Revenue Recovery Acts and other Acts creating special tribunals and procedure for the expeditious recovery of revenue and State dues are in the public interest and do not violate Article 14, see *Shri Manna Lal v. Collector of Jhalawar, Nav Rattanmal v. State of Rajasthan, Collector of Malabar v. Erimal Ebrahim Hajee, Purshottam Govindji Halai v. Shree B.M. Desai, Additional Collector of Bombay* and *Lachhman Das v. State of Punjab.* If quick recovery of revenue is in the public interest, expeditious recovery of State property from which revenue is derived is *a fortiori* in the public interest. The impugned Act has properly devised a special machinery for the speedy recovery of premises belonging to the government.

The class of public premises to which the benefit of the impugned Act extends includes premises belonging to the district board, municipal committee, notified area committee and panchayat. The classification has reasonable relation to the object of the Act and does not offend Article 14. We have upheld similar classification for the purpose of other Acts, see *Baburao Shantaram More v. Bombay Housing Board.*

The Government has the option of proceeding against an unauthorized occupant of public premises either under the Act or by a civil suit. On the question whether such an option offends Article 14, our decisions upholding the validity of the Revenue Recovery Acts are conclusive. The Revenue Recovery Acts do not deny the equal protection of the laws because the government has the free choice of recovering its revenue either by a suit or by a proceeding under those Acts.*

xxx xxx xxx

It is not pretended that the proceeding under the impugned Act is unfair or oppressive. The unauthorized occupant has full opportunity of being heard and of producing his evidence before the Collector. He may obtain a review of the order of the Collector by an appeal to the Commissioner. He may in appropriate cases ask for a writ of *certiorari* from the High

---

* Ibid., pp. 411–12.

Court. He is not denied the equal protection of the laws because the government has the option of proceeding against him either by a suit or under the Act. An unauthorized occupant has no constitutional right to dictate that the government should have no choice of proceedings. The argument based upon the option of the government to file a suit is unreal, because in practice the government is not likely to institute a suit in a case where it can seek relief under the Act.

Article 14 does not require a fanatical approach to the problem of equality before the law. It permits a free choice of remedies for the redress of grievances. The impugned Act makes no unjust discrimination. It promotes public welfare and is a beneficient measure of legislation. If we strike down the Act, we shall be giving a free charter to unauthorized occupants and to officers squatting on public premises after they have vacated their offices to continue in occupation for an indefinite time until they are evicted by dilatory procedure of a title suit. The Act does not suffer from any blemish and we uphold it.[*]

In *Maganlal Chhagganlal (P) Ltd. v. Municipal Corporation of Greater Bombay & Ors.* (1975),[†] a similar provision to that contained in the aforesaid Punjab Act was contained in the Bombay Government Premises (Eviction) Act, 1955, with the difference being that Section 8A of the Bombay Act provided that no civil court shall have jurisdiction to entertain any suit or proceeding in respect of matters covered by the 1955 Act. The constitutional validity of this Bombay Act was upheld by the majority judgment delivered by Alagiriswami, J. on behalf of himself and three other learned judges, in which the learned judge first noted:

The decision in *Northern India Caterers'* case led to the Public Premises (Eviction of Unauthorized Occupation) Act, 1958 being replaced by Public Premises (Eviction of Unauthorised Occupants) Act, 1971 which was given retrospective operation from the date of the 1958 Act and barred the jurisdiction of the Court to entertain a suit or proceeding in respect of eviction of any person in unauthorized occupation of

------
[*] Id., p. 414.
[†] (1975) 1 SCR 1.

public premises. It also led to the amendment of one of the Acts now under consideration, the Bombay Government Premises (Eviction) Act introducing therein Section 3-A, already referred to, barring resort to the civil court. In *Hari Singh v. Military Estate Officer* this Court referred to the decision in *Northern India Caterers* case and upheld the validity of the 1971 Act on the ground that there was only one procedure for ejectment of persons in unauthorized occupation of public premises under the 1971 Act and that there was no vice of discrimination under it.*

Thereafter, after setting out the majority and minority judgments in *Northern India Caterers*, the judgment proceeded to hold that the majority view in *Northern India Caterers* was incorrect:

The statute itself in the two classes of cases before us clearly lays down the purpose behind them, that is that premises belonging to the Corporation and the Government should be subject to speedy procedure in the matter of evicting unauthorized persons occupying them. This is a sufficient guidance for the authorities on whom the power has been conferred. With such an indication clearly given in the statutes one expects the officers concerned to avail themselves of the procedures prescribed by the Acts and not resort to the dilatory procedure of the ordinary civil court. Even normally one cannot imagine an officer having the choice of two procedures, one which enables him to get possession of the property quickly and the other which would be a prolonged one, to resort to the latter. Administrative officers, no less than the courts, do not function in a vacuum. It would be extremely unreal to hold that an administrative officer would in taking proceedings for eviction of unauthorized occupants of Government property or Municipal property resort to the procedure prescribed by the two Acts in one case and to the ordinary civil court in the other. The provisions of these two Acts cannot be struck down on the fanciful theory that power would be exercised in such an unrealistic fashion. In considering whether the officers would be discriminating between one set of persons and

---

* Ibid., p. 11.

another, one has got to take into account normal human behaviour and not behaviour which is abnormal. It is not every fancied possibility of discrimination but the real risk of discrimination that we must take into account. This is not one of those cases where discrimination is writ large on the face of the statute. Discrimination may be possible but is very improbable. And if there is discrimination in actual practice this Court is not powerless. Furthermore, the fact that the Legislature considered that the ordinary procedure is insufficient or ineffective in evicting unauthorized occupants of Government and Corporation property and provided a special speedy procedure therefore is a clear guidance for the authorities charged with the duty of evicting unauthorized occupants. We, therefore, find ourselves unable to agree with the majority in the *Northern India Caterers* case.[*]

Khanna, J., while agreeing with the ultimate conclusion of the majority judgment, however, held:

Applying the principle enunciated above also, I am of the view that no sufficient ground has been shown for overruling the view expressed by the majority in *Northern India Caterers* case. It may be that the view expressed by the minority in that case appears to be preferable, but that by itself would not show that the decision arrived at in the *Northern India Caterer* case was plainly erroneous and as such requires overruling. It also cannot be said that the aforesaid decision has given rise to public inconvenience and hardship. The legislature has in view of the decision in *Northern India Caterers* case made necessary amendments in many of the enactments so as to bar the jurisdiction of the civil courts in matters dealt with by those enactments. No constitutional amendment was required to set right the difficulty experienced as a result of the decision of this Court in *Northern India Caterers* case.

I am, therefore, of the view that it is not necessary for the purpose of this case to overrule the majority decision in the case of *Northern India Caterers*.[†]

---

[*] Id., p. 23.
[†] Id., pp. 29–30.

Bhagwati, J., in a separate concurring judgment, chartered his own course, stating:

> Bachawat, J., delivering judgment on behalf of himself and Hidayatullah, J., (as he then was) held that 'without violating Article 14, the law may allow a litigant a free choice of remedies, proceedings and tribunals for the redress of his grievances'. The learned Judge observed that 'it is not pretended that the proceeding under the impugned Act is unfair or oppressive. The unauthorized occupant has full opportunity of being heard and of producing his evidence. He is not denied the equal protection of the laws because the government has the option of proceeding against him either by a suit or under the Act', and added: 'an unauthorized occupant has no constitutional right to dictate that the government should have no choice of proceedings. The argument based upon the option of the government to file a suit is unreal, because in practice the government is not likely to institute a suit in a case where it can seek relief under the Act'. The learned Judge concluded by saying that 'Art. 14 does not require a fanatical approach to the problem of equality before law' and upheld the validity of the Act. We find it difficult to accept the reasoning of the majority as well as the minority decisions.[*]

He differed with Bachawat, J.'s minority view in *Northern India Caterers* as follows:

> It was then contended on behalf of the respondents that even where two procedures are available against a person, one substantially more drastic and prejudicial than the other, and there is no guiding principle or policy laid down by the Legislature as to when one or the other shall be adopted, there would be no violation of the equality clause, if both procedures are fair. The argument was that the special procedure provided by the Legislature would not fall foul of the equality clause even if it is substantially more drastic and prejudicial than the ordinary procedure, if it is otherwise fair and reasonable. This argument was

---

[*] Id., p. 38.

sought to be supported by reference to certain observations in the minority judgment in *Northern India Caterers Ltd. v. State of Punjab*. But we do not think this is sound in the context of the guarantee of equality although its relevance to reasonable restrictions under Article 19 is obvious. When we are dealing with a question under Article 14, we have to enter the comparative arena for determining whether there is equal treatment of persons similarly situated so far as the procedure for determination of liability is concerned. Mere fairness of the special procedure which is impugned as discriminatory is not enough to take it out of the inhibition of Article 14. The fairness of the special procedure would undoubtedly be relevant if the special procedure is challenged as imposing unreasonable restriction under Article 19(1)(f). It would also be relevant if the special procedure were assailed as being in violation of the due process clause in a country like the United States. But where the attack is under Article 14, what we have to consider is whether there is equality before law, and there the question that has to be asked and answered is whether the two procedures are so disparate substantially and qualitatively as to lead to unequal treatment. Equality before law cannot be denied to a person by telling him: 'It is true that you are being treated differently from others who are similarly situate with you and the procedure to which you are subjected is definitely more drastic and prejudicial as compared to the procedure to which others are subjected, but you should not complain because the procedure adopted against you is quite fair'. The question which such a person would legitimately ask is: 'why am I being dealt with under the more drastic and prejudicial procedure when others similarly situate as myself are dealt with under the ordinary procedure which is less drastic and onerous?' There would have to be a rational answer to this query in order to meet the challenge of Article 14. It is, therefore, no argument on the part of the respondents to say that the special procedure set out in Chapter V-A of the Municipal Act is fair and consequently it does not have to stand the test of Article 14.*

---

* Id., pp. 47-48.

The majority judgment of Alagiriswami, J. in *Maganlal Chhagganlal* was thereafter reiterated in *Ahmedabad Municipal Corporation and others v. Ramanlal Govindram and Others* (1975),[*] as follows:

> The majority decision of this Court in *Maganlal Chhagganlal (P) Ltd. v. Municipal Corporation of Greater Bombay* is that where the statute itself covers only a class of cases, the statute will not be bad on that ground. The feature that such cases are chosen by the statute to be tried under the special procedure laid down there will not affect the validity of the statute. The contention that the mere availability of two procedures will vitiate one of them, i.e. the special procedure is not supported by reason or authority. In *Maganlal Chhagganlal* case this Court held that the fact that the Legislature considered that the ordinary procedure is inefficient or ineffective in evicting unauthorized occupants of government and corporation property and provided a special procedure therefor is a clear guidance for the authorities charged with the duty of evicting unauthorized occupants. The correct law is now laid down in *Maganlal Chhagganlas* case and the view of this Court in the *Northern India Caterers'* case does not hold the field. In *Maganlal Chhagganlal* case it has been held that a statute which deals with premises belonging to the Corporation and the Government and lays down a special speedy procedure in the matter of evicting unauthorized persons occupying them is a sufficient reason to support such special procedure. The policy and the purpose of the Act make it clear that the Legislature intended to make the statute applicable to a special class and provide a speedy method of recovering possession of these properties.
>
> On the ruling of this Court in *Maganlal Chhagganlal* case the conclusion of the High Court that Section 437-A offends Article 14 on the ground that there is no clear guidance on the Municipal Commissioner to take proceedings is set aside. It may also be stated here that the respondents because of the decision of this Court in *Maganlal Chhagganlal* case did not support the conclusion of the High Court on the infraction of Article 14.[†]

---

[*] (1975) 3 SCR 935.
[†] Ibid., p. 940.

11. *Coffee Board v. Joint Commercial Tax Officer* (1969)

Another instance of a minority judgment being subsequently accepted as having expressed the correct view—and therefore becoming the law—is the minority judgment of S.M. Sikri, J. in *Coffee Board v. Joint Commercial Tax Officer* (1969).* This time, it was the legislature that amended the law to accord with Sikri J.'s minority view.

At issue in this case was whether export auctions held by the coffee board were 'sales in the course of export', or 'sales which occasion the export', within the meaning of Article 286(1)(b) of the Constitution of India, read with Section 5 of the Central Sales Tax Act, 1956, so as to be exempt from the levy of sales tax. The majority judgment of Hidayatullah, C.J., joined by three other learned judges, held that there was room for only one export sale, i.e. such sale which itself results in the movement of goods from the exporter to the importer,[†] there being no room for two or more sales in the course of export. Sikri, J. dissented. Referring to the earlier judgments of the Supreme Court, in particular *K.G. Khosla & Co. v. Deputy Commissioner of Commercial Taxes* (1966),[‡] Sikri, J. held:

> 45. . . . The heart of the matter lies in answering one question. Can two sales occasion an export? I find no difficulty in answering this question in the affirmative. Two sales can take place in the course of export if they are effected by a transfer of documents of title to the goods after the goods have crossed the customs frontier of India, and they both will to be protected under Section 5(1) of the Act. Therefore, it cannot be assumed that it is the intention of Section 5(1) that only one sale can enjoy the protection of Section 5 (1). Accordingly, apart from any assumption, can two sales occasion an export? As I have said, 'occasion' does not necessarily mean immediately cause; it also means to 'bring about especially in an incidental or subsidiary manner'. If the sale by the appellant brings about the export in an incidental or subsidiary manner it can be said to occasion the export. It was in view of these

---

* (1969) 3 SCC 349.
† Ibid., paragraph 29.
‡ (1966) 17 STC 473.

considerations that Shah, J., speaking for the Court, had observed in *Ben Gorm Nilgiri Plantations Co. v. Sales Tax Officer*:

'A sale in the course of export predicates a connection between the sale and export, the two activities being so integrated that the connection between the two cannot be voluntarily interrupted, without a breach of the contract or the compulsion arising from the nature of the transaction. In this sense to constitute a sale in the course of export it may be said that there must be an intention on the part of both the buyer and the seller to export, there must be an obligation to export, and there must be an actual export. The obligation may arise by reason of statute, contract between the parties, or from mutual understanding or agreement between them, or even from the nature of the transaction which links the sale to export. A transaction of sale which is a preliminary to export of the commodity sold may be regarded as a sale for export, but is not necessarily to be regarded as one in the course of export, unless the sale occasions export.

The learned judge then concluded:

49. On the facts of this case, the Coffee Board, the Sellers, have concern with the actual export of goods. They have made various provisions to see that the purchasers must export. Condition 26, quoted by the learned Chief Justice, clearly provides that the coffee shall be exported to stipulated or approved destinations and it shall not under any circumstances be diverted to another destination, sold or be disposed of or otherwise released in India. If the purchaser commits a default, apart from penalty, it is provided that unexported coffee may be seized. Thus the Coffee Board retains control over the goods. These conditions create a bond between the sale and eventual export. The possibility that in a particular case a purchaser might commit a breach of contract or law and not export does not change the nature of the transaction.

The Parliament stepped in, and amended Section 5 of the Central Sales Tax Act in 1975, by adding subsection (3) to the main provision, so as to incorporate Sikri, J.'s view, as follows:

(3) Notwithstanding anything contained in sub-section (1), the last sale or purchase of any goods preceding the sale or purchase occasioning the export of those goods out of the territory of India shall also be deemed to be in the course of such export, if such last sale or purchase took place after, and was for the purpose of complying with, the agreement or order for or in relation to such export.

12. *Associated Cement Co. Ltd. v. Commercial Tax Officer, Kota & Ors.* (1981)

In *Associated Cement Co. Ltd. v. Commercial Tax Officer, Kota & Ors.* (1981),* one of the questions that arose for consideration before a bench consisting of three learned judges is whether the assessee was liable, under Section 11-B of the Rajasthan Sales Tax Act, 1954, to pay interest on tax (in respect of an amount of freight), for the period between the date of filing of the original return and the date when such tax was actually paid while filing the revised return. The answer to this question depended on the correct interpretation of two sections of the said act, namely, sections 7(1) and (2), and section 11B. The said sections are set out hereinbelow:

7. Submission of returns.—(1) Every registered dealer, and such other dealer, as may be required to do so by the assessing authority by notice served in the prescribed manner, shall furnish prescribed returns, for the prescribed periods, in the prescribed forms, in the prescribed manner and within the prescribed time to the assessing authority:

Provided that the assessing authority may extend the date for the submission of such returns by any dealer or class of dealers by a period not exceeding fifteen days in the aggregate.

(2) Every such return shall be accompanied by a Treasury receipt or receipt of any bank authorized to receive money on behalf of the State Government, showing the deposit of the full amount of tax due on the basis of return in the State Government Treasury or bank concerned.

* * *

* (1981) 4 SCC 578.

11-B. Interest on failure to pay tax, fee or penalty.—(a) If the amount of any tax payable under sub-sections (2) and (2-A) of Section 7 is not paid within the period allowed, or

(b) If the amount specified in any notice of demand, whether for tax, fee, or penalty, is not paid within the period specified in such notice, or in the absence of such specification, within 30 days from the date of service of such notice, the dealer shall be liable to pay simple interest on such amount at one per cent per month from the day commencing after the end of the said period for a period of three months and at one and a half per cent per month thereafter during the time he continues to make default in the payments:

Provided that, where, as a result of any order under this Act, the amount, on which interest was payable under this section, has been reduced, the interest shall be reduced accordingly and the excess interest paid, if any, shall be refunded:

Provided further that no interest shall be payable under this section on such amount and for such period in respect of which interest is paid under the provisions of Sections 11 and 14.

Venkataramiah, J., speaking on behalf of the majority, held that such interest was payable. P.N. Bhagwati, J. dissented, reasoning as follows:

6. The language used in sub-section (2) of Section 7 is 'full amount of tax due on the basis of return'. The 'return' referred to is obviously the return filed by the assessee under sub-section (1) of Section 7. Now it is true that when sub-section (1) of Section 7 requires an assessee to file a return, the return filed must be correct and proper. If the return is not correct and proper, the Assessing Authority may not give credence to the return and may refuse to assess the tax on the basis of the return and if the Assessing Authority finds that the assessee has concealed any particulars from the return furnished by him or has deliberately furnished inadequate particulars in the return, the Assessing Authority may levy penalty on the assessee under Section 16, sub-section (1), clause (e) and the assessee may also be liable to be punished for an offence under Section 16, sub-section (3), clause (d) for making a false statement in the return. But, whether the return filed be correct or not, the tax payable by the assessee under sub-

section (2) of Section 7 would be the full amount of tax due on the basis of the return. We must look at the return actually filed by the assessee in order to see what is the full amount of tax due on the basis of such return. It is not the assessed tax nor is it the tax due on the basis of a return which ought to have been filed by the assessee but it is the tax due according to the return actually filed that is payable under sub-section (2) of Section 7. This provision is really in the nature of self-assessment and what it requires is that whatever be the amount of tax due on the basis of self-assessment must be paid up along with the filing of the return which constitutes self-assessment. I fail to see how the plain words of sub-section (2) of Section 7 can be tortured to mean full amount of tax due on the basis of return which ought to have been filed but which has not been filed.

7. It may also be noted that the construction contended for on behalf of the Revenue leads to a serious anomaly. If this construction were accepted, the tax payable under sub-section (2) of Section 7 would be the full amount of tax due on the basis of a correct and proper return and that would necessarily be the same as the tax assessed by the Assessing Authority, because what is a correct and proper return would be determinable only with reference to the assessment ultimately made. The assessment when made would show whether the return filed was correct and proper; it would be correct and proper if it accords with the assessment made; if it does not accord with the assessment, then to the extent to which it differs it would obviously have to be regarded as incorrect and improper. The consequence of the construction suggested on behalf of the Revenue would thus be that the tax payable under sub-section (2) of Section 7 would be the full amount of the tax as assessed, because that would represent the tax due on the basis of a correct and proper return and the assessee would have to deposit at the time of filing the return, an amount equivalent to the amount of the tax as assessed. If the assessee fails to do so, then apart from the liability to pay interest under Section 11-B, clause (a), the assessee would expose himself to penalty under Section 16, sub-section (1), clause (n) which provides *inter alia* that any person who fails to comply with any requirement of the provisions of the State Act, the requirement under sub-section (2) of Section 7 being to deposit the full amount of tax due on the basis of return, shall be liable to penalty in 'a sum not exceeding Rs 1000 and in the case of continuing default, a further penalty not exceeding Rs 50 for every day of such continuance'.

This is a consequence which it is difficult to believe could ever have been contemplated by the legislature. The legislature could never have intended that the assessee should be liable, on pain of imposition of penalty, to deposit an amount which is yet to be ascertained through assessment. How would the assessee know in advance what view the Assessing Authority would take in regard to the taxability of any particular category of sales or the rate of tax applicable to them and deposit the amount of tax on that basis? And this would be all the more problematic in the case of a statute like the sales tax law which is full of complexities and where it may be difficult to assert dogmatically that a particular view is right or wrong. Even in regard to the liability to pay interest, it does not stand to reason that the legislature should have subjected the assessee to such liability for non-payment of an amount of which the liability for payment is still to be ascertained. Moreover on the construction of the Revenue, if the assessee has not deposited at the time of filing the return an amount equivalent to the full amount of the tax assessed, the assessee would be liable to pay interest on the amount remaining unpaid from the date of filing of the return until payment . . .

. . . The Court must always prefer that interpretation which avoids repugnancy between two provisions of a statute and gives full meaning and effect to both. Therefore, on this principle of interpretation also the construction canvassed on behalf of the Revenue cannot be accepted, as it would create a direct conflict between the provisions of clauses (a) and (b) of Section 11-B. The only way in which clauses (a) and (b) of Section 11-B can be read harmoniously and full meaning and effect can be given to them is by construing them as dealing with distinct matters or situations. The tax payable under sub-section (2) of Section 7 dealt with in clause (a) of Section 11-B cannot, therefore, be equated with the amount of the tax assessed forming the subject-matter of clause (b) of Section 11-B and hence it must be held to be tax due on the basis of the return actually filed by the assessee and not on the basis of a correct and proper return which ought to have been filed by him.

In *J.K. Synthetics Ltd. v. Commercial Taxes Officer* (1994),[*] a five-judge bench of the Supreme Court took the view that the majority interpretation

---

[*] (1994) 4 SCC 276.

in *Associated Cement Co.* was incorrect, and that Justice Bhagwati's minority judgment was correct. A.M. Ahmadi, J., speaking on behalf of the bench, first referred to the majority judgment of Venkataramiah, J. in *Associated Cement Co.* as follows:

11. The majority view was expressed by Venkataramiah, J. on behalf of himself and Sen, J. with which Bhagwati, J. dissented. Venkataramiah, J. speaking for the majority points out that interest claimed on unpaid tax dues has been described as compensatory in character and not penal. Dealing with the assessee's contention that as it had deposited the full amount of tax due on the basis of the returns filed under Section 7(1), and had thereby complied with Section 7(2), and had subsequently deposited the additional tax on the basis that freight charges were includible in the taxable turnover while submitting the revised return under Section 7(3), the question of charging interest could not arise, Venkataramiah, J. observed:

'In the present case if we construe the words 'on the basis of return' occurring in sub-section (2) of Section 7 of the Act as on the basis of a true and proper return which ought to have been filed under sub-section (1) of Section 7 then all the three classes of persons viz. (i) those who have not filed any return at all and who are later on found to be liable to be assessed, (ii) those who have filed a true return but have not deposited the full amount of tax which they are liable to pay and (iii) those who have filed a return making a wrong claim that either the whole or any part of the turnover is not taxable and who are subsequently found to have made a wrong claim, would be placed in the same position and they would all be liable to pay interest on the amount of tax which they are liable to pay but have not paid as required by sub-section (2) of Section 7 of the Act. We are of opinion that this view is in conformity with the legislative intention in enacting Section 11-B of the Act.'

12. Referring to the Constitution Bench judgment in the case of *Ghasilal*, the learned Judge observes that the said decision was distinguishable because it related to the sustainability of the penalties imposed under Section 16(1) of the Act and not interest levied under Section 11-B of the Act and secondly because Section 16(1)(b) was attracted when there was a failure to pay the 'tax due', an expression not

employed by Section 11-B of the Act. The learned Judge also points out that if Sections 7 and 11-B are not interpreted in the manner indicated in the above-quoted passage, (i) a registered dealer who does not file a return and pays no tax (ii) a registered dealer who files a true return but does not pay the full amount of tax and (iii) a registered dealer who files a return but wrongly claims either the whole or any part of the turnover as not taxable and pays under Section 7(2) only that much amount of tax as he considers payable on the basis of the return, will escape the net of Section 11-B and render the provision either unworkable or meaningless and, therefore, it is essential, on a fair reading of Section 11-B, to hold that the law expects that all those liable to pay tax should file a 'true return' within the time allowed. The learned Judge concludes by saying 'We do not think . . . we have in any way disregarded the decision in *Ghasilal* case' and emphasizes 'we have to state that we depend upon *Ghasilal* case itself to hold that for the purpose of Section 11-B(a) the tax becomes payable before assessment is made by virtue of Section 3 read with Section 5 and sub-sections (2) and (2-A) of Section 7 of the Act and the Rules framed thereunder, even though, it becomes due when return is filed under Section 7(2) or ascertained under Section 10'. On this line of reasoning the majority upheld the demand made under Section 11-B of the Act.

Thereafter, passages from Bhagwati, J.'s minority judgment were set out. Agreeing with Bhagwati, J., the court, in an oft-quoted passage, held:

16. It is well-known that when a statute levies a tax it does so by inserting a charging section by which a liability is created or fixed and then proceeds to provide the machinery to make the liability effective. It, therefore, provides the machinery for the assessment of the liability already fixed by the charging section, and then provides the mode for the recovery and collection of tax, including penal provisions meant to deal with defaulters. Provision is also made for charging interest on delayed payments, etc. Ordinarily the charging section which fixes the liability is strictly construed but that rule of strict construction is not extended to the machinery provisions which are construed like any other statute. The machinery provisions must, no doubt, be so construed as

would effectuate the object and purpose of the statute and not defeat the same. (See *Whitney v. IRC, CIT v. Mahaliram Ramjidas, India United Mills Ltd. v. Commissioner of Excess Profits Tax, Bombay* and *Gursahai Saigal v. CIT, Punjab*). But it must also be realized that provision by which the authority is empowered to levy and collect interest, even if construed as forming part of the machinery provisions, is substantive law for the simple reason that in the absence of contract or usage interest can be levied under law and it cannot be recovered by way of damages for wrongful detention of the amount. (See *Bengal Nagpur Railway Co. Ltd. v. Ruttanji Ramji* and *Union of India v. A.L. Rallia Ram*). Our attention was, however, drawn by Mr Sen to two cases. Even in those cases, *CIT v. M. Chandra Sekhar* and *Central Provinces Manganese Ore Co. Ltd. v. CIT*, all that the Court pointed out was that provision for charging interest was, it seems, introduced in order to compensate for the loss occasioned to the Revenue due to delay. But then interest was charged on the strength of a statutory provision, may be its objective was to compensate the Revenue for delay in payment of tax. But regardless of the reason which impelled the Legislature to provide for charging interest, the Court must give that meaning to it as is conveyed by the language used and the purpose to be achieved. Therefore, any provision made in a statute for charging or levying interest on delayed payment of tax must be construed as a substantive law and not adjectival law. So construed and applying the normal rule of interpretation of statutes, we find, as pointed out by us earlier and by Bhagwati, J. in the *Associated Cement Co.* case, that if the Revenue's contention is accepted it leads to conflicts and creates certain anomalies which could never have been intended by the Legislature.

xxx xxx xxx

19. In the result we are of the view that the majority opinion expressed by Venkataramiah, J. in the *Associated Cement Company* case does not, with respect, state the law correctly and in our view the legal position was correctly stated by Bhagwati, J. in his minority judgment. We, therefore, overrule the majority view in that decision and affirm the minority view as laying down the correct law.

13. *I.T.C. Ltd. v. State of Karnataka and Ors.* (1985)

In *I.T.C. Ltd. v. State of Karnataka and Ors.* (1985),[*] there was a sharp cleavage of opinion between all the three learned judges who heard the case. The question which arose before the bench was regarding the validity of the Karnataka Agricultural Produce Marketing (Regulation) Amendment Act, 1980, which validated the levy and collection of market fees from sellers of specified agricultural produce under the Karnataka Agricultural Produce Marketing (Regulation) Act, 1966. Mukharji, J. upheld the constitutionality of the validation act, together with the levy of market fee, on the ground that the state act and the subsequent validating act were supported under Entry 28 of List II of the Seventh Schedule to the Constitution of India, which deals with 'markets and fairs'. Also, applying the test of *quid pro quo*, as laid down by decisions of the Supreme Court, and bypassing the five-judge-bench decision in *Kewal Krishan Puri v. State of Punjab* (1979),[†] the market fee that was levied was held to be valid.

Fazal Ali, J. disagreed with Mukharji, J. on the constitutional validity of the said acts, holding that Entry 52 of List I, which deals with 'Industries, the control of which by the Union is declared by Parliament by law to be expedient in the public interest' enabled the passing of the Tobacco Board Act, 1975, which then occupied the *entire* field of the tobacco industry, as a result of which the state act imposing market fee on tobacco would have to be held *ultra vires*. In this finding, Fazal Ali, J. was joined by Varadarajan, J., with Mukharji, J. in the minority.

However, insofar as the question of *quid pro quo* was concerned, Fazal Ali, J. joined Mukharji, J.—Varadarajan, J. being in the minority. Varadarajan, J., on this point, held that the five-judge bench in *Kewal Krishan Puri*, could not possibly be diluted by later judgments of benches of smaller strength, and would therefore have to be rigorously followed and applied.

In his minority judgment on the aspect of legislative competence, Mukharji, J. stated:

---

[*] (1985) Supp. SCC 476.
[†] (1979) 3 SCR 1217.

237. While it is true that in the spheres very carefully delineated the Parliament has supremacy over State Legislatures, supremacy in the sense that in those fields, parliamentary legislation would hold the field and not the State legislation—but to denude the State Legislature of its power to legislate where the legislation in question in pith and substance i.e. in its true nature and character, belongs to the State field, one should be chary to denude the State of its powers to legislate and mobilize resources—because that would be destructive of the spirit and purpose of India being a Union of States. States must have power to raise and mobilize resources in their exclusive fields. In the instant case by complying with the State Act, the Central Act can function to serve the purpose and object of the Central Act, but if only the Central Act was to prevail, the State Act of marketing for coffee would become non est—wholly unnecessary and undesirable. The Marketing Act is essentially an Act to regulate the marketing of agricultural produce, control of coffee industry would not be defeated if the marketing of coffee is done within the provisions of the Marketing Act. It must therefore be held that the State Act should prevail. One should avoid corroding the State's ambit of powers of legislation which will ultimately lead to erosion of India being a Union of States.

238. The contentions on behalf of the appellants therefore, on this point have to be rejected. As to who should obtain licence or as to who would have to be registered, the market committee or the Tobacco Board is a question which should be settled by proper adjudication.

239. Some argument has been built upon the fact that though more or less identical in nature, in respect of the Cardamom Act, 1965, it was held that the State Legislature was not competent to enact the Cardamom Act, 1965 in view of the declaration under Entry 52 of List I of the Seventh Schedule. It was therefore suggested that it would not be correct to take inconsistent views in respect of this Act as against the Tobacco Board Act. As noticed before, the contention of validity of the Cardamom Act on the ground of Entry 28 of List II of the Seventh Schedule was not canvassed. Furthermore, it was held that the rules under the Cardamom Act which were framed were in variance with the present Act. The Government had accepted the findings of the High Court so far as Cardamom Act is concerned. Had it been otherwise and

had it been examined by this Court for the reasons which are noted herein, what would have been the result it is difficult to state. In any event, in this background that cannot be any reason far less a compelling reason to hold that the Tobacco Board Act was within the competence of the State Legislature for the reasons indicated in this judgment. Therefore that cannot be any argument for consideration at all.

In *I.T.C. Limited v. Agricultural Produce Market Committee & Ors.*, (2002),* by a 3:2 majority decision, Mukharji, J.'s minority view was upheld by the court. Sabharwal, J. accepted Mukharji, J.'s dissenting judgment in the first *I.T.C.* case as follows:

> 16. In *ITC* case, by majority, it was held that the tobacco industry having been taken over by the Central Government under Entry 52 of the Union List by enactment of the Tobacco Board Act, the State Legislature ceases to have any jurisdiction to legislate for that field and, therefore, the provisions of the Karnataka Agricultural Produce and Marketing Act entitling the Market Committee to levy market fee in respect of sale and purchase of tobacco within the market area collide with the Tobacco Board Act. Thus, the State Act so far as it relates to tobacco was struck down. The minority view was that both the State and the Central Acts can operate in their respective fields and there is no repugnancy if both the Acts are considered in the light of their respective true nature and character.

> xxx xxx xxx

> 18. The minority view, however, was that there is nothing in the State Act or in the Rules which indicate that it is inconsistent with or cannot be operated along with the marketing regulations and both the Acts can operate in their respective fields and there is no repugnancy if both the Acts are considered in the light of their true nature and character.

> xxx xxx xxx

---

* (2002) 9 SCC 232.

21. In the minority opinion, Mukharji, J. noticed that the Karnataka Agricultural Produce Marketing (Regulation) Act, 1966 deals with the subject of market in Entry 28 read with Entry 66 of List II and that it had to be borne in mind that Entry 28 is not subject to withdrawal to List I by Parliament. The State Act is not on a subject in List III nor is the Central Act a law relating to any subject in List III. It was concluded that, therefore, there cannot be any question of repugnancy. The nature and character of the Acts, namely, the Karnataka Agricultural Produce Marketing (Regulation) Act, 1966 and the Central Act was noticed and it was held that it is fully manifest that both the Acts can operate in their respective fields. Further, in the minority opinion it was observed that while giving due weight to the Centre's supremacy in the matter of legislation, the States' legitimate sphere of legislation should not be unnecessarily whittled down because that would be unwarranted by the spirit and basic purpose of the constitutional division of powers—not merely allocation of power by the Constitution but invasion by parliamentary legislations. While it is true that in the spheres very carefully delineated, Parliament has supremacy over the State Legislatures, supremacy in the sense that in those fields, parliamentary legislation would hold the field and not the State legislation—but to denude the State Legislature of its power to legislate where the legislation in question in pith and substance i.e. in its true nature and character, belongs to the State field, one should be chary to denude the State of its powers to legislate and mobilize resources—because that would be destructive of the spirit and purpose of India being a Union of States. States must have power to raise and mobilize resources in their exclusive fields. The Marketing Act is essentially an Act to regulate the marketing of agricultural produce. Justice Mukharji said that:

'It must, therefore, be held that the State Act should prevail. One should avoid corroding the State's ambit of powers of legislation which will ultimately lead to erosion of India being a Union of States.'

He then concluded:

89. In view of the above, I see no compelling reason either on account of any binding precedent in the form of an earlier Constitution Bench judgment,

history and background of the framing of the Constitution or the words used in various entries or the language of any article in the Constitution of India, to take a view which will result in denuding the power of the State Legislatures to legislate not in respect of the field of legislation under Entry 24 but field of legislation covered by other entries on the State List on making of declaration under Entry 52 of the Union List. The Constitution Bench judgment in the case of *Tika Ramji* and other decisions following it confine the field of legislation of industries to 'the process of manufacture or production' and not to 'raw materials' which may be an integral part of industrial process or to the 'distribution of the product of the industry'.

90. In view of the aforesaid, I conclude as under:

1. The State legislations and the Tobacco Board Act, 1975 to the extent of sale of tobacco in market area cannot coexist.
2. The State Legislatures are competent to enact legislations providing for sale of agricultural produce of tobacco in market area and for levy and collection of market fee on that produce.
3. Parliament is not competent to pass legislation in respect of goods enumerated in the aforesaid Conclusion 2 while legislating in the field of legislation covered by Entry 52 of the Union List under which Parliament can legislate only in respect of industries, namely, 'the process of manufacture or production' as held in *Tika Ramji* case. The activity regarding sale of raw tobacco as provided in the Tobacco Board Act cannot be regarded as 'industry'.
4. *ITC* case is not correctly decided.

Ruma Pal, J., in her separate concurring judgment, also accepted the dissenting judgment of Mukharji, J.:

153. It was said that if the minority view (expressed by Mukharji, J.) was accepted, it would amount to
     'robbing the 1975 Act of its entire content and essential import by handing over the power of legislation to the State Government which per se has been taken over by Parliament under Article 246 by the 1975 Act'.
     Mukharji, J. had in fact followed Tika Ramji and held correctly that the Tobacco Act and the Markets Act operated in their respective fields

and that there was no repugnancy if both the Acts were considered in the light of their respective true nature and character. Tika Ramji and the other Constitution Bench decisions following it were not even referred to by the majority.

xxx xxx xxx

157. In the circumstances I would hold that *ITC v. State of Karnataka* was wrongly decided and would for the reasons discussed uphold the competence of the State Legislatures to levy market fee on tobacco.

Brijesh Kumar, J., the third learned judge who formed the majority of judges, agreed with Sabharwal, J.[*]

14. *Ashok Kumar Sharma & Anr. v. Chander Shekhar & Anr.* (1993)

In *Ashok Kumar Sharma & Anr. v. Chander Shekhar & Anr.* (1993),[†] the state of Jammu and Kashmir issued an advertisement on 9 June 1982, inviting applications for filling up of the posts of junior engineers. The last date for submission of such applications was 15 July 1982, and the educational qualification prescribed for junior engineers (civil) was a Bachelor of Engineering degree in civil engineering. The appellants had appeared in the BE (civil) examination, but their results had not yet been declared on the date of the advertisement. The results were declared on 21 August 1982, and interviews commenced thereafter on 24 August 1982. The appellants were allowed to be called in for the interview, though they may not have had the qualification on the date they sent in their applications. The question before the court was whether such persons could be allowed to appear in the interview. The majority, comprising T.K. Thommen, J. and V. Ramaswami, J., held as follows:

---

[*] *See* paragraph 164. The minority judgment of Patnaik, J., speaking on behalf of himself and Bharucha, C.J., is dealt with in Chapter III.

[†] (1993) Supp. 2 SCC 611.

15. The fact is that the appellants did pass the examination and were fully qualified for being selected prior to the date of interview. By allowing the appellants to sit for the interview and by their selection on the basis of their comparative merits, the recruiting authority was able to get the best talents available. It was certainly in the public interest that the interview was made as broad based as was possible on the basis of qualification. The reasoning of the learned Single Judge was thus based on sound principle with reference to comparatively superior merits. It was in the public interest that better candidates who were fully qualified on the dates of selection were not rejected, notwithstanding that the results of the examination in which they had appeared had been delayed for no fault of theirs. The appellants were fully qualified on the dates of the interview and taking into account the generally followed principle of Rule 37 in the State of Jammu & Kashmir, we are of opinion that the technical view adopted by the learned Judges of the Division Bench was incorrect and the view expressed by the learned Single Judge was, on the facts of this case, the correct view. Accordingly, we set aside the impugned judgment of the Division Bench and restore that of the learned Single Judge. In the result, we uphold the results announced by the recruiting authority. The appeal is allowed in the above terms. However, we make no order as to costs.

R.M. Sahai, J. dissented on the point of law, but concurred in the ultimate result. He held:

19. . . . The mandatory character of possessing the requirements as provided in the first part of the notification stands further strengthened from the third and last part of the notification which prohibited the candidates from applying if they did not possess the requisite qualifications. In view of these clear and specific conditions laid down in the advertisement those candidates who were not possessed of the B.E. qualifications were not eligible for applying nor their applications were liable to be entertained nor could they be called for interview. Eligibility for the post mentioned in the notification depended on possessing the qualification noted against each post. The expression, 'shall be possessed of such qualifications, is indicative of both the mandatory character of the requirement and its operation in praesenti. That is a candidate must

not only have been qualified but he should have been possessed of it on the date the application was made. The construction suggested by the learned counsel for the appellant that the relevant date for purposes of eligibility was the date of interview and not the date of application or July 15, 1982 the last date for submission of forms is not made out from the language of the notification. Acceptance of such construction would result in altering the first part of the advertisement prescribing eligibility on the date of applying for the post as being extended to the date of interview. If it is read in the manner suggested then the requirement that incomplete applications and those not accompanied by the requisite certificates shall not be entertained, shall become meaningless. Purpose of filing certificate along with application was to prove that the conditions required were satisfied. Non-filing of any of the certificates could have resulted in not entertaining the application as the requirements as specified would have been presumed to be non-existent. Fulfilment of conditions was mandatory and its proof could be directory. The former could not be waived or deferred whereas the defect in latter could be cured even subsequently. That is proof could be furnished till date of interview but not the eligibility to apply for the post. Any other construction would further be contrary to the last part of the notification.

A review petition was filed against the aforesaid judgment. Thus, in *Ashok Kumar Sharma & Ors. v. Chander Shekhar & Anr.* (1997),* a three-judge bench hearing this review petition, agreed with the dissenting judgment of Sahai, J. thus:

> 6. The review petitions came up for final hearing on 3-3-1997. We heard the learned counsel for the review petitioners, for the State of Jammu & Kashmir and for the 33 respondents. So far as the first issue referred to in our Order dated 1-9-1995 is concerned, we are of the respectful opinion that majority judgment (rendered by Dr T.K. Thommen and V. Ramaswami, JJ.) is unsustainable in law. The proposition that where applications are called for prescribing a particular date as the last date for filing the

---

* (1997) 4 SCC 18.

applications, the eligibility of the candidates shall have to be judged with reference to that date and that date alone, is a well-established one. A person who acquires the prescribed qualification subsequent to such prescribed date cannot be considered at all. An advertisement or notification issued/ published calling for applications constitutes a representation to the public and the authority issuing it is bound by such representation. It cannot act contrary to it. One reason behind this proposition is that if it were known that persons who obtained the qualifications after the prescribed date but before the date of interview would be allowed to appear for the interview, other similarly placed persons could also have applied. Just because some of the persons had applied notwithstanding that they had not acquired the prescribed qualifications by the prescribed date, they could not have been treated on a preferential basis. Their applications ought to have been rejected at the inception itself. This proposition is indisputable and in fact was not doubted or disputed in the majority judgment. This is also the proposition affirmed in *Rekha Chaturvedi v. University of Rajasthan*. The reasoning in the majority opinion that by allowing the 33 respondents to appear for the interview, the recruiting authority was able to get the best talent available and that such course was in furtherance of public interest is, with respect, an impermissible justification. It is, in our considered opinion, a clear error of law and an error apparent on the face of the record. In our opinion, R.M. Sahai, J. (and the Division Bench of the High Court) was right in holding that the 33 respondents could not have been allowed to appear for the interview.

Finally, however, the review petitions were dismissed on facts, with the view:

9. Having given our anxious and earnest consideration to the question and keeping in view the fact that we are sitting in review jurisdiction and that this particular aspect is a matter lying within the discretion of the Court, we do not think it appropriate to interfere with the unanimous opinion of the three learned Judges of this Court on this aspect. It is true that the Division Bench of the High Court had granted the relief not only to the four review petitioners/writ petitioners but to all the candidates falling in that category yet we cannot ignore the fact that even

Sahai, J. who agreed with the review petitioners on the first issue, thought it just and proper not to disturb the inter se seniority between these two groups of selected candidates. The said seniority was determined by the selecting authority. Though certain allegations are made with respect to the fairness of the process of selection, that issue is not open in these review applications nor was it gone into by this Court in the civil appeals.

15. *Gaurav Jain v. Union of India* (1997)

In *Gaurav Jain v. Union of India* (1997),[*] two learned judges of the Supreme Court in a 'Public Interest Litigation' for the rehabilitation of the children of prostitutes, passed certain directions. Ramaswamy, J., being the senior judge on the Division Bench, not only passed directions regarding the children of prostitutes but also passed certain directions on the question of whether prostitution itself should be allowed. Insofar as the latter directions were concerned, Wadhwa, J., the second learned judge of this Division Bench, differed. He held:

> 61. Thus considering the substratum of the judgment prepared by my learned brother relating to children of the prostitutes and establishment of the juvenile homes I would concur with the directions being issued by him in his Order. I would, however, record my respectful dissent on the question of prostitution and the directions proposed to be issued on that account and also, in the circumstances of the case, what my learned brother has to say on the directions proposed to be issued referring to the provisions of Articles 142 and 145(5) of the Constitution.

Despite this difference of opinion and the fact that the matter ought to have gone to three (instead of two) learned judges under the Rules of the Court, Ramaswamy, J., disagreeing with Wadhwa, J.'s dissent, held that all directions would have to be complied with, including those relating to prostitution:

> 52. By operation of Article 145(5), to the extent both of us have agreed, the Order constitutes as a binding precedent. It is to remember that

---

[*] (1997) 8 SCC 114.

this Court being composed of large number of Judges has evolved its own procedure to transact court management of its judicial work and to decide cases/causes sitting in appropriate Division Benches constituted by the Chief Justice of India as per the Supreme Court Rules. Any observation made by one of the Judges has persuasive obiter. When there is a dissent, the majority of opinion forms a binding precedent. Any difference of opinion between a Bench composed of two Judges, in an adversarial litigation requires resolution by a larger Bench of three Judges and/or if further reference is made to a Constitution Bench, it is to deal with the controversy and majority opinion forms a precedent. As stated earlier, public interest litigation is not adversarial in nature but is one of cooperation and coordination between the three wings of the State and it is the constitutional duty of this Court to ensure enjoyment of the fundamental rights by all citizens and in particular the poor and deprived social segments and in case of violation thereof, to prevent the same by giving appropriate directions in that behalf. In aid thereof, this Court has been armed by Article 142 to pass such orders as may be necessary for doing complete justice in a cause or pending matter before it. An order so made shall be enforceable throughout the Territory of India. Normally, if it were an adversarial dispute, we would have referred the matter to a three-Judge Bench in respect of the first part of the directions, namely, to prevent prostitution; to rehabilitate fallen women and to provide them facilities and opportunities by evolving suitable measures by all the Governments for enforcement of their economic empowerment and social integration with dignity of person which are fundamental rights to the unfortunate fallen women, i.e., the victims of circumstances. It is seen that this matter has been pending for nearly a decade. If a reference is made to a three-Judge Bench, it may further be delayed. Since 'delay defeats justice' it may amount to everyday denial of the fundamental rights to a large number of fallen women.

53. I put a caveat upon myself and I am aware that Article 142 would be used to enforce final judgment or order which, in given special or exceptional circumstances, would include directions of this type to mitigate injustice and to elongate enforcement of fundamental and human rights. Article 142 speaks of doing complete justice in a cause. The arm of the Court is long enough to reach injustice wherever it is found and to mete out

justice. Denial of the constitutional rights to the unfortunate fallen women outrages the quest for justice and pragmatism of constitutional ethos which constrain me to avail of Article 142 of the Constitution of India to direct the Union of India as well as all the State Governments to evolve, after in-depth discussion at Ministerial-level conference, such procedures and principles or programmes, as indicated in this Order, as guidance would help rescue and rehabilitate the fallen women. Otherwise, the fundamental and human rights remain pious platitudes to these miserable souls crushed in the cruel flesh trade with grinding poverty in the evening of their lives. Generally, Article 142 may not be invoked before the difference of opinion is resolved in an adversarial litigation and in keenly contested matters of even public interest litigation, in particular, of recent type cases. However, in the cases of the type in hand, where there would be no controversy on human problems of the most unfortunate women which require their careful planning, rescue and rehabilitation, the exercise of the power under Article 142, even by a single Member of the Bench, may be appropriate and efficacious to enforce fundamental and human rights of a large number of neglected and exploited segments of the society. Society is responsible for a woman's becoming victim of circumstances. The society should make reparation to prevent trafficking in women, rescue them from red-light areas and other areas in which the women are driven or trapped in prostitution. Their rehabilitation by socio-economic empowerment and justice, is the constitutional duty of the State. Their economic empowerment and social justice with dignity of person, are the fundamental rights and the Court and the Government should positively endeavour to ensure them. The State in a democratic polity includes its three constitutional organs—the Legislature, the Executive and the Judiciary. The Legislature has already done its duty. The Executive and the Judiciary are required to act in union to ensure enforcement of fundamental and human rights of the fallen women. I am also conscious that the Union of India as well as the State Governments are sensitive to the conscience of their constitutional duty under Article 23 and are desirous of having prostitution eradicated from the root with the aid of the ITP Act, IPC and other appropriate legislative or executive actions. Sequential rehabilitation of the fallen women rescued from the red-light areas and other areas requires enforcement. The observations made in this Order, the constitutional provisions, the human rights and other

International Conventions referred to in the Order and the National Policy would aid the Union of India and the State Governments as foundation and guide them to discuss the problems in Ministerial and Secretarial-level Conferences and as suggested in this Order to evolve procedures and principles to ensure that the fallen women also enjoy their fundamental and human rights mentioned in the Order.

A three-judge bench in *Gaurav Jain v. Union of India* (1998),* took exception to Ramaswamy, J.'s approach, holding:

4. Article 145(1) of the Constitution provides that subject to the provisions of any law made by Parliament, the Supreme Court may, from time to time, with the approval of the President, make rules for regulating generally the practice and procedure of the court. The Supreme Court Rules have been framed under this provision. Under clause (2) of Article 145, subject to the provisions of clause (3), rules made under this article may fix the minimum number of Judges who are to sit for any purpose, and may provide for the powers of Single Judges and Division Courts. Clause (5) of Article 145 provides as follows:

'145. (5) No judgment and no such opinion shall be delivered by the Supreme Court save with the concurrence of a majority of the Judges present at the hearing of the case, but nothing in this clause shall be deemed to prevent a Judge who does not concur from delivering a dissenting judgment or opinion.'

xxx xxx xxx

8. There is no provision under Order XXXV for any special procedure in respect of a public interest petition under Article 32. The petition will have to be served on the respondents who have a right to file a counter-affidavit. Although the proceedings in a public interest litigation may not be adversarial in a given case, there can clearly be different perceptions of the same problem or its solution and the respondents are entitled to put forth their own view before the Court which may or may not coincide with

* (1998) 4 SCC 270.

the view of the petitioner. The Court may come to a view different from that of any of the parties. Therefore, even in a public interest litigation, if the members of the Bench hold different views, the provisions of Article 145(5) will apply and the matter will have to be decided by a majority. When a Bench consists of two Judges and they differ, the matter must necessarily be referred to the Chief Justice for constituting a larger Bench. In fact this legal position is expressly noted by Ramaswamy, J. However, he has taken the view that despite the provisions of Article 145(5), he can take the assistance of Article 142 for the purpose of issuing directions even though his brother Judge has differed from these directions.

9. We do not find anything in Article 142 which enables the Court to do so. Article 142 provides as follows:

'142. Enforcement of decrees and orders of Supreme Court and orders as to discovery, etc.—(1) The Supreme Court in the exercise of its jurisdiction may pass such decree or make such order as is necessary for doing complete justice in any cause or matter pending before it, and any decree so passed or order so made shall be enforceable throughout the territory of India in such manner as may be prescribed by or under any law made by Parliament and, until provision in that behalf is so made, in such manner as the President may by order prescribe.'

10. It does not and cannot override Article 145(5). The decrees or orders issued under Article 142 must be issued with the concurrence of the majority of Judges hearing the matter. In the case of *Prem Chand Garg v. Excise Commr., U.P.* a Bench of five Judges of this Court considered a Rule made by this Court providing for imposition of terms as to costs and as to giving of security in a petition under Article 32. The Rule was sought to be justified, *inter alia*, on the ground that the powers conferred on this Court under Article 142 were very wide and could not be controlled by Article 32. Negativing this contention, this Court said:

'The powers of this Court are no doubt very wide and they are intended to be and will always be exercised in the interest of justice. But that is not to say that an order can be made by this Court which is inconsistent with the fundamental rights guaranteed by Part III of the Constitution. An order which this Court can make in order to do complete justice between the parties, must not only be consistent with the fundamental rights guaranteed by the Constitution, but it cannot even be inconsistent with the substantive provisions of the relevant statutory laws. Therefore, we do not think it would be possible to hold that Article 142(1) confers upon this Court powers which can contravene the provisions of Article 32.'

Similarly, powers conferred by Article 142(1) also cannot contravene the provisions of Article 145(5). Article 142 would not entitle a Judge sitting on a Bench of two Judges, who differs from his colleague to issue directions for the enforcement of his order although it may not be the agreed order of the Bench of two Judges. If this were to be permitted, it would lead to conflicting directions being issued by each Judge under Article 142, directions which may quite possibly nullify the directions given by another Judge on the same Bench. This would put the Court in an untenable position. Because if in a Bench of two Judges, one Judge can resort to Article 142 for enforcement of his directions, the second Judge can do likewise for the enforcement of his directions. And even in a larger Bench, a Judge holding a minority view can issue his order under Article 142 although it may conflict with the order issued by the majority. This would put this Court in an indefensible situation and lead to total confusion. Article 142 is not meant for such a purpose and cannot be resorted to in this fashion.

11. The learned Judge is in error in resorting to Article 142 for the purpose of enforcement of his directions although his brother Judge has dissented from those directions. The justification which is put forward for resorting to Article 142 is that reference to a larger Bench would cause delay. This cannot be a ground for not following the provisions of the Constitution under Article 145. Whenever a matter has to be referred to a larger Bench, there is bound to be some delay. But such a reference is necessary in the interest of justice. It is necessary that the Court speak with one voice and that voice is the voice of the majority as propounded in Article 145(5). Only then can its orders be enforced. When two Judges differ, the matter will have to be decided by a larger Bench.

12. We, therefore, allow this review petition. The directions given by the learned Judge relating to prostitution and/or its amelioration or eradication are set aside. This, however, should not be understood as preventing the Union or State Governments from formulating their own policies in this area or taking measures to implement them. His

observations relating to the use of Article 142 in this connection are also set aside and the question of giving any directions in relation to prostitution, its eradication or amelioration will have to be placed before a larger Bench if any directions are required to be given in that connection by this Court. The matter should be placed before the Hon'ble the Chief Justice for considering whether a larger Bench should be constituted for this purpose.

16. *Raj Deo Sharma (II) v. State of Bihar* (1999)

In *Raj Deo Sharma (II) v. State of Bihar* (1999),[*] a three-judge bench was requested by the Central Bureau of Investigation to modify/clarify certain directions issued by an earlier three-judge bench in *Raj Deo Sharma (I) v. State of Bihar* (1998),[†] in which the Supreme Court had issued directions for effective enforcement of the 'right to speedy trial', which flowed from Article 21 of the Constitution, laying down certain time-limits within which such trials must be conducted. K.T. Thomas, J., with whom M. Srinivasan, J. concurred, clarified the aforesaid directions laid down in *Raj Deo Sharma (I)* in certain respects. M.B. Shah, J., however, dissented, stating:

> 47. In this view of the matter, in my view, prescribing time-limit would be against the decisions rendered by the Constitution Bench of this Court in *A.R. Antulay* and *Kartar Singh* cases as well as other decisions stated above. It would be prescribing time-limit which is not provided by the Criminal Procedure Code or by any other statutory provision. And finally, it would have an adverse effect in implementation of criminal law.

In a seven-judge-bench decision in *P. Ramachandra Rao v. State of Karnataka* (2002),[‡] R.C. Lahoti, J., speaking on behalf of the court, and after undertaking an exhaustive review of all the judgments on this subject, referred to Shah, J.'s dissenting judgment in *Raj Deo Sharma (II)* as follows:

---

[*] (1999) 7 SCC 604.
[†] (1998) 7 SCC 507.
[‡] (2002) 4 SCC 578.

17. M.B. Shah, J. in his dissenting judgment noted the most usual causes for delay in delivery of criminal justice as discernible from several reported cases travelling up to this Court and held that the remedy for the causes of delay in disposal of criminal cases lies in effective steps being taken by the judiciary, the legislature and the State Governments, all the three. The dangers behind constructing time-limit barriers by judicial dictum beyond which a criminal trial or proceedings could not proceed, in the opinion of M.B. Shah, J., are (i) it would affect the smooth functioning of the society in accordance with law and finally the Constitution. The victims left without any remedy would resort to taking revenge by unlawful means resulting in further increase in the crimes and criminals. People at large in the society would also feel unsafe and insecure and their confidence in the judicial system would be shaken. Law would lose its deterrent effect on criminals; (ii) with the present strength of Judges and infrastructure available with criminal courts it would be almost impossible for the available criminal courts to dispose of the cases within the prescribed time-limit; (iii) prescribing such time-limits may run counter to the law specifically laid down by the Constitution Bench in *Antulay* case. In the fore-quoted thinking of M.B. Shah, J., we hear the echo of what the Constitution Bench spoke in *Kartar Singh v. State of Punjab* vide SCC p. 707, para 351:

'351. No doubt, liberty of a citizen must be zealously safeguarded by the courts; nonetheless the courts while dispensing justice in cases like the one under the TADA Act, should keep in mind not only the liberty of the accused but also the interest of the victim and their near and dear and above all the collective interest of the community and the safety of the nation so that the public may not lose faith in the system of judicial administration and indulge in private retribution.'

18. At the end, M.B. Shah, J. opined that order dated 8-10-1998 made in *Raj Deo Sharma* (I) requires to be held in abeyance and the State Government and Registrars of the High Courts ought to be directed to come up with specific plans for the setting up of additional courts/special courts (permanent/ad hoc) to cope up with the pending workload on the basis of available figures of pending cases also by taking into consideration the criteria for disposal of criminal cases prescribed by various High Courts. In conclusion, the Court directed the application filed by CBI to be disposed of in terms of the majority opinion.

The court finally concluded:

29. For all the foregoing reasons, we are of the opinion that in *Common Cause* case (I) [as modified in *Common Cause* (II) and *Raj Deo Sharma* (I) and (II)] the Court could not have prescribed periods of limitation beyond which the trial of a criminal case or a criminal proceeding cannot continue and must mandatorily be closed followed by an order acquitting or discharging the accused. In conclusion we hold:

(1) The dictum in *A.R. Antulay* case is correct and still holds the field.

(2) The propositions emerging from Article 21 of the Constitution and expounding the right to speedy trial laid down as guidelines in *A.R. Antulay* case adequately take care of right to speedy trial. We uphold and reaffirm the said propositions.

(3) The guidelines laid down in *A.R. Antulay* case are not exhaustive but only illustrative. They are not intended to operate as hard-and-fast rules or to be applied like a straitjacket formula. Their applicability would depend on the fact situation of each case. It is difficult to foresee all situations and no generalization can be made.

(4) It is neither advisable, nor feasible, nor judicially permissible to draw or prescribe an outer limit for conclusion of all criminal proceedings. The time-limits or bars of limitation prescribed in the several directions made in *Common Cause* (I), *Raj Deo Sharma* (I) and *Raj Deo Sharma* (II) could not have been so prescribed or drawn and are not good law. The criminal courts are not obliged to terminate trial or criminal proceedings merely on account of lapse of time, as prescribed by the directions made in *Common Cause* case (I), *Raj Deo Sharma* case (I) and (II). At the most the periods of time prescribed in those decisions can be taken by the courts seized of the trial or proceedings to act as reminders when they may be persuaded to apply their judicial mind to the facts and circumstances of the case before them and determine by taking into consideration the several relevant factors as pointed out in *A.R. Antulay* case and decide whether the trial or proceedings have become so inordinately delayed as to be called oppressive and unwarranted. Such time-limits cannot and will not by themselves be treated by any court as a bar to further continuance of the trial or proceedings and as

mandatorily obliging the court to terminate the same and acquit or discharge the accused.

(5) The criminal courts should exercise their available powers, such as those under Sections 309, 311 and 258 of the Code of Criminal Procedure to effectuate the right to speedy trial. A watchful and diligent trial Judge can prove to be a better protector of such right than any guidelines. In appropriate cases, jurisdiction of the High Court under Section 482 CrPC and Articles 226 and 227 of the Constitution can be invoked seeking appropriate relief or suitable directions.

(6) This is an appropriate occasion to remind the Union of India and the State Governments of their constitutional obligation to strengthen the judiciary—quantitatively and qualitatively—by providing requisite funds, manpower and infrastructure. We hope and trust that the Governments shall act.

D. Raju, J. pronounced a separate concurring judgment.

V

GREAT DISSENTS—THE SPIRIT OF THE LAW CONTINUES TO BROOD, NOT ACT

1. *Sardar Syedna Taher Saifuddin Saheb v. State of Bombay* (1962)

In *Sardar Syedna Taher Saifuddin Saheb v. State of Bombay* (1962),[*] the petitioner, who was the head of the Dawoodi Bohra community, challenged the Bombay Prevention of Excommunication Act, 1949—by which his power of excommunicating a member of the Dawoodi Bohra community was taken away—as violating Articles 25 and 26 of the Constitution of India. By a majority of 4:1, the aforesaid act was struck down. The majority reasoned that excommunication by the head of a community on religious grounds was viewed as an 'essential religious practice' by the community itself, and since excommunication even on these religious grounds had been invalidated by the act in question, the act violated the fundamental rights contained in Articles 25 and 26(b). Further, the majority held that this could not be said to be a measure of social reform so as to save the law under Article 25(2)(b), as barring excommunications on religious grounds per se cannot be considered to promote social welfare and reform.

Chief Justice B.P. Sinha, however, differed, speaking of Articles 25 and 26 as follows:

> It is not disputed that the petitioner is the head of the Dawoodi Bohra community or that the Dawoodi Bohra community is a religious denomination within the meaning of Article 26 of the Constitution. It is not even disputed by the State, the only respondent in the case, that the petitioner as the head of the community had the right, as found by the Privy Council in the case of *Hasanali v. Mansoorali* to excommunicate a particular member of the community for reasons and in the manner indicated in the judgment of Their Lordships of the Privy Council.

---

[*] (1962) Supp. (2) SCR 496.

But what is contended is that, as a result of the enactment in question, excommunication has been completely banned by the legislature, which was competent to do so, and that the ban in no way infringes Articles 25 and 26 of the Constitution. I have already indicated my considered opinion that the Bombay legislature was competent to enact the Act. It now remains to consider the main point in controversy, which was, as a matter of fact, the only point urged in support of the petition, namely, that the Act is void insofar as it is repugnant to the guaranteed rights under Articles 25 and 26 of the Constitution. Article 25 guarantees the right to every person, whether citizen or non-citizen, the freedom of conscience and the right freely to profess, practise and propagate religion. But this guaranteed right is not an absolute one. It is subject to (1) public order, morality and health, (2) the other provisions of Part III of the Constitution, (3) any existing law regulating or restricting an economic, financial, political or other secular activity which may be associated with religious practice, (4) a law providing for social welfare and reform, and (5) any law that may be made by the State regulating or restricting the activities aforesaid or providing for social welfare and reform. I have omitted reference to the provisions of Explanations I and II and other parts of Article 25 which are not material to our present purpose. It is noteworthy that the right guaranteed by Article 25 is an individual right, as distinguished from the right of an organized body like a religious denomination or any section thereof, dealt with by Article 26. Hence, every member of the community has the right, so long as he does not in any way interfere with the corresponding rights of others, to profess, practise and propagate his religion, and everyone is guaranteed his freedom of conscience. The question naturally arises: Can an individual be compelled to have a particular belief on pain of a penalty, like excommunication? One is entitled to believe or not to believe a particular tenet or to follow or not to follow a particular practice in matters of religion. No one can, therefore, be compelled, against his own judgment and belief, to hold any particular creed or follow a set of religious practices. The Constitution has left every person free in the matter of his relation to his Creator, if he believes in one. It is, thus, clear that a person is left completely free to worship God according to the dictates of his conscience, and that his right to worship as he pleased is unfettered so long as it does not come into conflict with any restraints, as aforesaid, imposed by the State in the interest of public order, etc. A person is not liable to answer for the verity of his religious views, and he cannot be questioned as to his religious beliefs, by the State or by any other person. Thus, though his religious beliefs are entirely his own and his freedom to hold those beliefs is absolute, he has not the absolute right to act in any way he pleased in exercise of his religious beliefs. He has been guaranteed the right to practise and propagate his religion, subject to the limitations aforesaid. His right to practise his religion must also be subject to the criminal laws of the country, validly passed with reference to actions which the legislature has declared to be of a penal character. Laws made by a competent legislature in the interest of public order and the like, restricting religious practices, would come within the regulating power of the State. For example, there may be religious practices of sacrifice of human beings, or sacrifice of animals in a way deleterious to the well-being of the community at large. It is open to the State to intervene, by legislation, to restrict or to regulate to the extent of completely stopping such deleterious practices. It must, therefore, be held that though the freedom of conscience is guaranteed to every individual so that he may hold any beliefs he likes, his actions in pursuance of those beliefs may be liable to restrictions in the interest of the community at large, as may be determined by common consent, that is to say, by a competent legislature. It was on such humanitarian grounds, and for the purpose of social reform, that so called religious practices like immolating a widow at the pyre of her deceased husband, or of dedicating a virgin girl of tender years to a God to function as a devadasi, or of ostracizing a person from all social contacts and religious communion on account of his having eaten forbidden food or taboo, were stopped by legislation.*

With regard to Article 26(b), the learned chief justice held:

What are exactly matters of religion are completely outside State interference, subject of course to public order, morality and health. But

---

* Ibid., pp. 518–20.

activities associated with religious practices may have many ramifications and varieties—economic, financial, political and other—as recognized by Article 25(2)(a). Such activities, as are contemplated by the clause aforesaid cover a field much wider than that covered by either Article 25(1) or Article 26(b). Those provisions have, therefore, to be so construed as to create no conflict between them. We have, therefore, to classify practices into such as are essentially and purely of a religious character, and those which are not essentially such.[*]

The learned chief justice then referred to the Privy Council decision in *Hasanali v. Mansoorali* (1947)[†] and added:

A matter which is purely religious could not come within the purview of the courts. That conclusion is further strengthened by the consideration that the effect of the excommunication or expulsion from the community is that the expelled person is excluded from the exercise of rights in connection not only with places of worship but also from burying the dead in the community burial ground and other rights to property belonging to the community, which are all disputes of a civil nature and are not purely religious matters. In the case before Their Lordships of the Privy Council, Their Lordships enquired into the regularity of the proceedings resulting in the excommunication challenged in that case, and they held that the plaintiff had not been validly expelled. It cannot, therefore, be asserted that the Privy Council held the matter of excommunication as a purely religious one. If it were so, the courts could be out of the controversy.[‡]

In a significant passage, the learned chief justice concluded:

It has further been contended that a person who has been excommunicated as a result of his non-conformity to religious practices is not entitled to use the communal mosque or the communal burial ground or other

---

[*] Id., p. 521.
[†] 75 IA 1 (1947).
[‡] (1962) Supp. (2) SCR 496, p. 524.

communal property, thus showing that for all practical purposes he was no more to be treated as a member of the community, and is thus an outcast. Another result of excommunication is that no other member of the community can have any contacts, social or religious, with the person who has been excommunicated. All that is true. But the Act is intended to do away with all that mischief of treating a human being as a pariah, and of depriving him of his human dignity and of his right to follow the dictates of his own conscience. The Act is, thus, aimed at fulfilment of the individual liberty of conscience guaranteed by Article 25(1) of the Constitution, and not in derogation of it. Insofar as the Act has any repercussions on the right of the petitioner, as trustee of communal property, to deal with such property, the Act could come under the protection of Article 26(d), in the sense that his right to administer the property is not questioned, but he has to administer the property in accordance with law. The law, in the present instance, tells the petitioner not to withhold the civil rights of a member of the community to a communal property. But as against this it is argued on behalf of the petitioner that his right to excommunicate is so bound up with religion that it is protected by clause (b) of Article 26, and is thus completely out of the regulation of law, in accordance with the provisions of clause (d) of that article. But, I am not satisfied on the pleadings and on the evidence placed before us that the right of excommunication is a purely religious matter. As already pointed out, the indications are all to the contrary, particularly the judgment of the Privy Council in the case of *Hasanali v. Mansoorali* on which great reliance was placed on behalf of the petitioner.

On the social aspect of excommunication, one is inclined to think that the position of an excommunicated person becomes that of an untouchable in his community, and if that is so, the Act in declaring such practices to be void has only carried out the strict injunction of Article 17 of the Constitution, by which untouchability has been abolished and its practice in any form forbidden. The article further provides that the enforcement of any disability arising out of untouchability shall be an offence punishable in accordance with law. The Act, in this sense, is its logical corollary and must, therefore, be upheld.

In my opinion, it has not been established that the Act has been passed by a legislature which was not competent to legislate on the subject, or that it infringes any of the provisions of the Constitution. This petition must, therefore, fail.[*]

The majority judgment was sought to be referred to a larger bench of seven judges of the Supreme Court by a two-judge bench.[†] However, Lahoti, C.J. in *Central Board of Dawoodi Bohra Community and Anr. v. State of Maharashtra and Anr.* (2005)[‡] stated that this reference to a larger bench was improper, and placed the matter for hearing before a five-judge bench:

13. So far as the present case is concerned, there is no reference made by any Bench of any strength at any time for hearing by a larger Bench and doubting the correctness of the Constitution Bench decision in the case of *Sardar Syedna Taher Saifuddin Saheb* case. The order dated 18-3-1994 by the two-Judge Bench cannot be construed as an order of reference. At no point of time has the Chief Justice of India directed the matter to be placed for hearing before a Constitution Bench or a Bench of seven Judges.

14. In the facts and circumstances of this case, we are satisfied that the matter should be placed for hearing before a Constitution Bench (of five Judges) and not before a larger Bench of seven Judges. It is only if the Constitution Bench doubts the correctness of the law laid down in *Sardar Syedna Taher Saifuddin Saheb* case that it may opine in favour of hearing by a larger Bench consisting of seven Judges or such other strength as the Chief Justice of India may in exercise of his power to frame a roster may deem fit to constitute.

Central Board remains pending before the Supreme Court. At present, a nine-judge bench is also reviewing the entire case law on Articles 25

---

[*] Ibid., pp. 527–28.
[†] Order dated 18.03.1994 in W.P. No. 740 of 1986.
[‡] (2005) 2 SCC 673.

and 26 of the Constitution in India,[*] in particular, with reference to the 'Sabarimala Temple' case.[†]

2. *Smt. Ujjam Bai v. State of Uttar Pradesh* (1963)

The opening paragraph of N. Rajagopala Ayyangar, J.'s dissenting judgment in *Smt. Ujjam Bai v. State of Uttar Pradesh* (1963)[‡] indicates the points for consideration before a bench of seven honourable judges of the Supreme Court of India, which was constituted in order to determine whether the decision rendered by a five-judge bench in *Kailash Nath & Anr. v. State of U.P. & Ors.* (1957),[§] was correct. This question is set out as follows:

> This bench has been constituted for deciding the following two questions set out at the conclusion of what might be termed the order of reference (1): Is an order of assessment made by an authority under a taxing statute which is *intra vires*, open to challenge as repugnant to Art. 19(1)(g) on the sole ground that it is based on a mis-construction of a provision of the Act or of a notification issued thereunder (2) Can the validity of such an order be questioned in a petition under Art. 32 of the Constitution? Though the matter was not discussed with any elaborateness, both these questions were answered in the affirmative by this Court in *Kailashnath v. The State of U.P.* In effect therefore the bench has been constituted for considering the correctness of the decision on these points in *Kailashnath's* case.

The learned judge's vision of the fundamental freedoms granted by the Constitution of India were then set out:

> The scheme therefore of the Constitution makers was to prescribe a code of conduct to which State action ought to conform if it

---

[*] A nine-judge bench was constituted pursuant to the majority decision in *Kantaru Rajeevaru v. Indian Young Lawyers Association and Ors.* ([2020] 2 SCC 1).
[†] *Indian Young Lawyers Association and Ors. v. State of Kerala and Ors.* ([2019] 11 SCC 1).
[‡] (1963) 1 SCR 778.
[§] AIR 1957 SC 790.

should pass the test of constitutionality. The rights included in the eighteen Articles, starting from 14 up to 31, comprehend provisions for ensuring guarantees against any State action for protecting the right to life, liberty, and property, to trade and occupation, besides including the right to freedom of thought, belief and worship. The general scheme of Part III may be stated thus: Certain of the freedoms are absolute, i.e., subject to no limitations, e.g., Art. 17, Art. 20(1). In respect of certain others the Articles (vide Art. 19) set out the precise freedom guaranteed as well as its content and the qualifications to which the exercise of that freedom might be subjected by enacted law or action taken under such law. Having thus enumerated these freedoms and laid down the limitations, if any to which they could be subjected Art. 32 vests in the Supreme Court the authority and jurisdiction to ensure that the fundamental rights granted by Part III are not violated, and even the right to move this Court for appropriate relief for infraction of a fundamental right is itself made a fundamental right which ordinary legislation may not affect. The purpose of my drawing attention to these features is two-fold: (1) to emphasize the great value which the Constitution-makers attached to the freedoms guaranteed as the *sine qua non* of progress and the need which they considered for marking out a field which was immune from State action, and (2) the function of this Court as a guardian of those rights for the maintenance of individual liberty enshrined in the Constitution.*

The question posed before the court was then narrowed down:

These exceptions having been conceded by learned Counsel for the respondent, it is sufficient if attention is confined to the question, whether a patently incorrect order passed on a misconstruction of a charging enactment would or would not result in the violation of a fundamental right and that is the very narrow question which this bench is called upon to answer.†

---

* (1963) 1 SCR 778, pp. 948–49.
† Ibid., pp. 951–52.

In a significant passage, the learned judge went on to state how, in his opinion, the breach of a fundamental right is independent of judicial, or quasi-judicial errors, correctable by way of appeal:

> In considering the proper answer to this question it is necessary to exclude one matter which is apt to cloud the issue and it is this. The statute under which the quasi-judicial authority functions or makes the decision or order may contain provisions for enabling the correctness of the decision reached or the order passed being challenged by an appeal or may provide for a gradation of appeals and further revisions. The existence of procedures for redressing grievances or correcting errors of primary or appellate authorities is obviously wholly irrelevant for a consideration of the question as to whether the order of the authority involves an infringement of fundamental rights or not. This Court has laid down in a large number of cases of which it is sufficient to refer to: *Union of India v. T.R. Varma, The State of Uttar Pradesh v. Mohammad Nooh*, and *A.V. Venkateswamn, Collector of Customs, Bombay v. Ramchand Sobharj Wadhwani* that the existence of an alternative remedy is no legal bar to the exercise of the jurisdiction of the High Court under Art. 226 of the Constitution. If that is so in the case of the jurisdiction under Art. 226 it must *a fortiori* be so in the case of a guaranteed remedy such as is vested in this Court under Art. 32 of the Constitution. Besides it cannot be predicated that there is a violation of a fundamental right if the party aggrieved has no appeal provided by the statute under which the authority acts, but that if other statutory remedies are provided there would be no violation of a fundamental right, for the question whether a fundamental right is violated or not is dependent on the action complained of having an impact on a guaranteed right, and its existence or non-existence or the action constituting a breach of a fundamental right cannot be determined by the absence or presence of procedures prescribed by the statute for correcting erroneous orders. The absence of any provision for redress by way of appeal may have a bearing on the reasonableness of the law, but it has none on the point now under discussion. Besides, it cannot be that if the remedies open under the statute are exhausted and the authority vested with the ultimate authority under the statute has

made its decision and there is no longer any possibility of an objection on the score of an alternative remedy being available, there would be a violation of a fundamental right with the consequence that this Court would have jurisdiction, but that if it was approached at an earlier stage there was no violation of a fundamental right and that it lacks jurisdiction to afford relief under Art. 32, for it must be admitted that in ultimate analysis there is no distinction between the nature and quality of an order passed by an original as distinct from one by an appellate or revisional authority—in its consequences vis-à-vis the fundamental right of the individual affected. It is common ground and that is a matter which has already been emphasized that if a petitioner made out to the satisfaction of the Court that he has a fundamental right in respect of the subject-matter and that the same has been violated by State action, it is imperative on the Court to afford relief to the petitioner the Court not having any discretion in the matter in those circumstances. On this basis the only ground upon which the jurisdiction could be denied would be that the order or decision of the authority which is impugned does not prejudicially affect the fundamental right of the petitioner, for it cannot be that the order of the ultimate authority under the statute could involve the violation of a fundamental right but that the same orders passed by authorities lower down in the rung under the statute would not involve such a violation.[*]

Interestingly, Nani Palkhivala's intervention did much to help Rajagopala Ayyangar, J. make up his mind:

The question for consideration is what exactly is meant when it is said that a statute is valid in the sense of: (a) being legally competent to the legislature to enact, and (b) being constitutional as not violative of the freedoms guaranteed by Part III. It is obvious that it can only mean that the statute properly construed is not legally incompetent or constitutionally invalid. In this connection it is of advantage to refer to a point made by Mr Palkhivala who appeared for some of the interveners in support of the petition. One of his submissions was this: Suppose there is an Act for the

_____

[*] Id., pp. 953–55.

levy of sales-tax which is constitutionally valid. On its proper construction it does not purport to or authorize the imposition of a tax on a sale 'in the course of export or import'. If it did so expressly authorize, it is obvious that such a provision in the enactment would be *ultra vires* and unconstitutional as violative of the prohibition contained in Art. 286(1)(a). Suppose further that an authority functioning under such an enactment vested with jurisdiction to assess dealers to sales tax proceeds to levy a tax and includes in the computation of the assessable turnover not merely those items which are properly within the legislative competence of the State Legislature to tax under the head 'Taxes on the sale of goods' but also the turnover in respect of transactions which are plainly 'sales in the course of export or import' and this it does on a patent misconstruction of the statute, could it be said that the fundamental right of the dealer guaranteed by Art. 19(1)(f) and (g) was not violated by the imposition of the sales tax in such circumstances? The logic behind this argument might be stated thus: If the legislature had in terms authorized the imposition of sales tax on such a transaction it would have been plainly void and illegal and hence ex-concessis the fundamental right in respect of property as well as of business under Art. 19(1)(f) and (g) would be violated by the levy of the tax and its collection. How is the position improved if without even the legislature saving so in express terms an officer who purports to act under the statute himself interprets the charging provision so as to bring to tax a transaction which it was constitutionally incompetent for the legislature itself to tax. I find the logic in this reasoning impossible to controvert, nor did the learned Additional Solicitor-General attempt any answer to this argument.[*]

Following upon this example, it was then held:

When once it is conceded that a citizen cannot be deprived of his property or be restricted in respect of the enjoyment of his property save by authority of law, it appears to me to be plain that in the illustration above there is no statutory authority behind the tax liability imposed upon him by the assessing authority. The Act which imposed the tax and created the machinery for its assessment, levy and collection is, no

---

[*] Id., p. 957.

doubt, perfectly valid but by reason of this circumstance it does not follow that the deprivation of property occasioned by the collection of a tax which is not imposed by the charging section does not involve the violation of a fundamental right merely because the imposition was by reason of an order of an authority created by the statute, though by a patent mis-interpretation of the terms of the Act and by wrongly reaching the conclusion that such a transaction was taxable.

I consider that the four concessions made by the respondent which I have set out earlier, all proceed on the basis that in these cases there is no valid legislative backing for the action of the authority—executive, administrative or quasi-judicial. I consider that the reason of that rule would equally apply to cases where the quasi-judicial authority commits a patent error in construing the enactment—for in such a case also there would obviously be no legislative backing for the action resulting from his erroneous decision.[*]

Summing up the legal position, the learned judge held:

To sum up the position: (1) If a statute is legally enacted in the sense of being within legislative competence of the relevant legislature and is constitutional as not violating any fundamental rights, it does not automatically follow that any action taken by quasi-judicial authorities created under it cannot violate fundamental rights guaranteed by Part III of the Constitution. The legislative competence, the existence of which renders the enactment valid, is confined to action by the authorities created under it, which on its proper construction could be taken. In an authority constituted under such a legal and valid enactment oversteps the constitutional limitations on the legislative power of the State Legislature, the acts of such an authority would be plainly unconstitutional and the consequences arising out of unconstitutional State action would necessarily attach to such action. If an 'unconstitutional Act' of the State Legislature would invade fundamental rights the same character and the same consequence must *a fortiori* follow when that act is not even by the State Legislature but by an authority constituted under an enactment

---

[*] Id., p. 960.

passed by it. (2) Where State action without legislative sanction behind it would violate the rights guaranteed under Part III, the result cannot be different because the State acts through the mechanism of a quasi-judicial authority which is vested with jurisdiction to interpret the enactment. The absence of legislative sanction for the imposition of an obligation or the creation of a liability cannot be filled in by the misinterpretation by an authority created under the Act.[*]

Thus, it was concluded:

> Though if the words of the Constitution were explicit, considerations such as there would be of no avail, yet even if the matter were ambiguous I am clearly of the opinion that the rejection of the broad contention raised on behalf of the respondent is justified as needed to give effect to the intentions of the framers of the Constitution. But as I have pointed out already, on no logical basis could it be held that where an act or order of a quasi-judicial authority lacks legislative backing, it cannot still impinge on a person's fundamental right and where an order suffers from patent error, it has no legislative sanction behind it.

In a very significant passage, which presaged the minority judgment of Hidayatullah, J. in *Naresh Shridhar Mirajkar and Ors. v. State of Maharashtra and Anr.* (1966),[†] the learned judge found that the judiciary would be included as 'State' within the meaning of Article 12 of the Constitution of India, given that Article 20(1) referred to a limitation imposed upon the judicial power of the state, as follows:

> Article 20(1) would admittedly refer to a limitation imposed upon the judicial power of the State and is obviously addressed also, if not wholly, to judicial authorities. Mr. Chari however sought to get over the implication arising from Art. 20(1) by suggesting that the definition in Art. 12 which excluded judicial and quasi-judicial authorities from

---

[*] Id., pp. 961–62.
[†] (1966) 3 SCR 744. Hidayatullah, J.'s dissent in *Naresh Shridhar Mirajkar* is discussed in detail in Chapter VI.

within the purview of the expression 'State' should be understood as applying only subject to express provision to the contrary. I feel wholly unable to accept the method suggested of reconciling the presence of Art. 20(1) with the interpretation of Art. 12 as excluding judicial and quasi-judicial authorities. No doubt, the definition in Art. 12 starts with the words 'unless the context otherwise requires'. That expression however could serve to cut down even further the reach of the definition and cannot serve to expand it beyond the executive and legislative fields of State action if the word 'includes' were understood as 'means and includes' which is the contention urged by learned Counsel. Again, Art. 12 winds up the list of authorities falling within the definition by referring to 'other authorities' within the territory of India which cannot, obviously be read as ejusdem generis with either the Government and the Legislatures or local authorities. The words are of wide amplitude and capable of comprehending every authority created under a statute and functioning within the territory of India. There is, no characterization of the nature of the 'authority' in this residuary clause and consequently it must include every type of authority set up under a statute for the purpose of administering laws enacted by the Parliament or by the State including those vested with the duty to make decisions in order to implement those laws (2). Among the reliefs which on the terms of Art. 32 this Court might afford to persons approaching it complaining of the violation of the fundamental right is the issue of a writ of *certiorari* specifically enumerated in that Article. It is common ground that that writ is available for issue only against judicial or quasi-judicial authorities and it would normally follow that quasi-judicial authorities could equally with other instruments of State action violate fundamental rights which could be redressed by the issue of this type of writ.*

It was also held:

Both this Court, as well as the High Court have vested in them the power to make rules, and it cannot be disputed that such rules would be 'laws' within the definition of the expression in Art. 13. If so, it is

---

* (1963) 1 SCR 778, pp. 969–70.

manifest that such rules might violate the fundamental rights, i.e., their validity would depend *inter alia* on their passing the test of permissible legislation under Part III. This would directly contradict any argument that Courts and quasi-judicial authorities are outside the definition of State in Art. 12.[*]

The answer to the reference was, therefore:

> I would therefore answer the question referred to the Bench by saying that the action of quasi-judicial authority could violate a fundamental right if on a plain mis-construction of the statute or a patent misinterpretation of its provisions such an authority affects any rights guaranteed under Part III. This would be in addition to the three broad categories of cases in regard to which it was conceded that there could be a violation of fundamental rights: (1) where the statute under which it functions was itself invalid or unconstitutional, (2) where the authority exceeds the jurisdiction conferred on it by the Act, and (3) where the authority though functioning under statute, contravenes mandatory procedure prescribed in the statute or violates the principles of natural justice and passes an order or makes a direction affecting a person's rights of property etc.[†]

Our constitutional law has not yet accepted that the judiciary, as an organ of the state, would yet be included within Article 12 of the Constitution of India, so as to be amenable to challenge on the ground that fundamental rights have been violated by it.

3.   *Golak Nath v. State of Punjab* (1967)

Yet another powerful dissent, given its depth of understanding of the subject and irrefutable logic, is that of Justice R.S. Bachawat in the celebrated case of *I.C. Golaknath & Ors. v. State of Punjab* (1967).[‡] This case was

---

[*] Ibid., p. 972.
[†] Id., p. 972–73.
[‡] (1967) 2 SCR 762.

argued before a bench of eleven judges of the Supreme Court of India, in view of the importance of the questions raised therein: whether the power of amendment lies outside Article 368 of the Constitution of India, and whether the expression 'law' in Article 13(2) of the Constitution of India would include constitutional law, which would preclude Parliament, in its constituent capacity, from abridging or abrogating the fundamental rights contained in Part III of the Constitution of India.

By a majority of 6:5, it was held that Article 368 provided only for the *procedure* of amendment, and not the *power* to amend, and that Article 13(2), when it spoke of 'law' included 'constitutional law', so that the fundamental rights chapter would be immune from being amended.

The judgment of Subba Rao, C.J. upheld the First, Fourth and Seventeenth Amendment Acts to the Constitution, despite the fact that they would have to be set at naught as they sought to abridge fundamental rights, applying the doctrine of 'prospective overruling'. The judgment of Subba Rao C.J. applied this doctrine by borrowing it from the United States, stating that it is a 'pragmatic solution' which reconciles two conflicting doctrines, namely, that a court finds the law unconstitutional, but restricts the invalidity of such law only to the future. Therefore, by application of this doctrine, past transactions may be preserved.[*] Hidayatullah, J., in a separate judgment, upheld the First, Fourth and Seventeenth Amendments on the ground that they had been acquiesced in for a long period. The learned judge noted that it was therefore good sense and sound policy for the court to decline to take up an amendment for consideration after a considerable lapse of time when it was not challenged earlier, or was sustained on earlier occasions.[†] On the other hand, the judgments of Wanchoo, Bachawat, Ramaswami, Bhargava and Mitter, JJ. all held that under the Indian Constitution, since the law which is declared by the Supreme Court to be violative of fundamental rights is void from inception under Article 13(2) of the Constitution, there is no scope for the application of the doctrine of prospective overruling. Therefore, on the point of prospective overruling, the judgment of Subba Rao C.J., is in no man's land. Despite the fact that the principle of prospective

---

[*] Ibid., pp. 813–14.
[†] Id., pp. 893 and 902.

overruling was not applied by a majority of six out of eleven judges, yet, Hidayatullah, J. did not comment upon its applicability with regard to the Indian Constitution.

Five learned judges dissented on all other points. The most powerful dissent, in terms of its reasoning, was that of Bachawat, J. The learned judge first rejected the contention that Article 368 did not contain the power of amendment but only prescribed the procedure for amendment:

> The contention that Article 368 prescribes only the procedure of amendment cannot be accepted, the article not only prescribes the procedure but also gives the power of amendment. If the procedure of Article 368 is followed, the Constitution 'shall stand amended' in accordance with the terms of the bill. It is because the power to amend is given by the article that the Constitution stands amended. The proviso is enacted on the assumption that the several articles mentioned in it are amendable. The object of the proviso is to lay down a stricter procedure for amendment of the articles which would otherwise have been amendable under the easier procedure of the main part. There is no other provision in the Constitution under which these articles can be amended.*

Attention was then drawn to the similarity between the marginal note to Article 368 and the marginal note to Section 128 of the Australian Constitution thus:

> Chapter VIII of the Australian Constitution consists of a single section (Section 128). The heading is 'Alteration of the Constitution'. The marginal note is 'Mode of altering the Constitution'. The body lays down the procedure for alteration. The opening words are: 'This Constitution shall not be altered except in the following manner'. Nobody has doubted that the section gives the power of amending the Constitution. Wynes in his book on *Legislative, Executive and Judicial Powers in Australia*, third edition, p. 695, stated 'The power of amendment extends to alteration of 'this Constitution' which includes

---

* Id., pp. 904–05.

Section 128 itself. It is true that Section 128 is negative in form, but the power is implied by the terms of the section.[*]

With reference to Article 13(2), the learned judge then commented:

> Now Article 368 gives the power of amending each and every provision of the Constitution. Article 13(2) is a part of the Constitution and is within the reach of the amending power. In other words Article 13(2) is subject to the overriding power of Article 368 and is controlled by it. Article 368 is not controlled by Article 13(2) and the prohibitory injunction in Article 13(2) is not directed against the amending power. Looked at from this broad angle, Article 13(2) does not forbid the making of a constitutional amendment abridging or taking away any right conferred by Part III.
>
> Let us now view the matter from a narrower angle. The contention is that a constitutional amendment under Article 368 is a law within the meaning of Article 13. I am inclined to think that this narrow contention must also be rejected.
>
> In Article 13 unless the context otherwise provides 'law' includes any ordinance, order, bye-law, rule, regulation, notification, custom or usage having in the territory of India the force of law. The inclusive definition of law in Article 13(3)(c) neither expressly excludes nor expressly includes the Constitution or a constitutional amendment.[†]

It was then pointed out that the legislative procedure for amending the Constitution was completely different from ordinary lawmaking procedure, as follows:

> Nor is the procedure for amending the Constitution under Article 368 an ordinary law-making procedure. The common feature of the amending process under Article 368 and the legislative procedure is that a bill must be passed by each House of Parliament and assented to by the President. In other respects the amending process under

---

[*] Id., pp. 905–06.
[†] Id., pp. 906–07.

Article 368 is very different from the ordinary legislative process. A constitution amendment Act must be initiated by a bill introduced for that purpose in either House of Parliament. The bill must be passed in each House by not less than two thirds of the members present and voting, the requisite quorum in each House being a majority of its total membership; and in cases coming under the proviso, the amendment must be ratified by the legislature; of not less than one half of the States. Upon the bill so passed being assented to by the President, the Constitution stands amended in accordance with the terms of the bill. The ordinary legislative process is much easier. A bill initiating a law may be passed by a majority of the members present and voting at a sitting of each House or at a joint sitting of the Houses, the quorum for the meeting of either House being one-tenth of the total number of members of the House. The bill so passed on being assented to by the President becomes a law. A bill though passed by all the members of both Houses cannot take effect as a Constitution Amendment Act unless it is initiated for the express purpose of amending the Constitution.

The essence of a written Constitution is that it cannot be changed by an ordinary law. But most written Constitutions provide for their organic growth by constitutional amendments. The main method of constitutional amendments are (1) by the ordinary legislature but under certain restrictions, (2) by the people through a referendum, (3) by a majority of all the units of a Federal State; (4) by a special convocation, see C.F. Strong Modern Political Institutions. Our Constitution has by Article 368 chosen the first and a combination of the first and the third methods.

The special attributes of constitutional amendment under Article 368 indicate that it is not a law or a legislative act. Moreover it will be seen presently that the Constitution-makers could not have intended that the term 'law' in Article 13(2) would include a constitutional amendment under Article 368.

If a constitutional amendment creating a new fundamental right and incorporation it in Part III were a law, it would not be open to the Parliament by a subsequent constitutional amendment to abrogate the new fundamental right for such an amendment would be repugnant to

Part III. But the conclusion is absurd for the body which created the right can surely take it away by the same process.*

The reasoning as to why Articles 13(2) and 368 operate in different fields is then stated as follows:

> I find no conflict between Articles 13(2) and 368. The two articles operate in different fields. Article 13(2) operates on laws; it makes no express exception regarding a constitutional amendment, because a constitutional amendment is not a law and is outside its purview. Article 368 occupies the field of constitutional amendments. It does not particularly refer to the articles in Part III and many other articles, but on its true construction it gives the power of amending each and every provision of the Constitution and necessarily takes in Part III. Moreover, Article 368 gives the power of amending itself, and if express power for amending the provisions of Part III were needed, such a power could be taken by an amendment of the article.
>
> It is said that the *non obstante* clause in Article 35 shows that the article is not amendable. No one has amended Article 35 and the point does not arise. Moreover, the *non obstante* clause is to be found in Articles 258(1), 364, 369, 370 and 371-A. No one has suggested that these articles are not amendable.
>
> The next contention is that there are implied limitations on the amending power. It is said that apart from Article 13(2) there are expressions in Part III which indicate that the amending power cannot touch Part III. Part III is headed 'fundamental rights'. The right to move the Supreme Court for enforcement of the rights conferred by this Part is guaranteed by Article 32 and cannot be suspended except as otherwise provided for by the Constitution—Article 32(4)]. It is said that the terms 'fundamental' and 'guarantee' indicate that the rights conferred by Part III are not amendable. The argument overlooks the dynamic character of the Constitution. While the Constitution is static, it is the fundamental law of the country, the rights conferred by Part III are fundamental, the right under Article 32 is guaranteed, and the principles

---

* Id., pp. 908–09.

of State policy enshrined in Part IV are fundamental in the governance of the country. But the Constitution is never at rest; it changes with the progress of time. Article 368 provides the means for the dynamic changes in the Constitution. The scale of values embodied in Parts III and IV is not immortal. Parts III and IV being parts of the Constitution are not immune from amendment under Article 368.[*]

In a significant passage as to how fundamental rights and Directive Principles of State Policy are to be viewed by the state, the learned judge then spoke of the fundamental rights chapter as containing 'passive' obligations, as opposed to the 'active' obligations contained in Part IV (speaking of the Directive Principles of State Policy), so far as the state was concerned. This is put thus:

> Part III contains the passive obligations of the State. It enshrines the right of life, personal liberty, expression, assembly, movement, residence, avocation, property, culture and education, constitutional remedies, and protection against exploitation and obnoxious penal laws. The State shall not deny these rights save as provided in the Constitution. Part IV contains the active obligations of the State.[†]

It was then pointed out that the first amendment to the Constitution, made by the provisional Parliament—which was none other than the Constituent Assembly itself—abridged fundamental rights in the following manner:

> The First amendment introduced clause (4) in Article 15 enabling the State to make special provisions for the benefit of the socially and educationally backward class of citizens, the scheduled castes and the scheduled tribes in derogation of Articles 15 and 29(2) with a view to

[*] Id., p. 910. Hidayatullah, J., in a separate concurring judgment, had argued in favour of unamendability of certain parts of the Constitution, and had pointed out Article 35 as being an article which cannot be amended. Bachawat, J.'s answer to this is found in the paragraphs above, pointing out that several other articles also contained *non-obstante* clauses, which happen to be there for reasons other than amendability.
[†] Id., p. 911.

implement Article 46 and to supersede the decision in *State of Madras v. Champakam* substituted a new clause (2) in Article 19 with retrospective effect chiefly with a view to bring in public order within the permissible restrictions and to supersede the decisions in *Romesh Thappar v. State of Madras, Brij Bhushan v. State of Delhi*, amended clause (6) of Article 19 with a view to free state trading monopoly from the test of reasonableness and to supersede the decision in *Moti Lal v. Government of the State of Uttar Pradesh*. Under the stress of the First amendment it is now suggested that *Champakam*'s case, *Romesh Thappar*'s case and *Motilal* case were wrongly decided, and the amendments of Articles 15 and 19 were in harmony with the original Constitution and made no real change in it. It is to be noticed however that before the First amendment no attempt was made to overrule these cases, and but for the amendments, these judicial interpretations of the Constitution would have continued to be the law of the land. The Zamindari Abolition Acts were the subject of bitter attack by the zamindars. The Bihar Act though protected by clause 6 of Article 31 from attack under Article 31 was struck down as violative of Article 14 by the Patna High Court see the *State of Bihar v. Maharajadhiraj Shri Kameshwar Singh*, while the Uttar Pradesh Act and the Madhya Pradesh Act, though upheld by the High Courts were under challenge in this Court. The First amendment therefore introduced Article 31-A, 31-B and the Ninth schedule with a view to give effect to the policy of agrarian reforms, to secure distribution of large blocks of land in the hands of the zamindars in conformity with Article 39, and to immunize specially 13 State Acts from attack under Part III. The validity of the First Amendment was upheld in *Shri Sankari Prasad Singh Deo* case.[*]

In answer to the argument that the Preamble secures liberties that were grouped together in Part III, and being not amendable, it also rendered Part III unamendable, the learned judge said:

It is argued that the preamble secures the liberties grouped together in Part III and as the preamble cannot be amended, Part III is not

---

[*] Id., pp. 911–12.

amendable. The argument overlooks that the preamble is mirrored in the entire Constitution. If the rest of the Constitution is amendable, Part III cannot stand on a higher footing. The objective of the preamble is secured not only by Part III but also by Part IV and Article 368. The dynamic character of Part IV may require drastic amendments of Part III by recourse to Article 368.*

In answer to the argument that the word 'amendment' means 'improvement', the learned judge had recourse to a United States Supreme Court decision as follows:

> It is urged that the word 'amend' imposes the limitation that an amendment must be an improvement of the Constitution. Reliance is placed on the dictum in *Livermore v. E.G. Waite*: 'On the other hand, the significance of the term 'amendment' implies such an addition or change within the lines of the original instrument as will effect an improvement, or better carry out the purpose for which it was framed'. Now an attack on the eighteenth amendment of the U.S. Constitution based on this passage was brushed aside by the U.S. Supreme Court in the decision in the *National Prohibition* case. The decision totally negatived the contention that 'an amendment must be confined in its scope to an alteration or improvement of that which is already contained in the Constitution and cannot change its basic structure, include new grants of power to the Federal Government nor relinquish in the State those which already have been granted to it', see Cooley on *Constitutional Law*, Chapter III, Article 5, pp. 46 & 47. I may also read a passage from *Corpus Juris Secundum* Vol. XVI, title 'Constitutional Law', p. 26 thus: 'The term 'amendment' as used in the constitutional article giving congress a power of proposal includes additions to, as well as corrections of, matters already treated, and there is nothing there which suggests that it is used in a restricted sense'.†

So far as the argument of unamendability of the 'basic features' of the Constitution is concerned, the learned judge held thus:

---

* Id., pp. 913, 914.
† Id., p. 915.

It is argued that under the amending power, the basic features of the Constitution cannot be amended. Counsel said that they could not give an exhaustive catalogue of the basic features, but sovereignty, the republican form of government the federal structure and the fundamental rights were some of the features. The Seventeenth Amendment has not derogated from the sovereignty, the republican form of government and the federal structure, and the question whether they can be touched by amendment does not arise for decision. For the purposes of these cases, it is sufficient to say that the fundamental rights are within the reach of the amending power.*

The judgment then goes on to refer to Sir B.N. Rau's suggestion that the Constitution be allowed to be amended by a process of ordinary legislation for the first five years after it comes into force, and the subsequent rejection of this suggestion, as follows:

In a special article written on August 15, 1948, Sir B.N. Rau remarked:

'It seems rather illogical that a constitution should be settled by a simple majority by an assembly elected indirectly on a very limited franchise and that it should not be capable of being amended in the same way by a Parliament elected—and perhaps for the most part elected directly—by adult suffrage' (see B.N. Rau's *India's Constitution in the Making*, 2nd Edn. p. 394).

The conditions in India were rapidly changing and the country was in a state of flux politically and economically. Sir B.N. Rau therefore recommended that the Parliament should be empowered to amend the Constitution by its ordinary law making process for at least the first five years. Earlier, para 8 of the Suggestions of the Indian National Congress of May 12, 1946 and para 15 of the Proposal of the Cabinet Mission of May 16, 1946 had recommended similar powers of revision by the

---

* Id., p. 916. This is a very interesting part of the judgment. Justice Bachawat did not state that the amending power can reach every part of the Constitution, including articles which reflected 'basic' structure. On the assumption that the 'basic structure' theory is correct, the learned judge went on to state that the Seventeenth Amendment does not in any manner violate a basic feature of the Constitution.

Parliament during the initial years or at stated intervals. The Constituent Assembly did not accept these recommendations.[*]

The learned judge then went on to state the importance of the amending power reaching every article of the Constitution as follows:

A static system of laws is the worst tyranny that any constitution can impose upon a country. An unamendable constitution means that all reform and progress are at a stand-still. If Parliament cannot amend Part III of the Constitution even by recourse to Article 368, no other power can do so. There is no provision in the Constitution for calling a convention for its revision or for submission of any proposal for amendment to the referendum. Even if power to call a convention or to submit a proposal to the referendum be taken by amendment of Article 368, Part III would still remain unamendable on the assumption that a constitutional amendment is a law. Not even the unanimous vote of the 500 million citizens or their representatives at a special convocation could amend Part III. The deadlock could be resolved by revolution only. Such a consequence was not intended by the framers of the Constitution. The Constitution is meant to endure.

It has been suggested that the Parliament may provide for another Constituent Assembly by amending the Constitution and that Assembly can amend Part III and take away or abridge the fundamental rights. Now if this proposition is correct, a suitable amendment of the Constitution may provide that the Parliament will be the Constituent Assembly and thereupon the Parliament may amend Part III. If so, I do not see why under the Constitution as it stands now, the Parliament cannot be regarded as a recreation of the Constituent Assembly for the special purpose of making constitutional amendments under Article 368, and why the amending power cannot be regarded as a constituent power as was held in *Shri Sankari Prasad Singh Deo* case.[†]

---

[*] Id., pp. 917–18.

[†] Id., pp. 918–19. The last quoted passage is a direct assault on Justice Hidayatullah's concurring judgment, in which the learned judge had suggested that if fundamental rights were to be abridged, a Constituent Assembly would have to be convened for the purpose.

Pointing out that revolutionary changes involving the abridgement of fundamental rights had been made, and which clock cannot now be reversed, the learned judge held:

> For the last 16 years the validity of constitutional amendments of fundamental rights have been recognized by the people and all the organs of the government including the legislature, the judiciary and the executive. Revolutionary, social and economic changes have taken place on the strength of the First, Fourth and Seventeenth Amendments. Even if two views were possible on the question of the validity of the amendments, we should not now reverse our previous decisions and pronounce them to be invalid. Having heard lengthy arguments on the question I have come to the conclusion that the validity of the constitutional amendments was rightly upheld in *Shri Shankari Prasad Singh Deo and Sajjan Singh* cases and I find no reason for overruling them.
>
> The First, Fourth and Seventeenth Amendment Acts are subjected to bitter attacks because they strike at the entrenched property rights. But the abolition of the zamindari was a necessary reform. It is the First Constitution Amendment Act that made this reform possible. No legal argument can restore the outmoded feudal zamindari system. What has been done cannot be undone. The battle for the past is lost. The legal argument necessarily shifts. The proposition now is that the Constitution Amendment Acts must be recognized to be valid in the past but they must be struck down for the future. The argument leans on the ready-made American doctrine of prospective overruling.
>
> Now the First, Fourth, Sixteenth and Seventeenth Amendment Acts take away and abridge the rights conferred by Part III. If they are laws they are necessarily rendered void by Article 13(2). If they are void, they do not legally exist from their very inception. They cannot be valid from 1951 to 1976 and invalid thereafter. To say that they were valid in the past and will be invalid in the future is to amend the Constitution. Such a naked power of amendment of the Constitution is not given to the Judges. The argument for the petitioners suffers from a double fallacy, the first that the Parliament has no power to amend Part III so as

to abridge or take away the entrenched property rights, and the second that the Judges have the power to make such an amendment.*

The judgment then ended with a powerful quote from Thomas Paine, as follows:

'The views of Jefferson echoed by Ambedkar and Nehru were more powerfully expressed by Thomas Paine in 1791:

'There never did there never will, and there never can, exist a parliament, or any description of men, or any generation of men, in any country, possessed of the right or the power of binding and controlling posterity to the 'end of time', or of commanding for ever how the world shall be governed, or who shall govern it; and therefore all such clauses, acts or declarations by which the makers of them attempt to do what they have neither the right nor the power to do, nor take power to execute, are in themselves null and void. Every age and generation must be as free to act for itself in all cases as the ages and generations which preceded it. The vanity and presumption of governing beyond the grave is the most ridiculous and insolent of all tyrannies. Man has no property in man; neither has any generation a property in the generations which are to follow. The parliament of the people of 1688 or of any other period, had no more right to dispose of the people of the present day, or to bind or to control them in any shape whatever, than the parliament or the people of the present day have to dispose of, bind or control those who are to live a hundred or a thousand years hence. Every generation is, and must be, competent to all the purposes which its occasions require. It is the living, and not the dead, that are to be accommodated. When man ceases to be, his power and his wants cease with him; and having no longer any participation in the concerns of this world, he has no longer any authority in directing who shall be its governors, or how its government shall be organized, or how administered.' (See *Rights of Man* by Thomas Paine, unabridged edition by H.B. Bonner, pp. 3 & 4).†

---

* Id., pp. 920–21.
† Id., p. 925.

This remarkable dissenting judgment was approved in part by the judgments delivered in *Kesavananda Bharati v. State of Kerala and Anr.* (1973).[*] In *Kesavananda Bharati*, Article 368 was held to contain the power of amendment as was provided by the Constitution (Twenty-fourth Amendment) Act.[†] The expression 'law' occurring in Article 13(2) was held to be applicable to ordinary, and not constitutional law. So far as the 'basic structure' doctrine is concerned, the wisdom of Justice Bachawat, in not rejecting it, but in acting on the supposition that it is correct in law, also found favour with a majority of 7:6 in *Kesavananda Bharati*. This continues to be the law in this country, despite the hiccup of Article 368(4) and (5), which invalidated the 'basic structure doctrine'. Article 368(4) and (5) were struck down in *Minerva Mills v. Union of India* (1981).[‡]

4. *Kesavananda Bharati v. State of Kerala & Anr.* (1973)

Even though as many as six dissenting judgments were delivered in the celebrated case of *Kesavananda Bharati v. State of Kerala* (1973),[§] the selection of Palekar, J.'s judgment in this chapter is a result of its close reasoning. Though the logic of the judgment would be difficult to dislodge, still, the statement of the great Justice Holmes comes to mind: 'The life of the law is not logic but experience.'[⁵] And experience has shown that the majority view is correct.

Palekar, J. begins his celebrated dissent with a few 'prefatory' remarks with regard to the Constitution of India as follows:

> 1219. Since fundamental questions with regard to the Constitution have been raised, it will be necessary to make a few prefatory remarks with regard to the Constitution. The Constitution is not an indigenous product. Those who framed it were, as recognized by this Court in *Automobile Transport (Rajasthan) Ltd. v. State of Rajasthan*, thoroughly

---

[*] (1973) 4 SCC 225.

[†] Brought into force on 5 November 1971.

[‡] (1981) 1 SCR 206.

[§] (1973) 4 SCC 225.

[⁵] Oliver Wendell Holmes Jr, *The Common Law* (London: Little, Brown and Company, 1938).

acquainted with the Constitutions and constitutional problems of the more important countries in the world, especially, the English-speaking countries. They knew the unitary and federal types of Constitutions and parliamentary and Presidential systems of Government. They knew what constitutions were regarded as 'flexible' constitution and what constitutions were regarded as 'rigid' constitutions. They further knew that in all modern written constitutions special provision is made for the amendment of the Constitution. Besides, after the Government of India Act, 1935 this country had become better acquainted at first hand, both with parliamentary system of Government and the frame of a Federal constitution with distribution of powers between the Centre and the States. All this knowledge and experience went into the making of our Constitution which is broadly speaking a quasi-Federal constitution which adopted parliamentary system of government based on adult franchise both at the Centre and in the States.

In the next paragraph, the learned judge deals with different kinds of constitutions as follows:

1220. The two words mentioned above 'flexible' and 'rigid' were first coined by Lord Bryce to describe the English constitution and the American constitution respectively. The words were made popular by Dicey in his *Law of the Constitution* first published in 1885. Many generations of lawyers, thereafter, who looked upon Dicey as one of the greatest expositors of the law of the Constitution became familiar with these words. A 'flexible' constitution is one under which every law of every description (including one relating to the Constitution) can legally be changed with the same ease and in the same manner by one and the same body. A 'rigid' constitution is one under which certain laws generally known as constitutional or fundamental laws cannot be changed in the same manner as ordinary laws. See: *Dicey's Law of the Constitution*, 10th Edn., 1964, p. 127. It will be noted that the emphasis is on the word 'change' in denoting the distinction between the two types of constitutions. Lord Birkenhead in delivering the judgment of the Judicial Committee of the Privy Council in *McCawley v. King* used the words 'uncontrolled' and 'controlled' for the words 'flexible' and 'rigid' respectively which were current then. He had to examine the type of Constitution Queensland possessed, whether it was a 'flexible' constitution or a 'rigid' one in order to decide the point in controversy. He observed at p. 703 'The first point which requires consideration depends upon the distinction between constitutions the terms of which may be modified or repealed with no other formality than is necessary in the case of other legislation, and constitutions which can only be altered with some special formality and in some cases by a specially convened assembly'. He had to do that because the distinction between the two types of constitutions was vital to the decision of the controversy before the Privy Council. At p. 704 he further said 'Many different terms have been employed in the text-books to distinguish these two contrasted forms of constitution. Their special qualities may perhaps be exhibited as clearly by calling the one a 'controlled' and the other an 'uncontrolled' constitution as by any other nomenclature'. Perhaps this was an apology for not using the words 'rigid' and 'flexible' which were current when he delivered the judgment. In fact, Sir John Simon in the course of his arguments in that case had used the words 'rigid' and 'flexible' and he had specifically referred to Dicey's *Law of the Constitution*. Strong in his textbook on *Modern Political Constitutions*, 7th Revised Edn., 1966— reprinted in 1970 says at p. 153 'The sole criterion of a rigid constitution is whether the Constituent Assembly which drew up the Constitution left any special directions as to how it was to be changed. If in the Constitution there are no such directions, or if the directions explicitly leave the legislature a free hand, then the Constitution is 'flexible'.

Pointing out that India's is a 'rigid' or 'controlled' Constitution, the learned judge held:

1222. Our Constitution provides for a legislature at the Centre and in the States. At the Centre it is Parliament consisting of the Lok Sabha and the Rajya Sabha. In the States the legislature consists of the State Assembly and, in some of them, of an Upper Chamber known as the Legislative Council. Legislative power is distributed between the Centre and the States, Parliament having the power to make laws with regard to subject-matters contained in List I of the Seventh Schedule and the

State legislatures with regard to those in List II. There is also List III enumerating matters in respect of which both Parliament and the State Legislatures have concurrent powers to make laws. This power to make laws is given to these bodies by Articles 245 and 248 and the law-making procedure for Parliament is contained in Articles 107 to 122 and for the State Legislatures in Articles 196 to 213. The three Lists in the Seventh Schedule no where mention the 'Amendment of the Constitution' as one of the subject-matters of legislation for either Parliament or the State Legislatures. On the other hand, after dealing with all important matters of permanent interest to the Constitution in the First 19 parts covering 367 articles, the Constitution makes special provision for the 'Amendment of the Constitution' in Part XX in one single article, namely, Article 368. A special procedure is provided for amendment which is not the same as the one provided for making ordinary laws under Articles 245 to 248. The principle features of the legislative procedure at the Centre are that the law must be passed by both Houses of Parliament by a majority of the members present and voting in the House, and in case of an impasse between the two Houses of Parliament, by a majority vote at a joint sitting. All that is necessary is that there should be a quorum which we understand is 10% of the strength of the House and if such a quorum is available the two Houses separately or at a joint meeting, as the case may be, may make the law in accordance with its legislative procedure laid down in Articles 107 to 122. The point to be specially noted is that all ordinary laws which Parliament makes in accordance with Articles 245 to 248 must be made in accordance with this legislative procedure and no other. Under Article 368 however, a different and special procedure is provided for amending the Constitution. A Bill has to be introduced in either House of Parliament and must be passed by each House separately by a special majority. It should be passed not only by 2/3rd majority of the members present and voting but also by a majority of the total strength of the House. No joint sitting of the two Houses is permissible. In the case of certain provisions of the Constitution which directly or indirectly affect inter-state relations, the proposed amendment is required to be ratified by the legislatures—which is not a legislative process—of not less than one-half of the States before the Bill proposing the amendment is presented to the President for his assent. The procedure is special in the sense that it is different and more exacting or restrictive than the one by which ordinary laws are made by Parliament. Secondly in certain matters the State Legislatures are involved in the process of making the amendment. Such partnership between Parliament and the State Legislatures in making their own laws by the ordinary procedure is not recognized by the Constitution. It follows from the special provision made in Article 368 for the amendment of the Constitution that our Constitution is a 'rigid' or 'controlled' constitution because the Constituent Assembly has 'left a special direction as to how the Constitution is to be changed'. In view of Article 368, when the special procedure is successfully followed, the proposed amendment automatically becomes a part of the Constitution or, in other words, it writes itself into the Constitution.

Five kinds of amending power, found in various constitutions across the world, were then set out:

1230. The next question which requires to be examined in the nature of this constituent power, specially in the case of 'controlled' or 'rigid' constitutions. A student of modern political Constitutions will find that the methods of modern constitutional amendment are: (1) by the ordinary legislature but under certain restrictions; (2) by the people through a referendum; (3) by a majority of all the unions of a Federal State; (4) by special convention; and (5) by a combination of two or more of the above methods which are mentioned in order of increasing rigidity as to the method.

Refuting the argument that a legislative procedure of Parliament being applied to amend a constitution is of a lesser order than other modes of amendment, the learned judge found:

1232. The amplitude and effectiveness of the constituent power is not impaired because it is exercised by this or that representative body or by the people in a referendum. One cannot say that the power is less when exercised by the ordinary legislature as required by the Constitution or more when it is exercised—say by a special convention. This point is relevant because it was contended that our Parliament is a constituted body—'a creature of the Constitution' and cannot exercise the power of amending the Constitution to the same extent that a Constituent Assembly specially convened for the purpose may do. It was urged that the sovereignty still continues with the people and while it is open to the people through a convention or a Constituent Assembly to make any amendments to the Constitution in any manner it liked, there were limitations on the power of an ordinary Parliament—'a constituted body', which precluded it from making the amendments which damaged or destroyed the essential features and elements of the Constitution. We shall deal with the latter argument in its proper place. But for the present we are concerned to see whether the power to amend becomes more or less in content according to the nature of the body which makes the amendment. In my view it does not.

It was then held that our founding fathers entrusted the power of amendment to Parliament, and not to the people, in order that it is made as easy as possible:

1235. Why the power to amend the Constitution was given in the main to Parliament is not fully clear. But two things are clear. One is that as in America the people who gave us the Constitution completely withdrew themselves from the process of amendment. Secondly, we have the word of Dr Ambedkar—one of the principal framers of our Constitution that the alternative methods of referendum or convention had been considered and definitely rejected. (See *Constituent Assembly Debates*, Vol. VII, p. 43). They decided to give the power to Parliament, and Dr Ambedkar has gone on record as saying that the amendment of the Constitution was deliberately made as easy as was reasonably possible by prescribing the method of Article 368. The *Constituent Assembly Debates* show that the chief controversy was as to the degree of flexibility which should be introduced into the Constitution. There may have been several historical reasons for the Constituent Assembly's preference for Parliament. Our country is a vast continent with a very large population. The level of literacy is low and the people are divided by language, castes and communities not all pulling in the same direction. On account of widespread illiteracy, the capacity to understand political issues and to rise above local and parochial interests is limited. A national perspective had yet to be assiduously fostered. It was, therefore, inevitable that a body which represented all India leadership at the Centre should be the choice. Whatever the reasons, the Constituent Assembly entrusted the power of amendment to Parliament and whatever others may think about a possible better way, that was not the way which the Constituent Assembly commanded. The people themselves having withdrawn from the process of amendment and entrusted the task to Parliament instead of to any other representative body, it is obvious that the power of the authorities designated by the Constitution for amending the Constitution must be coextensive with the power of a convention or a Constituent Assembly, had that course been permitted by the Constitution.

The raison d'etre for including a provision for the amendment of the Constitution is then set out thus:

> 1238. The raison d'etre for making provision for the amendment of the Constitution is the need for orderly change. Indeed no constitution is safe against violent extra-constitutional upheavals. But the object of making such a provision in a constitution is to discourage such upheavals and provide for orderly change in accordance with the Constitution. On this all the textbooks and authorities are unanimous. Those who frame a constitution naturally want it to endure but, however gifted they may be, they may not be able to project into the future, when, owing to internal or external pressures or the social, economic and political changes in the country, alterations would be necessary in the Constitutional instrument responding all the time to the will of the people in changed conditions. Only thus an orderly change is ensured. If such a change of constitution is not made possible, there is great danger of the Constitution being overtaken by forces which could not be controlled by the instruments of power created under the Constitution. Widespread popular revolt directed against the extreme rigidity of a constitution is triggered not by minor issues but by major issues. People revolt not because the so-called 'unessential' parts of a constitution are not changed but because the 'essential' parts are not changed. The essential parts are regarded as a stumbling block in their progress to reform. It is, therefore, evident

that if for any reason, whether it is the extreme rigidity of a constitution or the disinclination of those who are in power to introduce change by amendment, the essential parts looked upon with distrust by the people are not amended, the Constitution has hardly a chance to survive against the will of the people. If the Constitution is to endure it must necessarily respond to the will of the people by incorporating changes sought by the people. The survival of the American Constitution is generally attributed not so much to the amending Article 5 of the Constitution but to its vagueness which was exploited by the great Judges of the Supreme Court of America who by their rulings adapted the Constitution to the changing conditions. Legislative enactments, custom and usage also played a part. If the Constitution were to merely depend upon constitutional amendments there are many who believe that the Constitution would not have survived. The reason was the extreme rigidity of the process of amendment. But framers of modern constitutions as of India learning from experience of other countries have endeavoured to make their constitution as precise and as detailed as possible so that one need not depend upon judicial interpretation to make it survive. Correspondingly they have made it more flexible so that it is amenable to amendment whenever a change in the Constitution is necessary.

To the emotive argument that a *simpliciter* repeal of the Constitution would not fall within the amending power, the learned judge pointed out:

1239. A good deal of unnecessary dust was raised over the question whether the amendment of the Constitution would extend to the repeal of the Constitution. That is an interesting subject for speculation by purists and theoretical jurists, but politicians who frame a constitution for the practical purposes of government do not generally concern themselves with such speculations. The pre-eminent object in framing a constitution is orderly government. Knowing that no constitution, however, good it may seem to be when it was framed, would be able to bear the strain of unforeseen developments, the framers wisely provide for the alteration of the Constitution in the interest of orderly change. Between these two coordinates, namely, the need for orderly government and the demands for orderly change, both in accordance with the Constitution, the makers of the Constitution provide for its amendment to the widest possible limit. If any provision requires amendment by way of addition, alteration or repeal, the change would be entirely permissible. If one were to ask the makers of the Constitution the theoretical question whether they contemplated the repeal of the Constitution, this answer would be, in all probability, in the negative. They did not toil on the Constitution for years in order that it may be repealed by the agencies to whom the amendment of the Constitution is entrusted. They wished it to be permanent, if not eternal, knowing that as time moved, it may continue in utility incorporating all required changes made in an orderly manner. Declaring their faith in the Constitution they will express their confidence that the Constitution which they had framed with the knowledge of their own people and their history would be able to weather all storms when it is exposed to orderly changes by the process of amendment. To them the whole sale repeal would be unthinkable; but not necessary changes in response to the demands of time and circumstance which, in the opinion of the then amending authorities, the current constitutional instrument would be able to absorb. This is sufficient for the courts to go on as it was sufficient for the framers of the Constitution. Quibbling on the meaning of the word 'amendment' as to whether it also involved repeal of the whole Constitution is an irrelevant and unprofitable exercise. Luckily for us besides the word 'amendment' in Article 368 we have also the uncomplicated word 'change' in that article and thus the intention of the framers of the Constitution is sufficiently known. Then again the expression 'amendment of the Constitution' is not a coinage of the framers of our Constitution. That is an expression well known in modern Constitutions and it is commonly accepted as standing for the alteration, variation or change in its provisions.

It was then observed that there are no express or implied limitations on the amending power, unlike in the United States Constitution, where two excepted matters limit the power of amendment. This part of the reasoning of the judgment is particularly commendable for its logic, and needs to be set out in full:

1241. We shall now see if there are express or implied limitations in Article 368 itself. Article 368 is found in Part XX of the Constitution which deals with only one subject, namely, the Amendment of the Constitution. The article provides that when the special procedure directed by it is successfully followed the Constitution stands amended in terms of the proposal for amendment made in the Bill. Whatever provision of the Constitution may be sought to be amended, the amendment is an amendment of the Constitution. The range is the whole of this Constitution which means all the provisions of the Constitution. No part of the Constitution is expressly excepted from amendment. Part XX and Article 368 stand in supreme isolation, after the permanent provisions of the Constitution are exhausted in the previous 19 parts. The power to amend is not made expressly subject to any other provision of the Constitution. There are no governing words like 'subject to the Constitution' or this or that part of the Constitution. If the framers of the Constitution had thought it necessary to exclude any part or provision of the Constitution from amendment, they would have done so in this part only as was done in the American Constitution. Article 5 of that Constitution, which was undoubtedly consulted before drafting Article 368, made two specific exceptions. The language structure of Article 5 has a close resemblance to the language structure of our Article 368. Therefore, if any part of the Constitution was intended to be excluded from the operation of the power to amend it would have normally found a place in or below Article 368. As a matter of fact, in the draft Constitution below Article 304, which corresponds to the present Article 368, there was Article 305 which excluded certain provisions from amendment, but later on Article 305 itself was deleted. Even Article 368 itself was not safe from amendment because the proviso to Article 368 shows that the provisions of the article could be changed. Then again we find that when the people through the Constituent Assembly granted the power to amend, they made no reservations in favour of the people. The people completely withdrew from the process of amendment. In other words, the grant of power was without reservation. Another thing which is to be noted is that when the Constituent Assembly directed that amendments of the Constitution must be made by a prescribed method, they necessarily excluded every other method of amending the Constitution. As long as the article stood in its present form Parliament could not possibly introduce its own procedure to amend the Constitution by calling a Constituent Assembly, a convention or the like. Altogether, it will be seen that the grant of power under Article 368 is plenary, unqualified and without any limitations, except as to the special procedure to be followed.

xxx xxx xxx

1288. I have already discussed the amplitude of power conferred by the amending clause of the Constitution. In countries like America and Australia where express limitations have been imposed in the amending clause itself there is substantial authority for the view that even these express limitations can be removed by following the procedure laid down in the amending clause. According to them this could be done in two steps the first being to amend the amending clause itself. It is not necessary for us to investigate the matter further because Article 368 does not contain any express limitation. On the other hand, the power is wide enough even to amend the provisions of Article 368. (See: Proviso (e) of that Article). In other words, Article 368 contains unqualified and plenary powers to amend the provisions of the Constitution including the Amending clause. Prima facia, to introduce implied prohibitions to cut down a clear affirmative grant in a Constitution would be contrary to the settled rules of construction. (See the dissenting judgment of Issacs and Rich, JJ., in *McCawley v. King* 26 CLR 43-68, approved by the Privy Council in 1920 AC 691).

1289. When such an amending clause is amended without affecting the power of amendment will principally involve the Amending procedure. It may make amendment easier or more difficult. The procedure may also differ substantially. Parliament may be eliminated from the process leaving the amendment to the States. The proviso might be dropped, enlarging the role of the Parliament. On the other hand, the Parliament and State Assemblies may be divested of the function by providing for a referendum plebiscite or a special convention. While, thus the power remains the same, the instrumentalities may differ from time to time in accordance with the procedure prescribed. Hidayatullah,

J., with respect, was right in pointing out that the power to amend is not entrusted to this or that body. The power is generated when the prescribed procedure is followed by the instrumentalities specified in the Article. Since the instrumentalities are liable to be changed by a proper amendment it will be inaccurate to say that the Constituent Assembly had entrusted the power to any body. If the authority which is required to follow the procedure is the Parliament for the time being, it may be convenient to describe Parliament as the authority to whom the power is granted or entrusted, but strictly that would be inaccurate, because there is no grant to any body. Whichever may be the instrumentality for the time being the power remains unqualified.

1290. If the theory of implied limitations is sound—the assumption made being that the same have their origin in the rest of the constitutional provisions including the Preamble and the fundamental rights—then these limitations must clog the power by whatever agency it is exercised. The rest of the Constitution does not change merely because the procedure prescribed in Article 368 is changed. Therefore, the implied limitations should continue to clog the power. Logically, if Article 368 is so amended as to provide for a convention or a referendum, the latter will be bound to respect the implied limitations—a conclusion which Mr Palkhivala is not prepared to accept. He agrees with the jurists who hold that a convention or a referendum will not be bound by any limitations. The reason given is that the people directly take part in a referendum or, through their elected representatives in a convention. Even in *Golak Nath* case it was accepted that any part of the constitution including the fundamental rights could be amended out of existence by a Constituent Assembly.

1291. The argument seems to be that a distinction must be made between the power exercised by the people and the power exercised by Parliament. In fact Mr Palkhivala's whole thesis is that the Parliament is a creature of the Constitution and the limitation is inherent in its being a constituted authority. We have already examined the question and shown that where the people have withdrawn completely from the process of Amendment, the Constituent body to whom the power is entrusted and exercise the power to the same extent as a Constituent Assembly and that the power does not vary according to the Agency to whom the power is entrusted. Therefore, this reason also viz. that Parliament is a constituted body and, therefore, it suffers from inherent limitations does not hold good.

1292. From the conclusion that the power of Amendment remains unqualified by whomsoever it is exercised, it follows that there can be no implied or inherent limitations on the Amending power. If a special convention admittedly does not suffer from limitations, any other constituent body cannot be subject to it.

The dissenting judgment then noted that fundamental rights cannot be said to be immutable, as some of them are not 'natural' rights:

1277. The further argument that fundamental rights are inalienable natural rights and, therefore, unamendable so as to abridge or take them away does not stand close scrutiny. Articles 13 and 32 show that they are rights which the people have 'conferred' upon themselves. A good many of them are not natural rights at all. Abolition of untouchability (Article 17); abolition of titles (Article 18); protection against double jeopardy [Article 20(2)]; protection of children against employment in factories (Article 24); freedom as to attendance at religious instruction or religious worship in certain educational institutions (Article 28) are not natural rights. Nor are all the fundamental rights conceded to all as human beings. The several freedoms in Article 19 are conferred only on citizens and not non-citizens. Even the rights conferred are not in absolute terms. They are hedged in and restricted in the interest of the general public, public order, public morality, security of the State and the like which shows that social and political considerations are more important in our organized society. Personal liberty is cut down by provision for preventive detention which, having regard to the conditions prevailing even in peace time, is permitted. Not a few members of the Constituent Assembly resented the limitations on freedoms on the ground that what was conferred was merely a husk. Prior to the Constitution no such inherent inalienability was ascribed by law to these rights, because they could be taken away by law.

Dealing with the Preamble and 'basic structure', it was pointed out:

1305. It follows that if in implementing such a law the rights of an individual under Articles 14, 19 and 31 are infringed in the course of securing the success of the scheme of the law, such an infringement will have to be regarded as a necessary consequence and, therefore, secondary. The Preamble read as a whole, therefore, does not contain the implication that in any genuine implementation of the Directive Principles, a fundamental right will not suffer any diminution. Concentration and control of community resources, wealth and means of production in the hands of a few individuals are, in the eyes of the Constitution, an evil which must be eradicated from the social organization, and hence, any fundamental right, to the extent that it fosters this evil, is liable to be abridged or taken away in the interest of the social structure envisaged by the Constitution. The scheme of the fundamental rights in Part III itself shows that restrictions on them have been placed to guard against their exercise in an evil way.

1306. Nor is there anything in the Preamble to suggest that the power to amend the fundamental right to property is cut down. Actually there is no reference to the right to property. On the other hand, while declaring the objectives which inspired the framers of the Constitution to give unto themselves the Constitution which, they hoped, would be able to achieve them, they took good care to provide for the amendment of 'this Constitution'. It was clearly implied that if the operative parts of the Constitution failed to put us on the road to the objectives, the Constitution was liable to be appropriately amended. Even the Preamble, which, as we know, had been adopted by the Constituent Assembly as a part of the Constitution (*Constituent Assembly Debates*, Vol. X, p. 456) was liable to be amended. Right to property was, perhaps, deliberately not enthroned in the Preamble because that would have conflicted with the objectives of securing to all its citizens, justice, social, economic and political, and equality of opportunity, to achieve which Directive Principles were laid down in Articles 38 to 51.

Then, noticing the difficulties in discovering what are 'essential features' and what are not, the learned judge states:

1311. Since the 'essential features and basic principles' referred to by Mr Palkhivala are those culled from the provisions of the constitution it is clear that he wants to divide the constitution into parts—one of provisions containing the essential features and the other containing non-essential features. According to him the latter can be amended in any way the Parliament likes, but so far as the former provisions are concerned, though they may be amended, they cannot be amended so as to damage or destroy the core of the essential features. Two difficulties arise, who is to decide what are essential provisions and non-essential provisions? According to Mr Palkhivala it is the court which should do it. If that is correct, what stable standard will guide the court in deciding which provision is essential and which is not essential? Every provision, in one sense, is an essential provision, because if a law is made by the Parliament or the State Legislatures contravening even the most insignificant provision of the constitution, that law will be void. From that point of view the courts acting under the constitution will have to look upon its provisions with an equal eye. Secondly, if an essential provision is amended and a new provision is inserted, which in the opinion of the constituent body, should be presumed to be more essential than the one repealed, what is the yardstick the court is expected to employ? It will only mean that whatever necessity the constituent body may feel in introducing a change in the constitution, whatever change of policy that body may like to introduce in the Constitution, the same is liable to be struck down if the court is not satisfied either about the necessity or the policy. Clearly this is not a function of the courts. The difficulty assumes greater proportion when an amendment is challenged on the ground that the core of essential feature is either damaged or destroyed. What is the standard? Who will decide where the core lies and when it is reached? One can understand the argument that particular provisions in the constitution embodying some essential features are not amendable at all. But the difficulty arises when it is conceded that the provision is liable to be amended, but not so as to touch its 'core'. Apart from the difficulty in determining where the 'core' of an 'essential feature' lies, it does not appear to be sufficiently realized what fantastic results may follow in working the constitution. Suppose an amendment of a provision is made this year. The mere fact that an amendment is made will not give any body the right to come to this court to have the amendment nullified on the ground that it affects the core of an essential feature. It is only when a law is made under the amended provision and that law affects some individual's right, that he may come to this Court. At that time he will first show that the amendment is bad because it affects the core of an essential feature and if he succeeds there he will automatically succeed and the law made by the Legislature in the confidence that it is protected by the amended constitution will be rendered void. And such a challenge to the amendment may come several years after the amendment which till then is regarded as a part of the constitution. In other words, every amendment, however innocuous it may seem when it is made is liable to be struck down several years after the amendment although all the people have arranged their affairs on the strength of the amended constitution. And in dealing with the challenge to a particular amendment and searching for the core of the essential feature the court will have to do it either with reference to the original constitution or the constitution as it stood with all its amendments up-to date. The former procedure is clearly absurd; because the constitution has already undergone vital changes by amendments in the meantime. So the challenged amendment will have to be assessed on the basis of the constitution with all its amendments made prior to the challenged amendment. All such prior amendments will have to be accepted as good because they are not under challenge, and on that basis Judges will have to deal with the challenged amendment. But the other amendments are also not free from challenge in subsequent proceedings, because we have already seen that every amendment can be challenged several years after it is made, if a law made under it affects a private individual. So there will be a continuous state of flux after an amendment is made and at any given moment when the court wants to determine the core of the essential feature, it will have to discard, in order to be able to say where the core lies, every other amendment because these amendments also being unstable will not help in the determination of the core. In other words, the courts will have to go by the original constitution to decide the core of an essential feature ignoring altogether all the amendments made in the meantime, all the transformations of rights that have taken place after them, all the arrangements people have made on the basis of the validity of the amendments and all the laws made under them without question. An argument which leads to such obnoxious results can hardly be entertained. In this very case if the core argument were to be sustained several previous amendments will have to be set aside because they have undoubtedly affected the core of one or the other fundamental right. Prospective overruling will be the order of the day.

It was then pointed out that the majority judgment introduced an additional proviso to Article 368, which was a constituent, and not judicial exercise:

> 1316. In short, if the doctrine of unamendability of the core of essential features is accepted, it will mean that we add some such proviso below Article 368. 'Nothing in the above Amendment will be deemed to have authorized an Amendment of the Constitution, which has the effect of damaging or destroying the core of the essential features, basic principles and fundamental elements of the Constitution as may be determined by the Courts'. This is quite impermissible.

The final conclusion was reached as follows:

> 1333. My conclusions are:
>
> (1) The power and the procedure for the amendment of the Constitution were contained in the unamended Article 368. An Amendment of the Constitution in accordance with the procedure prescribed in that Article is not a law within the meaning of Article 13. An Amendment of the Constitution abridging or taking away a fundamental right conferred by Part III of the Constitution is not void as contravening the provisions of Article 13(2). The majority decision in *Golak Nath v. State of Punjab* is, with respect, not correct.
>
> (2) There were no implied or inherent limitations on the amending power under the unamended Article 368 in operation over the fundamental rights. There can be none after its amendment.
>
> (3) The Twenty-fourth, the Twenty-fifth and the Twenty-ninth Amendment Acts are valid.

Within a period of two years from the date of this judgment, in *Smt. Indira Nehru Gandhi v. Raj Narain & Anr.* (1976),* *all* five judges applied

---

* (1976) 2 SCR 347.

the basic-structure doctrine to invalidate the Constitution (Thirty-ninth Amendment) Act. It is significant that the five judges who struck down the Amendment Act on the ground that it violated certain essential features of the Constitution were all dissenting judges in *Kesavananda Bharati*, save and except Khanna, J. The vindication of the majority judgments in *Kesavananda Bharati*, tested on the anvil of experience, and not logic, has ultimately become irrefutable.

5. *Bachan Singh v. State of Punjab* (1980)

Bachan Singh v. State of Punjab (1980)[*] is a judgment in which the award of the 'death penalty' in case of certain heinous offences was challenged as being unconstitutional and violative of the fundamental rights contained in Articles 14 and 21 of the Constitution of India. The majority judgment of Sarkaria, J., speaking for himself and three other learned judges, upheld the imposition of the death penalty.[†] P. Bhagwati, J., in a powerfully worded dissent,[‡] exposed the hazards of sentencing a man to death, stressing the fact that any mistake committed in so doing was incapable of future correction. The learned judge began his judgment stating:

> These writ petitions challenge the constitutional validity of Section 302 of the Penal Code, 1860 read with Section 354, sub-section (3) of the Code of Criminal Procedure insofar as it provides death sentence as an alternative punishment for the offence of murder. There are several grounds on which the constitutional validity of the death penalty provided in Section 302 of the Penal Code, 1860 read with Section 354, sub-section (3) of the Code of Criminal Procedure is assailed before us, but it is not necessary to set them out at this stage, for I propose to deal with them when I examine the arguments advanced on behalf of the parties. Suffice it to state for the present that I find considerable force in some of these grounds and in my view, the constitutional validity of the death penalty provided as an alternative punishment in Section

---

[*] (1980) 2 SCC 684.
[†] Ibid., paragraph 209.
[‡] Reported as (1982) 3 SCC 24.

302 of the Penal Code, 1860 read with Section 354, sub-section (3) of the Code of Criminal Procedure cannot be sustained. I am conscious that my learned Brethren on the Bench who constitute the majority have taken a different view and upheld the constitutional validity of the death penalty but, with the greatest respect to them and in all humility, I cannot persuade myself to concur with the view taken by them. Mine is unfortunately a solitary dissent and it is therefore with a certain amount of hesitation that I speak but my initial diffidence is overcome by my deep and abiding faith in the dignity of man and worth of the human person and passionate conviction about the true spiritual nature and dimension of man. I agree with Bernard Shaw that 'Criminals do not die by the hands of the law. They die by the hands of other men. Assassination on the scaffold is the worst form of assassination because there it is invested with the approval of the society. . . . Murder and capital punishment are not opposites that cancel one another but similars that breed their kind.' It was the Father of the Nation who said years ago, reaffirming what Prince Satyavan said on capital punishment in Shanti Parva of Mahabharata that 'Destruction of individuals can never be a virtuous act' and this sentiment has been echoed by many eminent men such as Leonardo da Vinci, John Bright, Victor Hugo and Berdyaev. To quote again from Bernard Shaw from Act IV of his play *Caesar and Cleopatra*:

'And so to the end of history, murder shall breed murder, always in the name of right and honour and peace, until the Gods are tired of blood and create a race that can understand.

I share this sentiment because I regard men as an embodiment of divinity and I am therefore morally against death penalty. But my dissent is based not upon any ground of morality or ethics but is founded on constitutional issues, for as I shall presently show, death penalty does not serve any social purpose or advance any constitutional value and is totally arbitrary and unreasonable so as to be violative of Articles 14, 19, 21 of the Constitution.

The learned judge then referred to the Universal Declaration of Human Rights adopted by the UN General Assembly in paragraph 5, and spoke of the rule of law that the Constitution of India provides:

10. Now if we look at the various constitutional provisions including the Chapters on fundamental rights and Directive Principles of State Policy, it is clear that the rule of law permeates the entire fabric of the Constitution and indeed forms one of its basic features. The rule of law excludes arbitrariness; its postulate is 'intelligence without passion' and 'reason freed from desire'. Wherever we find arbitrariness or unreasonableness there is denial of the rule of law. That is why Aristotle preferred a government of laws rather than of men. 'Law' in the context of the rule of law, does not mean any law enacted by the legislative authority, howsoever arbitrary or despotic it may be. Otherwise even under a dictatorship it would be possible to say that there is rule of law, because every law made by the dictator howsoever arbitrary and unreasonable has to be obeyed and every action has to be taken in conformity with such law. In such a case too even where the political set up is dictatorial, it is law that governs the relationship between men and men and between men and the State. But still it is not rule of law as understood in modern jurisprudence, because in jurisprudential terms, the law itself in such a case being an emanation from the absolute will of the dictator it is in effect and substance the rule of man and not of law which prevails in such a situation. What is a necessary element of the rule of law is that the law must not be arbitrary or irrational and it must satisfy the test of reason and the democratic form of polity seeks to ensure this element by making the framers of the law accountable to the people. Of course, in a country like the United Kingdom, where there is no written constitution imposing fetters on legislative power and providing for judicial review of legislation, it may be difficult to hold a law to be invalid on the ground that it is arbitrary and irrational and hence violative of an essential element of the rule of law and the only remedy if at all would be an appeal to the electorate at the time when a fresh mandate is sought at the election. But the situation is totally different in a country like India which has a written Constitution enacting fundamental rights and conferring power on the courts to enforce them not only against the executive but also against the legislature. The fundamental rights erect a protective armour for the individual against arbitrary or unreasonable executive or legislative action.

The 'golden triangle' which Y.V. Chandrachud, C.J. referred to in *Minerva Mills & Ors.*, as being Articles 14, 19 and 21 of the Indian Constitution, was then considered by Bhagwati, J. in paragraph 11. The learned judge also noted a legislative attempt towards restricting and rationalizing the death penalty which, however, failed to become law:

> 21. It is also interesting to note that a further legislative attempt towards restricting and rationalizing death penalty was made in the late seventies. A Bill called Penal Code, 1860 (Amendment) Bill, 1972 for amending Section 302 was passed by the Rajya Sabha in 1978 and it was pending in the Lok Sabha at the time when *Rajendra Prasad* case was decided and though it ultimately lapsed with the dissolution of the Lok Sabha, it shows how strongly were the minds of the elected representatives of the people agitated against 'homicidal exercise of discretion' which is often an 'obsession with retributive justice in disguise'. This Bill sought to narrow drastically the judicial discretion to impose death penalty and tried to formulate the guidelines which should control the exercise of judicial exercise in this punitive area. But unfortunately the Bill though passed by the Rajya Sabha could not see its way through the Lok Sabha and was not enacted into law. Otherwise perhaps the charge against the present Section 302 of the Penal Code, 1860 read with Section 354, sub-section (3) of the Code of Criminal Procedure that it does not indicate any policy or principle to guide the exercise of judicial discretion in awarding death penalty, would have been considerably diluted, though even then, I doubt very much whether that section could have survived the attack against its constitutionality on the ground that it still leaves the door open for arbitrary exercise of discretion in imposing death penalty.

It is at this stage that the learned judge speaks of the irrevocability of the death penalty:

> 23. I may also at this stage make a few observations in regard to the barbarity and cruelty of death penalty, for the problem of constitutional validity of death penalty cannot be appreciated in its proper perspective without an adequate understanding of the true nature of death penalty and what it involves in terms of human anguish and suffering. In the first

place, death penalty is irrevocable; it cannot be recalled. It extinguishes the flame of life for ever and is plainly destructive of the right to life, the most precious right of all, a right without which enjoyment of no other rights is possible. It silences for ever a living being and despatches him to that 'undiscovered country from whose bourn no traveller returns' nor, once executed, 'can storied urn or animated bust back to its mansion call the fleeting breath'. It is by reason of its cold and cruel finality that death penalty is qualitatively different from all other forms of punishment. If a person is sentenced to imprisonment, even if it be for life, and subsequently it is found that he was innocent and was wrongly convicted, he can be set free. Of course, the imprisonment that he has suffered till then cannot be undone and the time he has spent in the prison cannot be given back to him in specie but he can come back and be restored to normal life with his honour vindicated, if he is found innocent. But that is not possible where a person has been wrongly convicted and sentenced to death and put out of existence in pursuance of the sentence of death. In his case, even if any mistake is subsequently discovered, it will be too late; in every way and for every purpose it will be too late, for he cannot be brought back to life. The execution of the sentence of death in such a case makes miscarriage of justice irrevocable. On whose conscience will this death of an innocent man lie? The State through its judicial instrumentality would have killed an innocent man. How is it different from a private murder? That is why Lafayatte said: 'I shall ask for the abolition of the penalty of death until I have the infallibility of human judgment demonstrated (to) me.

Concomitant with this, Bhagwati, J. commented upon the impossibility of eliminating the chance of judicial error when awarding the death sentence:

25. Howsoever careful may be the procedural safeguards erected by the law before death penalty can be imposed, it is impossible to eliminate the chance of judicial error. No possible judicial safeguards can prevent conviction of the innocent. Students of the criminal process have identified several reasons why innocent men may be convicted of crime. In the first place, our methods of investigation are crude and archaic. We are, by and large, ignorant of modern methods of investigation based on

scientific and technological advances. Our convictions are based largely on oral evidence of witnesses. Often, witnesses perjure themselves as they are motivated by caste, communal and factional considerations. Sometimes they are even got up by the police to prove what the police believes to be a true case. Sometimes there is also mistaken eyewitness identification and this evidence is almost always difficult to shake in cross-examination. Then there is also the possibility of a frame up of innocent men by their enemies. There are also cases where an overzealous prosecutor may fail to disclose evidence of innocence known to him but not known to the defence. The possibility of error in judgment cannot therefore be ruled out on any theoretical considerations. It is indeed a very live possibility and it is not at all unlikely that so long as death penalty remains a constitutionally valid alternative, the court or the State acting through the instrumentality of the court may have on its conscience the blood of an innocent man.

The barbaric and inhumane nature of the death penalty was then exposed in the following manner:

27. It is also necessary to point out that death penalty is barbaric and inhuman in its effect, mental and physical upon the condemned man and is positively cruel. Its psychological effect on the prisoner in the Death Row is disastrous. One Psychiatrist has described Death Row as a 'grisly laboratory' 'the ultimate experimental stress in which the condemned prisoner's personality is incredibly brutalized'. He points out that 'the strain of existence on Death Row is very likely to produce . . . acute psychotic breaks' (vide the article of West on 'Medicine and Capital Punishment'). 'Some inmates are driven to ravings or delusions but the majority sink into a sort of catatonic numbness under the overwhelming stress' (vide 'The Case against Capital Punishment' by the Washington Research Project). Intense mental suffering is inevitably associated with confinement under sentence of death. Anticipation of approaching death can and does produce stark terror (vide article on 'Mental Suffering under Sentence of Death'). Justice Brennan in his opinion in *Furman v. Georgia* gave it as a reason for holding the capital punishment to be unconstitutional that 'mental pain is an inseparable

part of our practice of punishing criminals by death, for the prospect of pending execution exacts a frightful toll during the inevitable long wait between the imposition of sentence and the actual infliction of death'. Krishna Iyer, J. also pointed out in *Rajendra Prasad*'s case that because the condemned prisoner had 'the hanging agony hanging over his head since 1973 (i.e. for six years) . . . he must by now be more a vegetable than a person'. He added that 'the excruciation of long pendency of the death sentence with the prisoner languishing near-solitary suffering all the time, may make the death sentence unconstitutionally cruel and agonizing'. The California Supreme Court also, in finding the death penalty per se unconstitutional remarked with a sense of poignancy:

The cruelty of capital punishment lies not only in the execution itself and the pain incident thereto, but also in the dehumanizing effects of the lengthy imprisonment prior to execution during which the judicial and administrative procedures essential to due process of law are carried out. Penologists and medical experts agree that the process of carrying out a verdict of death is often so degrading and brutalizing to the human spirit as to constitute psychological torture.

In Re Kemmler the Supreme Court of the United States accepted that 'punishments are cruel when they involve a lingering death, something more than the mere extinguishment of life'. Now a death would be as lingering if a man spends several years in a death cell awaiting execution as it would be if the method of execution takes an unacceptably long time to kill the victim. The pain of mental lingering can be as intense as the agony of physical lingering. (See David Pannick on *Judicial Review of the Death Penalty*.) Justice Miller also pointed out *in Re Medley* that 'when a prisoner sentenced by a court to death is confined to the penitentiary awaiting the execution of the sentence, one of the most horrible feelings to which he can be subjected during that time is the uncertainty during the whole of it . . . as to the precise time when his execution shall take place'. He acknowledged that such uncertainty is inevitably 'accompanied by an immense mental anxiety amounting to a great increase of the offender's punishment.

Equally, the physical pain and suffering, which the execution of the sentence of death involves would also, according to the learned judge, be cruel and inhuman:

29. The physical pain and suffering which the execution of the sentence of death involves is also no less cruel and inhuman. In India, the method of execution followed is hanging by the rope. Electrocution or application of lethal gas has not yet taken its place as in some of the western countries. It is therefore with reference to execution by hanging that I must consider whether the sentence of death is barbaric and inhuman as entailing physical pain and agony. It is no doubt true that the Royal Commission on Capital Punishment 1949–53 found that hanging is the most humane method of execution and so also in *Ichikawa v. Japan*, the Japanese Supreme Court held that execution by hanging does not correspond to 'cruel punishment' inhibited by Article 36 of the Japanese Constitution. But whether amongst all the methods of execution, hanging is the most humane or in the view of the Japanese Supreme Court, hanging is not cruel punishment within the meaning of Article 36, one thing is clear that hanging is undoubtedly accompanied by intense physical torture and pain. Warden Duffy of San Quentin, a high security prison in the United States of America, describes the hanging process with brutal frankness in lurid details:

'The day before an execution the prisoner goes through a harrowing experience of being weighed, measured for length of drop to assure breaking of the neck, the size of the neck, body measurements et cetera. When the trap springs he dangles at the end of the rope. There are times when the neck has not been broken and the prisoner strangles to death. His eyes pop almost out of his head, his tongue swells and protrudes from his mouth, his neck may be broken, and the rope many times takes large portions of skin and flesh from the side of the face that the noose is on. He urinates, he defecates, and droppings fall to the floor while witnesses look on, and at almost all executions one or more faint or have to be helped out of the witness-room. The prisoner remains dangling from the end of the rope for from 8 to 14 minutes before the doctor, who has climbed up a small ladder and listens to his heartbeat with a stethoscope, pronounces him dead. A prison guard stands at the feet of the hanged person and holds the body steady, because during the first few minutes there is usually considerable struggling in an effort to breathe.'

If the drop is too short, there will be a slow and agonizing death by strangulation. On the other hand, if the drop is too long, the head will be torn off. In England centuries of practice have produced a detailed chart relating a man's weight and physical condition to the proper length of drop, but even there mistakes have been made. In 1927, a surgeon who witnessed a double execution wrote:

> The bodies were cut down after fifteen minutes and placed in an antechamber, when I was horrified to hear one of the supposed corpses give a gasp and find him making respiratory efforts, evidently a prelude to revival. The two bodies were quickly suspended again for a quarter of an hour longer. . . . Dislocation of the neck is the ideal aimed at, but, out of all my post-mortem findings, that has proved rather an exception, which in the majority of instances the cause of death was strangulation and asphyxia.

> These passages clearly establish beyond doubt that the execution of sentence of death by hanging does involve intense physical pain and suffering, though it may be regarded by some as more humane than electrocution or application of lethal gas.

Referring to how the death sentence is disproportionate to an offence of murder, the learned judge held:

> 39 . . . Moreover, it is difficult to see how death penalty can be regarded as proportionate to the offence of murder when legislatively it has been ordained that life sentence shall be the rule and it is only in exceptional cases for special reasons that death penalty may be imposed. It is obvious from the provision enacted in Section 354(3) of the Code of Criminal Procedure that death sentence is legislatively regarded as disproportionate and excessive in most cases of murder and it is only in exceptional cases what Sarkaria, J. speaking on behalf of the majority, describes as 'the rarest of rare' cases, that it can at all be contended that death sentence is proportionate to the offence of murder. But, then the legislature does not indicate as to what are those exceptional cases in which death sentence may be regarded as proportionate to the offence and, therefore, reasonable and just. Merely because a murder is heinous or horrifying, it cannot be said that death penalty is proportionate to the offence when it is not so for a simple murder. How does it become proportionate to the offence merely because it is a 'murder most foul'.

I fail to appreciate how it should make any difference to the penalty whether the murder is a simple murder or a brutal one. A murder is a murder all the same, whether it is carried out quickly and inoffensively or in a gory and gruesome manner. If death penalty is not proportionate to the offence in the former case, it is difficult to see how it can be so in the latter. I may usefully quote in this connection the words of Krishna Iyer, J. in *Rajendra Prasad* case where the learned Judge said:

Speaking illustratively, is shocking crime, without more, good to justify the lethal verdict? Most murders are horrifying, and an adjective adds but sentiment, not argument. The personal story of an actor in a shocking murder, if considered, may bring tears and soften the sentence. He might have been a tortured child, an ill-treated orphan, a jobless starveling, a badgered brother, a wounded son, a tragic person hardened by societal cruelty or vengeful justice, even a Hamlet or Parasurama. He might have been an angelic boy but thrown into mafia company or inducted into dopes and drugs by parental neglect or morally-mentally retarded or disordered. Imagine a harijan village hacked out of existence by the genocidal fury of a kulak group and one survivor, days later, cutting to pieces the villain of the earlier outrage. Is the court in error in reckoning the prior provocative barbarity as a sentencing factor?

Another facet. Maybe, the convict's poverty had disabled his presentation of the social milieu or other circumstances of extenuation in defence. . . . When life is at stake, can such frolics of fortune play with judicial verdicts?

The nature of the crime—too terrible to contemplate—has often been regarded a traditional peg on which to hang a death penalty. Even Ediga Anamma has hardened here. But 'murder most foul' is not the test, speaking scientifically. The doer may be a patriot, a revolutionary, a weak victim of an overpowering passion who, given better environment, may be a good citizen, a good administrator, a good husband, a great saint. What was Valmiki once? And that sublime spiritual star, Shri Aurobindo, tried once for murder but by history's fortune acquitted.

I agree with these observations of the learned Judge which clearly show that death penalty cannot be regarded as proportionate to the offence of murder, merely because the murder is brutal, heinous or shocking. The nature and magnitude of the offence or the motive and purposes underlying it or the manner and extent of its commission cannot have any relevance to the proportionality of death penalty to the offence. It may be argued that though these factors may not of themselves be relevant, they may go to show that the murderer is such a social monster, a psychopath, that he cannot be reformed and he should therefore be regarded as human refuse, dangerous to society, and deserving to be hanged and in such a case, death penalty may legitimately be regarded as proportionate to the offence. But I do not think this is a valid argument. It is for reasons which I shall presently state, wholly untenable and it has dangerous implications. I do not think it is possible to hold that death penalty is, in any circumstances, proportionate to the offence of murder. Moreover, when death penalty does not serve any legitimate social purpose, and this is a proposition which I shall proceed to establish in the succeeding paragraphs, infliction of mental and physical pain and suffering on the condemned prisoner by sentencing him to death penalty cannot but be regarded as cruel and inhuman and therefore arbitrary and unreasonable.

The learned judge then referred to three justifications traditionally advanced in support of punishment in general, namely (1) reformation, (2) retribution and (3) deterrence.[*] According to the learned judge, no murderer, being first a human being, is beyond reformation.[†] Equally, according to the learned judge, mere retribution is the antithesis of a cultured society.[‡] Deterrence was then dealt with in paragraphs 47 and 48, concluding that studies had shown that the theory that the death penalty acts as a greater deterrent than life punishment is wholly unfounded. Certain figures were referred to in paragraph 52 to show that the incidents of the crime of murder did not increase during the period when capital punishment was in abeyance. Ultimately, it was found that the deterrent effect would be the same as that of life imprisonment.[§] This being so, the learned judge concluded:

---

[*] Ibid., paragraph 40.
[†] Id., paragraph 41.
[‡] Id., paragraph 42.
[§] Id., paragraph 62.

68. It will thus be seen that death penalty as provided under Section 302 of the Penal Code, 1860 read with Section 354, sub-section (3) of the Code of Criminal Procedure, 1973 does not subserve any legitimate end of punishment, since by killing the murderer it totally rejects the reformative purpose and it has no additional deterrent effect which life sentence does not possess and it is therefore not justified by the deterrence theory of punishment. Though retribution or denunciation is regarded by same as a proper end of punishment, I do not think, for reasons I have already discussed, that it can have any legitimate place in an enlightened philosophy of punishment. It must therefore be held that death penalty has no rational nexus with any legitimate penological goal or any rational penological purpose and it is arbitrary and irrational and hence violative of Articles 14 and 21 of the Constitution.

Bhagwati, J. also noted that the vagaries of the judicial process, and the difference in approach to the death sentence between different judges, would lead to arbitrary decisions for the following reason:

69. I must now turn to consider the attack against the constitutional validity of death penalty provided under Section 302 of the Penal Code, 1860 read with Section 354, sub-section (3) of the Code of Criminal Procedure, 1973 on the ground that these sections confer an unguided and standardless discretion on the court whether to liquidate an accused out of existence or to let him continue to live and the vesting of such discretion in the court renders the death penalty arbitrary and freakish. This ground of challenge is in my opinion well founded and it furnishes one additional reason why the death penalty must be struck down as violative of Articles 14 and 21. It is obvious on a plain reading of Section 302 of the Penal Code, 1860 which provides death penalty as alternative punishment for murder that it leaves it entirely to the discretion of the court whether to impose death sentence or to award only life imprisonment to an accused convicted of the offence of murder. This section does not lay down any standards or principles to guide the discretion of the court in the matter of imposition of death penalty. The critical choice between physical liquidation and lifelong incarceration is left to the discretion of the court and no legislative light is shed as to how this deadly discretion

is to be exercised. The court is left free to navigate in an uncharted sea without any compass or directional guidance. The respondents sought to find some guidance in Section 354, sub-section (3) of the Code of Criminal Procedure, 1973 but I fail to see how that section can be of any help at all in providing guidance in the exercise of discretion. On the contrary it makes the exercise of discretion more difficult and uncertain. Section 354, sub-section (3) provides that in case of offence of murder, life sentence shall be the rule and it is only in exceptional cases for special reasons that death penalty may be awarded. But what are the special reasons for which the court may award death penalty is a matter on which Section 354, sub-section (3) is silent nor is any guidance in that behalf provided by any other provision of law. It is left to the judge to grope in the dark for himself and in the exercise of his unguided and unfettered discretion decide what reasons may be considered as 'special reasons' justifying award of death penalty and whether in a given case any such special reasons exist which should persuade the court to depart from the normal rule and inflict death penalty on the accused. There being no legislative policy or principle to guide the court in exercising its discretion in this delicate and sensitive area of life and death, the exercise of discretion of the court is bound to vary from judge to judge. What may appear as special reasons to one judge may not so appear to another and the decision in a given case whether to impose the death sentence or to let off the offender only with life imprisonment would, to a large extent, depend upon who is the judge called upon to make the decision. The reason for this uncertainty in the sentencing process is two-fold. Firstly, the nature of the sentencing process is such that it involves a highly delicate task calling for skills and talents very much different from those ordinarily expected of lawyers. This was pointed out clearly and emphatically by Mr Justice Frankfurter in the course of the evidence he gave before the Royal Commission on Capital Punishment:

'I myself think that the Bench—we lawyers who become Judges— are not very competent, are not qualified by experience, to impose sentence where any discretion is to be exercised. I do not think it is in the domain of the training of lawyers to know what to do with a fellow after you find out he is a thief. I do not think legal training has given you any special competence. I, myself, hope that one of these days, and before long, we will divide the functions of criminal justice. I think the lawyers are people who are competent to ascertain whether or not a crime has been committed. The whole scheme of common law judicial machinery—the rule of evidence, the ascertainment of what is relevant and what is irrelevant and what is fair, the whole question of whether you can introduce prior crimes in order to prove intent—I think lawyers are peculiarly fitted for that task. But all the questions that follow upon ascertainment of guilt, I think require very different and much more diversified talents than the lawyers and judges are normally likely to possess.'

Even if considerations relevant to capital sentencing were provided by the legislature, it would be a difficult exercise for the judges to decide whether to impose the death penalty or to award the life sentence. But without any such guidelines given by the legislature, the task of the judges becomes much more arbitrary and the sentencing decision is bound to vary with each judge. Secondly, when unguided discretion is conferred upon the court to choose between life and death, by providing a totally vague and indefinite criterion of 'special reasons' without laying down any principles or guidelines for determining what should be considered to be 'special reasons', the choice is bound to be influenced by the subjective philosophy of the judge called upon to pass the sentence and on his value system and social philosophy will depend whether the accused shall live or die. No doubt the judge will have to give 'special reasons' if he opts in favour of inflicting the death penalty, but that does not eliminate arbitrariness and caprice, firstly because there being no guidelines provided by the legislature, the reasons which may appeal to one judge as 'special reasons' may not appeal to another, and secondly, because reasons can always be found for a conclusion that the judge instinctively wishes to reach and the judge can bona fide and conscientiously find such reasons to be 'special reasons'. It is now recognized on all hands that judicial conscience is not a fixed conscience; it varies from judge to judge depending upon his attitudes and approaches, his predilections and prejudices, his habits of mind and thought and in short all that goes with the expression 'social philosophy'. We lawyers and Judges like to cling to the myth that every decision which we make in the exercise of our judicial discretion is guided exclusively by legal principles and we refuse to admit the subjective element in judicial decision-making. But that myth now stands exploded and it is acknowledged by jurists that the social philosophy of the judge plays a not inconsiderable part in moulding his judicial decision and particularly the exercise of judicial discretion. There is nothing like complete objectivity in the decision-making process and especially so, when this process involves making of decision in the exercise of judicial discretion. Every judgment necessarily bears the impact of the attitude and approach of the judge and his social value system. It would be pertinent here to quote Justice Cardozo's analysis of the mind of a Judge in his famous lectures on Nature of Judicial Process:

'We are reminded by William James in a telling page of his lectures on Pragmatism that every one of us has in truth an underlying philosophy of life, even those of us to whom the names and the notions of philosophy are unknown or anathema. There is in each of us a stream of tendency, whether you choose to call it philosophy or not, which gives coherence and direction to thought and action. Judges cannot escape that current any more than other mortals. All their lives, forces which they do not recognize and cannot name, have been tugging at them—inherited instincts, traditional beliefs, acquired convictions; and the resultant is an outlook on life, a conception of social needs, a sense in James' phrase of 'the total push and pressure of the cosmos', which when reasons are nicely balanced, must determine where choice shall fall. In this mental background every problem finds its setting. We may try to see things as objectively as we please. Nonetheless, we can never see them with any eyes except our own.'

It may be noted that the human mind, even at infancy, is no blank sheet of paper. We are born with predispositions and the process of education, formal and informal, and, our own subjective experiences create attitudes which affect us in judging situations and coming to decisions. Jerome Frank says in his book *Law and the Modern Mind*, in an observation with which I find myself in entire agreement:

'Without acquired 'slants' preconceptions, life could not go on. Every habit constitutes a pre-judgment; were those pre-judgments which we call habits absent in any person, were he obliged to treat every event as an unprecedented crisis presenting a wholly new problem, he would go mad. Interests, points of view, references, are the essence of living. Only death yields complete dispassionateness, for such dispassionateness signifies utter indifference. . . . An 'open mind' in the sense of a mind containing no preconceptions whatever, would be a mind incapable of learning anything, would be that of an utterly emotionless human being.'

It must be remembered that 'a Judge does not shed the attributes of common humanity when he assumes the ermine'. The ordinary human mind is a mass of preconceptions inherited and acquired, often unrecognized by their possessor. 'Few minds are as neutral as a sheet of plain glass and indeed a mind of that quality may actually fail in judicial efficiency, for the warmer tints of imagination and sympathy are needed to temper the cold light of reason, if human justice is to be done.' It is, therefore, obvious that when a judge is called upon to exercise his discretion as to whether the accused shall be killed or shall be permitted to live, his conclusion would depend to a large extent on his approach and attitude, his predilections and preconceptions, his value system and social philosophy and his response to the evolving norms of decency and newly developing concepts and ideas in penological jurisprudence. One judge may have faith in the Upanishad doctrine that every human being is an embodiment of the divine and he may believe with Mahatma Gandhi that every offender can be reclaimed and transformed by love and it is immoral and unethical to kill him, while another judge may believe that it is necessary for social defence that the offender should be put out of way and that no mercy should be shown to him who did not show mercy to another. One judge may feel that the Naxalites, though guilty of murders, are dedicated souls totally different from ordinary criminals as they are motivated not by any self-interest but by a burning desire to bring about a revolution by eliminating vested interests and should not therefore be put out of corporal existence while another judge may take the view that the Naxalites being guilty of cold premeditated murders are a menace to the society and to innocent men and women and therefore deserve to be liquidated. The views of judges as to what may be regarded as 'special reasons' are bound to differ from judge to judge depending upon his value system and social philosophy with the result that whether a person shall live or die depends very much upon the composition of the Bench which tries his case and this renders the imposition of death penalty arbitrary and capricious.*

A reference was then made to the judgment in *Furman v. Georgia* (1972)[†] of the United States Supreme Court.[‡] Finding that the death penalty is discriminatory in nature—the incidence of poor persons being sentenced to death being far greater than the rich, the learned judge held:

81. There is also one other characteristic of death penalty that is revealed by a study of the decided cases and it is that death sentence has a certain class complexion or class bias inasmuch as it is largely the poor and the downtrodden who are the victims of this extreme penalty. We would hardly find a rich or affluent person going to the gallows. Capital punishment, as pointed out by Warden Duffy is 'a privilege of the poor'. Justice Douglas also observed in a famous death penalty case, 'Former Attorney Pamsey Clark has said: 'it is the poor, the sick, the ignorant, the powerless and the hated who are executed'.' So also Governor Disalle of Ohio State speaking from his personal experience with the death penalty said:

'During my experience as Governor of Ohio, I found the men in death row had one thing in common; they were penniless. There were other common denominators, low mental capacity, little or no

---

* In *Devender Pal Singh v. State of NCT of Delhi and Anr.* ([2002] 5 SCC 234) and *Krishna Mochi and Ors. v. State of Bihar* ([2002] 6 SCC 81), a majority of two learned judges of the Supreme Court, after examining the evidence, held that the death penalty must be awarded to the accused in each case. On the other hand, in both cases, M.B. Shah, J. would have either allowed the appeals by acquitting the accused; or if not acquitting them entirely, would have set aside the punishment of the death penalty awarded to them. Thus, despite the fact that one learned judge thought that the accused in these cases should be acquitted, or that the crimes of which they were guilty did not merit the award of a death penalty, by a majority of two out of three votes in both cases, the accused were ultimately hanged. This itself points out how Bhagwati, J. is perhaps correct in stating that differently trained judicial minds react differently to the same set of facts; and that if even one judicially trained mind could differ on a death sentence being awarded, the death penalty should be scrapped altogether.

† 408 U.S. 238.

‡ (1982) 3 SCC 24, paragraph 78.

education, few friends, broken homes—but the fact that they had no money was a principal factor in their being condemned to death. . . .'

The same point was stressed by Krishna Iyer, J. in *Rajendra Prasad*'s case with his usual punch and vigour and in hard hitting language distinctive of his inimitable style:

'. . . Who, by and large, are the men whom the gallows swallow? The white-collar criminals and the corporate criminals whose wilful economic and environmental crimes inflict mass deaths or who hire assassins and murder by remote control? Rarely. With a few exceptions, they hardly fear the halter. The feuding villager, heady with country liquor, the striking workers desperate with defeat, the political dissenter and sacrificing liberator intent on changing the social order from satanic misrule, the waifs and strays whom society has hardened by neglect into street toughs, or the poor householder—husband or wife—driven by dire necessity or burst of tantrums—it is this person who is the morning meal of the macabre executioner.

Historically speaking, capital sentence perhaps has a class bias and colour bar, even as criminal law barks at both but bites the proletariat to defend the proprietariat a reason which, incidentally, explains why corporate criminals including top executives who, by subtle processes, account for slow or sudden killing of large members by adulteration, smuggling, cornering, pollution and other invisible operations, are not on the wanted list and their offending operations which directly derive profit from mafia and white-collar crimes are not visited with death penalty, while relatively lesser delinquencies have, in statutory and forensic rhetoric, deserved the extreme penalty.'

There can be no doubt that death penalty in its actual operation is discriminatory, for it strikes mostly against the poor and deprived sections of the community and the rich and the affluent usually escape from its clutches. This circumstance also adds to the arbitrary and capricious nature of the death penalty and renders it unconstitutional as being violative of Articles 14 and 21.*

---

* Brennan, J. of the US Supreme Court holds the same view as Bhagwati, J. In fact, in his dissent in *McCleskey v. Kemp* (481 U.S. 279 [1981], p. 345), the learned judge found that the vagaries of sentencing in cases involving the death penalty invariably hit black communities disproportionately, which was buttressed by facts and figures set out in the

Pointing out the only method by which a death sentence could be sustained, the learned judge stated:

> 82. Before I part with this topic I may point out that the only way in which the vice of arbitrariness in the imposition of death penalty can be removed is by the law providing that in every case where the death sentence is confirmed by the High Court there shall be an automatic review of the death sentence by the Supreme Court sitting as a whole and the death sentence shall not be affirmed or imposed by the Supreme Court unless it is approved unanimously by the entire court sitting en banc and the only exceptional cases in which death sentence may be affirmed or imposed should be legislatively limited to those where the offender is found to be so depraved that it is not possible to reform him by any curative or rehabilitative therapy and even after his release he would be a serious menace to the society and therefore in the interest of the society he is required to be eliminated. Of course, for reasons I have already discussed such exceptional cases would be practically nil because it is almost impossible to predicate of any person that he is beyond reformation or redemption and therefore, from a practical point of view death penalty would be almost non-existent. But theoretically it may

---

dissenting judgments in this case. It was found that where a black criminal committed crimes upon a black victim, the death penalty would not be frequently given. However, where a black criminal did so upon a white victim, the death penalty was imposed much more frequently. Also, in a case where a white person was the criminal and a black person the victim, the death penalty was rarely given. Given this statistical analysis, the dissent of Brennan, J.—after setting out the history of racial discrimination in the United States and the Supreme Court's judgments in *Dred Scott* (supra) and *Plessy* (supra)—in a celebrated passage, holds thus: 'Once we can identify a pattern of arbitrary sentencing outcomes, we can say that a defendant runs a risk of being sentenced arbitrarily. It is thus immaterial whether the operation of an impermissible influence such as race is intentional. While the Equal Protection Clause forbids racial discrimination, and intent may be critical in a successful claim under that provision, the Eighth Amendment has its own distinct focus: whether punishment comports with social standards of rationality and decency. It may be, as in this case, that on occasion an influence that makes punishment arbitrary is also proscribed under another constitutional provision. That does not mean, however, that the standard for determining an Eighth Amendment violation is superseded by the standard for determining a violation under this other provision. Thus, the fact that McCleskey presents a viable equal protection claim does not require that he demonstrate intentional racial discrimination to establish his Eighth Amendment claim.'

be possible to say that if the State is in a position to establish positively that the offender is such a social monster that even after suffering life imprisonment and undergoing reformative and rehabilitative therapy, he can never be reclaimed for the society, then he may be awarded death penalty. If this test is legislatively adopted and applied by following the procedure mentioned above, the imposition of death penalty may be rescued from the vice of arbitrariness and caprice. But that is not so under the law as it stands today.

Despite this lone and brilliant dissent, subsequent judgments of the court have failed to respond—the death penalty continues to be awarded by the courts even today, Parliament not having stepped in to amend the law. Given the rise of crime, and of terrorism in particular, worldwide, it is unlikely that, in the foreseeable future, Bhagwati J.'s vision will ever be translated into law.

6.   *A.R. Antulay v. R.S. Nayak* (1988)

The dissenting judgment of Venkatachalaiah, J. in *A.R. Antulay v. R.S. Nayak & Anr.* (1988)* is remarkable, in that it is an emphatic repudiation of every single conclusion reached by the majority judges—being a majority of five in a seven-judge bench of the Supreme Court. What is even more remarkable is the courage shown by Venkatachalaiah, J. as the junior-most member of the bench, being certain that the law, as he saw it, was flouted on every score, only in order to set right what the majority saw as being an injustice done to the petitioner.

Among other things, the majority judgment held, contrary to a binding nine-judge bench in *Mirajkar*, that a judicial order by a Constitution Bench of the Supreme Court, *can* violate fundamental rights. The majority also held that the said judicial order being *per incuriam*, the Latin maxim '*actus curiae neminem gravabit*' must apply, i.e. that the act of the court can harm no man; and that therefore it was the duty of the court, even without a review petition being filed, to correct the error.

---

* (1988) 2 SCC 602.

As stated hereinabove, in his terse and well-reasoned judgment, Venkatachalaiah, J. dissented on all counts. Quotations from Justice Jackson, Lord Diplock and Justice Learned Hand were relied upon, to show that even erroneous decisions must finally bind parties to a litigation, as follows:

> 137. Courts are as much human institutions as any other and share all human susceptibilities to error. Justice Jackson said:
>
> '. . . Whenever decisions of one court are reviewed by another, a percentage of them are reversed. That reflects a difference in outlook normally found between personnel comprising different courts. Moreover, reversal by a higher court is not proof that justice is thereby better done. There is no doubt that if there were a super-Supreme Court, a substantial proportion of our reversals of State courts would also be reversed. We are not final because we are infallible, but we are infallible only because we are final.'
>
> 138. In *Cassell & Co. v. Broome*, Lord Diplock said:
>
> 'It is inevitable in a hierarchical system of courts that there are decisions of the supreme appellate tribunal which do not attract the unanimous approval of all members of the judiciary. When I sat in the Court of Appeal I sometimes thought the House of Lords was wrong in overruling me. Even since that time there have been occasions, of which the instant appeal itself is one, when, alone or in company, I have dissented from a decision of the majority of this House. But the judicial system only works if someone is allowed to have the last word and if that last word, once spoken, is loyally accepted.'
>
> 139. Judge Learned Hand, referred to as one of the most profound legal minds in the jurisprudence of the English speaking world, commended the Cromwellian intellectual humility and desired that these words of Cromwell be 'written over the portals of every church, over court house and at every cross road in the nation: 'I beseech ye . . . think that ye may be mistaken'.
>
> 140. As a learned Author said, while infallibility is an unrealizable ideal, 'correctness', is often a matter of opinion. An erroneous decision must be as binding as a correct one. It would be an unattainable ideal to require the binding effect of a Judgment to defend on its being correct

in the absolute, for the test of correctness would be resort to another court the infallibility of which is, again subject to a similar further investigation. No self-respecting judge would wish to act if he did so at the risk of being called a usurper whenever he failed to anticipate and predict what another judge thought of his conclusions. Even infallibility would not protect him; he would need the gift of prophecy—ability to anticipate the fallibilities of others as well. A proper perception of means and ends of the judicial process, that in the interest of finality it is inevitable to make some compromise between its ambitions of ideal justice in absolute terms and its limitations.

The *Anisminic** principle, relied upon by the majority judgments, was dealt with as follows:

143. In the course of the arguments there were references to the *Anisminic* case. In my view, reliance on the *Anisminic* principle is wholly misplaced in this case. That case related to the powers of Tribunals of limited jurisdiction. It would be a mistake of first magnitude to import these inhibitions as to jurisdiction into the concept of the jurisdiction of superior courts. A finding of a superior court even on a question of its own jurisdiction, however grossly erroneous it may, otherwise be, is not a nullity; nor one which could at all be said to have been reached without jurisdiction, susceptible to be ignored or to admit of any collateral attack. Otherwise, the adjudications of superior courts would be held up to ridicule and the remedies generally arising from and considered concomitants of such classification of judicial errors would be so seriously abused and expanded as to make a mockery of those foundational principles essential to the stability of administration of justice.

It was therefore concluded:

149. It would, in my opinion, be wholly erroneous to characterize the directions issued by the Five-Judge Bench as a nullity, amenable to be ignored or so declared in a collateral attack.

---

* (1969) 2 AC 147.

The learned judge also noted that the only way of correcting a final judgment of a superior court is by the review procedure laid down by the Constitution:

> 157. The pronouncements of every Division Bench of this Court are pronouncements of the court itself. A larger Bench, merely on the strength of its numbers, cannot undo the finality of the decisions of other Division Benches. If the decision suffers from an error the only way to correct it, is to go in review under Article 137 read with Order 40 Rule 1 framed under Article 145 before 'as far as is practicable' the same judges. This is not a matter merely of some dispensable procedural 'form' but the requirement of substance. The reported decisions on the review power under the Civil Procedure Code when it had a similar provision for the same judges hearing the matter demonstrate the high purpose sought to be served thereby.

It was then pointed out that if a party has no notice, and a judgment is passed against it, that judgment can then be set aside *ex debito justitiae* only by the same bench, and not by a separately constituted bench in a writ petition challenging such order. This was stated by the learned dissenting judge as follows:

> 160. Where a party has had no notice and a decree is made against him, he can approach the court for setting aside the decision. In such a case the party is said to become entitled to relief *ex debito Justitiae*, on proof of the fact that there was no service. This is a class of cases where there is no trial at all and the judgment is for default. D.M. Gordan, in his 'Actions to set aside judgments' says:
>
> 'The more familiar applications to set aside judgments are those made on motion and otherwise summarily. But these are judgments obtained by default, which do not represent a judicial determination. In general, judgments rendered after a trial are conclusive between the parties unless and until reversed on appeal. Certainly in general judgments of superior courts cannot be overturned or questioned between the parties in collateral actions. Yet there is a type of collateral action known as an action of review, by which even a superior court's judgment can be questioned, even between the parties, and set aside.

161. Cases of such frank failure of natural justice are obvious cases where relief is granted as of right. Where a person is not actually served but is held erroneously, to have been served, he can agitate that grievance only in that forum or in any further proceeding therefrom. In *Isaacs* case, Privy Council referred to

'a category of orders of such a court which a person affected by the order is entitled to apply to have set aside *ex debito justitiae* in exercise of the inherent jurisdiction of the court without needing to have recourse to the rules that deal expressly with proceedings to set aside orders for irregularity and give to the judge a discretion as to the order he will make.

162. In the present case by the order dated 5-4-1984 a Five-Judge Bench set out, what according to it, was, the legal basis and source of jurisdiction to order transfer. On 17-4-1984 appellant's writ petition challenging that transfer as a nullity was dismissed. These orders are not which appellant is entitled to have set aside *ex debito justitiae* by another Bench. Reliance on the observations in Isaacs case is wholly misplaced.

The learned judge then observed that the withdrawal of a criminal case from the trial court to the high court may be wrong, but it is still a *possible* view, as a result of which the earlier five-judge-bench decision cannot be collaterally challenged before a separate bench, admittedly not under the review jurisdiction. This was set out with great clarity as under:

165. The argument of nullity is too tall and has no place in this case. The earlier direction proceeded on a construction of Section 7(1) of the Act and Section 407 CrPC. We do not sit here in appeal over what the Five-Judge Bench said and proclaim how wrong they were. We are, simply, not entitled to embark, at a later stage, upon an investigation of the correctness of the very same decision. The same Bench can, of course, reconsider the matter under Article 137.

166. However, even to the extent the argument goes that the High Court under Section 407 CrPC could not withdraw to itself a trial from Special Judge under the 1952 Act, the view of the earlier Bench is a possible view. The submissions of Shri Ram Jethmalani that the exclusivity of the jurisdiction claimed for the special forum under the 1952 Act is in relation to courts which would, otherwise, be courts of competing or co-ordinate jurisdictions and that such exclusivity does

not affect the superior jurisdiction of the High Court to withdraw, in appropriate situations, the case to itself in exercise of its extraordinary original criminal jurisdiction: that canons of statutory construction, appropriate to the situation, require that the exclusion of jurisdiction implied in the 1952 Amending Act should not be pushed beyond the purpose sought to be served by the amending law; and that the law while creating the special jurisdiction did not seek to exclude the extraordinary jurisdiction of the High Court are not without force. The argument, relying upon *Kavasji Pestonji Dalal v. Rustomji Sorabji Jamadar* that while the ordinary competing jurisdictions of other courts were excluded, the extraordinary jurisdiction of the High Court was neither intended to be, nor, in fact, affected, is a matter which would also bear serious examination. In Sir Francis Bennion's Statutory Interpretation, there are passages (at p. 433) which referring to presumption against implied repeal, suggest that in view of the difficulties in determining whether an implication of repeal was intended in a particular situation it would be a reasonable presumption that where the legislature desired a repeal, it would have made it plain by express words. In Sutherland: Statutory Construction the following passages occur:

'Prior statutes relating to the same subject-matter are to be compared with the new provisions; and if possible by reasonable construction, both are to be so construed that effect is given to every provision of each. Statutes in pari materia although in apparent conflict, are so far as reasonably possible constructed to be in harmony with each other.

When the legislature enacts a provision, it has before it all the other provisions relating to the same subject-matter which it enacts at that time, whether in the same statute or in a separate Act. It is evident that it has in mind the provisions of a prior Act to which it refers, whether it phrases the later Act as amendment or an independent Act. Experience indicates that a legislature does not deliberately enact inconsistent provisions when it is recognizant of them both, without expressly recognizing the inconsistency.

That Article 14 could not possibly be applied in the facts of this case, following the decision in *Anwar Ali Sarkar v. State of West Bengal* (1952),* was set out as follows:

---

* (1952) SCR 284.

169. If the operation of Section 407 of the CrPC is not impliedly excluded and therefore, enables the withdrawal of a case by the High Court to itself for trial as, indeed, has been held by the earlier Bench, the argument based on Article 14 would really amount to a challenge to the very *vires* of Section 407. All accused persons cannot claim to be tried by the same judge. The discriminations—inherent in the choice of one of the concurrent jurisdictions—are not brought about by an inanimate statutory rule or by executive fiat. The withdrawal of a case under Section 407 is made by a conscious judicial act and is the result of judicial discernment. If the law permits the withdrawal of the trial to the High Court from a Special Judge, such a law enabling withdrawal would not, *prima facie*, be bad as violation of Article 14. The Five-Judge Bench in the earlier case has held that such a transfer is permissible under law. The appeal to the principle in *Anwar Ali Sarkar* case, in such a context would be somewhat out of place.

170. If the law did not permit such a transfer then the trial before a forum, which is not according to law, violates the rights of the accused person. In the earlier decision the transfer has been held to be permissible. That decision has assumed finality.

171. If appellant says that he is singled out for a hostile treatment on the ground alone that he is exposed to a trial before a judge of the High Court then the submission has a touch of irony. Indeed that a trial by a judge of the High Court makes for added reassurance of justice, has been recognized in a number of judicial pronouncements. The argument that a Judge of the High Court may not necessarily possess the statutory qualifications requisite for being appointed as a Special Judge appears to be specious. A Judge of the High Court hears appeals arising from the decisions of the Special Judge, and exercises a jurisdiction which includes powers co-extensive with that of the trial court.

Refuting the contention that the right of appeal from the special court to the highest court was taken away by the five-judge-bench order, which would result in its being declared a nullity, the learned judge held:

176. The contention that the transfer of the case to the High Court involves the elimination of the appellant's right of appeal to the High

Court which he would otherwise have and that the appeal under Article 136 of the Constitution is not as of right may not be substantial in view of Section 374, of the CrPC which provides such an appeal as of right, when the trial is held by the High Court.'

The learned judge went on to hold that since *Mirajkar* holds the field, *Prem Chand Garg v. Excise Commissioner, U.P.* (1963),[*] must be understood in such manner that it does not clash with the nine-judge-bench decision, as follows:

177. The argument is that the earlier order of the Five-Judge Bench insofar as it violates the fundamental rights of the appellant under Articles 14 and 21 must be held to be void and amenable to challenge under Article 32 in this very Court and that the decision of this Court in *Prem Chand Garg* case supports such a position. As rightly pointed out by Ranganath Misra, J. *Prem Chand Garg* case needs to be understood in the light of the observations made in *Naresh Sridhar Mirajkar v. State of Maharashtra*. In *Mirajkar*'s case, Gajendragadkar, C.J., who had himself delivered the opinion in *Garg* case noticed the contention based on *Garg*'s case thus:

'In support of his argument that a judicial decision can be corrected by this Court in exercise of its writ jurisdiction under Article 32(2), Mr Setalvad has relied upon another decision of this Court in *Prem Chand Garg v. Excise Commissioner.*'

178. Learned Chief Justice referring to the scope of the matter that fell for consideration in *Garg* case stated:

'It would thus be seen that the main controversy in the case of *Prem Chand Garg* centred round the question as to whether Article 145 conferred powers on this Court to make rules, though they may be inconsistent with the constitutional provisions prescribed by Part III. Once it was held that the powers under Article 142 had to be read subject not only to the fundamental rights, but to other binding statutory provisions, it became clear that the rule which authorized the making of the impugned order was invalid. It was in that context that

---

[*] (1963) Supp. (1) SCR 885.

the validity of the order had to be incidentally examined. The petition was made not to challenge the order as such, but to challenge the validity of the rule under which the order was made.

179. Repelling the contention, learned Chief Justice said:

'It is difficult to see how this decision can be pressed into service by Mr Setalvad in support of the argument that a judicial order passed by this Court was held to be subject to the writ jurisdiction of this Court itself.'

180. A passage from Kaddish and Kaddish: *Discretion to Disobey*, 1973 Edn. may usefully be recalled:

'On one view, it would appear that the right of a citizen to defy illegitimate judicial authority should be the same as his right to defy illegitimate legislative authority. After all, if a rule that transgresses the Constitution or is otherwise invalid is no law at all and never was one, it should hardly matter whether a court or a legislature made the rule. Yet the prevailing approach of the courts has been to treat invalid court orders quite differently from invalid statutes. The long established principle of the old equity courts was that an erroneously issued injunction must be obeyed until the error was judicially determined. Only where the issuing court could be said to have lacked jurisdiction in the sense of authority to adjudicate the cause and to reach the parties through its mandate were disobedient contemnors permitted to raise the invalidity of the order as a full defence. By and large, American courts have declined to treat the unconstitutionality of a court order as a jurisdictional defect within this traditional equity principle, and in notable instances they have qualified that principle even where the defect was jurisdictional in the accepted sense.'

Indeed Ranganath Misra, J. in his opinion rejected the contention of the appellant in these terms:

'In view of this decision in *Mirajkar* case it must be taken as concluded that judicial proceedings in this Court are not subject to the writ jurisdiction thereof.'

Dealing with the *per incuriam* doctrine, it was stated that it is applied only when the earlier judgment is to be considered as a precedent, and not otherwise. This was also felicitously stated as follows:

182. It is asserted that the impugned directions issued by the Five-Judge Bench was *per incuriam* as it ignored the statute and the earlier *Chadha* case.

183. But the point is that the circumstance that a decision is reached *per incuriam*, merely serves to denude the decision of its precedent value. Such a decision would not be binding as a judicial precedent. A co-ordinate Bench can disagree with it and decline to follow it. A larger Bench can overrule such decision. When a previous decision is so overruled it does not happen—nor has the overruling Bench any jurisdiction so to do—that the finality of the operative order, inter partes, in the previous decision is overturned. In this context the word 'decision' means only the reason for the previous order and not the operative order in the previous decision, binding inter partes. Even if a previous decision is overruled by a larger Bench, the efficacy and binding nature, of the adjudication expressed in the operative order remains undisturbed inter partes. Even if the earlier decision of the Five-Judge Bench is *per incuriam* the operative part of the order cannot be interfered with in the manner now sought to be done. That apart the Five-Judge Bench gave its reason. The reason, in our opinion, may or may not be sufficient. There is advertence to Section 7(1) of the 1952 Act and to the exclusive jurisdiction created thereunder. There is also reference to Section 407 of the Criminal Procedure Code. Can such a decision be characterized as one reached *per incuriam*? Indeed, Ranganath Misra, J. says this on the point:

'Overruling when made by a larger Bench of an earlier decision of a smaller one is intended to take away the precedent value of the decision without effecting the binding effect of the decision in the particular case. Antulay, therefore, is not entitled to take advantage of the matter being before a larger Bench.'

184. I respectfully agree.

Lastly, dealing with the maxim *actus curiae*, the learned judge held:

186. I am afraid this maxim has no application to conscious conclusions reached in a judicial decision. The maxim is not a source of a general power to reopen and rehear adjudication which have otherwise assumed finality. The maxim operates in a different and narrow area. The best

illustration of the operation of the maxim is provided by the application of the rule of nunc-pro-tunc. For instance, if owing to the delay in what the court should, otherwise, have done earlier but did later, a party suffers owing to events occurring in the interregnum, the court has the power to remedy it. The area of operation of the maxim is, generally, procedural. Errors in judicial findings, either of facts or law or operative decisions consciously arrived at as a part of the judicial exercise cannot be interfered with by resort to this maxim. There is no substance in contention (h).

187. It is true that the highest court in the land should not, by technicalities of procedure forge fetters on its own feet and disable itself in cases of serious miscarriages of justice. It is said that 'Life of law is not logic; it has been experience'. But it is equally true as Cardozo said: 'But Holmes did not tell us that logic is to be ignored when experience is silent'. Those who do not put the teachings of experience and the lessons of logic out of consideration would tell what inspires confidence in the judiciary and what does not. Judicial vacillations fall in the latter category and undermine respect of the judiciary and judicial institutions, denuding thereby respect for law and the confidence in the even-handedness in the administration of justice by courts. It would be gross injustice, says an author (Miller—'Data of Jurisprudence') to decide alternate cases on opposite principles. The power to alter a decision by review must be expressly conferred or necessarily inferred. The power of review—and the limitations on the power—under Article 137 are implicit recognitions of what would, otherwise, be final and irrevocable. No appeal could be made to the doctrine of inherent powers of the court either. Inherent powers do not confer, or constitute a source of jurisdiction. They are to be exercised in aid of a jurisdiction that is already invested. The remedy of the appellant, if any, is recourse to Article 137; nowhere else. This appears to me both good sense and good law.

7. *P. V. Narsimha Rao v. State* (1998)

In *P. V. Narsimha Rao v. State* (1998),* by a majority of 3:2, an extremely curious result was reached, namely, that a member of Parliament could claim immunity in a criminal court, under Article 105 of the Constitution,

---

* (1998) 4 SCC 626.

from prosecution under the ordinary law of the land on a charge of bribery. Justice S.C. Agrawal (joined by Justice A.S. Anand) dissented. The questions posed before the court were stated as follows:

> Whether by virtue of Article 105 of the Constitution a Member of Parliament can claim immunity from prosecution on a charge of bribery in a criminal court, and whether a Member of Parliament is a 'public servant' falling within the purview of the Prevention of Corruption Act, 1988 (hereinafter referred to as 'the 1988 Act').

The questions were then reformulated by the learned judge as follows:

> (1) Does Article 105 of the Constitution confer any immunity on a Member of Parliament from being prosecuted in a criminal court for an offence involving offer or acceptance of bribe?
>
> (2) Is a Member of Parliament excluded from the ambit of the 1988 Act for the reason that:
>
> (a) he is not a person who can be regarded as a 'public servant' as defined under Section 2(c) of the 1988 Act, and
>
> (b) he is not a person comprehended in clauses (a), (b) and (c) of sub-section (1) of Section 19 and there is no authority competent to grant sanction for his prosecution under the 1988 Act?

The dissenting judge then surveyed English law, Australian Law, Canadian Law and the US Law, and finally concluded that in India, a breach of parliamentary privilege must be related to the business of the House, and not be concerned with what happens outside the House.[*] At best, a proven allegation of bribery, being unbecoming of a member of Parliament, he/she would be held guilty of lowering the dignity of the House. This was held as follows:

> 25. It does not, however, constitute breach or contempt of the House if the offering of payment of bribe is related to the business other than that of the House. In 1974, the Lok Sabha considered the matter relating

---

[*] Ibid., pp. 652–60.

to offer or payment of bribe in the import licences case wherein it was alleged that a Member of Lok Sabha had taken bribe and forged signatures of the Members for furthering the cause of certain applicants. The question of privilege was disallowed since it was considered that the conduct of the Member, although improper, was not related to the business of the House. But at the same time it was held that as the allegation of bribery and forgery were very serious and unbecoming of a Member of Parliament, he could be held guilty of lowering the dignity of the House.

Article 105, with which the court was concerned, states:

105. Powers, privileges, etc. of the House of Parliament and of the Members and committees thereof—(1) Subject to the provisions of this Constitution and to the rules and standing orders regulating the procedure of Parliament, there shall be freedom of speech in Parliament.

(2) No Member of Parliament shall be liable to any proceedings in any court in respect of anything said or any vote given by him in Parliament or any committee thereof, and no person shall be so liable in respect of the publication by or under the authority of either House of Parliament of any report, paper, votes or proceedings.

(3) In other respects, the powers, privileges and immunities of each House of Parliament, and of the Members and the committees of each House, shall be such as may from time to time be defined by Parliament by law, and until so defined, shall be those of the House of Commons of Parliament of the United Kingdom, and of its Members and committees, at the commencement of this Constitution.

(4) The provisions of clauses (1), (2) and (3) shall apply in relation to persons who by virtue of this Constitution have the right to speak in, and otherwise to take part in the proceedings of, a House of Parliament or any committee thereof as they apply in relation to Members of Parliament.'

By the Constitution (Forty-fourth Amendment) Act, 1978 clause (3) was replaced by the following clause:

105. (3) In other respects, the powers, privileges and immunities of each House of Parliament, and of the Members and the committees

of each House, shall be such as may from time to time be defined by
Parliament by law, and, until so defined, shall be those of that House
and of its Members and committees immediately before coming into
force of Section 15 of the Constitution (Forty-fourth Amendment) Act,
1978.

The minority view that Articles 105(1) and 105(2) are interlinked, led to
the following result:

39. We may now examine whether the decision in Ex p Wason has
any bearing on the interpretation of Article 105(2). Clauses (1) and (2)
of Article 105 are interlinked, while clause (1) secures to the Members
freedom of speech in Parliament, clause (2) safeguards and protects the
said freedom by conferring immunity on the Members from liability in
respect of anything said or any vote given by him in Parliament or in
any committee thereof. This is necessary because for a regulatory body
like Parliament, the freedom of speech is of the utmost importance and
a full and free debate is of the essence of parliamentary democracy. In
England this freedom of speech in Parliament is secured by Article 9 of
the Bill of Rights. Though clause (2) of Article 105 appears to be similar
to Article 9 of the Bill of Rights a closer look would show that they differ
in certain aspects. Article 9 of the Bill of Rights, by prescribing that
'freedom of speech and debates or proceedings in Parliament ought not
to be impeached or questioned in any court or place out of Parliament',
confers immunity in respect of speech, debates or proceedings in
Parliament being questioned in any court or place out of Parliament.
The said immunity has been construed to preclude what was said or
done in Parliament in the course of proceedings there from being
examined outside Parliament for the purpose of supporting a cause of
action even though the cause of action itself arose out of something done
outside Parliament. In an Australian case *R. v. Murphy* a question arose
whether in the course of criminal trial, the witness's earlier evidence to
the Select Committee could be put to him in cross-examination with
a view to showing a previous inconsistent statement. Hunt, J. in the
Supreme Court of New South Wales, held that Article 9 of the Bill of
Rights did not prohibit such cross-examination even if the suggestion

was made that the evidence given to the Select Committee was a lie. He further held that the statements of the Select Committee could be used to draw inferences and could be analysed and be made the basis of submission.

The protection under Article 105(2) was then stated to be narrower than that conferred under Article 9 of the Bill of Rights, as follows:

40. . . The protection given under clause (2) of Article 105 is narrower than that conferred under Article 9 of the Bill of Rights in the sense that the immunity conferred by that clause is personal in nature and is available to the Member in respect of anything said or in any vote given by him in the House or any committee thereof. The said clause does not confer an immunity for challenge in the court on the speech or vote given by a Member of Parliament. The protection given under clause (2) of Article 105 is thus similar to protection envisaged under the construction placed by Hunt, J. in *R. v. Murphy* on Article 9 of the Bill of Rights which has not been accepted by the Privy Council in *Prebble v. Television New Zealand Ltd.* The decision in Ex p Wason which was given in the context of Article 9 of the Bill of Rights, can, therefore, have no application in the matter of construction of clause (2) of Article 105. Ex p Wason which holds that the information laid by Wason did not disclose any indictable offence, proceeds on the basis that statements made by Members of either House of Parliament in their places in the House, though they might be untrue to their knowledge, could not be made the foundation of civil or criminal proceedings. The position under clause (2) of Article 105 is, however, different. The said clause does not prescribe that a speech made or vote given by a Member in Parliament cannot be made the basis of civil or criminal proceedings at all. The said clause only gives protection to the Member who has made the speech or has given the vote from liability in any proceeding in a court of law. Therefore, on the basis of the decision in Ex p Wason it cannot be said that no offence was committed by those who are alleged to have offered the illegal gratification and by those who had received such gratification to vote against the no-confidence motion and for that reason the charge of conspiracy and abetment must also fail. On the

basis of Article 105(2) the claim for immunity from prosecution can be made only on behalf of A-3 to A-5 and A-16 to A-21 who are alleged to have voted against the no-confidence motion. As to whether they are entitled to such immunity under Article 105(2) will, however, depend on the interpretation of the provisions of Article 105(2).

It was then stated, after referring to various judgments, that a member of Parliament who is found to have accepted a bribe in connection with the business of Parliament can be punished by the House for contempt. These punishments may be suspension or expulsion, but not fines. This was expressed in the following terms:

> 45. It is no doubt true that a Member who is found to have accepted bribe in connection with the business of Parliament can be punished by the House for contempt. But that is not a satisfactory solution. In exercise of its power to punish for contempt the House of Commons can convict a person to custody and may also order expulsion or suspension from the service of the House. There is no power to impose a fine. The power of committal cannot exceed the duration of the session and the person, if not sooner discharged by the House, is immediately released from confinement on prorogation. (See: May's Parliamentary Practice, 21st Edn., pp. 103, 109 and 111.) The Houses of Parliament in India cannot claim a higher power. The Salmon Commission has stated that 'whilst the theoretical power of the House to commit a person into custody undoubtedly exists, nobody has been committed to prison for contempt of Parliament for a hundred years or so, and it is most unlikely that Parliament would use this power in modern conditions'. (para 306) The Salmon Commission has also expressed the view that in view of the special expertise that is necessary for this type of inquiry the Committee of Privileges do not provide an investigative machinery comparable to that of a police investigation.

Referring to the object of the immunity conferred under Article 105(2), the learned judge then went on to hold:

> 47. As mentioned earlier, the object of the immunity conferred under Article 105(2) is to ensure the independence of the individual

legislators. Such independence is necessary for healthy functioning of the system of parliamentary democracy adopted in the Constitution. Parliamentary democracy is a part of the basic structure of the Constitution. An interpretation of the provisions of Article 105(2) which would enable a Member of Parliament to claim immunity from prosecution in a criminal court for an offence of bribery in connection with anything said by him or a vote given by him in Parliament or any committee thereof and thereby place such Members above the law would not only be repugnant to healthy functioning of parliamentary democracy but would also be subversive of the rule of law which is also an essential part of the basic structure of the Constitution. It is settled law that in interpreting the constitutional provisions the court should adopt a construction which strengthens the foundational features and the basic structure of the Constitution. The expression 'in respect of' precedes the words 'anything said or any vote given' in Article 105(2). The words 'anything said or any vote given' can only mean speech that has already been made or a vote that has already been given. The immunity from liability, therefore, comes into play only if a speech has been made or vote has been given. The immunity would not be available in a case where a speech has not been made or a vote has not been given. When there is a prior agreement whereunder a Member of Parliament has received an illegal consideration in order to exercise his right to speak or to give his vote in a particular manner on a matter coming up for consideration before the House, there can be two possible situations. There may be an agreement whereunder a Member accepts illegal gratification and agrees not to speak in Parliament or not to give his vote in Parliament. The immunity granted under Article 105(2) would not be available to such a Member and he would be liable to be prosecuted on the charge of bribery in a criminal court. What would be the position if the agreement is that in lieu of the illegal gratification paid or promised the Member would speak or give his vote in Parliament in a particular manner and he speaks and gives his vote in that manner? As per the wide meaning suggested by Shri Rao for the expression 'in respect of', the immunity for prosecution would be available to the Member who has received illegal gratification under such an agreement for speaking or giving his vote and who has spoken or given his vote in Parliament as per the said agreement because such acceptance of illegal gratification has a nexus or connection with such speaking or giving of vote by that Member. If the construction placed by Shri Rao on the expression 'in respect of' is adopted, a Member would be liable to be prosecuted on a charge of bribery if he accepts bribe for not speaking or for not giving his vote on a matter under consideration before the House but he would enjoy immunity from prosecution for such a charge if he accepts bribe for speaking or giving his vote in Parliament in a particular manner and he speaks or gives his vote in Parliament in that manner. It is difficult to conceive that the framers of the Constitution intended to make such a distinction in the matter of grant of immunity between a Member of Parliament who receives bribe for speaking or giving his vote in Parliament in a particular manner and speaks or gives his vote in that manner and a Member of Parliament who receives bribe for not speaking or not giving his vote on a particular matter coming up before the House and does not speak or give his vote as per the agreement so as to confer an immunity from prosecution on charge of bribery on the former but denying such immunity to the latter. Such an anomalous situation would be avoided if the words 'in respect of' in Article 105(2) are construed to mean 'arising out of'. If the expression 'in respect of' is thus construed, the immunity conferred under Article 105(2) would be confined to liability that arises out of or is attributable to something that has been said or to a vote that has been given by a Member in Parliament or any committee thereof. The immunity would be available only if the speech that has been made or the vote that has been given is an essential and integral part of the cause of action for the proceedings giving rise to the liability. The immunity would not be available to give protection against liability for an act that precedes the making of the speech or giving of vote by a Member in Parliament even though it may have a connection with the speech made or the vote given by the Member if such an act gives rise to a liability which arises independently and does not depend on the making of the speech or the giving of vote in Parliament by the Member. Such an independent liability cannot be regarded as liability in respect of anything said or vote given by the Member in Parliament. The liability for which immunity can be claimed under Article 105(2) is the liability that has arisen as a consequence of the speech that has been made or the vote that has been given in Parliament.

In a significant passage in the judgment, it was held that the offence of bribery is complete by accepting the bribe. The member of Parliament may default later by either not speaking, or by speaking contrary to the agreement by which he accepted by bribe. This therefore snaps the link between the offence, which is complete outside the four walls of the House, and is therefore not 'in respect of' the speech or vote to be given *in* Parliament. This reasoning of the judgment on this aspect is as follows:

> 50. The construction placed by us on the expression 'in respect of' in Article 105(2) raises the question: Is the liability to be prosecuted arising from acceptance of bribe by a Member of Parliament for the purpose of speaking or giving his vote in Parliament in a particular manner on a matter pending consideration before the House an independent liability which cannot be said to arise out of anything said or any vote given by the Member in Parliament? In our opinion, this question must be answered in the affirmative. The offence of bribery is made out against the receiver if he takes or agrees to take money for promise to act in a certain way. The offence is complete with the acceptance of the money or on the agreement to accept the money being concluded and is not dependent on the performance of the illegal promise by the receiver. The receiver of the money will be treated to have committed the offence even when he defaults in the illegal bargain. For proving the offence of bribery all that is required to be established is that the offender has received or agreed to receive money for a promise to act in a certain way and it is not necessary to go further and prove that he actually acted in that way.

xxx xxx xxx

> 52. The criminal liability incurred by a Member of Parliament who has accepted bribe for speaking or giving his vote in Parliament in a particular manner thus arises independently of the making of the speech or giving of vote by the Member and the said liability cannot, therefore, be regarded as a liability 'in respect of anything said or any vote given' in

Parliament. We are, therefore, of the opinion that the protection granted under Article 105(2) cannot be invoked by any of the appellants to claim immunity from prosecution on the substantive charge in respect of the offences punishable under Section 7, Section 13(2) read with Section 13(1)(d) and Section 12 of the 1988 Act as well as the charge of criminal conspiracy under Section 120-B IPC read with Section 7 and Section 13(2) read with Section 13(1)(d) of the 1988 Act.

The law in Australia and Canada was then referred to, which provide that even if bribery constitutes a breach of privilege, prosecution for a criminal offence may continue.[*] It was pointed out that even in the UK, there was a move to change the law in this regard, and bring it in line with that of Australia and Canada.[†] On the point as to whether a member of Parliament is a 'public servant' and would therefore require sanction for prosecution under the Prevention of Corruption Act, 1988, the dissenting judgment held that an MP certainly holds an 'office' and is performing a constitutional duty and is therefore a public servant. However, Parliament, even though it can expel an MP, cannot be regarded as an authority for grant of sanction to prosecute, as it cannot be regarded as the authority which either appoints, or removes, an MP. Resultantly, the dissenting opinion exhorted Parliament to amend the law. In the meanwhile, in order to obtain sanction, the learned judge noted that the Speaker of the House may be regarded as the authority for doing so.[‡]

The conclusion therefore reached by the learned dissenting judges was as follows:

98. On the basis of the aforesaid discussion we arrive at the following conclusion:

1. A Member of Parliament does not enjoy immunity under Article 105(2) or under Article 105(3) of the Constitution from being prosecuted before a criminal court for an offence involving offer or

---

[*] Id., paragraph 54.
[†] Id., paragraph 55.
[‡] Id., pp. 686, 699 and 701.

acceptance of bribe for the purpose of speaking or by giving his vote in Parliament or in any committees thereof.

2.   A Member of Parliament is a public servant under Section 2(c) of the Prevention of Corruption Act, 1988.

3.   Since there is no authority competent to remove a Member of Parliament and to grant sanction for his prosecution under Section 19(1) of the Prevention of Corruption Act, 1988, the court can take cognizance of the offences mentioned in Section 19(1) in the absence of sanction but till provision is made by Parliament in that regard by suitable amendment in the law, the prosecuting agency, before filing a charge-sheet in respect of an offence punishable under Sections 7, 10, 11, 13 and 15 of the 1988 Act against a Member of Parliament in a criminal court, shall obtain the permission of the Chairman of the Rajya Sabha/Speaker of the Lok Sabha, as the case may be.'

8. *Kihoto Hollohan v. Zachillhu & Ors.* (1992)

The important judgment of *Kihoto Hollohan v. Zachillhu & Ors.* (1992)* dealt with a challenge to the Tenth Schedule of the Constitution of India, in which an elaborate anti-defection law was enacted. The principal grounds of challenge were that since paragraph 7 of the Tenth Schedule excludes judicial review of a superior Court, it would need ratification of the states under the proviso to Article 368(2) of the Constitution of India, and this not having been done, the entire amendment would fall to the ground. It was also contended that paragraph 6, which gave a limited judicial review to the court to review a Speaker's decision, together with the fact that the Speaker has been made the sole authority to decide anti-defection petitions, would violate the basic structure of the Constitution of India, making the entire amendment void.

The majority judgment of Venkatachalaiah, J., speaking on behalf of himself and two other learned judges, held that paragraph 7 did indeed require ratification and would therefore be contrary to the proviso to Article 368(2), but that paragraph 7, being severable, could be segregated from the rest of the Tenth Schedule. Thus, only paragraph 7 was struck

---

* (1992) Supp. (2) SCC 651.

down on this score. Otherwise, the majority judgment did not find the rest of the Tenth Schedule to be violative of, or contrary to, the basic structure of the Constitution.

Verma, J., for himself and Sharma, J., dissented. The learned judge held that paragraph 7 of the Tenth Schedule clearly violated the proviso to Article 368(2):

> 169. There can thus be no doubt that Paragraph 7 of the Tenth Schedule which seeks to make a change in Article 136 which is a part of Chapter IV of Part V and Articles 226 and 227 which form part of Chapter V of Part VI of the Constitution, has not been enacted by incorporation in a Bill seeking to make the constitutional amendment in the manner prescribed by clause (2) read with the proviso therein of Article 368. Paragraph 7 of the Tenth Schedule is, therefore, unconstitutional and to that extent at least the Constitution does not stand amended in accordance with the Bill seeking to make the constitutional amendment. The further question now is : its effect on the validity of the remaining part of the Tenth Schedule and consequently the Constitution (Fifty-second Amendment) Act, 1985 itself.

The dissenting judgment then went on to hold that the doctrine of severability did not apply to a stillborn legislation:

> 171. On this view, the question of applying the Doctrine of Severability to strike down Paragraph 7 alone retaining the remaining part of Tenth Schedule does not arise since it presupposes that the Constitution stood so amended on the President's assent. The doctrine does not apply to a still-born legislation.

xxx xxx xxx

> 177. Apart from inapplicability of the Doctrine of Severability to a Bill to which the proviso to clause (2) of Article 368 applies, for the reasons given, it does not apply in the present case to strike down Paragraph 7 alone retaining the remaining part of the Tenth Schedule. In the first place, the discipline for exercise of the constituent power was consciously and deliberately adopted instead of resorting to the

mode of ordinary legislation in accordance with sub-clause (e) of clause (1) of Articles 102 and 191, which would render the decision on the question of disqualification on the ground of defection also amenable to judicial review as in the case of decision on questions relating to other disqualifications. Moreover, even the test applicable for applying the Doctrine of Severability to ordinary legislation as summarized in *R.M.D. Chamarbaughwalla v. Union of India* indicates that Paragraph 7 alone is not severable to permit retention of the remaining part of the Tenth Schedule as valid legislation. The settled test whether the enactment would have been made without Paragraph 7 indicates that the legislative intent was to make the enactment only with Paragraph 7 therein and not without it. This intention is manifest throughout and evident from the fact that but for Paragraph 7 the enactment did not require the discipline of Article 368 and exercise of the constituent power. Paragraph 7 follows Paragraph 6 the contents of which indicate the importance given to Paragraph 7 while enacting the Tenth Schedule. The entire exercise, as reiterated time and again in the debates, particularly the speech of the Law Minister while piloting the Bill in the Lok Sabha and that of the Prime Minister in the Rajya Sabha, was to emphasize that total exclusion of judicial review of the speaker's decision by all courts including the Supreme Court, was the prime object of enacting the Tenth Schedule. The entire legislative history shows this. How can the Doctrine of Severability be applied in such a situation to retain the Tenth Schedule striking down Paragraph 7 alone? This is a further reason for inapplicability of this doctrine.

In an instructive passage, the dissenting judgment held that giving the power of decision, in all anti-defection cases, to the Speaker of the House would violate the basic structure of the Constitution:

180. The Speaker's office is undoubtedly high and has considerable aura with the attribute of impartiality. This aura of the office was even greater when the Constitution was framed and yet the framers of the Constitution did not choose to vest the authority of adjudicating disputes as to disqualification of Members to the Speaker; and provision was made in Articles 103 and 192 for decision of such disputes by the

President/Governor in accordance with the opinion of the Election Commission. The reason is not far to seek.

181. The Speaker being an authority within the House and his tenure being dependent on the will of the majority therein, likelihood of suspicion of bias could not be ruled out. The question as to disqualification of a Member has adjudicatory disposition and, therefore, requires the decision to be rendered in consonance with the scheme for adjudication of disputes. Rule of law has in it firmly entrenched, natural justice, of which, rule against bias is a necessary concomitant; and basic postulates of rule against bias are: *nemo judex in causa sua*—'A Judge is disqualified from determining any case in which he may be, or may fairly be suspected to be, biased'; and 'it is of fundamental importance that justice should not only be done, but should manifestly and undoubtedly be seen to be done.' This appears to be the underlying principle adopted by the framers of the Constitution in not designating the Speaker as the authority to decide election disputes and questions as to disqualification of members under Articles 103, 192 and 329 and opting for an independent authority outside the House. The framers of the Constitution had in this manner kept the office of the Speaker away from this controversy. There is nothing unusual in this scheme if we bear in mind that the final authority for removal of a Judge of the Supreme Court and High Court is outside the judiciary in the Parliament under Article 124(4). On the same principle the authority to decide the question of disqualification of a Member of Legislature is outside the House as envisaged by Articles 103 and 192.

182. In the Tenth Schedule, the Speaker is made not only the sole but the final arbiter of such dispute with no provision for any appeal or revision against the Speaker's decision to any independent outside authority. This departure in the Tenth Schedule is a reverse trend and violates a basic feature of the Constitution since the Speaker cannot be treated as an authority contemplated for being entrusted with this function by the basic postulates of the Constitution, notwithstanding the great dignity attaching to that office with the attribute of impartiality.

183. It is the Vice-President of India who is ex-officio Chairman of the Rajya Sabha and his position, being akin to that of the President of India, is different from that of the Speaker. Nothing said herein relating to the office of the Speaker applies to the Chairman of the Rajya

Sabha, that is, the Vice-President of India. However, the only authority named for the Lok Sabha and the Legislative Assemblies is the Speaker of the House and entrustment of this adjudicatory function fouls with the constitutional scheme and, therefore, violates a basic feature of the Constitution. Remaining part of the Tenth Schedule also is rendered invalid notwithstanding the fact that this defect would not apply to the Rajya Sabha alone whose Chairman is the Vice-President of India, since the Tenth Schedule becomes unworkable for the Lok Sabha and the State Legislatures. The statutory exception of Doctrine of Necessity has no application since designation of authority in the Tenth Schedule is made by choice while enacting the legislation instead of adopting the other available options.

184. Since the conferment of authority is on the Speaker and that provision cannot be sustained for the reason given, even without Paragraph 7, the entire Tenth Schedule is rendered invalid in the absence of any valid authority for decision of the dispute.

185. Thus, even if the entire Tenth Schedule cannot be held unconstitutional merely on the ground of absence of ratification of the Bill, assuming it is permissible to strike down Paragraph 7 alone, the remaining part of the Tenth Schedule is rendered unconstitutional also on account of violation of the aforesaid basic feature. Irrespective of the view on the question of effect of absence of ratification, the entire Tenth Schedule must be struck down as unconstitutional.*

9. *TMA Pai Foundation & Ors. v. State of Karnataka* (2002)

In *TMA Pai Foundation & Ors. v. State of Karnataka & Ors.* (2002)[†] an eleven-judge bench was specially constituted in order to set at rest all

---

* In a recent judgment of *Keisham Meghachandra Singh v. Hon'ble Speaker Manipur Legislative Assembly and Ors.* (2020 SCC OnLine SC 55), a three-judge bench of the Supreme Court, after considering the experience of decisions by various Speakers in the recent past, came to the conclusion that this part of Verma, J.'s judgment was both correct and prophetic. The Supreme Court has therefore in *Keisham* called upon Parliament to amend the Constitution so as to replace the Speaker as the decision-making authority for disputes that fall within the Tenth Schedule, whether in Parliament or the state legislature, with a permanent election tribunal headed by a retired Supreme Court judge (*see* paragraph 31).

[†] (2002) 8 SCC 481.

controversies relating to admission of students in minority educational institutions, given the fundamental right contained in Article 30(1) of the Constitution of India. The majority judgment of six learned judges, delivered by Chief Justice B.N. Kirpal, found that an 'aided' minority educational institution would be entitled to admit students belonging to the particular minority group, but at the same time would be required to admit, to a reasonable extent, non-minority students, on a 'balancing' of the rights of all citizens under Article 29(2), and the fundamental right of minority institutions under Article 30(1) of the Constitution.

A separate judgment, authored by S.N. Variava, J., speaking for himself and Ashok Bhan, J., arrived at the conclusion that Article 29(2) would have to be given precedence over Article 30(1). The moment aid is received by a minority educational institution, it would then not be able to refuse admission to *any* citizen of India on the grounds of religion, race, caste, language or any of them. In other words, it cannot then give preference to students of its own community or group.

Ruma Pal, J. held the diametrically opposite view to that of Variava, J. and Bhan, J. This remarkable dissent, eloquent for both its reasoning, and the importance to be given to a fundamental right which is not subject to reasonable restrictions in the public interest, truly reflects the vision of the founding fathers of the Constitution of India.

The learned judge first begins with what is to be understood by the word 'secular':

331. The word 'secular' is commonly understood in contradistinction to the word 'religious'. The political philosophy of a secular government has been developed in the West in the historical context of the pre-eminence of the established Church and the exercise of power by it over society and its institutions. With the burgeoning presence of diverse religious groups and the growth of liberal and democratic ideas, religious intolerance and the attendant violence and persecution of 'non-believers' was replaced by a growing awareness of the right of the individual to profession of faith, or non-profession of any faith. The democratic State gradually replaced and marginalized the influence of the Church. But the meaning of the word 'secular State' in its political context can and has assumed different meanings in different countries, depending broadly on historical

and social circumstances, the political philosophy and the felt needs of a particular country. In one country, secularism may mean an actively negative attitude to all religions and religious institutions; in another it may mean a strict 'wall of separation' between the State and religion and religious institutions. In India the State is secular in that there is no official religion. India is not a theocratic State. However the Constitution does envisage the involvement of the State in matters associated with religion and religious institutions, and even indeed with the practice, profession and propagation of religion in its most limited and distilled meaning.

332. Although the idea of secularism may have been borrowed in the Indian Constitution from the West, it has adopted its own unique brand of secularism based on its particular history and exigencies which are far removed in many ways from secularism as it is defined and followed in European countries, the United States of America and Australia.'

The learned judge therefore concludes that the Constitution of India, as it stands, does not proceed on the 'melting pot' theory, but rather represents a 'salad bowl', where there is homogeneity, without an obliteration of identity.* Going on to distinguish the US Constitution from the Indian Constitution, the learned judge then refers to Articles 27 and 28 of the Constitution of India, finding no wall of separation between the Church and the state, as in the United States, observing:

344. In the ultimate analysis the Indian Constitution does not unlike the United States, subscribe to the principle of non-interference of the State in religious organizations but it remains secular in that it strives to respect all religions equally, the equality being understood in its substantive sense as is discussed in the subsequent paragraphs.

In a closely reasoned analysis of the various facets of Article 30(1), the learned judge finds:

350. The question then is does this special right in an admitted linguistic or religious minority to establish and administer an educational

---

* Ibid., paragraph 340.

institution encompass the right to admit students belonging to that particular community?

351. Before considering the earlier decisions on this, a semantic analysis of the words used in Article 30(1) indicates that the right to admit students is an intrinsic part of Article 30(1).

352. First—Article 30(1) speaks of the right to set up an educational institution. An educational institution is not a structure of bricks and mortar. It is the activity which is carried on in the structure which gives it its character as an educational institution. An educational institution denotes the process or activity of education not only involving the educators but also those receiving education. It follows that the right to set up an educational institution necessarily includes not only the selection of teachers or educators but also the admission of students.

353. Second—Article 30(1) speaks of the right to 'administer' an educational institution. If the administration of an educational institution includes and means its organization then the organization cannot be limited to the infrastructure for the purposes of education and exclude the persons for whom the infrastructure is set up, namely, the students. The right to admit students is, therefore, part of the right to administer an educational institution.

354. Third—the benefit which has been guaranteed under Article 30 is a protection or benefit guaranteed to all members of the minority as a whole. What is protected is the community right which includes the right of children of the minority community to receive education and the right of parents to have their children educated in such institution. The content of the right lies not in merely managing an educational institution but doing so for the benefit of the community. Benefit can only lie in the education received. It would be meaningless to give the minorities the right to establish and set up an organization for giving education as an end in itself, and deny them the benefit of the education. This would render the right a mere form without any content. The benefit to the community and the purpose of the grant of the right is in the actual education of the members of the community.

355. Finally—the words 'of their choice' is not qualified by any words of limitation and would include the right to admit students of the minority's choice. Since the primary purpose of Article 30(1) is to give

the benefit to the members of the minority community in question that 'choice' cannot be exercised in a manner that deprives the community of the benefit. Therefore, the choice must be directed towards fulfilling the needs of the community. How that need is met, whether by general education or otherwise, is for the community to determine.

Finding then that Article 30(2) also reinforces the position that the receipt of aid makes no difference to the reach of the fundamental right contained in Article 30(1), the learned judge holds:

363. An institution set up by minorities for educating members of the minority community does not cease to be a minority institution merely because it takes aid. There is nothing in Article 30(1) which allows the drawing of a distinction in the exercise of the right under that article between needy minorities and affluent ones. Article 30(2) of the Constitution reinforces this when it says:

'30. (2) The State shall not, in granting aid to educational institutions, discriminate against any educational institution on the ground that it is under the management of a minority, whether based on religion or language.'

This assumes that even after the grant-of-aid by the State to an educational institution under the management of the minority, the educational institution continues to be a minority educational institution. According to some, Article 30(2) merely protects the minority's right of management of the educational institution and not the students who form part of such institution. Such a reading would be contrary to Article 30(1) itself. The argument is based on the construction of the word 'management'. 'Management' may be defined as 'the process of managing' and is not limited to the people managing the institution. In the context of Article 30(1) and having regard to the content of the right, namely, the education of the minority community, the word 'management' in Article 30(2) must be construed to mean the 'process' and not the 'persons' in management. 'Aid' by definition means to give support or to help or assist. It cannot be that by giving 'aid' one destroys those to whom 'aid' is given. The obvious purpose of Article 30(2) is to forbid the State from refusing aid to a minority educational institution merely because it is being run as a minority educational institution. Besides, Article 30(2) is an additional right conferred on minorities under Article 30(1). It cannot be construed in a manner which is destructive of or as a limitation on Article 30(1). As has been said earlier by this Court in *Rev. Sidhajbhai Sabhai* clause (2) of Article 30 is only another non-discriminatory clause in the Constitution. It is a right in addition to the rights under Article 30(1) and does not operate to derogate from the provisions in clause (1). When in decision after decision, this Court has held that aid in whatever form is necessary for an educational institution to survive, it is a specious argument to say that a minority institution can preserve its rights under Article 30(1) by refusing aid.

Coming to the most difficult aspect of the case, namely, the interplay of Articles 29(2) and 30(1), the learned judge holds:

369. To the extent that legislation is enacted under Article 15(4) making special provision in respect of a particular caste, there is a denial of admission to others who do not belong to that caste. Nevertheless, Article 15(4) does not contradict the right under Article 29(2). This is because of the use of the word 'only' in Article 29(2). Article 15(4) is based on the rationale that Scheduled Castes and Tribes are not on a par with other members of society in the matter of education and, therefore, special provision is to be made for them. It is not, therefore, only caste but this additional factor which prevents clause 15(4) from conflicting with Article 29(2) and Article 14.

370. Then again, under Article 337, grants are made available for the benefit of the Anglo-Indian community in respect of education, provided that any educational institution receiving such grant makes available at least 40 per cent of the annual admissions for members of communities other than the Anglo-Indian community. Hence 60 per cent of the admission to an aided Anglo-Indian school is constitutionally reservable for members of the Anglo-Indian community. To the extent of such reservation, there is necessarily a denial of admission to non-Anglo-Indians on the basis of race.

371. Similarly, the Constitution has also carved out a further exception to Article 29(2) in the form of Article 30(1) by recognizing the rights of special classes in the form of minorities based on language

or religion to establish and administer educational institutions of their choice. The right of the minorities under Article 30(1) does not operate as discrimination against other citizens only on the ground of religion or language. The reason for such classification is not only religion or language per se but minorities based on religion and language. Although, it is not necessary to justify a classification made by the Constitution, this fact of 'minorityship' is the obvious rationale for making a distinction, the underlying assumption being that minorities by their very numbers are in a politically disadvantaged situation and require special protection at least in the field of education.

372. Articles 15(4), 337 and 30 are therefore facets of substantive equality by making special provision for special classes on special considerations.

373. Even on general principles of interpretation, it cannot be held that Article 29(2) is absolute and in effect wipes out Article 30(1). Article 29(2) refers to 'any educational institution'—the word 'any' signifying the generality of its application. Article 30(1) on the other hand refers to 'educational institutions established and administered by minorities'. Clearly, the right under Article 30(1) is the more particular right and on the principle of generalia specialibus non derogant, it must be held that Article 29(2) does not override the educational institutions even if they are aided under Article 30(1).

374. Then again Article 29(2) appears under the heading 'Protection of interests of minorities'. Whatever the historical reasons for the placement of Article 29(2) under this head, it is clear that on general principles of interpretation, the heading is at least a pointer or aid in construing the meaning of Article 29(2). As Subba Rao, J. said: 'if there is any doubt in the interpretation of the words in the section, the heading certainly helps us to resolve that doubt.' Therefore, if two interpretations of the words of Article 29(2) are possible, the one which is in keeping with the heading of the article must be preferred. It would follow that Article 29(2) must be construed in a manner protective of minority interests and not destructive of them.

375. When 'aid' is sought for by the minority institution to run its institution for the benefit of students belonging to that particular community, the argument on the basis of Article 29(2) is that if such

an institution asks for aid it does so at the peril of depriving the very persons for whom aid was asked for in the first place. Apart from this anomalous result, if the taking of aid implies that the minority institution will be forced to give up or waive its right under Article 30(1), then on the principle that it is not permissible to give up or waive fundamental rights, such an interpretation is not possible. It has then been urged that Article 29(2) applies to minority institutions under Article 30(1) much in the same way that Articles 28(1) and 28(3) do. The argument proceeds on the assumption that an educational institution set up under Article 30(1) is set up for the purposes and with the sole object of giving religious instruction. The assumption is wrong. At the outset, it may also be noted that Articles 28(1) and (3) do not in terms apply to linguistic minority educational institutions at all. Furthermore, the right to set up an educational institution in which religious instruction is to be imparted is a right which is derived from Article 26(a) which provides that every religious denomination or any section thereof shall have the right to establish and maintain institutions for religious and charitable purposes, and not under Article 30(1). Educational institutions set up under Article 26(a) are, therefore, subject to clauses (1) and (3) of Article 28. Article 30(1) is a right additional to Article 26(a). This follows from the fact that it has been separately and expressly provided for and there is nothing in the language of Article 30(1) making the right thereunder subject to Articles 25 and 26. Unless it is so construed Article 30(1) would be rendered redundant. Therefore, what Article 30 does is to secure the minorities the additional right to give general education. Although in a particular case a minority educational institution may combine general education with religious instruction that is done in exercise of the rights derivable from Article 26(a) and Article 30(1) and not under Article 30(1) alone. Clauses (1) and (3) of Article 28, therefore, do not apply to Article 30(1). The argument in support of reading Article 30(1) as being subject to Article 29(2) on the analogy of Articles 28(1) and 28(3) is, I would think, erroneous.'

The conclusion is then reached:

376. For the reasons already stated I have held the right to admit minority students to a minority educational institution is an intrinsic

part of Article 30(1). To say that Article 29(2) prevails over Article 30(1) would be to infringe and to a large extent wipe out this right. There would be no distinction between a minority educational institution and other institutions and the rights under Article 30(1) would be rendered wholly inoperational. It is no answer to say that the rights of unaided minority institutions would remain untouched because Article 29(2) does not relate to unaided institutions at all. Whereas if one reads Article 29(2) as subject to Article 30(1) then effect can be given to both. And it is the latter approach which is to be followed in the interpretation of constitutional provisions. In other words, as long as the minority educational institution is being run for the benefit of and catering to the needs of the members of that community under Article 30(1), Article 29(2) would not apply. But once the minority educational institution travels beyond the needs in the sense of requirements of its own community, at that stage it is no longer exercising rights of admission guaranteed under Article 30(1). To put it differently, when the right of admission is exercised not to meet the need of the minorities, the right of admission given under Article 30(1) is to that extent removed and the institution is bound to admit students for the balance in keeping with the provisions of Article 29(2).

Given this conclusion, it is clear that both Articles 29(2) and 30(1) are harmonized by stating that when aid is received by a minority educational institution, Article 29(2) would only apply to the extent that non-minority students are admitted to the minority educational institution, such admission being within the sole discretion of the minority educational institution.

Coming to the rights of linguistic minorities, the learned judge held:

382. I need only add that the rights of linguistic minorities assumed special significance and support when, much after independence, the imposition of a 'unifying language' led not to unity but to an assertion of differences. States were formed on linguistic bases showing the apparent paradox that allowing for and protecting differences leads to unity and integrity and enforced assimilation may lead to disaffection and unrest. The recognition of the principle of 'unity in diversity' has continued to

be the hallmark of the Constitution—a concept which has been further strengthened by affording further support to the protection of minorities on linguistic bases in 1956 by way of Articles 350-A and 350-B and in 1978 by introducing clause (1-A) in Article 30 requiring

'the State, that is to say, Parliament in the case of a Central legislation or a State Legislature in the case of State legislation, to make a specific law to provide for the compulsory acquisition of the property of minority educational institutions, the provisions of which law should ensure that the amount payable to the educational institution for the acquisition of its property will not be such as will in any manner impair the functioning of the educational institution'.

Any judicial interpretation of the provisions of the Constitution whereby this constitutional diversity is diminished would be contrary to this avowed intent and the political considerations which underlie this intention.

Dealing with *Re: Kerala Education Bill* (1959),* the learned judge held:

383. The earlier decisions of this Court show that the issue of admission to a minority educational institution almost invariably arose in the context of the State claiming that a minority institution had to be 'purely' one which was established and administered by members of the minority community concerned, strictly for the members of the minority community, with the object only of preserving of the minority religion, language, script or culture. The contention on the part of the executive then was that a minority institution could not avail of the protection of Article 30(1) if there was any non-minority element either in the establishment, administration, admission or subjects taught. It was in that context that the Court in Kerala Education Bill, 1957 held that a 'sprinkling of outsiders' being admitted into a minority institution did not result in the minority institution shedding its character and ceasing to be a minority institution. It was also in that context that the Court in St. Xavier's College came to the conclusion that a minority institution based on religion and language had the right to establish and administer

---

* (1959) SCR 995.

educational institution for imparting general secular education and still not lose its minority character. While the effort of the executive was to retain the 'purity' of a minority institution and thereby to limit it, 'the principle which can be discerned in the various decisions of this Court is that the catholic approach which led to the drafting of the provisions relating to minority rights should not be set at naught by narrow judicial interpretation'

The striking of a 'balance' between Articles 29(2) and 30(1), as was done by the majority judgment, was expressly disapproved, as follows:

386. There is thus no question of striking a balance between Articles 29(2) and 30(1) as if they were two competing rights. Where once the Court has held:

'Equality of opportunity for unequals can only mean aggravation of inequality. Equality of opportunity admits discrimination with reason and prohibits discrimination without reason. Discrimination with reasons means rational classification for differential treatment having nexus to the constitutionally permissible object.'

and where Article 29(2) is nothing more than a principle of equality, and when

'the whole object of conferring the right on minorities under Article 30 is to ensure that there will be equality between the majority and the minority, if the minorities do not have such special protection they will be denied equality'

it must follow that Article 29(2) is subject to the constitutional classification of minorities under Article 30(1).

The learned judge then concludes, stating:

388. I agree with the view as expressed by the learned Chief Justice that there is no question of fixing a percentage when the need may be variable. I would only add that in fixing a percentage, the Court in St. Stephen's in fact 'reserved' 50 per cent of available seats in a minority institution for the general category ostensibly under Article 29(2). Article 29(2) pertains to the right of an individual and is not a class

right. It would therefore apply when an individual is denied admission into any educational institution maintained by the State or receiving aid from the State funds, solely on the basis of the ground of religion, race, caste, language or any of them. It does not operate to create a class interest or right in the sense that any educational institution has to set apart for non-minorities as a class and without reference to any individual applicant, a fixed percentage of available seats. Unless Articles 30(1) and 29(2) are allowed to operate in their separate fields then what started with the voluntary 'sprinkling' of outsiders, would become a major inundation and a large chunk of the right of an aided minority institution to operate for the benefit of the community it was set up to serve, would be washed away.

389. Apart from this difference with the views expressed by the majority view on the interpretation of Article 29(2) and Article 30(1), I am also unable to concur in the mode of determining the need of a minority community for admission to an educational institution set up by such community. Whether there has been a violation of Article 29(2) in refusing admission to a non-minority student in a particular case must be resolved as it has been in the past by recourse to the courts. It must be emphasized that the right under Article 29(2) is an individual one. If the non-minority student is otherwise eligible for admission, the decision on the issue of refusal would depend on whether the minority institution is able to establish that the refusal was only because it was satisfying the requirements of its own community under Article 30(1). I cannot therefore subscribe to the view expressed by the majority that the requirement of the minority community for admission to a minority educational institution should be left to the State or any other governmental authority to determine. If the executive is given the power to determine the requirements of the minority community in the matter of admission to its educational institutions, we would be subjecting the minority educational institution in question to an 'intolerable encroachment' on the right under Article 30(1) and let in by the back door as it were, what should be denied entry altogether.

INDEX OF CASES

S.NO.	PARTICULARS	CITATION	PAGE NO.
1.	A. and J. Mucklow Ltd. v. IRC	(1954) Ch.615	201
2.	A.K. Gopalan v. State of Madras	1950 SCR 88	118,231
3.	A.R. Antulay v. R.S. Nayak & Anr.	(1988) 2 SCC 602	380
4.	A.V. Venkateswaran, Collector of Customs, Bombay v. Ramchand Sobharj Wadhwani	(1962) 1 SCR 753	325
5.	Abrams v. United States	250 U.S. 616 (1919)	33
6.	Additional Collector of Bombay and Lachhman Das v. State of Punjab	(1963) 2 SCR 353	279
7.	Additional District Magistrate, Jabalpur v. Shivakant Shukla (ADM Jabalpur)	(1976) 2 SCC 521	96
8.	ADM, Jabalpur v. Shivakant Shukla	(1976) 2 SCC 521	120
9.	Ahmedabad Municipal Corporation and others v. Ramanlal Govindram and Others	(1975) 3 SCR 935	285

10.	Ahmedabad St. Xavier's College Society v. State of Gujarat	(1974) 1 SCC 717	155-156,158-159
11.	Ajay Hasia v. Khalid Mujib Sehravardi & Ors.	(1981) 1 SCC 722	192
12.	Ajoy Kumar Mukerjee v. Local Board of Barpeta	(1965) 3 SCR 47	205
13.	A.K. Gopalan v. State of Madras	(1950) SCR 88	118,231
14.	Al-Kateb v. Godwin	[2004] HCA 37	22
15.	Alpha Cement Company v. Massachusetts	268 U.S. 203 (1925)	30
16.	Alton v. Midland Rly Co.	(1865) 19 C.B., N.S. 213	61
17.	Anderton v. Ryan	[1985] AC 560	86
18.	Anisminic Ltd. v Foreign Compensation Commission	(1969) 2 AC 147	382
19.	Anwar Ali Sarkar v. State of West Bengal	(1952) SCR 284	385
20.	Ashby v. White	(1703) 92 ER 126	38
21.	Ashok Kumar Sharma & Anr. v. Chander Shekhar & Anr.	(1993) Supp. 2 SCC 611	300
22.	Ashok Kumar Sharma & Ors. v. Chander Shekhar & Anr.	(1997) 4 SCC 18	302
23.	Associated Cement Co. Ltd. v. Commercial Tax Officer, Kota & Ors.	(1981) 4 SCC 578	288
24.	Atiabari Tea Co. Ltd. v. State of Assam and Ors.	(1961) 1 SCR 809	249
25.	Atkins v. Virginia	536 U.S. 304 (2002)	78
26.	Attorney General v. Guardian Papers Ltd.	(1987) 3 All ER 316	72
27.	Attorney-General for N.S.W. v. Perpetual Trustee Co. Ltd.	[1940] HCA 12	132
28.	Automobile Transport (Rajasthan) Ltd. v. The State of Rajasthan and Others	(1963) 1 SCR 491	253,344

29.	Baburao Shantaram More v. Bombay Housing Board	1954 SCR 572	279
30.	Bachan Singh v. State of Punjab	(1980) 2 SCC 684	361
31.	Baker v. Carr	369 U.S. 186 (1962)	32
32.	Baltic Mining Company v. Massachusetts	231 U.S. 68 (1913)	30
33.	Assistant Commissioner, Assessment (ii), Bangalore & Ors. v. M/s. Velliappa Textiles Ltd. & Anr.	(2003) 11 SCC 405	215
34.	Bangalore Water Supply & Sewerage Board, etc. v. R. Rajappa	(1978) 2 SCC 213	166-72
35.	Barnard v. Gorman	[141] AC 378	66
36.	Ben Gorm Nilgiri Plantations Co. v. Sales Tax Officer	(1964) 7 SCR 706	287
37.	Bengal Immunity Co. Ltd. v. State of Bihar and Ors.	(1955) 2 SCR 603	38,125-40,243
38.	Bengal Nagpur Railway Co. Ltd. v. Ruttanji Ramji	AIR 1938 PC 67	294
39.	Bernheimer v. Converse	206 U.S. 516,535 (1907)	17
40.	Betts v. Brady	316 U.S. 455 (1942)	32
41.	Bhagat Raja v. The Union of India & Ors.	[1967] 3 SCR 302	277
42.	Bhagwandas Goverdhandas Kedia v. Girdharilal Parshottamdas and Co.	[1966] 1 SCR 656	147-52
43.	Gursahai Saigal v. CIT, Punjab	(1963) 3 SCR 893	294
44.	Ben Gorm Nilgiri Plantations Co. v. Sales Tax Officer	(1964) 7 SCR 706	287
45.	Bonsor v. Musicians' Union	1956 A.C. 104	201
46.	Bowditch v. Balchin	[1850] 5 Exch 278	66
47.	Bradley Egg Farm Ltd. v. Clifford and Ors.	(1943) 2 All ER 378	34
48.	Brenham v. German American Bank	144 U.S. 173 (1892)	30

49.	Brij Bhushan v. State of Delhi	(1950) SCR 605	231,241,338
50.	Briscoe v. Bank of Kentucky	36 U.S. 257 (1837)	19
51.	British Coal Corp. v. The King	1935 AC 500	9
52.	Brown v. Board of Education	347 U.S. 483 (1954)	32
53.	Bryers v. Canadian Pacific Steamships Ltd.	(1957) 1 QB 134	201
54.	Buck v. Bell	274 U.S. 200 (1927)	116
55.	Builders Supply Corporation v. Union of India	(1957) ILR 2Cal 897	278
56.	Queen v. Burah	(1878) UKPC 26	5
57.	C.I.R. v. Carron Co.	1967 S.C (H.L.) 47,61	18
58.	Burdett v. Abbot	(1811) 14 East 1	147
59.	Canadian Pacific Steamships Ltd. v. Bryers	[1957] 3 All ER 572	201
60.	Candler v. Crane, Christmas and Co.	(1951) 2 K.B. 164	37
61.	Carlill v. Carbolic Smoke Ball Co.	[1892] EWCA Civ 1	149, 60-69,89-96, 104-108,145-147, 149-152,185-198,200-202, 275-277,280-283,285-287,290-297,311-312,320-323,363-367,382-389
62.	Cassell & Co. v. Broome	[1972] 2 WLR 645	381
63.	Central Board of Dawoodi Bohra Community and Anr. v. State of Maharashtra and Anr.	(2005) 2 SCC 673	322
64.	Central Provinces Manganese Ore Co. Ltd. v. CIT	1986 SCR (3) 140	294
65.	Chester v. Bateson	1920 1 K.B. 829	55-56

66.	CIT v. M. Chandra Sekhar	1985 SCR (2) 215	294
67.	CIT v. Mahaliram Ramjidas	(1940) 42 BOMLR 997	294
68.	Coffee Board v. Joint Commercial Tax Officer	(1969) 3 SCC 349	286
69.	Coffee Board, Bangalore v. JCT, Madras	(1969) 3 SCC 349	39,286
70.	Colegrove v. Green	319 U.S. 624 (1943)	32
71.	Collector of Malabar v. Erimal Ebrahim Hajee	[1962] 2 SCR 324	279
72.	Cooper v. Aaron	358 U.S. 1 (1958)	25
73.	In Re: Delhi Laws Act	(1951) 2 SCR 747	5
74.	Dennis v. United States	341 U.S. 494 (1951)	32
75.	Devender Pal Singh v. State of NCT of Delhi	(2002) 5 SCC 234	377
76.	Di Santo v. Pennsylvania	273 U.S. 34 (1927)	16
77.	Director of Rationing and Distribution v. The Corporation of Calcutta	(1961) 1 SCR 158	107,152,245,248
78.	Donoghue v. Stevenson	[1932] A.C. 562	38
79.	Doyle v. Continental Insurance Company	94 U.S. 535 (1876)	30
80.	Dr Ram Manohar Lohia v. State of Bihar	(1966) 1 SCR 709	105
81.	Dred Scott v. Sandford	60 U.S. 393 (1957)	75
82.	Elder, Dempster and Co Ltd v Paterson, Zochonis and Co Ltd	[1924] AC 522	61
83.	Entores Ltd. v. Miles Far East Corp.	(1955) 2 QBD 327	148
84.	Fabrigas v. Mostyn	(1774) 1 Cowp 161	106
85.	Farey v. Burvett	(1916) HCA 36	86
86.	Federal Trade Commission v. Beech-Nut Packing Co.	257 U.S. 441 (1922)	17
87.	'First Judges' case—S.P. Gupta and Ors. v. Union of India and Ors.	(1981) Supp. SCC 87	172,177,179

88.	Rajnarain Singh v. Chairman, Patna Administration Committee	(1955) 1 SCR 290	5
89.	Florida v. Royer	460 U.S. 491 (1983)	75
90.	Furman v. Georgia	408 U.S.238 (1972)	366,377
91.	The Gandhi Faiz-E-Am College, Shahjahanpur v. University of Agra and Ors	(1975) 2 SCC 283	155-60
92.	Gaurav Jain v. Union of India	(1997) 8 SCC 114	304
93.	Gaurav Jain v. Union of India	(1998) 4 SCC 270	307
94.	Ghasilal v The State of Rajasthan	1968 (1) WLN 31	292-293
95.	Gideon v. Wainwright	372 U.S. 335 (1963)	32
96.	Golak Nath v. State of Punjab	(1967) 2 SCR 762	331,355,360
97.	Granatino v. Radmacher	(2010) UKSC 42	63
98.	Grovey v. Townsend	295 U.S. 45 (1935)	27
99.	Guardians of the Poor of the West Derby Union v. Guardians of the Poor of the Atcham Union	(1889) 24 QBD 117	278
100.	Gurbachan Singh v. State of Bombay	1952 SCR 737	278
101.	Habeas Corpus case	(1976) 2 SCC 521	119
102.	Hammer v. Dagenhart	247 U.S. 251 (1918)	38
103.	Hanover fire Insurance Co. v. Harding	272 U.S. 494 (1926)	30
104.	Hari Singh v. Military Estate Officer	(1972) 2 SCC 239	281
105.	Hasanali v. Mansoorali	AIR 1948 PC 66	317,320-321
106.	Henry v. A.B. Dick Company	224 U.S. 1 (1912)	30
107.	Himmatlal Harilal Mehta v. State of Madhya Pradesh	(1954) 1 SCR 1122	131
108.	Hingir Rampur Coal Co. Ltd. v. State of Orissa	(1961) 2 SCR 537	204-5
109.	Hirabayashi v United States	320 U.S. 81 (1943)	89-90
110.	Huddersfield Police Authority v. Watson	(1947) 2 All ER 193	201

111.	I.C. Golaknath & Ors. V. State of Punjab & Anr.	(1967) 2 SCR 762	274,331
112.	I.R. Coelho v. State of T.N.	(2007) 2 SCC 1	120
113.	I.T.C. Limited v. Agricultural Produce Market Committee & Ors.	(2002) 9 SCC 232	185-91,297
114.	I.T.C. Ltd. v. State of Karnataka and Ors.	(1985) Supp. SCC 476	185,295,300
115.	Ichikawa v. Japan	15 KEISHU 7, 1106 (Sup. Ct., July 19, 1961), translated in THE CONSTITUTIONAL CASE LAW OF JAPAN: SELECTED SUPREME COURT DECISIONS, 1961-70, at 161-164 (Hiroshi Itoh & Lawrence Ward Beer eds., 1978)	368
116.	India Cement Ltd. v. State of Tamil Nadu	(1990) 1 SCC 12	203
117.	India United Mills Ltd. v. Commissioner of Excess Profits Tax	[1955] 1 SCR 810	294
118.	Indian Young Lawyers Association and Ors. v. State of Kerala and Ors.	(2019) 11 SCC 1	323
119.	Indira Nehru Gandhi v. Raj Narain & Anr.	(1976) 2 SCR 347	155,360
120.	Indra Sawhney v. Union of India	(1992) Supp 3 SCC 217	166,269
121.	Inland Revenue Commissioners v. Rossminster Ltd.	(1980) AC 952	71
122.	I.R. Coelho v. State of T.N.	(1997) 7 SCC 580	120
123.	I.T.C. Limited v. Agricultural Produce Market Committee & Ors	(2002) 9 SCC 232	185-191,297,299

124.	Jackson v. Metropolitan Edison Co.	419 U.S. 345 (1974)	40
125.	Jagdish v. State of Madhya Pradesh	(2020) 14 SCC 156	228
126.	J.K. Synthetics Ltd. v. Commercial Taxes Officer	(1994) 4 SCC 276	291
127.	Jackson v. Metropolitan Edison Co.	419 U.S. 345 (1974)	40
128.	James v. Commonwealth	[1939] HCA 9; 62 CLR 339	137
129.	Jindal Stainless Steel v. State of Haryana	(2017) 12 SCC 1	254
130.	Justice K.S. Puttaswamy (Retd.) v. Union of India	(2017) 10 SCC 1	115
131.	K.G. Khosla & Co. v. Deputy Commissioner of Commercial Taxes	(1966) 17 STC 473	286
132.	K.K. Narula v. State of Jammu and Kashmir & Ors.	(1967) 3 SCR 50	198
133.	Kailash Nath & Anr. v. State of U.P. & Ors.	AIR 1957 SC 790	323
134.	Kalyani Stores v. State of Orissa and Ors.	(1966) 1 SCR 865	197,198-200,202
135.	Kantaru Rajeevaru v. Indian Young Lawyers Association and Ors.	(2020) 2 SCC 1	323
136.	Kartar Singh v. State of Punjab	(1991) 2 SCC 635	311
137.	Katz v. United States	389 U.S. 347 (1967)	32
138.	Kavasji Pestonji Dalal v. Rustomji Sorabji Jamadar	AIR 1949 Bom 42	385
139.	Keisham Meghachandra Singh v. Hon'ble Speaker Manipur Legislative Assembly and Ors.	2020 SCC OnLine SC 55	404
140.	Kesavananda Bharati Sripadagalvaru & Ors. v. State of Kerala & Anr.	(1973) 4 SCC 225	274,344

141.	Keshav Singh v Speaker, Legislative Assembly & Ors.	AIR 1965 All 349	143
142.	Kewal Krishan Puri v. State of Punjab	(1979) 3 SCR 1217	295
143.	Kharak Singh v. State of U.P. & Ors.	(1964) 1 SCR 332	262,266
144.	Kihoto Hollohan v. Zachillhu & Ors.	(1992) Supp. (2) SCC 651	
145.	King v. Burwell	576 U.S. 988 (2015)	79
146.	Konkan Railway Corpn. Ltd. & Ors v. M/s. Mehul Construction Co.	(2000) 7 SCC 201	219
147.	Konkan Railway Corporation Ltd. & Anr. v. Rani Construction Pvt. Ltd.	(2002) 2 SCC 388	217-18
148.	Korematsu v. United States	323 U.S. 214 (1944)	88,94-95,116
149.	Krishna Mochi and Ors. v. State of Bihar	(2002) 6 SCC 81	377
150.	Lancaster Motor Co. (London) Ltd. v. Bremith Ltd.	(1941) 1 KB 675: (1941) 2 All ER 11 CA	201
151.	Lee v. Weisman	505 U.S. 304 (2002)	78
152.	Livermore v. E.G. Waite	102 Cal. 113 (1894)	339
153.	Liversidge v. Sir John Anderson	(1941) UKHL 1	27,57,69,71-72,110,238-39
154.	Lochner v. State of New York	198 U.S. 45 (1905)	16
155.	Loh Wai Kong v. Government of Malaysia	(1979) 2 MLJ 33	41
156.	M. Nagaraj and Ors. v. Union of India and Ors.	(2006) 8 SCC 212	166
157.	M. Nagaraj v. Union of India	(2010) 12 SCC 526	117
158.	M.C. Mehta v. Union of India	(1987) 1 SCC 395	195
159.	M.R. Balaji v. State of Mysore	1963 Supp (1) SCR 439	165
160.	M/s New India Sugar Mills Ltd. v. Commissioner of Sales Tax, Bihar	(1963) Supp. (2) SCR 459	258
161.	MacLeod v. MacLeod	[2008] UKPC 64, [2010] 1 AC 298	64

162.	Madhya Pradesh Industries Ltd. v. Union of India	(1966) 1 SCR 466	274,277
163.	Mafatlal Industries v. Union of India	(1997) 5 SCC 536	181-84
164.	Maganlal Chhagganlal (P) Ltd. v. Municipal Corporation of Greater Bombay & Ors.	(1975) 1 SCR 1	280,285
165.	Mahnich v. Southern S.S.	321 U.S. 96 (1944)	25
166.	Makhan Singh v. State of Punjab	(1964) 4 SCR 797	104
167.	Management of Safdarjung Hospital, New Delhi v. Kuldip Singh Sethi	(1970) 1 SCC 735	169
168.	Maneka Gandhi v. Union of India	(1978) 1 SCC 248	118,241,266
169.	Manohar Lal Chopra v. Rai Bahadur Rao Raja Seth Hiralal	(1962) Supp. (1) SCR 450	140-42
170.	McCawley v. King	(1920) 28 CLR 106	345,354
171.	McCleskey v. Kemp	481 U.S. 279 (1987)	378
172.	M.C. Mehta v. Union of India	(1987) 1 SCC 395	195
173.	Md. Mannan v. State of Bihar	(2019) SCC OnLine 737	228
174.	Millar v. Taylor	(1769) 4 Burrows 2303,2395	25
175.	Mineral Area Development Authority v. Steel Authority of India and Ors.	(2011) 4 SCC 450	208
176.	Minersville School District v. Gobitis	301 U.S. 586 (1940)	32
177.	Minerva Mills v. Union of India	(1981) 1 SCR 206	344
178.	Mohd. Arif v. The Registrar, Supreme Court of India & Ors.	(2014) 9 SCC 737	224,227
179.	Mohd. Hanif Quareshi v. State of Bihar	(1959) SCR 629	209
180.	Kunnathat Thathunni Moopil Nair v. The State of Kerala and Ors.	(1961) 3 SCR 77	205

181.	Morelle Ltd. v. Wakeling	(1955) 2 QB 379	201
182.	Morrison v. Olson	487 U.S. 654 (1988)	77
183.	Moti Lal v. Government of the State of Uttar Pradesh	(1979) 4 SCC 343	338
184.	Motion Picture Patents Company v. Universal Film Company	243 U.S. 502 (1917)	30
185.	M.R. Balaji v. State of Mysore	(1963) Supp 1 SCR 439	165
186.	Mr Fazlul Quader Chowdhry v. Mr. Mohd. Abdul Haque	1963 PLC 486	272
187.	M/s New India Sugar Mills Ltd. v. Commissioner of Sales Tax, Bihar	(1963) Supp. (2) SCR 459	258
188.	Nakkuda Ali v. Jayaratne	(1951) A.C. 66	71
189.	Naresh Shridhar Mirajkar and Ors. v. State of Maharashtra and Anr.	(1966) 3 SCR 744	329,387,388
190.	National Insurance Co. Ltd. v. Boghara Polyfab (P) Ltd.	(2009) 1 SCC 267	222
191.	National Prohibition Cases	253 U.S. 350 (1920)	339
192.	National Union of Commercial Employees v. M.R. Meher	AIR 1962 SC 1080	168
193.	Nav Rattanmal v. State of Rajasthan	(1962) 2 SCR 324	278-79
194.	New India Sugar Mills Ltd. v. Commissioner of Sales Tax, Bihar	(1963) Supp. (2) SCR 459	258
195.	Nicholas v. Penny	(1950) 66 T.L.R. 1122	201
196.	Northern India Caterers Private Ltd., & Anr. v. State of Punjab	(1967) 3 SCR 399	278,281-82,284
197.	Northern Securities Company v. The United States	193 U.S. 197 (1903)	15
198.	Obergefell v. Hodges	576 U.S. 644 (2015)	82
199.	Oliver v. City of Raleigh	193 S.E. 853 (1937)	36
200.	Olmstead v. United States	277 U.S. 483 (1928)	32

201.	Overseers of Manchester v. Guardians of Ormskirk Union	(1890) 24 QBD 678	7
202.	P. Ramachandra Rao v. State of Karnataka	(2002) 4 SCC 578	310
203.	P.N. Eswara Iyer v. The Registrar, Supreme Court of India	(1980) 4 SCC 680	225
204.	P.V. Narsimha Rao v. State	(1998) 4 SCC 626	390
205.	Padam Sen v. State of Uttar Pradesh	(1961) 1 SCR 884	140,141
206.	Pandit M.S.M. Sharma v. Shri Sri Krishna Sinha and Ors.	(1959) Supp. (1) SCR 806	144,145,146
207.	Pasley v. Freeman	100 Eng. Rep. 450 (K.B. 1789)	38
208.	PGA Tour, Inc. v. Martin	532 U.S. 661 (2001)	77
209.	Pickering v. John Tye & Son Ltd.	163 U.S. 537 (1896)	18
210.	Plessy v. Ferguson	163 U.S. 537 (1896)	31,36-37
211.	Re: Powers, Privileges and Immunities of State Legislatures	(1965) 1 SCR 413	142-47
212.	Prabhakar Kesheo Tare v. Emperor	AIR 1943 Nag. 26	97
213.	Pradeep Kumar Biswas v. Indian Institute of Chemical Biology & Ors.	(2002) 5 SCC 111	191-97
214.	Prebble v. Television New Zealand Ltd.	(1994) 3 NZLR 1	394
215.	Prem Chand Garg v. Excise Commissioner, U.P.	1963 Supp (1) SCR 885	308,387
216.	Province of Bombay v. Municipal Corporation of the City of Bombay	AIR 1944 Bom 26	246-47
217.	Purshottam Govindji Halai v. Shree B.M. Desai	(1955) 2 SCR 887	279
218.	R. v. Murphy	5 NSWLR 18 (1986)	393-94
219.	Rajendra Prasad v. State of Uttar Pradesh	(1979) 3 SCR 78	364,367,370,378

220.	Ramana Dayaram Shetty Vs. International Airport Authority of India and Ors.	(1979) 3 SCR 1014	193
221.	Ramkrit Singh and Ors. Vs.The State of Bihar and Ors.	1979 (1) PLJR 161	202
222.	R. v. Secretary of State for the Home Department, Ex parte Simms	(1999) UKHL 33	56
223.	R.C. Cooper v. Union of India	(1970) 3 SCR 530	240-41,267
224.	R.D. Shetty v. International Airport Authority of India	(1979) 3 SCC 489	40, 196
225.	R.M.D. Chamarbaughwalla v. Union of India	1957 SCR 930	402
226.	Raj Deo Sharma (I) v. State of Bihar	(1998) 7 SCC 507	310,312
227.	Regina v. Secretary of State for the Home Department	(2013) 1 W.L.R. 2224	72
228.	Rekha Chaturvedi v. University of Rajasthan	1993 Supp (3) SCC 168	303
229.	Rex v. Halliday	(1917) UKHL 1	45,55-58,110,238-39
230.	Richardson v. Shaw	209 U.S. 365,385 (1908)	17
231.	Rogers v. Burlington	70 U.S. 654 (1865)	29
232.	Romesh Thappar v. State of Madras	1950 SCR 594	231,338
233.	Sabarimala Temple case - Indian Young Lawyers Association and Ors. v. State of Kerala and Ors.	(2019) 11 SCC 1	323
234.	S.P. Gupta and Ors. v. Union of India and Ors.	(1981) Supp. SCC 87	172
235.	S.R. Bommai v. Union of India	(1994) 3 SCC 1	6,8
236.	Sabhajit Tewary v. Union of India	(1975) 1 SCC 485	191
237.	Saheb v. State of Bombay	(1962) Supp. (2) SCR 496	317

238.	Sajjan Singh v. State of Rajasthan	(1965) 1 SCR 933	270
239.	Sakal Papers (P) Ltd. v. Union of India	(1962) 3 SCR 842	118
240.	Sales Tax Officer, Benaras & Ors. v. Kanhaiya Lal Mukundlal Saraf	(1959) SCR 1350	181
241.	Sanguinetti v. Moore Dry Dock Co.	36 Cal. 2d 812,823-45 (1951)	76
242.	Sardar Syedna Taher Saifuddin Saheb v The State of Bombay	(1962) Supp (2) SCR 496	322
243.	Satwant Singh Sawhney v. D. Ramarathnam	(1967) 3 SCC 525	41
244.	SBP & Co. v. Patel Engineering Ltd.	(2005) 8 SCC 618	217-24
245.	Scruttons Ltd v. Midland Silicones	1962 1 All ER 1	60
246.	Second Judges' case - Supreme Court Advocates-on-Record Association and another v. Union of India	(1993) 4 SCC 441	172
247.	Secretary, Madras Gymkhana Club Employees Union v. Management of the Gymkhana Club	AIR 1968 SC 554	169
248.	Security Mutual Life Insurance Company v. Prewitt	202 U.S. 246	30
249.	Shaw v. Director of Public Prosecutions	(1962) AC 220	59
250.	Shayara Bano v. Union of India	(2017) 9 SCC 1	210
251.	Shin-Etsu Chemical Co. Ltd. v. Aksh Optifibre Ltd.	(2005) 7 SCC 234	223
252.	Sims v. Slacum	7 U.S. 300 (1806)	14
253.	Smith v. Allright	8 L.ed. 987 (1943)	25
254.	Spycatcher case - Attorney General v. Guardian Papers Ltd.	(1987) 3 All ER 316	72

255.	Smt. Ujjam Bai v. State of Uttar Pradesh	(1963) 1 SCR 778	323
256.	Standard Chartered Bank v. Directorate of Enforcement	(2005) 4 SCC 530	213,216
257.	State legislation case - Re: Kerala Education Bill	(1959) SCR 995	413
258.	State of Bihar v. Kalika Kuer	(2003) 5 SCC 448	202
259.	State of Bihar v. Maharajadhiraj Shri Kameshwar Singh	(1952) 1 SCR 889	338
260.	State of Bombay v. Hospital Mazdoor Sabha	AIR 1960 SC 610	166,169
261.	State of Bombay v. The United Motors (India) Ltd	(1953) 4 SCR 1069	38,125,127-28,134,136-37,243
262.	State of Gujarat v. Mirzapur Moti Kureshi Kassab	(2005) 8 SCC 534	208-13
263.	State of J&K v. T.N. Khosa	(1974) 1 SCC 19	165
264.	State of Kerala v. N.M. Thomas	(1976) 2 SCC 310	160-66,269
265.	State of Madras v. Champakam	1951 SCR 525	338
266.	State of Madras v. Gannon Dunkerley & Company (Madras) Ltd.	(1959) 1 SCR 379	258
267.	State of Maharashtra v. Prabhakar Pandurang Sangzgiri	(1966) 1 SCR 702	105
268.	State of Punjab v. Devans Modern Breweries Ltd.	(2004) 11 SCC 26	197-203
269.	State of Travancore-Cochin v. Shanmugha Vilas Cashew Nut Factory	(1954) 1 SCR 53	134
270.	State of Uttar Pradesh v. Jai Bir Singh	(2017) 3 SCC 311	172
271.	State of Uttar Pradesh v. Mohammad Nooh	(1958) 1 SCR 595	325
272.	State of West Bengal v. Kesoram Industries Ltd. & Ors	(2004) 10 SCC 201	203-8

273.	Steelworkers v. Weber	433 U.S. 193 (1979)	75
274.	Superintendent & Legal Remembrancer, State of West Bengal v. Corporation of Calcutta	(1967) 2 SCR 170	152-55, 247
275.	Supreme Court Advocates-on-Record Association v. Union of India	(1993) 4 SCC 441	172-81
276.	Supreme Court Advocates on Record Association v. Union of India	(2016) 5 SCC 1	181
277.	Supreme Court in Her Majesty's Treasury v. Mohommed Jabad Ahmed and Others	(2010) UKSC 2	56
278.	Tata Iron and Steel case - The Tata Iron & Steel Co., Ltd. vs. The State of Bihar	(1958) 1 SCR 1355	260
279.	T. Devadasan v. The Union of India	(1964) 4 SCR 680	267
280.	Taylor v. Taylor	(1875) 1 Ch.D 426	142
281.	Terral v. Burke Construction Company	257 U.S. 529 (1922)	30
282.	Tika Ramji v. State of U.P.	(1956) SCR 393	185
283.	TMA Pai Foundation & Ors. v. State of Karnataka	(2002) 8 SCC 481	404
284.	Travancore Rayon Ltd. v. Union of India	(1970) 3 SCR 40	277
285.	Trump, President of the United States v. Hawaii	138 S. Ct 2392	94
286.	Union of India v. A.L. Rallia Ram	(1964) 3 SCR 164	294
287.	Union of India v. Bhanudas Krishna Gawde	(1977) 1 SCC 834	116
288.	Union of India v. T.R. Varma	AIR 1957 SC 882	325
289.	United States v. Darby Lumber Co.	312 U.S.100 (1941)	38
290.	United States v. Lehigh Valley R. Co	254 U.S. 255 (1920)	17

291.	United States v. Rabinowitz	339 U.S. 56 (1950)	25
292.	University of Strathclyde v. Carnegie Trustees	(1968) S.C. (H.L.) 27,47	17
293.	Purviance v. Angus	1 U.S. 180 (1786)	14
294.	Vandervell Trustees Ltd. v. White	(1970) 46 T.C. 341	18
295.	Vijay Laxmi Sadho (Dr.) v. Jagdish	(2001) 2 SCC 247	201
296.	Vijay Narain Singh v. State of Bihar	(1984) 3 SCC 14	35
297.	Virendra Singh v. State of Uttar Pradesh	(1955) 1 SCR 415	245
298.	Vishnu Agencies (Pvt.) Ltd. Etc. v. Commercial Tax Officer & Ors.	(1978) 1 SCC 520	261
299.	V.S. Rice and Oil Mills v. State of Andhra Pradesh	(1964) 7 SCR 456	248
300.	Western Australia v. Ward	(2002) 191 ALR 1	29
301.	West Virginia Board of Education v. Barnette	319 U.S. 624 (1943)	32
302.	Whitney v. IRC	(1926) AC 37; 10 TC 88	294
303.	Williams v. Glasbrook Bros. Ltd.	(1947) 2 All ER 884 CA	201
304.	Winterbottom v. Wright	(1842) 10 M. &W. 109	61
305.	Wolf v. Colorado	338 U.S. 25 (1949)	264
306.	Yates v. United States	354 U.S. 298 (1957)	32
307.	Young v. Bristol Aeroplane Co. Ltd.	(1944) KB 718 CA	201
308.	Zee Telefilms Ltd. & Anr. v. Union of India	(2005) 4 SCC 649	195

INDEX

A

Ackner, Lord 74
'acting in private' 78
Act of 1939 239
Advocates-on-Record Association 172,
    181
Affordable Care Act 79–82
Agrawal, B.N. (J) 6–7, 198, 200
Agrawal, S.C. (J) 391
Agricultural Produce Marketing
    (Regulation) Amendment Act,
    1980 295
Agricultural Produce Markets Acts
    185–86, 191
Ahmadi, A.M. (J) 172, 174, 177, 180,
    292
Aiyar, Venkatarama 139–40
Alagiriswami (J) 157, 280, 285
Ali, Ameer (J) 103
Ali, Fazl 177, 231, 241, 243, 263, 295
Alito (J) 79
Allen, C.K. 70
Ambedkar, B.R. 343, 349
Amendment of the Constitution 36, 37,
    341–42, 345, 347–53, 360
Anamma, Ediga 370
Anand, A.S. (J) 391
Anglo-Indian community 409
Anisminic principle 382

anti-defection cases 402
Appellate or Revisional Tribunal 276
appointment of judges 172, 173;
    American system of 173
Arbitral Tribunal 218, 220–23
arbitrary power 48, 98, 100, 175
Arbitration Act 220, 224
Arbitration and Conciliation Act, 1996
    217, 223
Aristotle 363
assassination 362
Atkin, Lord 27, 57–59, 65–72, 86,
    98–100, 102, 110, 121, 239
Atkin, Nancy 70
Australian Constitution 333
Australian Law 391
Avory (J) 55–56
Ayyangar, N. Rajagopala (J) 263, 323, 326
Ayyar, Venkatarama (J) 131, 133, 138,
    140

B

Bachawat, R.S., (J) 261, 262, 274, 278,
    283, 331–33, 344
backward classes 162–65, 337
bail 35, 142, 143
Balasubramanian, P.K. (J) 217
Banumathi (J) 256
Barth, Alan 31

Beg, (J) 114, 143, 168, 262
Bengal Cess Act, 1880 207
Bengal Immunity 127–28, 131, 191
Benjamin's Sale of Goods 262
Bennett (J) 34–35
Bennion, Francis, Sir., Statutory
    Interpretation of 385
Berdyaev 362
Bhagwati, N.H. (J) 38, 126, 127, 128,
    131, 133, 177, 193, 195, 283, 292,
    293, 294, 364, 365, 372, 380
Bhan, Ashok (J) 405
Bhan, (J) 405
Bhargava, (J) 332
Bharucha, B., CJ. 185
Bickel, Alexander 16
Bihar Act 338
Bihar Control of Crimes Act, 1981 35
Bihar Sales Tax Act, 1947 258
Bill of Rights 23, 83, 115, 393–94
Bingham, Lord 4
Birkenhead, Lord 345
Biswas, Pradeep Kumar 191, 195, 197
Black: (J) 32, 88; Hugo 85
blacks, discrimination on 37
Blom-Cooper, Louis 17
Bombay Animal Preservation (Gujarat
    Amendment) Act, 1994 208, 210,
    280
Bombay Animal Preservation (Gujarat
    Amendment) Ordinance, 1993 209
Bombay Government Premises
    (Eviction) Act, 1955 280–81
Bombay Prevention of
    Excommunication Act, 1949 317
Bombay Sales Tax Act, 1952 244
Bose, Vivian (J) 5, 97, 126–27, 131,
    134, 243
Bracton 154–55
Bradley, Justices 30
Brandeis, Louis (J) 16, 32, 85
Brennan, Justice 74, 366
bribery 391–92, 396–99

Bridge, Lord 72
Bright, John 362
Brougham, Lord 10
Brown, Lord 56
Bryce, Lord 345
Buller (J) 61
Burah case 5
Burger, CJ 75

C
Calcutta Gas 187
Calcutta Municipal Act 154, 245
California Supreme Court 367
Canadian Law 391
capital punishment 362, 366–68, 371,
    373, 377
capital sentencing 374
Cardamom Act 1965 296
Cardozo, Benjamin (J) 23, 39, 85, 93,
    375, 390
Central Act 186–87, 296–98
Central Bureau of Investigation 310
Central Excise Tariff Act, 1985 182, 184
Central Sales Tax Act 1975 39, 140,
    286–87
certiorari 279, 330
Chandrachud, D.Y. J 120, 158, 166
Charles I 8, 52, 67, 70
Chase, CJ 30
Chelameswar, (J) 181, 227
Chief Justice of India 113, 172–81,
    217–18, 305, 322
Chief Minister 7, 174
Church 381, 405–6
civil law systems 3, 22
Civil Liberties Act 94–95
Civil Rights Act of 1964 37, 94
Clark, Ramsey 377
Clarkson, (J) 36
Code of Criminal Procedure 1973 372–73
code of criminal procedure 1898 97,
    107, 142, 310, 313, 361–62, 364,
    369, 372–73, 389

Coke, Edward, Sir. 154
Committee of Privileges 395
committee of public safety 51–52
common law tradition 3, 12, 21, 22–23
communal property, entitlement over
    320–21
Compensatory Tax Theory 258
Constituent Assembly 176, 235–36,
    243, 272, 337, 341, 346, 348–50,
    353–57
Constitution 21; amendments of 133,
    180, 282, 334–36, 341–42, 351,
    401; Amendment Acts 335, 342;
    of America 235–36, 345, 351,
    353; Article 1 of 109; Article 4 of
    271; Article 5 of 339, 351, 353;
    Article 9 of 109, 393–94; Article
    10 of 73; Article 11 of 271; Article
    12 of 41, 191–97, 271, 329–31;
    Article 13 of 334; Article 13 (2)
    of 194, 274, 332, 334–36, 342,
    344, 360; Article 13 (3) (c) of 334;
    Article 14 of 119, 161, 199, 203,
    268, 278–80, 283–85, 338, 357,
    361–62, 364, 372, 378, 385–87,
    409; Article 15 of 233, 337; Article
    15 (2) of 196; Article 15 (4) of
    165, 409–10; Article 16 of 160–64,
    267–68; Article 16 (1) of 160,
    164, 268; Article 16 (4) of 160,
    164, 267–68; Article 17 of 321;
    Article 19 of 143, 145–46, 184,
    198–99, 211, 232–35, 237–38,
    241–43, 263, 266–67, 270, 338,
    356–57; Article 19 (1) of 143,
    145, 184, 198–99, 231–35, 241,
    264–67, 284; Article 19 (1) (a) of
    143, 145, 241, 266; Article 19 (1)
    (d) of 231–35, 263–66; Article 19
    (1) (f) of 233, 284, 327; Article
    19 (1) (g) of 184, 198–99, 327;
    Article 19 (2) of 241–43, 264,
    267; Article 19 (5) of 238; Article
    20 of 120, 232; Article 21 of 96,
    104–6, 108, 111–12, 114, 117–20,
    146–47, 196, 225, 227, 231–33,
    235, 263–65, 267, 310, 312, 372;
    Article 22 of 231, 237; Article 23
    of 176, 306; Article 25 of 317–18,
    322, 411; Article 25 (1) of 320–21;
    Article 25 (2) (a) of 320; Article 25
    (2) (b) of 317; Article 25A of 63;
    Article 26 of 317–18, 321, 323;
    Article 26 (a) of 411; Article 26 (b)
    of 319–20; Article 26 (d) of 321;
    Article 28 (1) of 411; Article 29 (1)
    of 212–13; Article 29 (2) of 337,
    405, 409–12, 414–15; Article 30
    of 155–59, 405–15; Article 30 (1)
    of 155–59, 405–15; Article 30 (2)
    of 408–9; Article 31 of 338, 357;
    Article 31-A of 270, 338; Article
    31-B of 270, 338; Article 32 of
    144, 147, 271, 307–9, 323–26,
    330, 336, 387; Article 35 of 336–
    37; Article 39 of 209, 338; Article
    46 of 162, 164, 338; Article 47 of
    209; Article 48 of 209, 211; Article
    48A of 211; Article 51 of 211;
    Article 51A (g) of 212; Article 74
    (1) of 175, 177; Article 75 of 235;
    Article 103 of 402–3; Article 105
    of 390–99; Article 105 (1) of 393;
    Article 105 (2) of 172, 176, 178,
    393–99; Article 107 of 347; Article
    124 (4) of 403; Article 127 176;
    of Article 128 176; Article 136 of
    218–19, 277, 387, 401; Article 137
    of 383–84, 390; Article 141 of 7,
    127, 132, 137, 204; Article 142 of
    305–6, 308–10, 387; Article 143
    (1) of 143; Article 145 of 176, 228,
    304, 307–8, 383, 387; Article 145
    (1) of 307; Article 145 (5) of 304,
    308–9; Article 192 of 403; Article
    194 143–44, 146–47; Article 194

(3) of 143–47; Article 196 of 347; Article 217 of 174; Article 217 (1) of 174, 176, 178–79; Article 217 (3) of 178; Article 222 of 173; Article 222 (1) of 178–79; Article 224-A of 174, 176; Article 226 of 104, 109–10, 112, 142, 147, 271, 313, 325, 401; Article 227 of 277, 313; Article 233 (1) of 176; Article 240 of 271; Article 245 of 119, 347; Article 246 of 139, 299; Article 248 of 347; Article 253 of 208; Article 258 (1) of 336; Article 265 of 182, 184; Article 286 of 125–31, 244, 286; Article 286 (1) of 126–30, 132–35, 138–40, 243–44, 286; Article 286 (2) of 126–30, 132–35, 138, 243; Article 301 139, 197–200, 203, 249–57; Article 303 (2) of 252; Article 304 (a) of 200, 252, 257–58; Article 304 (b) of 250, 252, 258; Article 305 of 252, 353; Article 329 of 403; Article 335 of 162, 164, 267–68; Article 337 of 409–10; Article 350-A of 413; Article 350-B of 413; Article 356 of 6; Article 359 of 109, 112, 120; Article 359 (1) of 96, 109, 112; Article 364 of 336; Article 368 of 270–72, 274, 332–37, 339, 341, 344, 347–49, 352–55, 360, 400–402; Article 368 (2) of 400–401; Article 368 (4) of 344; Article 369 of 336; Article 370 of 336; Article 371-A of 336; Article 372 of 107, 111, 115, 152–53, 246, 248–49; Article 395 of 107; First Amendment Act of 332; Fourth Amendment Act of 332, 342; Sixteenth Constitution Amendment 342; Seventeenth Amendment Act, 1964 270, 332, 340, 342; Thirty-ninth

Amendment Act 361; Forty-fourth Amendment Act, 1978 392–93; Fifty-second Amendment Act, 1985 401; power to amend 349; Preamble of 271, 338–39, 355–57; Seventh Schedule of 185–86, 190, 200, 203–4, 206–8, 258, 295–96, 346–47; Tenth Schedule of 400–404; constitutional law 332, 339

Constitutional Law: Keith 235; by Willis 236–37

Constitutional Law of India, by Seervai 114

Constitutional Limitations, by Cooley 273

Constitution of India 406

contempt 142–43, 147, 391, 395; of court 241, 243; of Parliament 395

Cooley, Thomas 85, 273, 339

Cornelius, C.J. 273

corporate criminals 378

Court, as collective body 3

criminal cases 97, 311–12, 384

Cromwell, Oliver 31, 381

culture 19, 92, 212–13, 337, 413

D

Das, S.K. (J) 253

Das, S.R. (J) 127–28, 131, 139

da Vinci, Leonardo 362

Dawoodi Bohra Community 317

Day (J) 30

Dayal, Raghubar (J) 140

death penalty 78, 228, 361–62, 364–67, 369–74, 377–80; as discriminatory 377–78

death penalty acts 371

Death Row 226, 366, 377

decency 241, 243, 376

defamation 241, 243

Defence (General) Regulations, 1939 57

Defence of India Act (Act 35 of 1939) 97, 99, 102, 104

Defence of the Realm Consolidation
      Act, 1914 45–46, 48
Defence Regulations 66–67
Delhi Laws Act, 1912 (1951) 5
Denning, L. (J) 37, 60, 62, 65, 150
de Pencier Wright, John 10
Desai (J) 177, 279
DeWitt, General 93
Dicey 234, 345
Diplock, Lord 71, 381
Directive Principle of State Policy 203,
      211, 275, 336–37, 357, 363
Discretion to Disobey, by Kadish and
      Kadish 388
discrimination 37, 163, 199, 252–53,
      278, 280–82, 386, 410, 414
dissenting/dissenting opinion 4, 7–8,
      10, 12, 14–16, 18–20, 23–25,
      27–35, 37–38, 45, 58–63, 68–69,
      71–72, 74–75, 77–79, 85, 87, 89,
      92, 94, 102, 117, 126, 131, 249,
      289, 304–5, 309–10, 331, 333,
      399; Atkin and 86; Cardozo on
      39–40; Hailsham on 39; Harlan
      and 36; L'Heureux-Dube on 40;
      Little on 34; by Shah 141; Thomas
      on 82
dissenting judgment 3–4, 21, 23, 25,
      27–28, 31, 33–35, 37–41, 75,
      113–14, 125, 131–34, 216, 262–
      63, 297, 299, 310–11, 344, 354,
      401–2; of Hidayatullah (J) 148,
      258, 261; Scalia on 39; Sikri and
      39; by Sinha 138; of Srikrishna (J)
      215; of Venkatachaliah 380
District Judges, designation of 218
Dixon (J) 132
Dock Labour Board 171
Doctrine of Severability to a Bill 401
Dominion or Colonial Courts 9
Donovan, Lord 18
Douglas, William O. (J) 19–20, 32, 40,
      377

Dred Scott Case 36
Drewry, Gavin 17
Duffy, Gavan (J) 87
Duffy, Warden 368, 377
Dunedin, Lord 54–55
Dwivedi 187–89

E
East Punjab Public Safety Act, 1949 241
Educational institutions 155–59, 356,
      405–15
Election Commission 403
Ellenborough, Lord CJ. 147
'Emergency' 96
English law 4, 65, 391
English Sale of Goods Act, 1893 258
Eswara Iyer, P.N. 225–27
Ethics in Government Act, 1978 77
European Convention on Human
      Rights 73
European Court of Human Rights 74
excommunication 317–18, 320–21
ex debito Justitiae 141, 383–84
Ex parte Endo 90

F
Farquhar 104
Fazal Ali (J) 177, 231, 241, 243, 263,
      295
Federal constitution 345
Federal Constitutional Court,
      Karlsruhe 3
*Federal Trade Commission v. Beechnut
      Co.* (1922) 17
Field (J) 30
First Constitution Amendment Act 342
Foreign Exchange Regulation Act, 1973
      213
Frankfurter, Felix (J) 4, 23, 25, 85, 264,
      373
*Frank in his book review of Alexander
      Bickel's The Unpublished Opinions
      of Mr Justice Brandeis* 16

Frank, Jerome 375

Frank, John P. 16

freedom of speech 20, 34, 73, 143–46, 233–34, 241–42, 266, 392–93

Friendly, Henry 85

fundamental rights 97–99, 112, 116–19, 144–47, 156, 159–60, 199, 231–32, 263–65, 267, 270, 305–6, 308, 324–32, 335–37, 340–42, 355–57, 360–61, 363, 405; of 'life and personal liberty' 96; violation of 330

G

Gajendragadkar, P.B., CJ. 12, 165, 169, 249, 253, 270, 387

Gandhi, Mahatma 376

Ganga Sugar 187

Ginsburg, Ruth Bader (J) 13

Goddard, Lord, CJ 34–35

Gopalan, A.K. 118, 231, 241, 263

Gordan, D.M. 383

Government of India Act, 1935 127, 258, 345

Great Seal 10, 107

Grier (J) 30

Gujarat Amendment Act 208–10

Gujarat University (Amendment) Act, 1972 156

Gujarat University Act, 1949 156

Gupta, S.P. (J) 160, 163, 177, 179

H

habeas corpus 96–7, 100, 104, 106–07, 109–10, 112–13, 116, 119–20

Habeas Corpus Acts 97, 110

Hailsham, Lord 39, 99

Haldane, Viscount 10–11

Hale, Baroness 63, 65

Hand, Learned (J) 15, 85, 381

Harding, Warren 28

Harlan, John (J) 24, 30, 31, 36, 85

Hart, H.L.A. 14

Hasia, Ajay 192–95

Hearst, William Randolph 28

Hidayatullah, M. (J) 41, 148, 258, 261–62, 270, 283, 286, 329, 332–33, 337, 354

High Court 103, 109, 112, 154, 162, 175, 217–18, 224–25, 240, 245, 277, 285, 296, 303, 313, 325, 330, 379, 384–87; Ahmadi on 174; Allahabad 143; appointment to 174–75, 178; bypassing of 113; cases withdrawal by 386; and disposal of criminal cases 311; extraordinary jurisdiction of 385; Lucknow 142

Hindu Law 12

Holdsworth, William, Sir. 70

Holmes, Oliver Wendell (Jr.) 85, 116

Holmes, Oliver Wendell, (J) 15, 17, 31, 33, 45, 75, 88, 116, 161, 344, 390

Holmes, Valentine 70

Hoover, Herbert 28

Hope, Lord 56

Hospital Mazdoor Sabha 166–69

hostile association 57

House of Commons of Parliament, UK 144, 239, 392, 395

Houses of Parliament in India 144, 239, 334–35, 347, 392, 394–95

Hughes, Charles Evans, CJ 23, 28, 31, 75, 113

Hugo, Victor 362

I

illegal gratification 394, 396–97

immunity 38, 125, 127–28, 131, 191, 214, 234–35, 243, 390–91, 393–97, 399

independence 29, 83, 113–14, 177–79, 395–96, 412

Indian Contract Act 1872 148, 152, 181–82

Indian Penal Code 242

Industrial Disputes Act 166, 168
industries 166–71, 183, 185–86, 188–
    90, 295, 299
Industries (Development and
    Regulation) Act 187, 189
Intellectual integrity 23
intra vires 55, 323
*Introduction to the Study of the Law of the
    Constitution*, by Dicey 234
IPC (Amendment) Bill, 1972 215
ipse dixit 68, 77
Isaacs (J) 354
ITP Act 306
Iyer, Krishna (J) 168, 225–26, 169, 367,
    370, 378

J
Jackson, Robert (J) 15, 85, 92, 95–6, 381
Jaffer Imam, (J) 131
Jagannadhadas (J) 131, 138
James, William 375
Japanese Constitution 105, 236, 368
Japanese Supreme Court 368
Jayakar, M.R. (J) 12
Jefferson, Thomas 13–14, 20, 343
Jethmalani, Ram 384
Jews 53–54; in Nazi concentration
    camps 114
'jiggery-pokery' 80, 82
Jim Crow laws 37
J.J. group of hospitals 167
Johnson, William (J) 13–14
judicial authorities 202, 240, 329–31, 388
Judicial Committee of Privy Council
    8–11, 242, 345

K
Kaddish 388
Kannan Devan 187
Kapur, (J) 261
Karnataka Agricultural Produce
    Marketing (Regulation) Act, 1966
    295, 298

Kaul (J) 120
Kerala Education Bill 413
Khanna (J) 104–5, 113–17, 157, 160,
    163–65, 282, 361
King's Bench 4, 67, 70
Kirby, Michael (J) 3, 21–22, 32
Kirpal, B.N., CJ 405
Korematzu, Fred 88, 92, 94–96
Kumar Brijesh, (J) 300

L
Lahoti, C.J. (J) 191, 210, 310, 322
Lahoti, R.C. (J) 203, 310
Lal, Kanhaiya 182
'Law' 363; in Australia 399; in Canada
    399, *see also* English Law
Law and the Modern Mind, by Frank
    375
Law Lords, The 23–24, 38, 58, 65, 60,
    69, 99, 101
Law of the Constitution, by Dicey
    345–46
*Legislative, Executive and Judicial Powers
    in Australia*, by Wynes 333
Lewis, Geoffrey 57, 70
L'Heureux-Dubé, Claire 40
liberal approach 161
liberty 31, 49–51, 53–54, 58, 66–67,
    73, 83–84, 89, 95, 97–99, 104–8,
    111, 115–17, 119, 146, 214, 233,
    239–40, 311, 324
liberty of the press 242
life imprisonment 228, 371–73, 380; *see
    also* capital punishment
Little, Rory K. 34
Liversidge 59, 65, 71, 97, 121
Lochner v. State of New York (1905) 16
Lok Sabha 346, 364, 391–92, 400, 402,
    404
Luthra, Shri 226

M
Macmillan, Lord 58, 98, 101, 110, 239

Madhya Pradesh Act 338
Madison, James 20
Madras Maintenance of Public Order Act, 1949 241
Magna Carta 105, 154, 236, 239
Maitland, F.W. 52
majority judgment 6–7, 16, 23, 25–26, 32, 35, 38–41, 57–58, 64, 70, 71, 75, 88, 94, 97, 114–15, 119–20, 125, 127, 131, 141, 145, 147, 152, 155, 160, 166, 172, 180, 181, 186, 191, 195, 198, 202–3, 205, 208–10, 214–15, 217, 221, 225, 231, 241, 245, 247, 249, 253, 261–63, 269, 274, 277–78, 280, 281, 282, 285, 286, 292, 302, 303, 322, 360–61, 382, 400, 401, 405, 414
Mansfield, Lord 61, 105–6
Marketing Act 296–98
Marshall, John, CJ. 13–14, 31, 85–86
Mathur, A.K. (J) 210
Maugham, Viscount 58, 69–70
Maugham, William Somerset 58
Members of Parliament 10, 272, 390–92, 394–400; exclusion and 391; as public servant 399
Mikva, Abner 74
Miller (J) 30, 367, 390
Mines and Minerals (Regulation and Development) Act, 1957 206
minority: community 156, 158, 407–8, 413, 415; institution 155, 157–58, 160, 405, 408–11, 413–15, 412
minority judgment 7, 40–41, 95, 115, 128, 145, 186–87, 190–91, 195, 212, 215–16, 262, 281, 284, 286, 292–95, 329; in *Bangalore Water Supply* 170; Douglas and 40
MISA 113
Misra, Ranganath (J) 387–89
Mitter, (J) 332
Modern Political Constitutions, Strong 346
morality 241, 243, 318–19, 362

Mudholkar, (J) 267, 271, 274
Mukharjea, (J) 5
Mukharji (J) 190, 295, 297–99
Municipal Act 284
Municipal Commissioner 285
Murphy, (J) 90, 95
Muslim-minority educational institution 155

N
Nariman (J) 116, 120, 220, 225, 227
Naxalites 376
Nehru, Jawaharlal 343
nemo judex in causa sua 403
The Nereide 18
Neuberger, Lord 11
1940 Act 219
1952 Amending Act 385
1975 Act 299
Non-Detention Act of 1971 96

O
Other Backward Classes 160, 165
overrulings 26–27, 30, 32, 39, 94–95, 114–18, 120, 125, 127, 133, 136, 138, 152, 163, 166, 172, 181, 185, 201–2, 254–55, 258, 269, 274, 277, 282, 332, 333, 342, 360, 381, 389

P
Paine, Thomas 20, 343
Palekar (J) 156, 344
Palkhivala, Nani 114, 326, 355, 357–58
Pal, Radhabinod (J) 4
Pal, Ruma (J) 299, 405
Pandian (J) 6–7, 180
Pannick, David 367
pari materia 158, 160, 385
Paterson, (J) 14
Patient Protection and Affordable Care Act (Obamacare) 79, 82
Patnaik, G.B. (J) 185
per incuriam 200–202, 380, 388–89
Perlzweig, Jack 57

'Personal liberty' 96, 107–9, 111–12, 115, 117–20, 147, 226, 231–35, 239–40, 263–67, 337, 356

Plantations Labour Act, 1951 171

Post, Robert 16

Presidential Orders 96, 105, 108–9, 111–12

Presidential Proclamation (under Article 356) 6

Prevention of Corruption Act, 1988 391, 399–400

Prima facie 131, 196–97, 220, 223, 271, 386

Privy Council 8–12, 64, 71, 98, 101, 103, 136, 246–48, 317, 320–21, 345–46, 354, 384, 394; Judicial Committee of 8, 10

'procedure established by law' 111, 118–19, 235–37

prohibition against slaughter of progeny of cow 209

property 98, 107, 126, 207, 214, 233–34, 236, 244, 259, 281–82, 285, 320–21, 324, 327–28, 331, 337, 343, 357, 413

property rights 342–43

Prophets with Honour, by Barth 31

prosecution 186, 213–14, 391, 395–97, 399–400

prospective overruling, doctrine of 332–33, 342, 360, *see also* overrulings

Protection of Human Rights Act, 1993 117

Provincial Government 5, 103–4

public order 108, 241, 243, 318–19, 338, 356

Public Premises (Eviction of Unauthorised Occupants) Act, 1971 280

Punchhi (J) 172, 180

Punjab Public Premises and Land (Eviction and Recovery) Act of 1955 278, 280

'pure applesauce' 81–2

Puri, Kewal Krishan 295

Q

quasi-judicial authorities 328–31

'quod Rex non debet esse sub-homine sed sub Deo et lege' 154–55

R

racial discrimination 25, 31, 92–94, 196

racism, legalization of 92

Radcliffe, Lord 24, 68, 71

Rajasthan Sales Tax Act, 1954 288

Raju, D. (J) 191, 313

Rajya Sabha 346, 364, 400, 402–4

Ramana, (J) 256

Ramaswami, V. (J) 300, 302, 332

Ramaswamy, (J) 7, 304, 307–8

Ramji, Tika 186–89, 190, 299, 300

Rao, Subba, CJ. 145, 247, 263, 266–69, 274–75, 277, 332, 410

Rau, B.N., Sir. 340

Raveendran, (J) 222

Reddy, Chinnappa, (J) 35

Reddy, Jaganmohan (J) 157

Reddy, Jeevan B.P. (J) 6–7, 181, 269

Reed, Stanley (J) 25–26

Rehnquist, (J) 75

Reid, Lord 4, 18, 59, 65

religious: practices 318–20; propagation 319

reservation 7–8, 160, 166, 163–64, 269, 353, 409

res integra 137, 211

Revenue Recovery Acts 279

review petitions 224–28, 302–3, 309, 380

Revolution of 1776 83

Rich, (J) 87, 354

right of movement 234–35

Rights of Man by Paine 343

rights to property 320, 357

right to life 96, 104, 108, 111, 115, 117, 119, 226, 231, 264, 267, 324, 337, 365

Roberts, (CJ) 25, 89, 94
Roman Catholics 53–54
Roman Law 259
Romer, Lord 58, 101
Roosevelt, Theodore 28
Royal Commission on Capital
    Punishment 1949-53 368, 373
Rule of Law 116, 245
Rush, Justice 14

S
Sabarimala Temple 323
Sabhai, Sidhajbhai Rev. 409
Sahai, R.M., (J) 301–4
Sahgal (J) 143
Sale of Goods Act, 1930 184, 259
Sandburg, Carl 19
Sankey, Viscount 8–9
Santosh Hegde, N. (J) 215
Sarkar, (J) 142, 145–46, 245
Sarkaria, (J) 361, 369
Sastri, Patanjali, CJ 126–27
Sawant, (J) 6–7
Scalia (J) 39, 78–79, 82
Scheduled Castes 160, 162–63, 165,
    267, 269, 337, 409
Scheduled Tribes 160, 162–65, 209,
    267, 337
Scott, L. (J) 34
Scrutton, Lord (J) 60, 63
Secretary of State 28, 45–46, 48, 50, 53,
    56–58, 67–68, 72, 101–2, 239
secularism 406
Seervai, H.M. 114, 119
Sen, A.P., (J) 35, 292
Sen, Padam 140–42
Sen, S.C. (J) 182
seriatim 4–5, 12–13
Setalvad 387–88
Shah, Ajit Prakash (J) 221, 249, 253
Shah, J.C. (J) 147, 254, 263
Shah, M.B. (J) 310–11
Shankar, Har 198

Shaw of Dunfermline, Lord 47, 51,
    54–58, 239
Sikri, S.M. (J) 39, 286–87
Simon, John, Sir. 68–69, 346
Singh, Jaswant (J) 166, 168
Singh, Kartar 310
Singh, Keshav 142–43
Singh, Kuldip (J) 6–7, 180
Singh, Rajnarain 5
Singh, S.K. (J) 255
Sinha, B.P. CJ 131, 138, 200, 203–5,
    245, 247, 249, 252–57, 317
Sinha, S.B. (J) 198, 203
Smith Act 32
social philosophy 374–76
Social Security Act 82
social welfare 317–18
'somersaults of statutory interpretation' 82
Sommersett, James 106
Sorabjee, Soli 6
Sotomayor (J) 95
Spycatcher 72–73
Srikrishna, B.N. (J) 215
Srinivasan, M. (J) 310
Stare decisis 21, 27, 211–13
State: definition of 331; and religion
    406
State Act 50, 187, 189, 290, 295–98,
    329, 338
State Governments 129, 152, 160, 246,
    275, 277, 288, 299, 306–7, 309,
    311, 313; corruption or abuse of
    power by 7
State Legislatures 88, 129, 142–44,
    186–87, 189–90, 205, 207, 209,
    249, 272, 296–300, 327–28, 347–
    48, 358, 404, 413; unconstitutional
    Act of 328
State of Jammu & Kashmir 302; Rule of
    37 in 301
Stone, CJ. 23, 32
Story, Joseph (J) 18–19, 86
subjective satisfaction, theory of 67–68

Subordinate Services Rules 1958 160, 164
Sugar and Sugar Products Order 1946
    258
Sugarcane Act 187
Sugar Products Control Order, 1946 258
Superior Court of Ontario 10
superior courts 3, 10, 45, 96, 105, 273,
    382–83, 400
Supreme Court of India 5, 31, 41, 104,
    125, 127, 152, 160, 166, 224–25,
    231, 323, 332, 402
Supreme Court of New South Wales 393
Supreme Court of USA 13, 17, 19, 28,
    31, 74, 75, 77, 82, 116, 236, 339,
    351, 367, 377
Supreme Court Rules 305, 307
Swayne (J) 30

T
TADA Act 311
Taft-Hartley Act 82
Taft, William Howard 28, 85
taxation 31, 84, 126, 129, 133, 135,
    138–39, 206, 208, 244, 249–52,
    254, 256–57
taxes on the sale of goods 327
Tea Act 1953 206, 208
Templeman, Lord 74
Thakker, C.K. (J) 219, 224
Thakur, T.S. CJ 254
Thomas, K.T. (J) 79, 82, 310
Thommen, T.K. (J) 300, 302
Tobacco Board Act, 1975 185–86,
    190–91, 295–97, 299
Tokyo War Crimes Trials 4
To the Best of My Memory, by
    Gajendragadkar 12
trial court 225, 384, 386
trials 4, 45, 47–48, 51–54, 100–101,
    103, 110, 112, 222, 232, 240, 310,
    312, 383–84, 386–87
tribunals 26, 36, 65–66, 99, 109, 221,
    236–37, 275–77, 279, 283, 382

Tulzapurkar (J) 166, 168

U
ultra vires 45, 47–48, 51, 54, 56, 185,
    203–4, 207, 244, 295, 327
United States of America 13, 73, 368,
    406; Constitution of 88, 92, 109,
    113, 339, 352; Law in 391
University of Agra 155
Upjohn, Lord 18
U.P. Police Regulations, Regulation 236
    of 262

V
Varadarajan (J) 295
Variava, S.N. (J) 405
Venkatachalaiah (J) 380–81, 400
Venkataramiah (J) 35, 177, 179, 289,
    292, 294
Verma, (J) 180, 401
Vice-President of India 403–4

W
Wadhwa (J) 304
Wanchoo (J) 148, 204–5, 245, 247,
    332
Wason 393–94
white-collar criminals 378
Wilberforce, Lord 17
Winfield 149
women 84, 305–6, 376; denial of
    constitutional right to fallen 306;
    fundamental rights of fallen 305–7;
    human problems and 306; rights of
    306; trafficking of 306
World War 1 45, 86, 258
World War 2 4, 88–89, 97
Wright, Lord 58, 61, 66, 98, 101
Wynes 333

Z
Zadig, Arthur 45–47
Zamindari Abolition Acts 338